GW00543895

Braidwood &c.

Raymond Lee

History never ends.

Doreen E. Woodford
(1926 - 2011)

Contents

Foreword

Preface

Acknowledgements

Fore-Index

The Braidwood Family and the Education of the Deaf

The Braidwoodian Pupils

The Appendices

Foreword

The year 1760 is a momentous one as one of the landmarks in the history of British education. In that year Thomas Braidwood, a Scot, established his Academy for the Deaf and Dumb based at the foot of Arthur's Seat in Edinburgh. It became the first ever regularly-organised school for deaf students in the world. What about its history? Raymond Lee remarked -

> "The history of the life and times of the founder of British deaf education, Thomas Braidwood, and his subsequent family members, has not been well researched and documented over the past 200 years or so by various historians."

One wonders what prompted Raymond Lee to take up the challenge to research the lives of Thomas Braidwood and his family when many historians constantly refer to the pioneering schoolmaster for 200 years when dealing with the issues on historical side of the education of the Deaf. The answer is the discovery of the gravestone of Thomas Braidwood and some of his family members in a cemetery adjoining the Presbyterian Dissenters' Meeting House on the south side of St. Thomas Square in Hackney, east London, in April 1993. The sight of the sadly neglected gravestone, which sank partly into the ground, led both Lee and his colleague John A. Hay of Edinburgh to consider how best to preserve it - hence their co-founding of the British Deaf History Society (BDHS) on 14 April 1993.

The aims of BDHS are to encourage the study of Deaf history and to preserve and to collect Deaf-related materials and artefacts for museum and archival purposes. It produces its own Deaf History Journal, publishes its own books and administers its National Deaf Museum and Archives at Warrington, Lancashire.

Raymond Lee was aware of the enormity of the task in researching the Braidwood family and, with the support of some members of the BDHS, he decided to trace the lives and work of the Braidwood family members, the Deaf students whom they taught and the training of their assistant teachers. It is very difficult to write up the biographies of Thomas Braidwood and his family members because of lack of archival evidence and documents relating to them and their academy.

Many times during the past 22 years research and writing, it was thought all of the facts relating to Braidwood and his work were collected, but something new always turned up and still does today. Like a jigsaw puzzle, the story of Thomas Braidwood's educational development with the Deaf slowly unfolded, but is not possible to complete it at present.

We have to remember that Edinburgh had been undergoing huge changes during the 1760s and 1770s. This city became renowned as the City of Enlightenment. Thomas Braidwood contributed in no small way to the reputation of Edinburgh, but, alas, his pioneering teaching efforts did not reach the public at large; nor did his work gain greater renown that it deserved. It was only when Samuel Johnson and James Boswell visited their school and gave accounts of his efforts that brought fame to Braidwood. We know from advertisements in the newspapers of the day that the members of the Braidwood family idolised Thomas Braidwood and made use of his name. However, they never wrote any articles on him, their shining star. Dr Joseph Watson, a kinsman of Thomas Braidwood, only mentioned a few lines about Braidwood and yet in spite of his literary talents, he never wrote a biography of the man who taught and trained him as a teacher of the Deaf. Both the scarcity of information and lack of evidence on Braidwood defeat the purpose of analysing the man that he was. Again it is surprising to see that Braidwood's pioneering success with the Deaf students never reached the ears of the Royal Society, and yet two of his students, John Goodricke of York and Francis Humberston Mackenzie, Lord Seaforth, were honoured with membership of the Royal Society, Goodricke for astronomy and Mackenzie for botany.

As a result of the author's sheer hard work, done on a voluntary and unpaid basis in the past 22 years, he has achieved his task of producing this wonderful book *Braidwood &c.* It contains many archival materials, some rare and previously unpublished, along with illustrations.

Having known Raymond Lee since the formation of the BDHS, I recommend his new book to the public. He is well known in the world of Deaf education as his literary contributions to Deaf history, numerous articles published in specialised journals and books have gained him national reputation. In recognition of his work in the field of Deaf history, the British Deaf History Society bestowed him with a Fellowship in December 2012.

Lee worked with John A. Hay and Isobel Watson, the chair of the Friends of Hackney Archives, in locating Hackney sites where the Braidwood families were known to have resided. This led to an event in March 1996, when the *Braidwood commemorative plaque* was placed at Rowe House at the corner of Chatham Place and Retreat Place in Hackney. It used to be the site of Grove House where the Braidwood family opened the Academy for the Deaf in May 1783 after their transfer from Edinburgh to London. Joseph Watson, one of the assistant teachers trained by Thomas Braidwood, later became the first headmaster of the London Asylum for the Deaf and Dumb located at New Kent Road, the first ever British public school for the Deaf in November 1792. This move later paved the way for other British cities and towns to set up their schools for the Deaf. Thomas Braidwood's hopes for education to be made available to the Deaf of poor families bore fruition and many public schools for the Deaf prospered nationwide.

Lee is to be congratulated for his thorough investigations, efforts and achievements. His extensive research has allowed us to have a glimpse of how Deaf students in the Braidwood Academy progressed and also how they fared when they left the academy. There are, of course, many more questions on this issue, but the book is meant to be a springboard for aspiring readers who may wish to delve into the subject further.

The book is intended not merely for educationalists and historians, but also for members of the public wishing to learn something about British Deaf history and Thomas Braidwood, whose work and example led to many deaf children receiving their education. This book provides the most comprehensive, accurate, and readable account of the history of the education of the Deaf relating to Thomas Braidwood's pioneering efforts at present available, and I feel privileged to be asked to write a foreword in commending it.

Anthony J. Boyce,
Hon. President,
British Deaf History Society.
May 2015

Preface

My interest in Thomas Braidwood and the education of the Deaf in Britain was triggered by a letter from a friend John Alexander Hay, of Edinburgh, dated 29 March 1993. A part of the letter read:

> You may recall I was looking for the location of the final resting place of Thomas Braidwood. Well, I have just uncovered a piece of information from the photostats of the *Clinical Excerpts Vol 32, Autumn*, which I got from my local public library. He was buried in the cemetery adjoining the Presbyterian Dissenters' Meeting House on the south side of what is now St Thomas Square, Hackney.

It was on April Fools' Day of the same year that I visited the St Thomas Square cemetery. The tombstones had been uprooted from their original positions and leant against the perimeter walls running all the way round the boundary of St Thomas Square cemetery. After much searching, I located the Braidwood tombstone, and it was numbered 16. I was able to relay this discovery to John by letter the following day. This aroused my curiosity about Thomas Braidwood and in order to learn more about him, I decided to pay a visit to the Royal National Institute for the Deaf (RNID) Library in London.

While I was at the RNID Library after browsing through a number of old British Deaf magazines, I came across *The Deaf and Dumb Times* (Vol 2, no.7, January 1891, page 107). I read an account about the last day of the Paris International Deaf and Dumb Congress under the heading REMINISCENCES OF THE PARIS INTERNATIONAL DEAF AND DUMB CONGRESS (1890) BY ONE WHO WAS THERE. I was attracted to a small section of the report on the final day's proceedings:

> The Congress was then declared closed with the cries of *Vive la France! Vive l'Abbé de l'Epée! Vive l'Emancipation des Sourd-Muets!*
>
> It will be observed that Mr. Thomas Braidwood, who had the honour of being the first to introduce the method of teaching the deaf in Great Britain, on his own method, at the very time when the Abbé de

l'Epée began his work, by establishing his school at Leith in 1760, was not mentioned at this meeting. The British delegates, if there were any present, however, were so disgusted at the mismanagement of the Congress that they took no further part in the proceedings.

I hope, however, that when the time comes when an International Congress shall be held in Great Britain, our deaf will take care that Mr. Braidwood is not forgotten. For Braidwood really has every right to rank with such men as the Abbé de l'Epée, Gallaudet, and others.

After reading this part of the report, I resolved to unearth all I could on Thomas Braidwood, his family and his method of education. Many questions were raised in my head — what was Thomas Braidwood like as a man? — was he a good teacher? — did his pupils benefit greatly from his method of education?

My initial thought was that someone must have written something on him, celebrating his work and his life. I was truly taken aback when I found that no one had ever written anything about Braidwood: there was, and still is, a token mention of him in the *Dictionary of National Biography*, which is presently no better than a passage mentioning him in the 1801 *Encyclopædia Britannica* under the heading 'Deaf and Dumb.' I thought to myself that there were surely more books around mentioning Braidwood. I came across Kenneth W. Hodgson's *The Deaf and Their Problems* (1953) and Thomas Arnold's *The Education of Deaf Mutes: A Manual for Teachers* (1888), but the mention of Braidwood in these two books were minimal. There were also various short references to Braidwood in various early issues of *The American Annals of the Deaf*. I came into possession of Joseph Watson's *The Instruction of the Deaf and Dumb* (1809) and I was disappointed that the book contained no history on Thomas Braidwood, Watson's mentor. I was even more disappointed to read Watson mentioning in *Introduction xxii* —

> ... I have not thought it incumbent on me to give anything like a history of the discovery and practice of the science of teaching the Deaf and Dumb.

Watson, a distant relation of Braidwood, had the opportunity to create a history of Braidwood but elected not to do so and we are left with a blank canvas. I was also able to gather more information from another wonderful source – Deaflore. That was just about all.

I pondered why so little had been written about Thomas Braidwood. Was it because hearing people in Britain had not shown any interest in the Deaf and their history? The answer to that question, based on my experience living as a Deaf person in Britain, is an emphatic yes. An extremely large proportion of the hearing population of the United Kingdom are so untrained in Deaf Awareness that they fail to recognise the existence of Deaf people and they are also ignorant of the history of Deaf people. The same criticism applies to hearing people in the past, or should I say, throughout history. I believe my assessment stands true as I write this preface.

My research has been a journey filled mainly with frustration and disappointment due to the scarcity of information not only on Thomas Braidwood and the education of his Deaf pupils, but family and historical events that would greatly enhance the construction of a picture of the man and the pioneering days of the education of Deaf people.

My good friend, the late Doreen Emily Woodford, offered to assist me on the Braidwood project by doing some of the legwork on my behalf. She had ample time on her hands and expressed a desire to keep fit by travelling around the country, visiting various regional archives and institutions on my behalf. I readily accepted her kind offer and we formed a wonderful partnership which I treasured greatly, and which I still hold dear in my memory. However, like me, Doreen became frustrated and disappointed at not being able to get more information on Thomas Braidwood and his family members. One good thing did come out of our partnership: Doreen decided not to pursue Braidwood any further, leaving this to me and she embarked on a search for the Deaf pupils of Thomas Braidwood. I had an initial list of 27 Braidwoodian pupils supplied to me by John Hay, and Doreen expanded it to 37 pupils before her death at the age of 85 on 31 December 2011. Since then I have managed to discover nine more pupils.

I also received an instruction from the British Deaf History Society to "include everything and anything connected with Braidwood in my research" for publication. On top of that, along with the importance of getting the names of Braidwood's pupils, there was a need to include Braidwoodian teachers and their influences. My task became larger than I envisaged and my research has taken longer to complete.

After 22 years working on the project in my spare time, I have come to a decision that I could not do any more. A comprehensive historical account on Thomas Braidwood cannot be achieved due to the lack of information and sources. If I am to describe honestly what this publication is, I must say it is a collection of historical and research notes and nothing more. I think I have achieved in creating a body of work that is rich in information and details, all put into one basket. However, much research remains necessary as there is yet more to discover about Thomas Braidwood. It is my hope that future researchers will be encouraged to take up the challenge to complete the full picture of the history of Thomas Braidwood.

My task has been to simply gather facts and piece them all together. I hope this is what I have achieved and I have avoided making in depth commentaries, leaving it to the reader to come to his/her conclusions.

I would like to raise a question here, for this question had always been in the back of my mind throughout my research. The question –

"Why was Thomas Braidwood greatly disliked and vilified by those who are non-British and who were associated with the Deaf?"

PLACING TEACHERS UNDER A BOND

This question still interests me even now. Old publications, especially from America, carried articles accusing Braidwood of secrecy by not revealing his methods; some articles accused Braidwood of being oralist; some accused Braidwood of being a fraud and some accused Braidwood of being greedy for money by creating a system of placing teachers under bond of some thousands of pounds not to reveal his method for a number of years. I am not going into lengthy details to try and answer the question, for I am confident that my research will answer the question to some extent.

I must make it clear here that the stories of Braidwood placing teachers under oath not to reveal his method for a number of years were greatly exaggerated by our past friends across the Atlantic. During my research

I looked for a list of teachers who were placed on a bond of certain sum of money not to reveal the Braidwoodian system to anyone and I am pleased to report I have found only one person – and he was Robert Kinniburgh (1780-1851), who had no connection with Thomas Braidwood (1715-1806). I must repeat here, only one person! History must be re-written for the sake of clarifying the truth and righting the wrong placed upon Thomas Braidwood. The true problem was with Isabella Braidwood who was trying, very foolishly, to protect her alcoholic son John in America.

It must be pointed out here that the Deaf French, Laurent Clerc, was placed under a three-year bond by Thomas Gallaudet not to reveal teaching methods and suchlike, and yet no one accused Gallaudet in the same way that Thomas Gallaudet and others accused Braidwood.

ACCUSATIONS OF SECRECY

As for secrecy, it depends on what one means by secrecy. "Keeping it in the family" cannot be construed as "keeping it secret." When one thinks of "secrecy" the root phrase for this word is surely "deliberately concealed from public knowledge." It is known from newspaper articles that Thomas Braidwood did demonstrate his method of teaching the Deaf on a good number of occasions to various visitors such as Lord Monboddo, Dr Samuel Johnson, Dr Alexander Crombie, Sir David Dalrymple, members of various professional bodies and also the editors of the 1801 *Encyclopædia Britannica*. There were also several occasions when Braidwood offered to train young men to become teachers of the Deaf if funds could be raised to finance their training, but no one showed interest. The Braidwood Academy was in reality a family business and was run as such: it was their primary source of income. To the reader this may sound strange, but Braidwood was living at a time when every business needed to guard its "main ingredient" or "formula" from being snatched by others as they needed to protect their income. This was no different for Thomas Braidwood, although he was happy to impart his knowledge should he get assistance to finance the training of new teachers.

There was a letter published in *Science*, January 6, 1888, Vol. XI, page 12 and it is copied here:

> In a foot-note to a page of Sir Walter Scott's "Heart of Midlothian," I read, "'Dumbiedykes' is really the

name of the house bordering on the King's Park (Edinburgh) so called because the late Mr Braidwood, an Instructor of the Deaf and Dumb, resided there with his Pupils."

Now, I happen to know that Thomas Braidwood sold his estate (that goes by the name of our family, and is situated next to the Duke of Hamilton's, some twenty miles beyond Glasgow) in order to use the proceed to start his institution for educating the deaf and dumb; and if Professor Bell, in his address at the Gallaudet anniversary, a notice of which is published in *Science*, of December 23, meant it as a reproach to the memory of Mr Braidwood, when he says the school "was a money making institution," and its principal "had bound all his teachers under a heavy fine not to reveal his methods to any one," it may be pertinent to ask if, under the circumstances, it was not only prudent, but a duty of Mr Braidwood, to make his institution to pay its own way. His all was involved in it; and, had he not used what people will call a necessary precaution, his school might have perished for want of funds, and himself been impoverished. At all events, this is the view his relations take of the matter.

And when one reviews the dreary centuries preceding, when every now and again some gentle soul proposed to educate the deaf and dumb only for it to drop out of thought again, perhaps it would be best to guard with caution the acts of him who staked his entire wealth in the venture, and spent forty-six years of life in establishing as a living fact what was but as a grand dream for centuries.

Signed,
THOMAS W. BRAIDWOOD.
Vineland, N. J.
December 29, 1887.

Accusing Braidwood of secrecy seems like the action of a frustrated and impatient person, or persons. And Braidwood's reputation was not made any better by the "copy and paste" researchers throughout history. To be fair, the grumblings about secrecy did not begin with Thomas Braidwood (1715-1806), but with Isabella Braidwood (1758-1819). It was Isabella's mismanagement of the Braidwood Institution that led to its downfall.

Thomas Braidwood's reputation was not enhanced by a small breed of sub-standard researchers in the early part of the 20th century. To give one example, there was a totally negative comment made by Merle E. Frampton, Professor of Education, Teachers College, Columbia University, and Hugh Grant Rowell, Assistant Professor of Education, Teachers College, Columbia University. They both edited and published *The Education of the Handicapped* (1938, World Book Company, Yonkers-on-Hudson, New York). In Volume 1, History, they wrote on page 66:

THE BRAIDWOODS

> Paralleling the manual work of de l'Épée and the oral methods of Heinecke came, in England, what would be considered today an unethical monopoly and possibly a racket – the Braidwood School. It has had the greatest influence of all the European developments upon the education of the deaf in America.

Frampton and Rowell's opening comment alone reveals how little they know of the education of the Deaf in Britain and their comment that Braidwood was possibly running a racket makes one wonder about their professionalism as researchers. They even got the name of the school wrong.

DEAFLORE

I use the word Deaflore rather than British Deaf Folklore because I identify myself more with Deaflore. The term "British Deaf Folklore" does not seem to me to belong to the Deaf, of whom I am one. Deaflore embraces numerous features that are a part of "folklore" — signed narratives, signed histories, deaf cultural traditions, deaf humour, signed stories, signed poems and suchlike.

In the case of Deaf history, apart from some accounts published in newspapers in the 18th and 19th centuries, my knowledge and information regarding the Braidwoods came mainly from the late Jim

Mackenzie (1908-1979), a former pupil at Northern Counties School for the Deaf in Newcastle-upon-Tyne. I first met Mackenzie (his sign name was fingerspelled and ended with the pipe sign) in 1966 in Gateshead Deaf Centre which was then situated at the corner of Prince Consort Road and Bensham Road. Mackenzie enthralled me with stories and histories of Deaf people in the past, and some of these stories were about the pupils of Thomas Braidwood. I am ashamed now to admit I should have paid greater attention to these stories and ask questions at that time, but there I go. Mackenzie mentioned a trio of three deaf ladies from Shropshire who attended the Braidwood Academy; two deaf men who went on to become excellent artists; one deaf man who became a governor of Barbados and one deaf man who became a teacher of the deaf. At that time, being only seventeen years old and just out of school, I was merely fascinated by his story-telling, and, to my eternal regret, that was just that.

I did, however, ask Mackenzie about the source of the stories. My memory is a bit fuzzy at present, but I clearly remember Mackenzie saying that these stories were passed down from Deaf person to Deaf person starting with one Alexander Atkinson, a Newcastle-born and based Deaf person who attended the Edinburgh Institution for the Deaf and Dumb under Robert Kinniburgh in 1815. Clearly Atkinson met some former Braidwoodian pupils while in Scotland and on returning home to Newcastle, he conveyed stories about these pupils and through a good number of generations of pupils at the Northern Counties School for the Deaf down to Mackenzie and then finally to me.

When I set out to research the history of Thomas Braidwood and his deaf pupils, I never thought I would later be hit on the head when I recalled Mackenzie's stories. Along with Doreen Woodford, I unearthed some deaf ladies from Shropshire who attended the Braidwood Academy – Anne Walcott, Jane Poole, Sarah Dashwood and one more, Elizabeth Metcalfe. There was Francis Humberston Mackenzie, a Braidwoodian pupil, who went on to become a Governor of Barbados. The two excellent artists turned out to be Charles Shirreff, Braidwood's very first pupil, and Thomas Arrowsmith. The deaf man who became a teacher of the Deaf was none other than John Creasy, the man who inspired the Rev. John Townsend and the Rev. Henry Cox Mason to found the London Asylum for the Instruction of the Deaf and Dumb of the Poor in 1792. The Mackenzie's stories fitted in well with what I was able to discover. And, Alexander Atkinson (1806–1879) attended the Edinburgh Institution for the Deaf and Dumb in Chessel's Court, Canongate, in June 1815. He received an education under the headship of Robert Kinniburgh and he left the school in October 1820.

Atkinson published his autobiography *Memoirs of My Youth* in 1865, in which he gave a very detailed account of his progress at school, his relationship with Robert Kinniburgh, and his adventures with his school friends whilst at school and travelling around Scotland. Being in Edinburgh, Mackenzie assured me, Atkinson met some old Braidwoodian pupils and from that point on stories were passed down, starting in Edinburgh and ending up in Newcastle. These stories have become a part of Deaflore. The value of Deaflore must never be underestimated, but sadly a lot of stories and historical accounts have begun to vanish due to the closure of schools for the Deaf and the introduction of mainstreaming education of the Deaf.

I hope I have gone some way to answer the British Deaf delegates' protests at the closing ceremony of the 1890 International Congress of the Deaf and Dumb at Paris by building a picture of Thomas Braidwood and the pioneering days of the education of the Deaf in Britain.

Raymond Lee
Feltham
Middlesex

26 May 2015.

Acknowledgements

This book on Braidwood and the education of the Deaf in Britain took up considerable spare time and my research, which faltered on numerous occasions, was continually buoyed by members of the British Deaf History Society (BDHS). Their interest in the work on Braidwood and their encouragement for me to continue brought a new lease of life and determination on my part to complete the research. A good number of BDHS members gave some of their time and assistance with the legwork part of my research and I wish to express my gratitude to the following BDHS members – John A. Hay (Chairman of the BDHS); Peter W. Jackson (Executive Director of the BDHS); Anthony J. Boyce (President of the BDHS); Geoffrey J. Eagling, Martin Colville and Jemima Buoy.

I give my grateful thanks to Isobel Watson of the Friends of Hackney Archives and the archivist David Mander of Hackney Archives Department for their generous assistance and expertise on the Hackney side of the Braidwood history. Their help contributed immensely to a clear picture of the Braidwoods' situation in Hackney, and the Hackney Archives Department has been exceedingly generous in allowing me to use their sources and illustrations in the book.

I am indebted to Robert and Sally Burrows of Wolverhampton for their patience not only in proofreading the book, but for offering suggestions for alterations that would remove any misunderstandings on the part of the reader. There has been some further additions and changes to the book after the final proofreading, so any grammatical and spelling errors in this book will be down to me alone. I also express my thanks to Siobhan Charnay for her proofreading and suggestions on the first section of the book, advising me on the degree of readability for young readers.

I want to thank Geoffrey J. Eagling for his assistance in setting out the Braidwood Family Tree on page 1 and also for creating an illustration of a layout of surroundings in Hackney where Grove House was located (page 72). I would like to thank and compliment my good friend Alain Holcroft of Portsmouth for his artistic constructions of both Grove House (page 73) and Pembroke House (page 81).

There are others who helped me in no small way and I am grateful to the following for their assistance and contributions:

Marcus Green of Birmingham for his knowledge of the Edgbaston Institute for the Deaf and Dumb, and also for providing the photograph of The Mount and the old map of Edgbaston, both of which are featured on page 110.

Brian Southwell, the secretary of the Friends of Key Lane and Warstone Lane cemeteries, Birmingham. His photographs showing the final resting places of Isabella Braidwood and her son Thomas are on pages 118 and 119.

The late Louis M. Balfour of Chevy Chase, Maryland, USA, for the copy of the Circular of the Braidwood Institution for the Deaf and Dumb, Hackney.

Bill Beer of Kent Family History Society for his work on Ann Barksdale.

Mary Plackett, retired head of the RNID Library at Grays Inn Road, London, (now sadly known as UCL Ear Institute and Action on Hearing Loss Library) for allowing me to copy Alexander Graham Bell's articles on John Braidwood in America from *The Association Review* 1900.

My thanks are also due to Chelsea Raker of Columbus, Ohio, for her efforts in obtaining the Braidwood/Bolling documents from the Library of Virginia.

I also wish to thank the following for their kind permission to allow me to reproduce images used in the book:

The National Records of Scotland, Edinburgh
The British Deaf History Society, Warrington
Sarah Davis of Shropshire Archives, Shrewsbury
Hackney Archives Department, Hackney
Lincolnshire Archives, Lincoln
The British Library, London
Edinburgh City Library, Edinburgh
The Victoria & Albert Museum, London
Claudia Hill of Ellison Fine Art, Beaconsfield
Deirdre Magarelli of Pook & Pook Inc., Downingtown, PA, USA
Katharine Neil of The Highlanders' Museum (Queen's Own Highlander Collection), Ardersier, Scotland

Mark Griffith-Jones of Sotheby's, London
Fiona Keates of the Royal Society, London
Graham Budd of Graham Budd Auctions, London
Deaf Action, Edinburgh
Tom Nelthorpe of Scawby Estates, Lincolnshire
Sian Prosser of the Royal Astronomical Society, London
James Pearn of Brightwells Ltd., Leominster
Woolley & Wallis Salisbury Salerooms, Salisbury

There are images in this book in photocopy form which originated from the collections of Doreen E. Woodford and the late Arthur Frederick Dimmock (1918 - 2007). I have made every effort to trace the copyright owners of the images over the past two years or so and I have not been particularly successful in this task in the case of the following images:

Two images of Dumbie House on page 35.
Thomas Pennant on page 41.
William Burnett on page 245.
Engraving of James Burnett, Lord Monboddo, on page 245.
Caleb Whitefoord on page 278.
David Garrick on page 278.
Mary Proby on page 318.
Governor's House, Barbados, page 332.

Finally I must mention the contribution to my book by the late Doreen E. Woodford, a former teacher of the Deaf and a tireless campaigner for the establishment and improvement of the education of the Deaf in underprivileged African countries and Afghanistan. Doreen's assistance to me was immense and almost fast-paced in the last two years of her life. Come rain or shine, she travelled all over England using public transport and Shank's pony on my behalf in search of evidence to unearth the names of the Deaf pupils of Thomas Braidwood and her legwork contributed greatly to the research. In the last few weeks before she met her demise, I was able to produce quickly a draft booklet on the Braidwoodian pupils for her to peruse and I was heartened to receive her thumbs up of approval. Her contribution will never be forgotten as this book will be, in no small way, a living tribute to her assistance on The Braidwoodian Pupils section. Her presence and help is still sorely missed.

Index

The Braidwood Family
and the
Education of the Deaf

1 - THE BRAIDWOOD FAMILY

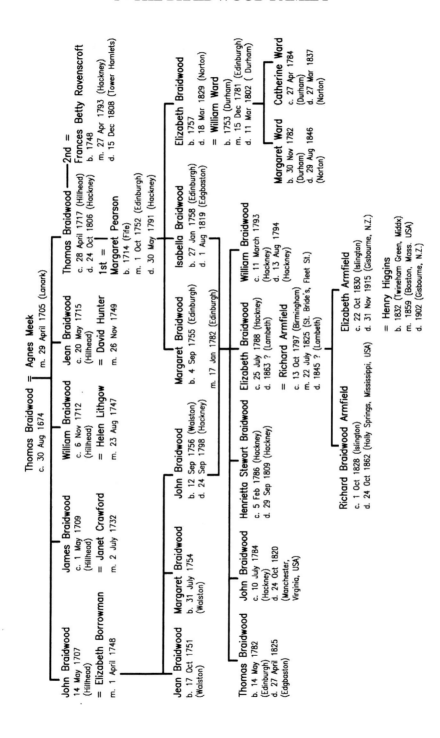

Thomas Braidwood = Agnes Meek
c. 30 Aug 1674   m. 29 April 1705 (Lanark)

John Braidwood
14 May 1707
(Hillhead)
= Elizabeth Borrowman
m. 1 April 1748

James Braidwood
c. 1 May 1709
(Hillhead)
= Janet Crawford
m. 2 July 1732

William Braidwood
c. 6 Nov 1712
(Hillhead)
= Helen Lithgow
m. 23 Aug 1747

Thomas Braidwood——2nd = **Frances Betty Ravenscroft**
c. 28 April 1717 (Hillhead)   b. 1748
d. 24 Oct 1806 (Hackney)   m. 27 Apr 1793 (Hackney)
1st =   d. 15 Dec 1808 (Tower Hamlets)
Margaret Pearson
b. 1714 (Fife)
m. 1 Oct 1752 (Edinburgh)
d. 30 May 1791 (Hackney)

Jean Braidwood
c. 20 May 1715
(Hillhead)
= David Hunter
m. 26 Nov 1749

Jean Braidwood
b. 17 Oct 1751
(Walston)

Margaret Braidwood
b. 31 July 1754
(Walston)

John Braidwood
b. 12 Sep 1756 (Walston)
d. 24 Sep 1798 (Hackney)

Margaret Braidwood
b. 4 Sep 1755 (Edinburgh)
m. 17 Jan 1782 (Edinburgh)

Isabella Braidwood
b. 27 Jan 1758 (Edinburgh)
d. 1 Aug 1819 (Edgbaston)

Elizabeth Braidwood
b. 1757
d. 18 Mar 1829 (Norton)
= **William Ward**
b. 1753 (Durham)
m. 15 Dec 1781 (Edinburgh)
d. 11 Mar 1802 (Durham)

Margaret Ward
b. 30 Nov 1782
(Durham)
d. 29 Aug 1846
(Norton)

Catherine Ward
c. 27 Apr 1784
(Durham)
d. 27 Mar 1837
(Norton)

Thomas Braidwood
b. 14 May 1782
(Edinburgh)
d. 27 April 1825
(Edgbaston)

John Braidwood
c. 10 July 1784
(Hackney)
d. 24 Oct 1820
(Manchester,
Virginia, USA)

Henrietta Stewart Braidwood
c. 5 Feb 1786 (Hackney)
d. 29 Sep 1809 (Hackney)

Elizabeth Braidwood
c. 25 July 1788 (Hackney)
d. 1863 ? (Lambeth)
= **Richard Armfield**
c. 13 Oct 1797 (Birmingham)
m. 22 July 1825 (St. Bride's,
Fleet St.)
d. 1845 ? (Lambeth)

William Braidwood
c. 11 March 1793
(Hackney)
d. 13 Aug 1794
(Hackney)

Richard Braidwood Armfield
c. 1 Oct 1828 (Islington)
d. 24 Oct 1862 (Holly Springs, Mississippi, USA)

Elizabeth Armfield
c. 22 Oct 1830 (Islington)
d. 31 Nov 1915 (Gisbourne, N.Z.)
= **Henry Higgins**
b. 1832 (Twineham Green, Middx)
m. 1859 (Boston, Mass. USA)
d. 1902 (Gisbourne, N.Z.)

HILLHEAD

Conflicting accounts of members of the Braidwood family and their connections were given by numerous authors in various historical accounts and publications over the past two centuries; quite a large number of these were, and still are, erroneous and needed to be corrected. There is no intention here to establish a genealogical account and study of Thomas Braidwood's lineage but to outline a simple and straightforward presentation of facts discovered so far without delving into the misty past of the Braidwood family tree.

Research was also conducted into the extended families of Thomas Braidwood in order to discover whether his relatives continued to run schools for the deaf long after the death of members of his immediate family.

There is an unpublished 1996 article by the author on the origins of Thomas Braidwood and it is reproduced here:—

The Lanarkshire Parish of Covington and Thankerton is bound on the north-west by Pettinain, east by Libberton, south-east by Symington and west by Carmichael. It measures some five miles in length from the river Clyde below Brown Ford in the north to the top of Tinto in the south; its greatest breadth measures around two and three-quarter miles from the Clyde in the east to the boundary with Carmichael in the west.

The dominant feature of that part of Scotland is Tinto Hill by the village of Symington. Standing 2335 feet high, Tinto, generally known as *"Hill of Fire"* in the days when the Druids ruled, was also once called *"a Sphinx brooding over Clydesdale."* An equally important feature of the parish is the Covington Tower, a former moated stronghold of the Lindsay family and now an impressive ruin, standing between a church and a well-preserved circular dovecot containing about 500 boxes.

The church, the ruined tower and the dovecot are situated a short stroll away from a large farmhouse, Covington Mains. Opposite this farmhouse, known locally as Mains, a road forks right from the main northbound road and it leads up quite steeply to an area known as Northflats Hill. At the top of the hill, the road continues to just veer eastwards, still climbing slightly, to a large farm bordering on the edge of the hill. The main residential building, Hillhead Farm, is in a unique situation; its front door overlooks the magnificent snaking river Clyde.

Hillhead Farm, the birthplace of Thomas Braidwood
Photograph taken by Raymond Lee in June 1998.

This farmhouse stands a proud and formidable building some 830 feet above sea level.

In the 19th century, this farm was at one time a close-knit community and it was once known as Covington Hillhead, containing within its boundary a number of buildings, now in ruins, to lodge its workers, weavers and crofters. The name of the place is now Hillhead. Despite the ravages of Time and the elements unleashed by Nature, the main building is at present in superb condition although the face of the stonework is now mainly covered in a rendering of cement to afford insulation and protection against fierce winds and inclement weather in the winter seasons. Hillhead Farm was where Thomas Braidwood first saw the light of day between early November and mid-December 1715…

According to the Sasine, John Braidwood was recorded as both the proprietor and resident of a building known as Hillhead of Covington in 1656 and his building was described as a farm. It was at that time no ordinary farm like it is at present; Hillhead was a settlement containing a collection of houses where workers and their families resided. There were good numbers of crofters' houses occupied by families of weavers. "The Braidwoods of Hillhead were important local employers and they were also a wealthy family; the wealth of John Braidwood can be measured by reading one Sasine transcript written and sealed on 12 May 1656 between John and one James Wynrahame of Wiston. Sasines were written in lengthy process and sentences were often repeated. The gist of the Wadsett of 1656 is as follows:

> *The instrument of seasing given by Robert Struth (?) baillie in that part constitute be James Wynrahame of Wiston to John Braidwood of Covington of all and haill the said James Wynrahame his just and equall third part of the town and lands of Littlegalla ...*

> *In the name of god Amen, be it known... to all men by these presents public instrument that upon the 12 day of May the year of God 1656 years ... compeared personally John Braidwood in Hillhead of Covington upon the ground of lands of Littlegallia having ... a contract betwixt him ... and James Wynrahame of Wiston ...of the date of the 11th day of August 1654 containing in the end thereof the precept of Sasine underwritten whereby the said James Wynrahame sold and disposed from him his heirs and assignees to the said John Braidwood his heirs and assignees heretablie with reversion of a thousand merks Scots ... money ... the said James Wynrahame his Just and equall third part of the town and lands of Littlegallia ...*

[National Records of Scotland RS42/5 ff 56R-58R.]

This original contract of the Wadsett was discharged in Edinburgh on 19 January 1672.

Thomas (c.30 August 1674), the son of John Braidwood, was recorded to have married Agnes Meek, the daughter of John Meek, at Lanark on 29 April 1705. Proceeding a stage further, Thomas appeared to have inherited Hillhead Farm and this was made evident by the fact that the birth register of Covington Kirk recorded all six children of his marriage to Agnes were born in Hillhead:

John Braidwood	*c.5 May 1706*
John Braidwood	*c.14 May 1707*
James Braidwood	*c.1 May 1709*
William Braidwood	*c.6 November 1712*
Jean Braidwood	*c.20 May 1715*
Thomas Braidwood	*c.28 April 1717*

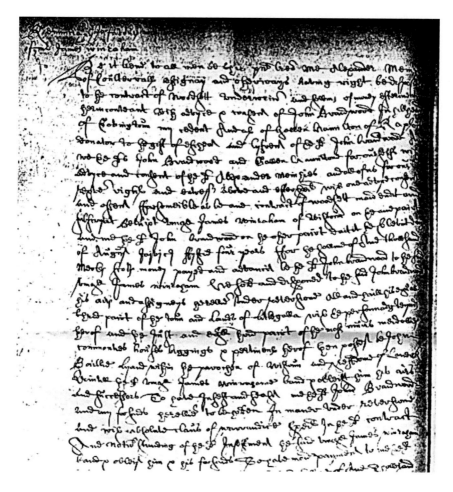

Part of the original page of Sasine
[National Records of Scotland RS42/5 ff 56R-58R]

It must be mentioned here that it was a custom for christening/baptism dates, rather than actual birth dates, to be recorded in church registers. Most religious denominations, with the exception of the Quakers and sometimes the Baptists, record dates of baptisms from 1538 up to 1837 when Parliament passed an act that every person born in Britain must be registered. The information contained in baptismal records varied over time and there was no standardised entry until 1 January 1813. From their starting date in 1538, many registers contained the name only of the child along with the name of his/her parents. Almost all religious sects in Britain baptise early in infancy; late baptisms, however, was not uncommon and records exist to show people having been baptised over 21 years of age.

5

[It is of interest to note that until 1752, New Year's Day was celebrated on 25 March, not 1 January, and therefore December 1715 was followed by January 1715. In a Christian country it was quite logical to use the day of Christ's conception as the beginning of the New Year. The first John Braidwood who was christened on 5 May 1706 is presumed to have died around or shortly after his birth.]

Further tracking of the offsprings of the five children of Thomas and Agnes of Hillhead yielded a significant twist in the Braidwoods' history; none of the offspring of these five children were born in Hillhead. This gave rise to an inkling that the Hillhead had been sold by Thomas Braidwood and the proceeds of the sale shared among his children. The marriages of the five children of Thomas and Agnes were as recorded:

John Braidwood m. Elizabeth Borrowman at Walston on 1 April 1748.
James Braidwood m. Janet Crawford at Edinburgh on 2 July 1732.
William Braidwood m. Helen Lithgow at Edinburgh on 23 August 1747.
Jean Braidwood m. David Hunter at Edinburgh on 26 November 1749.
Thomas Braidwood m. Margaret Pearson at Edinburgh on 1 October 1752.

From the time of the marriage of James Braidwood in 1732, there were no records of the Braidwoods of that particular family residing in Hillhead. With the exception of John Braidwood, four went to live and work in Edinburgh. Hillhead Farm contained over 40 acres of land along with dairy cows and black-faced sheep. There might be a possibility that none of the children were keen on farming which often involved long hours and laborious physical exertions. The young offsprings of Thomas and Agnes might have preferred to join in with the mainstream in the metropolis of Edinburgh which was at that time gaining a growing reputation as the *City of Learning and Enlightenment* in Europe. In view of the lack of evidence to support events leading to the sale and the Braidwoods' departure from Hillhead, an assumption based on an educated analysis had to be made in this respect and one would not be too wide of the mark in suggesting that Thomas sold Hillhead Farm and shared the proceeds of the sale almost equally among his children.

This guess was based on two lines of reasoning. One was that the Braidwoods were landowner farmers and therefore quite wealthy: the second was that the share of the proceeds of the sale of Hillhead was more than sufficient for each child to purchase a house and live in Edinburgh which was quite an expensive city compared with the parish of Covington and Thankerton.

Adding further to that, John Braidwood was able to purchase a small plot of land in the picturesque village of Walston, where he chose to settle with his wife Elizabeth. Their marriage produced three children viz.:

Jean Braidwood	b.17 October 1751
Margaret Braidwood	b.31 July 1754
John Braidwood	b.12 September 1756

The youngest of the five children of Thomas and Agnes, Thomas Braidwood, followed the footsteps of his other three siblings, James, William and Jean, leaving Hillhead for Edinburgh.

EDINBURGH

Edinburgh in the early 18th Century became the seat of wisdom and learning throughout Europe; any person with a thirst for learning and knowledge made it a personal rule to study in that great city and this was probably likewise for the Braidwood children.

Young Thomas Braidwood most probably resided with one of his brothers upon first arriving in Edinburgh. Thomas later enrolled as a student in Edinburgh College and it was said mainly through oral tradition that he studied mathematics to degree level. It must be stated here that Edinburgh University at present does not have any record of Thomas Braidwood as a student. The university stressed, however, that there were a good number of records missing for those who were admitted during the period Thomas was supposed to be a student. Consequently, there is no official record or evidence to show that Thomas studied mathematics.

After his supposedly successful graduation, Thomas took a position as a teacher in the prestigious Hamilton Grammar School near Glasgow. Again it was cited in various works that he was a mathematics teacher at that school, but these sources were not able to offer either proof or evidence. No documentary records exist to indicate either the employment or the duration of Thomas' stay as a mathematics teacher in Hamilton Grammar School. Thomas later returned to Edinburgh around 1750-1.

Still a man of sufficient means through his share of inheritance from his father's sale of Hillhead Farm, Thomas set out to purchase a house, or a number of houses. Being a person born of farming origins, it came as no surprise that Thomas was attracted to a medium sized house at the foot of the Old Town between Canongate and St Leonard's Hill, bordering onto Arthur's Seat. St Leonard's Hill was at that time probably for the most part covered with wild, scraggy grass, as is Arthur's Seat at the present day. As far as can be ascertained from old city maps of the district, only two houses were standing on the hill, one of these near the summit, the world-famed Jeanie Dean's cottage, and the other at the base of the hill, at the end of "the road leading to St Leonard's Hill" from Holyrood Place. Thomas purchased the latter property and turned his home into a private academy for young gentlemen and he earned his living as a teacher. He also obtained another house near Nicholsons Park which was populated by affluent house owners.

The measure of Thomas Braidwood's financial status can be found in the Sasine - written and sealed at Edinburgh on 14 April 1759:

> *... upon 12 April 1759 ... compeared Patrick Hunter, writer in Edinburgh as procurator and attorney for Thomas Braidwood, writing master in Edinburgh, having ... an heritable bond and disposition in security of the date underwritten ... granted by James McPherson, architect at the Dean to and in favour of the said Thomas Braidwood, in favour of (whom) ... James McPherson bound ... him ... to contract and pay to ... Thomas Braidwood ... the sum of £800 sterling against the term of Martinmas next ... and for (his) further security ... the said James McPherson bound ... him ... to infest and sease the said Thomas Braidwood ... in an annual rent of £40 sterling ... furth of ... that great lodging or dwelling house presently building by the said James McPherson upon part of a piece of ground lying in Nicholsons park ...*

[National Records of Scotland RS27/183 ff 286R-291R]

There also exists another Sasine dated 15 January 1770 at Edinburgh:

> *Seasine ... presented by William Anderson writer in Edinburgh ... that upon the 10 January 1770 ... compeared Robert Meikle, writer in Edinburgh as procurator and attorney for Thomas Braidwood, writing master in Edinburgh ... having ... a heritable bond and disposition in surety ... granted by James McPherson Architect and masson in Dean to ... Thomas Braidwood*

whereby the said James McPherson obliged him ... to pay ... to Thomas Braidwood ... the sum of £459 sterling against the term of Whitsunday next ... and for the said Thomas Braidwood and his forsaids their ... security and more sure payment of the said sums ... the said James McPherson ... bound ... him ... to infest and sease the said Thomas Braidwood heritably ... not only in an annual rent of £22-19 shillings sterling ... annual rent ... ffurth of ... that great lodging or dwelling house presently (building) by ... James McPherson ... lying within Nicholsons Park ...

[National Records of Scotland RS27/186 ff 341R-348R]

Both the above Sasine extracts made it clear that Thomas Braidwood was a writing master by profession, not a mathematics teacher as a number of past historians stated.

THOMAS BRAIDWOOD'S IMMEDIATE FAMILY

Thomas probably led a dull, mundane existence that was temporarily interrupted when he met and fell in love with a lady by the name of Margaret Pearson. After a short courtship, they married in the magnificent church of St. Cuthbert's on 1 October 1752. The newlyweds stayed in Thomas' house at St Leonards Hill. According to known birth registers of St Cuthbert's church, Margaret gave birth to two daughters, the first Margaret, who was born on 4 September 1755 and the other Isobel born on 27 January 1758. Isobel would in later years become known as Isabella. There is, however, a mystery yet to be solved at present. Thomas had a daughter named Elizabeth who was born in 1757, but her name was nowhere to be found in any of the Scottish church registers. The evidence of Elizabeth as Thomas' daughter was found in the St Cuthbert's marriage register for 15 December 1781 as shown in the extract from the register.

Extract from the St Cuthbert register of marriages
Showing the marriage of William Ward to Elizabeth Braidwood

(Doreen E. Woodford Collection)

9

Nothing much is known of Thomas' eldest daughter Margaret. Although she was an assistant teacher at the Braidwood Academy during its Edinburgh era, she was known not to have moved to Hackney with her family in 1783 and she could not be traced from that point onwards.

Isabella Braidwood married her first cousin John Braidwood (1756-1798), the son of Thomas' elder brother John Braidwood and his wife Elizabeth Borrowman. It appears that the marriage between Isabella and her cousin was hastily arranged as a marriage of necessity to preserve family honour since Isabella was about 4 months pregnant at the time of her marriage at St Cuthbert's, Edinburgh, on 17 January 1782. John Braidwood was employed by Isabella's father, Thomas, as a trainee teacher of the deaf at the Braidwood Academy in Edinburgh, where Isabella was also employed as a teacher of the deaf. Their firstborn, Thomas, who was born on 14 May 1782, turned out to be their only child to be born in Edinburgh for the whole Braidwood family, with the exception of Thomas' daughter Margaret, and the academy for the deaf and dumb transferred to Hackney on the outskirts of East London in May 1783.

HACKNEY

John and Isabella Braidwood had four more children when in Hackney:

John Braidwood	b. 10 July 1784
Henrietta Stewart Braidwood	b. 5 Feb 1786
Elizabeth Braidwood	b. 25 July 1788
William Braidwood	b. 11 March 1793

The eldest Edinburgh-born Thomas, John, Henrietta and Elizabeth were trained as teachers at the Braidwood Academy in Hackney. John took to alcoholism and left Hackney to take up a position as the first head teacher of the newly founded school for the deaf in Edinburgh in 1810. However, his drinking problems continued and he departed for America to seek a new life and to establish a school for the deaf there. His uncontrollable reliance on alcohol persisted and he eventually died of cirrhosis in Manchester, Virginia, in 1820.

William Braidwood died in infancy. Henrietta Stewart Braidwood died at the young age of 23 years, cause unknown. And Isabella's husband John passed away in September 1798 due to what the newspapers of the day reported as a "pulmonary complaint" which was suspected to be pulmonary embolism.

10

Margaret Braidwood, nee Pearson, passed away at the age of 77 in May 1791. Following this, Thomas Braidwood got married for the second time in April 1793 to a lady who was 33 years younger than him, a widow named Frances Betty Ravenscroft, to the displeasure of his daughter Isabella. Frances Betty was born Frances Betty Springall in London in June 1748, the daughter of Godfrey and Catherine Springall. She married a London attorney-at-law Samuel Ravenscroft on 1 June 1770; in April 1788 her husband passed away.

Isabella and her two children, Thomas and Elizabeth, became the surviving Braidwoodian teachers; Thomas took on an appointment as the first head teacher of the Edgbaston Institute for the Education of the Deaf and Dumb in Birmingham in 1814, where he remained until his early and unexpected death in April 1825. He never married.

Isabella and Elizabeth closed the Braidwood Institution in Mare Street, moving to Barclay House, but the establishment did not last long and had to be closed when Isabella found her income dwindling due to diminishing intake of pupils and they all moved from Hackney to 7 Great Ormond Street where they established a small seminary for young deaf children. In 1816 Isabella and Elizabeth moved to Edgbaston where they established the same seminary, but the true reason was that they needed to be close to Thomas. Isabella passed away after a short illness in August 1819. Elizabeth married Richard Armfield (christened on 13 October 1797), the son of the Birmingham plated and gilt button factory owner, Edward Armfield, at St Bride's church in Fleet Street, London, on 23 July 1825. Richard was a partner in the factory with his father and brother William Thomas Armfield. The partnership was dissolved on Richard's insistence on May 11 1826 and Richard established his own factory in King Street, London. The business continued until 1843 when Richard Armfield was declared bankrupt. He died not long after in 1845.

Elizabeth and Richard Armfield had two children Richard Braidwood Armfield (baptised on 1 October 1828) and Elizabeth Armfield (baptised on 22 October 1830). Richard Braidwood Armfield was known living in England up to 1851, when he left for America. As for Elizabeth, she became a teacher of the deaf for a very short period. The mother and daughter worked together and established a private school for the education of both deaf children and slow-learning children, who were not necessarily deaf. Where the school was initially situated is not known, but one location of the school surfaced in an advertisement printed in the Caledonian Mercury dated 12 March 1858:

DEAF and DUMB and CHILDREN
of WEAK INTELLECT

PRIVATE ESTABLISHMENT, conducted by Mrs
ARMFIELD
(assisted by her Daughter, and competent
Masters)

———

MRS ARMFIELD is the grand-daughter and only
descendant of the late *Mr Braidwood,* the *Inventor*
of the Art of Teaching the Deaf and dumb
to Speak. By this system Children and Adults
are Taught to Speak and enjoy ordinary
Conversation, and are fitted to fill any station in
society, besides receiving a First-Class Education
and Medical advantages.

References to many of the Nobility and Parents
of Pupils.

———

ADDRESS—
21 NORLAND SQUARE, NOTTING HILL, LONDON
W.

This 1858 advertisement showed that the Braidwood family continued
teaching and it indicated that the Braidwood family had been involved
in the education of the deaf in a private capacity for 98 years by 1858.
Elizabeth Armfield and her daughter Elizabeth went to America when
they received news of availability of land south of the Potomac in
Virginia came to their attention and they went to put in a claim that the
land belonged to them. This matter is dealt with in CHAPTER 6 (Page
187) .

For interest purposes, Elizabeth Braidwood, (the one who had no
christening records) Thomas Braidwood's second daughter, who
married the Durham surgeon William Ward, went to reside in
Durham. William Ward (born 1753) was the son of Humphrey Ward
and Catherine Kirton and he was apprenticed to one Mr Bainbridge, a
surgeon at Durham in 1770. After his apprenticeship and studies,
which included undertaking medical courses in Edinburgh, Ward was
employed as a surgeon in Durham Infirmary. With Elizabeth, two
daughters were born into the family, the first Margaret who was born

on 30 November 1782 and the other Catherine, born on 27 April 1784. Elizabeth and her daughters appeared never to have got involved in teaching deaf children.

The Ward families of Durham, Norton and Billingham were extremely rich families and they all wanted for nothing. Initially Thomas Braidwood left quite a large part of his fortune in his Will to Margaret and Catherine, but on being informed that his grand-daughters were left a tidy sum in the Will of William Ward's uncle, Thomas Ward, a gentleman of Norton who died on 6 December 1804, Braidwood removed them from his Will and distributed the amounts among his daughter Isabella and her children.

There was an interesting announcement in the *Newcastle Courant* dated May 24 1794:

> To the TRUSTEES of the DURHAM INFIRMARY
>
> Ladies and Gentlemen,
>
> The resignation of MR WARD, one of   the surgeons to the Infirmary, having occasioned a vacancy permit me to solicit your votes and interest to succeed him. Should I be so happy as to meet your approbation on the day of the election, every exertion in my power shall be devoted to the service of the charity.
>
> I have the honour to be,
> Your most obedient servant,
> Thomas Salked
> May 19th 1794.

From that newspaper announcement, it is now known that William Ward relinquished his post at Durham Infirmary in 1794. His demise came on 11 March 1802 at the age of 49 years. He was buried on 15 March at St Mary-le-Bow, a small chapel next to Durham Cathedral.

After Ward's death, Elizabeth and her two daughters relocated to Norton near Stockton. Both Margaret and Catherine associated with Ann Sleigh, nee Ward, the wife of William Sleigh, and immersed themselves in Ann's charity work with the poor in the region, which involved helping out in workhouses and assisting unfortunate and needy women. Elizabeth Ward passed away on 18 March 1829 and was buried at St Cuthbert's Church, Billingham.

13

Margaret and Catherine never married and continued with their charity work. Ann Sleigh passed away in 1835 and in her Will, she left Margaret and Catherine £4000 each for investment. They were paid interest every quarter from their respective investment by the trustees of Ann's Will.

Catherine Ward died on 27 March 1837 at Norton and she was followed by her sister Margaret on 29 August 1846, also at Norton. Both sisters were buried in St Cuthbert's Church, Billingham.

In order to avoid the repetition of mistakes and confusion, which past historians often made, an outline is made here to link the individual names of the family members with the places and buildings involved and this can be a basis for reference throughout this book Their birth and death dates are added to assist the reader to locate them on the family tree at the beginning of the chapter.

EDINBURGH ACADEMY 1760-1783

Thomas Braidwood (Founder, 1715-1806)
Margaret Braidwood (Dau. of Thomas, b. 1755)
Isabella Braidwood (Dau. of Thomas, 1758-1819)
John Braidwood (Nephew of Thomas, 1751-1798)

BRAIDWOOD ACADEMY HACKNEY 1783-1806

Thomas Braidwood (founder, 1715-1806)
Isabella Braidwood (Dau. of Thomas, 1758-1819) until 1799
John Braidwood (Nephew of Thomas, 1751-1798) until 1798
Thomas Braidwood (Son of Isabella & Thomas' grandson, 1782-1825) until 1799

BRAIDWOOD INSTITUTION, HACKNEY 1799-1813

Isabella Braidwood (Dau. of Thomas, 1758-1819)
Thomas Braidwood (Son of Isabella & Thomas' grandson, 1782-1825)
John Braidwood (Son of Isabella & Thomas' grandson, 1784-1820) until 1810
Henrietta Stewart Braidwood (Dau. of Isabella & Thomas' grand-dau., 1786-1809) until 1809
Elizabeth Braidwood (Dau. of Isabella & Thomas' grand-dau., 1788-1861)

14

GREAT ORMOND STREET, LONDON, 1814-1816

Isabella Braidwood (Dau. of Thomas, 1758-1819)
Elizabeth Braidwood (Dau. of Isabella & Thomas' grand-dau., 1788-1861)

EDINBURGH INSTITUTION FOR THE DEAF AND DUMB 1810 - 1811

John Braidwood (Son of Isabella & Thomas' grandson, 1784-1820) until 1811

GENERAL INSTITUTION FOR THE INSTRUCTION OF DEAF & DUMB CHILDREN, EDGBASTON 1814 - 1825

Thomas Braidwood (Son of Isabella & Thomas' grandson, 1782-1825) until 1825

BRAIDWOOD SEMINARY FOR DEAF CHILDREN, EDGBASTON 1816 - 1819

Isabella Braidwood (Dau. of Thomas, 1758-1819) until 1819
Elizabeth Braidwood (Dau. of Isabella & Thomas' grand-dau., 1788-1861)

USA - BOLLING HALL, COBBS & MANCHESTER PRIVATE SCHOOLS 1812 - 1820

John Braidwood (Son of Isabella & Thomas' grandson, 1784-1820)

NOTTING HILL, LONDON - KNOWN DATES 1858

Elizabeth Braidwood (Dau. of Isabella & Thomas' grand-dau. 1788-1861) married name Armfield
Elizabeth Armfield (Dau. of Elizabeth, b. 1830; &Thomas' great granddaughter. She later married Henry Higgins.)

2 - THE BRAIDWOOD ACADEMY FOR THE DEAF AND DUMB
EDINBURGH

Very little is known about Braidwood's Academy for the Deaf and Dumb. Most of the information were gleaned from antiquarian books, defunct magazines, 18th century newspapers and deaf people's signed history, known as Deaflore.

Braidwood's Academy was said to be primarily run as a family business, established at a time when every man had to fight to fend for himself not only in harsh economic conditions, but also during an era when many inventions were taking place. Inventors were guarding their prizes with ferocity because they all needed to protect the incomes that their inventions generated. On the other hand, many hearing schools were either privately managed, or mainly run by the church and a few charitable hospitals, with almost nothing in between to offer an education to every child, both deaf and hearing, who was unfortunate not only to be born into poverty, but also born disabled.

Nothing of particular interest appeared to have entered Thomas Braidwood's life and routine until one day when one man came round to pay him a visit sometime in the first quarter of 1760. For reasons that were neither explained nor discovered this man chose Thomas Braidwood, then 45 years old, as the focus of his particular yearning; perhaps the discreet and isolated location of Braidwood's Private Academy for Young Gentlemen situated at St Leonard's Hill at the foot of Canongate and also the excellent reputation of its teacher appealed to him. There was a possibility that Braidwood was recommended to this man through this man's connections in the wine trade, especially the wine merchants' federation in Edinburgh. This man called on Thomas Braidwood and introduced himself as a wealthy wine merchant from the nearby port of Leith and the name of the merchant was Alexander Shirreff.

A resident of Bernard Street, Leith, Alexander Shirreff had one misfortune in spite of his wealth and a successful wine business; he had a son who was both deaf and speech impaired since the age of three years old. His son, Charles, the youngest of Alexander's five children, was in dire need of an education when scholarly provisions for the deaf and dumb at that time in Edinburgh and its surrounds were non-existent. Thomas Braidwood did not appear to have had any connection with the deaf prior to the time of Alexander Shirreff's visit and he was very much pre-occupied with the running of his private academy for young gentlemen. No one will ever know the actual discussions that took place on that day between Shirreff and Braidwood, but Shirreff somehow succeeded in persuading Braidwood to accept the task of teaching his son Charles for an agreed sum.

There was a possibility that Braidwood was in a small way renowned for the correction of speech defects and stammering, as well as conducting elocution lessons as a part of his teaching package along with core subjects such as English, mathematics, geography and suchlike within his private academy. It was these speech correction elements which might have drawn Alexander Shirreff's notice and interest; Shirreff was in all likelihood hoping that Braidwood would be the best person who could help his deaf son.

Upon meeting 10 year old Charles Shirreff on Alexander's next visit, Braidwood examined the deaf child to assess his chances of success educationally and the main prerequisite for acceptance would be that the child must be of sound and capable mind. Braidwood certainly saw the task of teaching Charles a personal challenge and accepted Alexander's offer. Alexander Shirreff's desire for his son Charles to obtain an education must have been great if Alexander went to great lengths to find a suitable person to become his son's teacher. Alexander apparently had no objection to using sign language and also the additional benefit of speech would be very welcome, but a well-rounded educational provision, complete with the aim to equip the deaf child for the outside world of work and social interaction, would most certainly be the desired target for his deaf son. No known recorded facts exists to show exactly which communication mode Braidwood initially adopted to instruct his deaf pupil. It is hardly conceivable that Braidwood began with speech, and it is more likely that he used both writing and gestures to start off with Charles. In the 1760s, there was no shortage of fingerspelling charts, with the *Digiti Lingua* chart published in 1698 and the Duncan Campbell chart published in 1720 in Daniel Defoe's *The History of the Life and Adventures of Mr Duncan Campbell.*

Long before both the *Digiti Lingua* and *Duncan Campbell* charts, John Wilkins made the first published mention of the two-handed manual alphabet signs for vowels and consonants in his 1641 *Mercury, Or the Secret and Swift Messenger.* On page 117, Wilkins wrote:

> As for example: Let the tops of the fingers
> signifie the five vowels; the middle parts the
> five consonants; the bottoms of them the next

18

five consonants; the spaces betwixt the fingers the four next. One finger laid on the side of the hand may signifie T, two fingers V the consonant, three W, the little finger crossed X, the wrist Y, the middle of the hand Z.

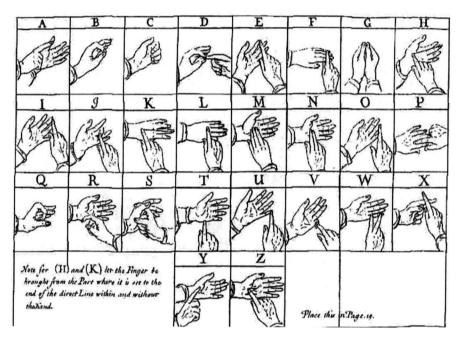

Digiti Lingua, 1698.
These hand alphabets were to quickly develop into positions that were used in Defoe's 1720 book on Duncan Campbell.

There exists a number of sources that described Braidwood's methods, but their accuracies will have to be taken with utmost care. *Encyclopaedia Britannica* in its early years gave some erroneous accounts, such as the wrong date of the foundation of the academy and its article made too much emphasis on speech. This may be because the authors of the *Britannica* were fascinated with the idea of making deaf children speak to the exclusion of other methods, including signs. The same can be said of other periodicals and publications of the mid-18th century; it must be remembered that people had a fascination about making the dumb speak more than about making the deaf well educated. There is no doubt that Braidwood was proficient in both teaching speech and enabling the deaf to speak, but at the same time there is no disputing the fact that Braidwood was also proficient in the use of the manual

19

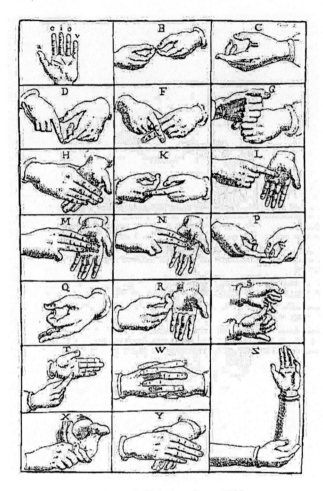

Manual Alphabet chart, 1720.
From Daniel Defoe's The History of the Life and Adventures of
Duncan Campbell.

alphabet, and later the sign language; he was reported very able in educating the deaf through this mode of communication. *The Christian's Penny Magazine* (no.133, December 20, 1834) contained a four page article entitled "Deafness and Dumbness - Early Efforts for their Cure." In this article, they praised Dr John Wallis, an Oxford mathematician and a founding member of the Royal Society, in teaching a deaf person to utter sounds in 1662 and they also praised Thomas Braidwood who *"undertook the instruction of a single pupil, the son of a merchant at Leith, upon the principles laid before the Royal Society, and published in the Philosophical Transactions."* This statement is common in other sources of writing by those who were fascinated by the deaf being taught to speak. It must be noted, however, that no concrete evidence exists to date to show that Braidwood started off teaching Shirreff using speech. A question therefore arises: "Which Philosophical Transactions linked with Wallis were the journals of the day referring to, and were they aware that Wallis also advocated the use of signs?"

John Wallis
(From frontispiece in his 1685 *A Treatise on Algebra*)

In his *The Instruction of the Deaf and Dumb; or, A Theoretical and Practical View of the means by which they are taught a Language* (Darton & Harvey, London, 1809) Joseph Watson wrote (Introduction, xxii-xxiii):

> ... I have not thought it incumbent on me to give anything like a history of the discovery and practice of the science of teaching the Deaf and Dumb. Suffice it to say, that our learned countryman, Dr John Wallis, near a hundred and fifty years ago, taught "a person dumb and deaf to speak and understand a language," (I use his own words in a letter to Robert Boyle Esq.) upon principles such as I have endeavoured to unfold. Various other persons in this country, at different periods, since his time, have made attempts of some sort, with unequal success. But, as far as I know, the late Mr Braidwood, formerly of Edinburgh, and latterly, till his death, in 1806, of Hackney, near London, was the first who kept a regular academy in this island, for the instruction of the Deaf and Dumb. His method was founded upon the same principles...

This Letter of Dr John Wallis to Robert Boyle Esq. (*Philosophical Transactions of the Royal Society 1665-1678, Vol. 5, 1670, pp. 1087-1099*), as mentioned in Joseph Watson's quote, imparted very little sense of how to educate a deaf person to speak and acquire a language although Wallis' fundamental method was laid out in this letter. It is not far off the mark if one were to say that there were many learned people who had studied Wallis' letter to Boyle and failed in their tasks in applying Wallis' principles as that Joseph Watson mentioned in his Introduction to his book. It is hard to envisage that Thomas Braidwood would have taken all the contents of Wallis' Letter to Boyle with ease and mastered the stated principles without any difficulty.

There also existed another letter written by Dr John Wallis to one Thomas Beverly, concerning his method for instructing deaf and dumb persons. This letter, dated 30 September 1698, was included in the Royal Society's *Philosophical Transactions (1683-1775), Vol. 20, 1698, pp. 353-360* — that magical year date that also saw the emergence of the *Digiti Lingua* manual alphabet chart. In his letter to Beverly, Wallis described how deaf children could be taught to read, write, speak and fingerspell and thus achieve an education. An extract from Wallis' Letter to Beverly on the method of teaching language reads:

> ... In order to do this, it is necessary in the first Place that the Deaf & Dumb Person be taught to write. That there may be something to express to the Eye what the sound of the Letter represent to the Ear.
>
> 'Twill next be very convenient, because Pen & Ink is not always to Hand, that he be taught, How to design each Letter, by some certain place, position or motion of a Finger, Hand or other part of the body, which may serve instead of writing. As for Instance. The five vowels a, e, i, o, u, by pointing to the top of the five fingers; & the other letters b, c, d &c. By such other place or Posture of a finger or otherwise as shall be agreed upon.
>
> After this a Language is to be taught this Deaf Person; by like methods as children are first taught a Language; tho' the Thing perhaps be not heeded, only with this difference: children learn sounds by the Ear. But both the one & the other do equally signify the same things or motions; & are equally (significantia ad placitum) of mere arbitrary Signification...

The method outlined in the Letter to Thomas Beverly, who was a father of four deaf children, appeared to come closest to that which Braidwood must have adopted because the clue lies in the last sentence of the first paragraph of the extract of John Wallis' letter above – *Vox oculis subjecta*, the motto of the Braidwood Academy. There is another account given by Edward Miner Gallaudet in page 189, Vol. 1 of the *American Annals of the Deaf,* suggesting that it was Alexander Shirreff who came across the *Philosophical* Transactions containing Wallis' letter to Thomas Beverly. It appears that Gallaudet obtained this information from reliable sources during his visit to Britain.

There is also a small contribution from a deaf pupil of the Manchester Deaf and Dumb School which was printed in the *Manchester Courier and Lancashire General Advertiser* dated Saturday 11 June 1842. On page 3, column 5 under the heading *Manchester Deaf and Dumb School, Public Examination of the Pupils*:

> ... I remember James Ainsworth telling me that Mr Braidwood has met a deaf and dumb boy, and he was speaking with him, but he cannot hear or speak, and Mr Braidwood will be wondered and surprised, and then he first made to spell with his hands about the alphabet, and the people reported him to the deaf and dumb children which must go to school and learn their lessons. Now Mr Braidwood is dead (Mr Pattison explained that Mr Braidwood was the original teacher of the deaf and dumb, in Edinburgh about 90 years ago)...
>
> G. Goodwin.

This simple contribution, written in "Deaf English," from a pupil's lesson book is a classic example of Deaflore/signed history being passed down from one deaf person to another and since it is inconceivable that although having proven ability in the correction of stammering and certain speech impairments, Braidwood began with speech. He began teaching Charles Shirreff using writing, gesticulations and signs long before attempting speech.

The earliest mention of Braidwood's progress was seen in a letter by J. H. to *The Scots Magazine* in January 1766, and this letter was also printed in the *London Chronicle* dated 3-5 June 1766:

> Edinburgh, January 1766.
>
> Sir,
>
> Those who have the misfortune to be deaf commonly spend their lives in ignorance and idleness, are useless to Society and a burden to their friends... and anyone who can remedy these evils

23

certainly deserves the thanks of the public. It is with pleasure, therefore, that I send you the following account:-

Mr Braidwood, writing master in Edinburgh, has, by his own ingenuity and industry, discovered a method of teaching the deaf and dumb to speak, and has certainly brought that art to the highest perfection ever yet known.

In September last, two of Mr Braidwood's pupils were examined at Edinburgh, in presence of the Earl of Morton President of the Royal Society, Sir David Dalrymple of Hales, Bart. George Clerk, Esq; one of the Commissioners of the Customs, Andrew Crosbie, Esq; Advocate, Doctor Robertson, Principal, and Mr James Russell, Professor of Natural Philosophy in the University of Edinburgh, Doctor Jardine, one of the Ministers of that City, and Doctor Blinshall, one of the Ministers of Dundee.

The first (who lost his hearing when about three years of age) son to Alexander Shirreff, Esq; of Craigleith, near Edinburgh, a lad of fifteen, who has been for some time under Mr Braidwood's care, reads any English book distinctly, and understands both the meaning and the grammatical construction of the passages which he reads. He answers questions put to him with great readiness, and his manner of pronouncing is articulate and distinct. He understands what is spoken by persons with whom he is familiar, and even by anyone who speaks distinct and slow, from the motion of their lips. Strangers also propose questions to him by writing with their finger on a table; and as he can follow the most rapid motion of that sort, there is little difficulty in holding conversation with him. He writes with elegance; is thoroughly master of arithmetic, book-keeping and geography; and is no inconsiderable proficient in drawing. He is to be bred a merchant, and it is thought he will excel in that business.

His other pupil, who was born deaf, was son to Doctor John Douglas, Physician in London, is a boy of thirteen. He had been only four months under Mr Braidwood's care, but his progress is remarkable; and in some things, particularly the tone of his voice, and his manner of articulation, he excels the former; owing chiefly to the superior skill which Mr Braidwood has acquired by experience.

The noble Lord and Gentlemen above mentioned, were highly pleased with Mr Braidwood's method, and the success he has already had in that way, and therefore they gave him a public attestation, and recommended him as well qualified in that art.

I am, &c., J. H.

The 1766 examination of Shirreff and Douglas set Braidwood on the road to renown, attracting the attention of the wealthy and the monied gentry whose deaf children were sorely in need of education. There, it seemed, was a small problem. Braidwood's Academy was not only a private school, it was also a home to his family and there was insufficient room for expansion. His pupils resided at his house, which became known among the locals as Dumbie House.

The announcements in the press by "J. H." in the early part of the 1760's was an attempt by a group of men fronted by "J. H." to promote Braidwood's work to the public at large. Although the initial move appears to have been that these men were seeking recognition of Braidwood's work and achievements, there are tones of an appeal to the public to offer their support to expand Braidwood's academy, perhaps with an idea or a hint of seeking funding to enable the training of teachers and therefore give an opportunity for numerous deaf people of poor parents to receive an education. "J. H." appears to be strongly linked with Alexander Shirreff and other respectable people through, perhaps, the Wine Merchants Federation or suchlike, and this person is revealed later.

Charles Shirreff left the Braidwood Academy around the first quarter of 1767 and it was understood that he went on to study the limner business. Braidwood took on several new deaf pupils. This was mentioned in a letter published in *The Scots Magazine* in August 1767 by the same J. H. who had written a letter to the same paper over a year earlier. The letter, which was also printed in the *London Chronicle*, read:-

Edinburgh, July 28th, 1767.

Sir,

You some time ago [xxviii. 31] published an account of Mr Braidwood, writing-master of Edinburgh, his success in teaching the deaf and dumb. I do not know if any discovery yet made deserves the thanks and notice of the public more than this. For, as it will appear by the following account, those who have the misfortune to be deaf, may now, not only be made acquainted with the great end and design of their being, and their concern in a future state, but also may become very useful members of Society, be enabled to do business, to act and judge for themselves, and so relieve their parents and relations of a very great burden, both in points of concern in mind, and experience of estate.

Mr Braidwood's first pupil, a lad of seventeen, son to Alexander Shirreff, Esq., left him some time ago. He is now studying the limning business. He reads any English book distinctly, and understands both the meaning and grammatical construction of the English language thoroughly. He either composes or makes an answer to a letter, equal, if not superior, to most people of his age. He writes with elegance, is thoroughly master at arithmetic, book-keeping, geography &c. and converses with ease.

Mr Braidwood has several deaf pupils who are making surprising progress in their education. I shall only mention the following as a specimen.

A boy of nine who has been eight months with him reads any English book slowly and pronounces distinctly, so that anyone who hears him understands with ease what he says. He writes readily, can vary any verb, according to person, number, time, and mood, and is begun to learn arithmetic.

Two young ladies, one of nine and the other of seven, daughters of the Rev. Mr Rogers at Shroton, near Blandford, Dorsetshire, have been six weeks under Mr Braidwood's care. They can pronounce all the letters and simple syllables distinctly.

Miss Medcalfe, aged about twelve, daughter to Mr James Medcalfe of Church Stretton in Shropshire, has been four weeks with him. She can pronounce near as distinctly as the Miss Rogers. They were all born deaf.

Mr Braidwood thinks, from the experience he has had in teaching the deaf, he may undertake to teach anyone of tolerable genius, in the space of about three years, to speak and read distinctly, to write readily, to perform the common rules of arithmetic, to understand the meaning and the grammatical construction of the English language, (so as to be able to compose, or to write an answer to a letter), and to have tolerable notion of the principles of morality and religion. He has had deaf pupils from twenty-five to seven years of age; he finds the younger they are, they pronounce the easier. He has likewise had considerable success in correcting the defects of persons who stutter, or have other impediments in their speech.

I am, etc.,
J. H.

The first two letters to The Scots Magazine revealed names of some of the pupils of Thomas Braidwood: Charles Shirreff (b.1st October 1749), John Douglas (b.1752) and Elizabeth Metcalfe (baptised on 2nd September 1755 - Medcalfe was incorrect and misspelt in the letter). The two deaf sisters from Shroton - Anna Colmer Rogers, who was born in 1758, and the other Mary ,who was born in 1762 - were both mentioned, but not by their full names.

Due to the fact that the Braidwood family did not retain and pass on a register of pupils or donate any documents for archival purposes, the odds of unearthing a list of pupils who attended the Academy are stacked against any researcher into the history of the Braidwood Academy. Since the school was run as a private establishment, and therefore as a company, the Braidwoods were under no legal obligation at that time to submit their records to public authorities. Over years of research and interviewing people, a small list of twelve deaf pupils who attended the Braidwood Academy in Edinburgh in its early years was drawn up:

Charles Shirreff	father: Alexander Shirreff, Leith wine merchant
John Douglas	father: John Douglas, London doctor
Francis H. Mackenzie	father: William Mackenzie.
Elizabeth Metcalfe	father: James Metcalfe of Church Stretton, Salop
Anna Colmer Rogers	father: Rev. Rogers of Shroton, Dorset
Mary Rogers	father: Rev. Rogers of Shroton, Dorset.
Robert Burns	
Alexander Inglis	
Archibald Douglas	
Miss Graham of Airth Castle	
Anne Burnett of Linton - later Mrs Graigie	
Mary Brunton	

The above were the known pupils who attended the Braidwood Academy up to the time of mid-1770s. There were some more pupils, but they cannot be traced.

Braidwood's pioneering work with the deaf attracted the attention and admiration of a few prominent people in and around Edinburgh; they felt that Braidwood deserved greater recognition for his work and set out to promote his name. One of those was a wine merchant and later Lord Provost of Edinburgh Thomas Elder (1737-1799) who took to writing letters to people he felt capable of raising the profile of Braidwood and his contribution to the education of the deaf. Elder wrote to John Stewart, Alexander Small, Elizabeth Delavery and John Hepburn at the same time about Braidwood's academy:

> Edin 20th Aug 1768
>
> I am strongly sollicited by several of my friends here that I am under the necessity of going to the trouble of a few lines to tell you there is one Braidwood, an English teacher who has of late years personified the

words amazing, wonders, in teaching the Deaf & Dumb to speak, read, write and figure. But he has no relation that can be of service in recommending him or making his extraordinary genius this way known to the world. He has been advised to go to London and try what can be done for him there, and that, if he were recommended to the Society of Arts, he may be taken notice of by them in some way that may be of service to him and make him much better known than by any advertisement which he could make in Print which people pay little attention to.

There is one Mr Hepburn a cousin of Mrs Elder going up at same time, who has seen his pupils & seems greatly inclined to serve him, and if you would choose to see Braidwood he will perhaps go along with him. Tho' I am very conscious to serve this man to raise my own consequence by any attention you may pay to my recommendation. I should be sorry to ask you to do anything that I thought would be disagreeable or inconvenient to you that I would therefore humbly request of you is that if your time will permit and from your natural inclination will encourage merit of all kinds you choose to converse with him if you think his talents will merit any attention from the public, you would give him your advice and assist him to follow it; on the contrary if from want of time or other circumstances this may be inconvenient for you, I beg you would think no more of the matter.

(Taken from Acc65, Letterbook of Thomas Elder, wine merchant of Edinburgh, 26 July 1767-7 Feb 1784, Page 57. Edinburgh City Library)

From Thomas Elder's letter, J. H. was revealed as John Hepburn, a cousin of Elder's wife Emilia. There were people who felt that Braidwood's pioneering work in the education of the deaf deserved greater respect and recognition.

The following year in 1769 another letter from John Hepburn was sent to both *The Scots Magazine* and *The London Magazine*:

Edinburgh, July 15, 1769,

Sir,

When the melancholy situation of such as are born deaf is considered, it must give the greatest pleasure to every benevolent mind, to be informed, that it is possible to bring relief to those objects of compassion; to rescue them from that ignorance and idleness in which they commonly live; and, instead of being useless in the world, and a burden upon their relations, to render them capable of business, and a comfort to all concerned in them.

MR BRAIDWOOD, writing-master in Edinburgh, claims the notice of the public, as having, in consequence of the greatest labour and attention, discovered a method, by which he is able to teach the deaf and dumb to speak, read, write, and cipher; to understand the meaning and grammatical construction of the English language; to acquire a proper knowledge of the principles of morality and religion, &c. However astonishing this fact may appear, it is sufficiently known to many who have attended at the public examination of his pupils, both here and at London, and who have, in the newspapers and magazines (xxix. 421), declared their great satisfaction with Mr B.'s method and success. Among others, the late Lord Morton, Lord Hailes, Commissioner Clerk, Dr Robertson, Dr Russel, Dr Blinshall, and Andrew Crosbie, Esq.; here; and Sir John Pringle, Dr Wilbraham, Dr Hunter, Dr Watson, Dr Huck, Dr Franklin, Dr Orme, Dr Monro, and Dr Gifford, at London, have had the opportunity of attending these examinations, and of observing the proficiency of Mr B.'s scholars.

Mr B. has at present several deaf pupils from six to twenty-eight years of age, who are all advancing in their education as well as could be wished; but it is to be regretted, that he has been obliged to refuse above thirty deaf persons, whose friends have applied for his assistance, as he can teach only a few at the same time, which of necessity renders the expence of this kind of education greater than some parents can afford.

In order to render Mr B.'s art universally useful, two things are necessary. The first is, That he shall communicate his skill to three or four ingenious young men, who may assist and succeed him in this business: and the second is, That some fund be established under the direction of proper managers, to be applied for defraying the expence of educating such, whose parents are unable to take that burden on them. N.B. Most of those who have applied, could not afford part of the expence. By these means, so useful and art would be preserved, and no unfortunate object be deprived of the benefit arising from it.

Mr B. has generously declared his readiness to communicate his skill to others upon the above plan; and in an age distinguished by so many public charities, and so ready to encourage every invention in arts or science, a fund sufficient for the purpose might be obtained, either by an application to his Majesty, or otherwise.

The design of this letter is, to excite the generous and compassionate among the nobility and gentry, to inquire into the facts already mentioned, and to afford them the opportunity of patronizing a scheme, so truly charitable, and so useful to society. If Mr B. receives no public encouragement, he will be obliged to move in the same confined track as hitherto, and teach only such deaf persons as he can afford the expence; and when he dies, this valuable art will probably die with him.

P.S. Mr B. has been very successful in perfectly correcting stuttering, and many other defects in speech, both in young persons, and those more advanced in years.

I am, etc.,
J. H.

According to the 1769 contribution to *The Scots Magazine*, Braidwood made an offer to train three or four men to become teachers of the deaf. A question must be asked why no one took up his offer; not only can one accuse Thomas Braidwood of not being open about his newly-found profession as a teacher of the deaf, but also that no one can ever accuse Braidwood of not trying to encourage moves for charitable sponsorship of deaf children for places in his academy. This is an interesting situation and it throws light on the fact that many people at that time may not have been made fully aware of the success of Braidwood's method up to the time of the published 1769 letter. The reason appeared to be that he taught a small number of select deaf pupils and the number was not sufficiently high to convince the wider public of the success of his method. It was also mentioned that Braidwood, being a professional teacher, did not catch the public's fascination during that period compared with a French priest, the Abbe de l'Epee, who devoted his time to rescuing the "poor deaf and dumb children from both a world of isolation and the harsh streets of Paris," giving them shelter and later an education. Religion was undoubtedly powerful and influential in assisting people to determine whether to contribute to worthy causes or not, and Braidwood was not religion-connected. Strange as it may seem, Charles Michel de l'Epee was in fact a wealthy man, born of an extremely rich family in Versailles. He was able to afford to spend a good proportion his wealth on deaf children and their education on top of accepting funds from the public. Braidwood, however, did take on teaching quite a good number of deaf children of poor families at his own expense. His academy was often visited by deaf children of poverty-stricken families begging for education, but Braidwood had to reluctantly turn them away.

In the next ten years following the 1769 letter, Braidwood continued to appeal for assistance and funds to train a number of men to become teachers of the deaf, with the hope that at the end of their training, these men would be able to establish new schools for the deaf in places across Britain. Braidwood never asked for much money, nor did he seek financial profit in his appeals. He was more concerned about the lack of opportunity for the deaf children of the poor to receive an education. Despite Braidwood's best efforts, his appeals and attempts to raise funds had fallen on deaf ears.

The number of deaf pupils in 1769 was small; Braidwood, as the 1769 letter indicated, was taking on some hearing people who had speech impediments, and not only that, there was the case where Braidwood claimed to have turned away over thirty deaf persons. This was most likely because the school was small, and all lessons were taken in one room. One must at all times note that Dumbie House in the early years of its base as an academy for the deaf and dumb was Braidwood's family home and also that deaf pupils from outside Edinburgh were residents in the house for the duration of their education.

Dumbie House was built in mid-18th century and it was quite new when Thomas Braidwood purchased the property to establish his academy for young men. The house consisted of a lower ground floor, an upper ground floor, a second floor and an attic with a small outhouse connected to the main house at the rear and an annexe connected on the upper ground floor to the west. Dumbie House had four rooms per floor except for two rooms in the attic, not counting the annexe and the rear outhouse. With a total of fourteen rooms in all it was indeed a large house but every room was of small to medium size. With the kitchen situated on the west side on the upper ground floor annexe of the south elevation, there were eleven rooms for family use, and the academy was most likely situated in the front west room of the north elevation upper ground floor because it was the largest room of the house. The size of that room used for classroom would be some sixteen feet square, which would be enough to hold about twelve to fifteen pupils with sufficient space for tables, chairs and elbow room for each pupil. There would hardly be enough room for more pupils unless another room was turned into a classroom, but Braidwood, being the sole teacher, would be in need of more help in the form of teachers. Along with Dumbie House, Braidwood owned another large three storey house in nearby Abbey Hill. This house contained seven bedrooms, an elegant dining room, dressing room, drawing room, large hall, lobby and a large completely fitted kitchen. Adjoining the kitchen was a house consisting of servants' apartments and an ale-cellar with catacombs. In addition, there was a washhouse, a pump well, a coach house, a large hay loft, a cow house, a hen house and a stable with six stalls. The grounds were about an acre and a half, containing numerous fine fruit trees as shown in Robert Kirkwood's 1817 map on the next page.

Braidwood's pupils came from England and the far corners of Scotland. This meant they had to reside with the Braidwood family on a board and lodging basis – they were known as "pupils with benefits." Two rooms would be set aside on the top floor in Dumbie House to lodge the pupils, one for females and the other for males. The board and

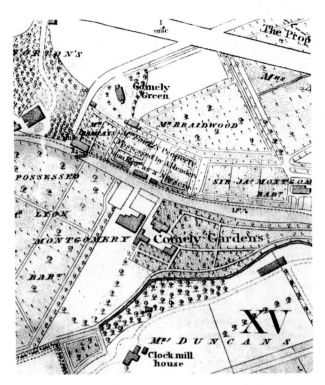

Robert Kirkwood's 1817 map showing Thomas Braidwood's residence at Abbeyhill, next to Comely Green

lodging fees would include a laundry service and some expenses for taking the pupils out to places of interest at weekends or perhaps even at any time of the week. This "with benefits" cost added greatly to tuition fees. Without support from the government, the various authorities, the local charities and private sponsors that would contribute to the costs for deaf pupils' education, Braidwood had no option but set his own fees and confine himself to teaching the fortunate few deaf pupils from affluent families, restricting the free places for deaf children of the poor to a manageable minimum.

There is no evidence, however, to indicate that Braidwood's fees were extortionate nor was there any evidence indicating that Braidwood was grasping as he was indeed accepting a few deaf children of the poor without charge. It appears that Braidwood's fees were in line with other private academies of his time.

It appeared that people were more interested in speech and this generated greater publicity and income for Braidwood whenever he was

North (above) and south (below) faces of the
Braidwood Academy, Dumbie House (1935)
The building was demolished in 1942.

taking on mainly hearing and hard of hearing day pupils whose needs were only speech correction and perhaps reading lessons. Literacy problems among the hearing still is a prevalent fact and was even ongoing in Braidwood's era. It must be stressed that Braidwood did attempt to teach speech to the profoundly deaf pupils. Whether he was successful or not is open to question, but it appears that Braidwood would discontinue to teach speech to those who could not gain success from it. The approach taken by Braidwood appears to be that every child must be given an opportunity to speak and this is no different in schools for the deaf at the present. An example of Braidwood's fees for speech correction and literacy can be seen in the case of one supposedly partially deaf pupil, Charlotte Carter.

There is an indication of the fees charged by Braidwood at his academy. In the Lincolnshire Archives, under Redbourne, Personal - ref. RED3 (Wills, Settlements, Executorships), there are documents relating to the executorship for Robert Carter Thelwall. Among the papers are "Accounts - ref. RED 3/1/4/6 - date 1753-1787; item: Disbursements, a further account book of Robert Carter - ref. RED 3/1/4/6/2 - date 1770-1787". In page 81 of the account book there is a note which reads:

> To Mr Braidwood for 5 months teaching Charlotte
> to speak and read without any Benefit at the rate of
> 1 guinea per hour and at his own school - £315
>
> (1780)

Three hundred and fifteen pounds for five months, and it is no wonder that the publicity about the speech achievement of pupils was generating income for the Braidwood Academy. It is inconceivable that signing and fingerspelling played an inferior role; it must have cost a pretty penny to educate those who could not achieve speech proficiency because such pupils needed greater reading and writing skills to compensate for their inability both to master speech and to hear, and on the other hand Braidwood had to justify costs to the parents and guardians of deaf pupils who could not achieve normal speech. Another indication of the private school fees in Braidwood's time can be seen in the book *Education in Edinburgh in the Eighteenth Century* by Alexander Law (University of London Press, 1965). On page 183 the author referred to fees for private girls' schools:

> The fees for boarding schools show an increase as
> the century wears on. In 1748, they are at £5 a

quarter, and remain on an average at about that figure until 1761. Thereafter they range between £7 and £11 a quarter. The Misses Lythgoe in 1779 charged for girls under 14 £22 a year for board, and for those over 14 £28 a year. Day boarders in this school were charged £14 a year. For these sums the Misses Lythgoe gave instruction in all kinds of needlework, writing, arithmetic, music and French, and Miss Jean Lythgoe accompanied her pupils to dancing schools.

From Alexander Law's account, a rough idea of the fees charged by the Braidwood Academy can be formed: its fees would have been much higher at between £60 and £100 per child per annum to reflect the specialist nature of educating the deaf and the endeavours to familiarise them with the hearing world around them.

The management of the Braidwood academy appears to follow the methods adopted by contemporary grammar schools; the normal school hours would be similar to that of the grammar schools. It would mean that, in the winter, the hours would be 9am to 12pm and 2pm to 5pm, whereas, in the summer, it would be 7am to 9am, 10am to 1pm and 3pm to 5pm. Seven in the morning may sound incredible, but in Francis Green's *Vox oculis subjecta* (1783), in page 141 Green mentioned:

> ... As soon as they rise in the morning they all repair to the same schoolroom for an hour or two before breakfast.

Periods of recreation were set aside each day and the deaf pupils were initially supervised by Braidwood and his wife Margaret. As the two Braidwood daughters got older, they became involved with the deaf pupils and participated in the running of the academy.

Since Braidwood was a devout member of the Presbyterian church, it is fair to assume that Sundays were religiously observed and were also used for Bible class where religious and moral training were given. Community and cultural integration was not ruled out; it is known Braidwood took his pupils to the theatre, and that information was gleaned from various sources on the life of Charles Shirreff. Tours of the city of Edinburgh and its surrounds were undertaken as a part of the academy's social, historical and environmental studies.

The situation would have been different had there been some positive response to his appeal in the 1769 letter in *The Scots Magazine* for the establishment of a fund to help parents of deaf children who could not afford to pay his fees, and also to help Braidwood to take on three or four young men to train them in his teaching skills. Due to the fact that Braidwood's offer had fallen on deaf ears, he was left with no option but to communicate his skill to close members of his own family. This decision, however, did not completely shut the door to opportunity for those outside the family to enter training to become teachers of the deaf. The opportunity was always open, subject to one simple condition: that funding to teach such persons become available.

John Hepburn's 1769 letter to *The Scots Magazine* also revealed that Braidwood and his pupils gave a demonstration of their educational capabilities and prowess in front of an audience of prominent people in London. Travelling appears to be one of the features of the educational package offered by Braidwood. Despite the lack of response to Braidwood's 1769 offer, his academy continued to attract more deaf children of the wealthy classes, the school growing steadily in its reputation and pulling in the attention of reputable people and journalists. In the 1st edition of *Encyclopaedia Britannica (vol.2)* published in 1771, under the heading of Dumbness on page 457, an article referring to Braidwood was given lengthy space. The article referred to dumbness as the privation of the faculty of speech and concentrated mainly on that topic; the public's fascination with the speech of the deaf continued to prevail over the important and vital use of signing in the education of the deaf which Braidwood clearly used as a major part of a communication package.

The relevant section on Braidwood in this article read:

> ... The organs of hearing and of speech have little or no connection. Persons deprived of the former generally possesses the latter in such perfection, that nothing further is necessary, in order to make them articulate, than to teach them how to use these organs. This is indeed no easy task; but experience shews that it is practicable. Mr THOMAS BRAIDWOOD, of Edinburgh, is perhaps the first who ever brought this surprising art to any degree of perfection. For these some years past, he has taught many people, born deaf, to speak distinctly, to read,

to write, to understand figures, the principles of religion and morality, &c. This, at first sight, may appear to be altogether incredible; but the fact is certain Mr Braidwood has, at present, ten or a dozen of deaf pupils, some of them above twenty years of age, all making a rapid and amazing progress in those useful branches of education. Mr Braidwood's principal difficulty, after he has discovered this art, was to make people believe in the practicability of it. He advertised in the public papers; he exhibited his pupils to many noblemen and gentlemen; still he found the generality of mankind unwilling to believe him. A remarkable instance of this incredulity occurred some years ago:

A gentleman in England sent a deaf girl of his to Mr Braidwood's care. A year or two afterwards, Mr Braidwood wrote to the father, that his daughter could speak, read and write distinctly. The father returned an answer, begging Mr Braidwood's excuse, as he could not believe it; however, he desired a friend of his, who was occasionally going to Edinburgh, to call at Mr Braidwood, and inquire into the truth of what he had wrote him: he did so; conversed with Mr Braidwood, saw the young lady, heard her read, speak and answer any questions he put to her.

On his return, he told the father the surprising progress his child had made; but the father thought the whole an imposition: the girl herself wrote to her father, but he looked upon the letter as a forgery. About this time, the father died, and the mother sent an uncle and cousin of the deaf lady's from Shrewsbury, in order to be satisfied with the truth. When they arrived, Mr Braidwood told the girl her uncle and cousin were in the parlour, and desired her to go and ask them how they did, and how mother and other friends did. The friends were astonished, and could hardly credit their own ears and eyes.

We have conversed with Mr Braidwood, concerning the nature and method of teaching this wonderful art: he seems to be very desirous of communicating and transmitting his discovery to posterity: but says, and, from the nature of the thing, we believe it to be true, that he cannot communicate it so fully in writing as to enable any other person to teach it. The first thing in the method is, to teach the pupil to pronounce the simple sounds of the vowels and consonants. We have even seen him performing this operation; but are unable to give a clear idea of it. He pronounces the sound of 'a' slowly, pointing out the figure of the letter at the same time; makes his pupil observe the motion of his mouth and throat; he then puts his finger into the pupil's mouth, depresses or elevates the tongue, and makes him keep the parts in that position; then he lays hold of the outside of the windpipe, and gives it some kind of squeeze, which it is impossible to describe: all the while he is pronouncing 'a', the pupil is anxiously imitating him, but at first seems not to understand what he would have him to do. In this manner, he proceeds, till the pupil has learned to pronounce the sounds of the letters. He goes on in the same manner to join a vowel and a consonant, till at length the pupil is enabled both to speak and to read.

It is altogether in vain for us to attempt to say any more concerning the mode of operation. Mr Braidwood undertakes every deaf person, who is not at the same time foolish or idiotical. The greatest misfortune is, that this art is confined to a single man, and that his pupils must live in the house with him for some years. The expence necessary in attending education of this kind excludes all but people in opulent circumstances from deriving any advantages from it. Mr Braidwood says that the only way for preserving the art, and communicating it to a number, is to take people in the way of apprentices: this he is unable to do at his own expence. What a pity, that such a useful and curious art should live and die with a single man! There are many sums mortified in this kingdom, both by government and private persons, for less important purposes, than the preservation and extension of the art of raising a great number of our fellow-creatures from the rank of brutes, to that of reasonable beings, and useful members of society.

The deaf girl referred to in the above article was Elizabeth Metcalfe of Church Stretton, a small town situated almost midway between Shrewsbury and Ludlow in Shropshire.

From the 1770s onwards the following deaf pupils were admitted:

John Philp Wood	father: John Wood.
Pelham Maitland	admitted 1773.
John Goodricke	father: Sir Henry Goodricke
Sarah Dashwood	father: Sir John Dashwood-King
John Creasy	parents: John and Mary Creasy, London
Girl 3	from Shepton Mallet
Boy 2	unidentified; Edinburgh Messenger VIII, 1844
Lister Sagar	father: Richard Sagar of Colne, Lancashire.
John Bolling	father: Thomas Bolling, Virginia, Admitted 1771
Mary Bolling	ditto. Admitted 1775
Thomas Bolling	ditto. Admitted 1775
Charles Green	father: Francis Green, Boston, USA
Charlotte Carter	father: Robert Carter

In 1772 Thomas Pennant (right) visited Braidwood's Academy and he reported in his *A Tour in Scotland and a Voyage to the Hebrides, 1772* (pages 256-258):

On returning into the city, I called at Mr Braidwood's academy of dumb and deaf. This extraordinary professor had under his care a number of young persons, who had received the Promethean heat, the divine inflatus; but from the unhappy construction of their organs, were ('till they had received his instructions) denied the power of utterance. Every idea was locked up, or appeared but in their eyes, or at their fingers ends, till their master instructed them in arts unknown to us, who have the faculty of hearing. Apprehension reaches us by the grosser sense. They see our words, and our uttered thoughts become to them visible. Our ideas expressed in speech strike their ears in vain: their eyes receive them as they part from our lips. They conceive by intuition, and speak by imitation. Mr Braidwood first teaches them the letters and their powers; and the ideas of words written, beginning with the most simple. The art of speaking is taken from the motion of his lips; his words being uttered slowly and distinctly. Their answers are slow and somewhat harsh.

When I entered the room, and found myself surrounded with numbers of human forms so oddly circumstanced, I felt a sort of anxiety, such as I might be supposed to feel had I been environed by another order of beings. I was soon relieved, by being introduced to the most angelic young creature, of about the age of thirteen. She honoured me with her new-acquired conversation; but I may truly say that I could scarcely bear the power of her piercing eyes: she looked me through and through. She soon satisfied me that she was an apt scholar. She readily apprehended all I said, and returned me the answers with utmost facility. She read, she wrote well. Her reading was not by rote. She could cloath the same thoughts in a new set of words, and never vary from the original sense. I have forgot the book she took up, or the sentences she made a new version of; but the effect was as follows:

Original Passage

Lord Bacon has divided the whole of human knowledge into history, poetry and philosophy, which are referred to the three powers of the mind, memory, imagination and reason.*

Version

A nobleman has parted the total or all of man's study, or understanding, into an account of the life, manners, religion and customs of any people or country, verse or metre, moral or natural knowledge, which are pointed to the three faculties

42

of the soul or spirit; the faculty of remembering what is past, thought or conception, and right judgement.

*This was read since, by another young lady; but that which I heard was not less difficult, nor less faithfully translated.

I left Mr Braidwood and his pupils with the satisfaction which must result from a reflection on the utility of his art, and the merit of his labours: who, after receiving under his care a Being that seemed to be merely endowed with a human form, could produce the divina particula aurae, latent, and, but for his skill, condemned to be even latent in it; and who could restore a child to its glad parents with a capacity of exerting its rational powers, by expressive sounds of duty, love and affection.

This "most angelic young girl of thirteen" was most probably Mary Brunton, the daughter of Benjamin Brunton, the owner of a shoe-making factory in Newcastle-upon-Tyne. Again here, we have another writer who was more fascinated by speech, reading and writing rather than exploring what he could find "at their fingers ends," an indication that signing was seen at Braidwood's academy. Thomas Pennant left very little of interest in terms of historical value.

The following year in late 1773, Braidwood received a visit by the celebrated Dr Samuel Johnson (right) who was on his journey through Scotland and the Hebrides. In his book *A Journey to the Western Islands of Scotland* (*1775*, pages 380-383), Dr Johnson wrote:

There is one subject of philosophical curiosity to be found in Edinburgh, which no other city has to shew; a college of the deaf and dumb, who are taught to speak, to read, to write, and to practice arithmetick, by a gentleman, whose name is Braidwood. The number which attends him is, I think, about twelve, which he brings together into a little school, and instructs according to their several degrees of proficiency.

43

I do not mean to mention the instruction of the deaf as new. Having been first practiced upon the son of a constable of Spain, it was afterwards cultivated with much emulation in England, by Wallis and Holder, and was latterly professed by Mr Baker, who once flattered me with hopes of seeing his method published. How far any former teachers have succeeded, it is not easy to know; the improvement of Mr Braidwood's pupils is wonderful. They not only speak, write and understand what is written, but if he that speaks looks towards them, and modifies his organs by distinct and full utterance, they know so well what is spoken, that is an expression scarcely figurative to say, they hear with the eye. That any have attained to the power mentioned by Burnet, of feeling sounds, by laying a hand on the speaker's mouth, I know not; but I have seen so much, that I can believe more; a single word, or a short sentence, I think, may possibly be so distinguished.

It will readily be supposed by those that consider this subject that Mr Braidwood's scholars spell accurately. Orthography is vitiated among such as learn first to speak, and then to write, by imperfect notions of the relations between letters and vocal utterance; but to those students every character is of equal importance; for letters are to them not symbols of names, but of things; when they write they do not represent a sound, but delineate a form.

This school I visited, and found some of the scholars waiting for their master, whom they are said to receive at his entrance with smiling countenances and sparkling eyes, delighted with the hope of new ideas. One of the young Ladies had her slate before her, on which I wrote a question consisting of three figures, to be multiplied by two figures. She looked upon it, and quivering her fingers in a manner which I thought very pretty, but of which I know not whether it was art or play, multiplied the sum regularly in two lines, observing the decimal place; but did not add the two lines together, probably disdaining so easy an operation. I pointed at the place where the sum total should stand, and she noted it with such expedition as seemed to shew that she had it only to write.

It was pleasing to see one of the most desperate of human calamities capable of so much help: whatever enlarges hope, will exalt courage; after having seen the deaf taught arithmetick, who would be afraid to cultivate the Hebrides?

There was a little more to what Dr Johnson wrote in his book. James Boswell (right) published *A Journal of a Tour to the Hebrides with Samuel Johnson, LL.D.* (Part V of Boswell's *The Life of Dr Johnson,* 1785) and he wrote:

> Near the end of his "Journey," Dr Johnson has given liberal praise to Mr Braidwood's academy for the deaf and dumb. When he visited it, a circumstance occurred which was truly characteristical of our great lexicographer. "Pray," said he, "can they pronounce any long words?" Mr Braidwood informed him they could. Upon which Dr Johnson wrote one of his *sesquipedalia verba,* which was pronounced by the scholars, and he was satisfied. My readers may perhaps wish to know what the word was; but I cannot gratify their curiosity. Mr Braidwood told me, it remained long in his school, but had been lost before I made my inquiry.*

> *One of the best critics of our age "does not wish to prevent the admirers of the incorrect and nerveless style which generally prevailed for a century before Dr Johnson's energetic writings were known, from enjoying the laugh that his story may produce, in which he is very ready to join them." He, however, requests me to observe that, "my friend very properly chose a long word on this occasion, not, it is believed, from any predilection for polysyllables (though he certainly had a due respect for them), but in order to put Mr

45

Braidwood's skill to the strictest test, and to try the efficacy of his instruction by the most difficult exertion of the organs of his pupils."

- *BOSWELL.*

Previous to the visits by both Thomas Pennant and Dr Johnson, James Burnett (Lord Monboddo) visited Braidwood's academy during the course of his research for a forthcoming publication and his observations and comments were included in his work published in 1773, *Of the Origin and Progress of Language* (Book 1, Chapter 14, pages 177-186) and this part pertaining to Braidwood is in Appendix 1.

Another writer John Herries also made a brief mention of Braidwood in his *Elements of Speech*, which was published in 1773.

Towards the end of 1779, Hugo Arnot, an advocate and a friend of Lord Monboddo, published his *History of Edinburgh* (1816 edition, Book 2, Chapter 3, page 425) in which he described Braidwood's method:

> He begins with learning the deaf articulation or the use of their vocal organs; and at the same time, teaches them to write the characters and compose words for them. He next shows them the use of words in expressing visible objects and their qualities. After this he proceeds to instruct them in the proper arrangement of words, or grammatical construction of language.
>
> The deaf (Mr Braidwood observes) find great difficulty in attaining pronunciation, but still more in acquiring a proper knowledge of written language. Their only method is conversing by signs and gestures. Their ideas are few, being entirely confined to visible objects and to the passions and senses, the former of which they delineate by figures, the latter by gestures. The connection between our ideas and written language being purely arbitrary, it is a very hard task to give the deaf any notion of that mode of conversing, theirs being only hieroglyphical. Another and still a greater difficulty is to enable them to comprehend the meaning of the figurative part of language. For

instance, they don't understand high, low, hard, tender, cloudy, etc., when applied to matter, but have not the slightest conception of these qualities when applied to mind. Notwithstanding these difficulties, the deaf attain a perfect knowledge of written language and become capable of speaking and writing their sentiments in the most distinct manner, and of understanding fully what they read. Being thus advanced they are capable to learn any art or science (musick excepted) and to translate one language into another. Mr Braidwood's pupils are under his tuition from three to six years, according to their age, capacity, and conveniency.

When we visited this academy we found that the boys not only could converse by the help of the artificial alphabet they learned by putting fingers onto certain positions, but they understood us, although perfect strangers to them, by the motion of our lips. In this manner they actually conversed with us, returning an answer to us distinctly, yet slowly, viva voce.

Hugo Arnot's account of his visit to the Braidwood Academy is probably the most honestly written and his observations the truest in that he mentioned fingerspelling, signing and gestures on top of speech, lipreading and writing. It showed that Thomas Braidwood was employing a full range of communication modes that would assist his pupils greatly. This was the Braidwoodian method, employing and applying all ranges of modes of communication in the education of the deaf child, not the oralist, or oral-only, method that many previous historians and researchers into the history of the education of the deaf wrote about. Arnot also mentioned that there were about 12 pupils at the time of his visit.

Of all the modes of communication, speech was probably the most profitable and, as has been said, Braidwood also took on hearing children and adults with speech impediments of varying degrees and he certainly displayed his proficiency in that area; his public claims were verifiable and he offered exactly what his customers wanted. Braidwood was taking on as many pupils as he could accommodate along with those on a "fees without benefits" basis - better known as day pupils who did not reside at the academy on a board and lodging basis.

The main subjects taught by Braidwood would include English, Mathematics, Geography and French as gleaned from what is known from various sources. Additional instructions in social affairs and etiquette would most certainly have been applied since the children came from wealthy families and they would be required to exercise both manners, besides obligation to display gestures of common courtesies, and knowledge of what was going on around them. Some sources mentioned that quite a number of Braidwoodian pupils found employment as accountants or similar in Counting Houses.

Braidwood's fame spread to the Colonies in America and his work came to the attention of the Bolling family of Virginia. This family were noteworthy as direct descendants of the Native American Indian princess Pocahontas, in the sixth generation after her marriage to the colonist John Rolfe. Major Thomas Bolling (left), of Cobbs, Chesterfield County, on the north bank of the Appomattox River (about nine miles from the city of Petersburg), had three children who were born deaf. They were John (b. 31 January 1761), Mary (b. 27 January 1765) and Thomas (b. 1 July 1766). Thomas Bolling sent his first son John to the Braidwood Academy in 1771, and pleased with his progress, he then sent his other two children Mary and Thomas to join their elder brother in 1775. Another American, Francis Green of Boston, Massachusetts, sent his son Charles, aged 8 years old, to Braidwood's academy in February 1780.

Contrary to long held belief that Braidwood only catered for the children of the opulent classes, it is known that Braidwood took on one or two deaf children annually and educated them without charging fees. This began in 1773 when the governors of Heriot's Hospital took on a deaf and dumb boy, Pelham Maitland, a son of a poor shoemaker, and sent him to Braidwood's academy on a day pupil basis, donating only £10 annually to the Braidwood Academy.

Since Braidwood was taking on pupils of varying ages, from six to twenty-five years old, he was teaching his pupils as individuals in accordance with their ages, intellect and needs. This kind of teaching situation was becoming burdensome, and following the lack of public response to his 1769 offer to train more young men in becoming teachers of the deaf, Braidwood took on and trained his immediate family members — firstly his daughters Margaret and Isabella — in teaching the deaf. Later in 1770, Braidwood engaged his 14 year old nephew John Braidwood as a trainee teacher of the deaf. This John Braidwood, born on 12 September 1756 in Walston, was the son of Thomas' eldest brother John and his wife Elizabeth (nee Borrowman). The number of teachers at Braidwood Academy grew to four and the teaching became more manageable.

Braidwood's fame attracted a competitor in the form of Cortes Telfair who professed to be better than Braidwood himself in the correction of speech defects. Cortes Telfair (b. 1749) was the son of a tailor James Telfair (b. 1712). Although he was born in Edinburgh, Cortes and his Scottish father lived in London. Cortes travelled from London and opened his private school in Edinburgh in 1772, naming it the College for the Deaf and Dumb and it was initially based in Niddery's Wynd. At Easter 1773, Telfair removed his college to Skinner's Close, locating it on the first floor of the second stairs. The main aim of Telfair's college was "to cure dumbness, stammering and all impediments in speech," indicating a very oralist approach, as opposed to Braidwood's all round educational provision delivered via the use of signs, fingerspelling, speech, reading and writing – known as the Braidwoodian method.

Telfair temporarily closed his school in Skinner's Close in the summer of 1773, possibly to travel to London for family affairs or business. In late September of the same year, Telfair returned to Edinburgh and reopened his school in the same place, on the same first floor in Skinner's Close. He added English, reading, writing and pronunciation to his teaching package; Telfair also changed teaching and class times to the hours to suit his students. Telfair, however, made one bold move – he banned spoken Scotch in his school.

In June 1775, Telfair published *The Town and Country Spelling Book* (Pub: Charles Elliot, Parliament Square) and continued his educational establishment in Edinburgh until around 1779 when he moved back to London. Telfair's College for the Deaf and Dumb did not achieve the same renown as Braidwood's Academy for the Deaf and Dumb and this appeared to have caused some resentment on Telfair's part towards Thomas Braidwood, with Telfair often accusing Braidwood of making fraudulent claims of his success in teaching the deaf and exaggerating their achievements.

Telfair College for the Deaf and Dumb (on 1st floor of right stair)
Skinners Close, Castle Hill, High Street, Edinburgh.

It appeared that, because Telfair found little success in Edinburgh, in 1779 he moved south of the border to try his luck in England. There were various newspaper advertisements announcing Telfair's school, and his successful "cures" of stammering and impediments of speech. His advertisements covered wide areas of England such as Bath and Bristol in the west to London in the east. Telfair made some claims of his teaching prowess and success through a number of press announcements – one in the *Bath Chronicle/Weekly Gazette* dated 24 August 1780 had this inclusion:

Dumbness and Impediments in Speech

> Mr TELFAIR teaches the Deaf and Dumb to speak, and to understand what is spoken by others. He likewise removes all Impediments in Speech. This useful art he has practised for several years in Edinburgh, and now practises in London; where he makes a quarterly exhibition of his Deaf and Dumb Scholars, who are examined by the most eminent Gentlemen of the Royal Society and of the Faculty. The truth of this can be ascertained by some

distinguished Gentlemen of the Faculty in Bath and Bristol; by applying to Mr Rack, on St. James' Parade; or Mr Cruttwell, printer, in Bath; where Mr Telfair may be heard of during his stay in Bath, which will probably not be longer than six or seven days.

In 1780, Cortes and his father James took occupation of a very large house belonging to the Countess of Salisbury at the west end of Knightsbridge Terrace near Hyde Park Corner. The College for the Deaf and Dumb was re-established at these premises. Whether this was the first school for the Deaf and dumb in England or not is open to question: it is most likely that Telfair's college was not a true establishment for the education of the deaf. The institution was mainly concerned with the correction of all forms of speech impediments along with accompanying educational provisions, rather than the education of the deaf and dumb. The number of deaf children taught by Telfair appeared small and whether his claim that these children were actually fully deaf and dumb is open to question; Telfair appeared to harbour bitterness towards Braidwood, rubbishing his claims and making counter claims of his own success. This was made known in many newspaper advertisements, and one such example from the *Caledonian Mercury* dated 28 May 1784 read:

At the College of DEAF and DUMB,
Knightsbridge, London,

MR TELFAIR in six years teaches Youth born without hearing *to speak, and pretty commonly know by the eye what is said very slowly spoken, and to read, write, and cipher.*

Of this art many deceptious accounts have been given both in Britain and France. Counterfeit specimens are published of the poetry of Mr Braidwood's scholars at Edinburgh, who, it is pretended, "attain to translate one language into another, and any art or science, practical (but not theoretical) music excepted, and to repeat with a better tone and "accent than many Clergymen." Mr T. humbly reminds his Patrons, that he professes to instruct the unfortunate Deaf, only to exchange their thoughts in an English style: that verse requires certain musical accents, of which they can have no idea; and that though he affords the consolation of producing from their organs sounds articulated, so as to be pretty generally intelligible; yet their voice can never be modulated to melody, nor their pronunciation marked with accent or emphasis, but their utterance, somewhat like the dialect of the Foreigners, is at first uncouth, and only becomes familiar upon acquaintance. Mr T. also removes impediments in Speech.

P.S. Some Children are received upon subscriptions.

Telfair's father James, who was assisting his son, passed away in 1796 and it was left to Cortes to manage the college on his own.

There was also a family relative engaged as an assistant teacher under Braidwood. This was mentioned in an advertisement of the same wording in both *The Leeds Intelligencer* dated 26 February 1782 and *Manchester Mercury* dated 5 March 1782:

FEBRUARY 26TH 1782

WHEN the melancholy Situation of such as are DEAF is considered, it must give the highest Pleasure to every benevolent Mind to be informed that it is possible to give them Relief, to rescue them from Ignorance and Idleness, and enable them to become happy Members of Society.

Mr. MACPHERSON, who has been regularly instructed by the ingenious and *celebrated* Mr. BRAIDWOOD of Edinburgh, TEACHER of the DEAF and DUMB, takes this Opportunity to acquaint the Public, that he has served a regular Apprenticeship with him for seven Years, besides acting for some Time afterwards in the Character of Assistant, and now is sufficiently qualified to instruct those who have the Misfortune to be born deaf and dumb to speak, read, understand what they read, write and cypher.

As some have assumed the Name of being taught this Art by Mr. Braidwood, Mr. MACPHERSON can assure the Public, that he himself is the first who ever appeared in England, or anywhere else, instructed by him; therefore he flatters himself his Success in Business will be such as may continue his Residence in YORK, being a Place very commodious for his Business.

In the Time Mr. MACPHERSON was with Mr. Braidwood, he likewise attained his infallible Method of correcting IMPEDIMENTS in SPEECH.

Mr. MACPHERSON will wait on any Gentleman or Lady on the shortest Notice sent to him at his Lodgings at Mr. Vicker's, Confectioner in Petergate, York.

This Macpherson would have commenced his training as a teacher of the deaf under Thomas Braidwood around 1775. He put in further advertisements in the *Leeds Intelligencer* on 13 August 1782 and another on May 20 1783. In the 13 August 1782 advertisement, he printed a reference from one Charles Campbell whose son suffered from speech impediment. Campbell was pleased with Macpherson's work and mentioned that his son had been "cured" of stammering:

To the PUBLIC

I HAVE a SON, who from his infancy hath been so great a STAMMERER, that it was with Difficulty he could express himself so as to be understood; he is now Thirteen Years of Age, and you may be sure I was under a great Affliction for my Son's Misfortune; when I happened to see an Advertisement in the Papers, that Mr. MACPHERSON, who served an Apprenticeship with the celebrated Mr. BRAIDWOOD, at Edinburgh, intended to fix his Abode at York, and take Persons under his Care, and to cure such as were dumb, deaf, or laboured under any Impediment of Speech, &c. after Mr. Braidwood's Method.

I immediately took my Son to York, and left him with Mr. Macpherson, who in the Space of a few Weeks had so much improved my Son's Speech, that he could talk and converse without Hesitation, to the utmost Surprize and Admiration of all his Friends and Acquaintance.

Mr. Macpherson being under the Necessity of going into the North, my Son came home; but I purpose sending him again to York, on Mr. Macpherson's Return, in full Persuasion that he will perform a perfect and lasting Cure.

For the information of all who labour under the great Misfortune of Dumbness, in Impediments of Speech, &c. I desire you will give this to the Public, and am, Sirs, Your's, &c.

Skipton, Aug. 1st, 1782. CHARLES CAMPBELL.

Mr. MACPHERSON is expected in York in the Course of this Week, and may be spoke to at Mr. Vicar's, Confectioner, in Petergate.

The later advertisement of 20 May783 read:

Mr. Macpherson
(*Formerly* an APPRENTICE to the *ingenious*
Mr. BRAIDWOOD *of* EDINBURGH,)

BEGS Leave to acquaint the Public, that he has during his residence in York, taken a commodious House in Gillygate, where he proposes to board and teach YOUNG GENTLEMEN who are born DEAF, (consequently DUMB) to speak, read, write, &c. He will likewise continue to correct impediments in Speech, which originates from either of these causes, viz a bad habit in the Formation of articulate Sounds, an extension in the Tonsils, Split-Uvula, Cleft-Palate, Hair-Lip, &c.

A Letter from GENERAL HALE to Mr. MACPHERSON,

54

In Gillygate, York.

SIR,   GUISBROUGH, May 4, 1783.

I have the pleasure to find that my Son has been cured, under your Care, of an Impediment in his Speech—an Obligation I take the first Opportunity to acknowledge.

I am your obliged and most humble Servant,

JOHN HALE.

The two advertisements showed that Macpherson dealt with speech impediments to the satisfaction of the parents of the hearing children concerned. (John Hale was a colonel with General Woolfe in the battle of Quebec and was present at Woolfe's death.) Not much was known of Macpherson until an advertisement appeared in the *Norfolk Chronicle* on Saturday 19 July 1794:

> **Home News.**
>
> **Mr. MACPHERSON.**
>
> FORMERLY Affiftant to his Uncle, Mr. BRAID-wood, TEACHER of the DEAF and DUMB to SPEAK, WRITE and CYPHER, and CORRECTOR of IMPEDI-MENTS in SPEECH of thofe who hear, mentioned in the publications of Dr. JOHNSON, Dr. BUCHAN, Lord MON-BODDO, and other eminent Auth rs, is at prefent in Nor-wich, and may be fp ke or wrote to at Yarington and Bacon's.
>
> ☞ Mr. MACPHERSON removes Hefitations in Speech of thofe who hear, in a fhort period of time and with little ex-pence to the Parent.

Twelve years after announcing his arrival in England and establishing his business, Macpherson claimed to be the nephew of Thomas Braidwood. This claim, whether genuine or otherwise, is open to investigation as the link between Macpherson and Braidwood could not be established.

There is a possibility, albeit not proven, that Braidwood may have taught some pupils about farming. It is known that Braidwood rented a farm from one William Brown for a period of nine years between 1772 and 1781. That farm, Harehope Farm in the parish of Eddlestone in the shire of Peebles, consisting of 600 acres of both sheep pasture and arable land with a good herd of cattle, was rented for a sum of £120 per annum and it was initially taken on by Braidwood to help his friend who had fallen into dire circumstances. It was a large farm and there is a possibility that deaf children were taught in ploughing, cultivating and tending the land. As it turned out, Braidwood fell into dispute with Brown and this culminated in a bitter court case in early 1781, in which Braidwood took action against Brown for his failure to adhere to the terms of their contract (see CHAPTER 6).

Braidwood's tireless battle for assistance in rising funds and support to train young men to become teachers of the deaf continued and in July 1779 he presented a petition to the Commissioners of the Annexed Estates (National Records of Scotland 02024 E728-39-3-00001/2/3). His petition was read on 26 July 1779:

To the Honble Commissioners of the Annexed Estates

The Petition of Mr. Thos Braidwood

The condition of people born deaf and of course dumb is so lamentable not only to themselves but to all concerned in them, that a remedy must be esteemed of the highest importance. Your Petitioner by trials without number and long experience has brought a remedy to perfection, by which all of them are made capable to enjoy the comforts of society, to acquire knowledge by reading and writing; and such of them as cannot live independent, to gain a livelihood by their own industry. Many of your Petitioner's Scholars are at present employed in public offices, Counting Houses, and various other branches of business. And the perfection of his method as known so generally, as that for some years he has had as many Scholars as he could do justice to, tho' his whole time is taken up in that laborious employment.

It however distresses him not a little to be obliged to refuse admittance to persons daily applying for aid, whom it is not in his power to serve. It is deplorable that so many innocent persons should be deprived of the chief comforts of life for want of instruction, which must deeply affect every person of humanity.

The only thing in your Petitioner's power is to instruct young men from time to time in his method, who may set up schools in different parts of the Kingdom. But without proper encouragement this cannot be expected from the Petitioner, a private man who gains his bread by his industry; for tho' he has the satisfaction of having done his duty to many gratis Scholars, yet he must pay some regard to his own family; and it would be hard to load him singly with serving the public in this important task.

The patriotic endeavours of your Honours to be serviceable to your native country, and your gracious reception of every project that may contribute to that end, encourage me to present to you the following offer on my part, which is to instruct some well qualified young men in my art, who after being perfected and thoroughly tried, may take up a school where directed by your Honours. Your Petitioner has no merit of making profit by this offer. He shall be satisfied with what reward your Honours shall think barely adequate to his labour. One merit he indeed has that goes near his heart, which is to have the patronage of this Honourable Board; as by your patronage and example men of benevolence and opulence may be moved to enlarge the plan, and in time to provide the sufficient labourers for this fruitful harvest.

Thos Braidwood

The outcome and response from the Commissioners is as yet unknown and no further records can be found, although Braidwood's later move to Hackney might have been connected with this appeal.

In May 1781 the American colonist Francis Green visited Braidwood's Academy to see his son Charles and to learn how he was getting on with his education. On the first visit, Green stayed at Edinburgh for

Francis Green

"VOX OCULIS SUBJECTA;"

A

DISSERTATION

ON THE

Moft *Curious* and Important Art of

Imparting Speech, and the Knowledge of Language, to the *naturally* Deaf, and (confequently) Dumb;

With a particular Account of

The Academy of Meffrs. BRAIDWOOD of Edinburgh,

AND

A PROPOSAL

To perpetuate, and extend the Benefits thereof.

" Per varios ufus artem experientia fecit,
" Exemplo monftrante viam." —

By a PARENT.

LONDON:

Sold by Benjamin White, Nº 63, Fleet-ftreet,
MDCCLXXXIII.

around six weeks. Green next visited the Braidwood school in September of the following year and he stayed for about four weeks. Francis Green was forced to leave Colonial America at the outbreak of the war between Britain and the colonists and he lived in England during the war. Before Green left England for America at the end of the war in 1783, he published a pamphlet around March 1783 entitled *Vox oculis subjecta.* He did not put his name to the pamphlet and he merely put down the authorship as "by a Parent". The title of the book was borrowed from the motto of the Braidwood Academy.

In Part Two of his book, Green mentioned that the number of scholars at Braidwood's school *at present (of both sexes) amounts near to twenty, including several who have only impediments in speech, without being deaf.* Green went on to give a little description of the school and its daily routine around the time of his visit:

> These are all lodged and boarded under the same roof with the teachers; and have all possible attention paid to their health and comfort. The apartments for the lads or boys being separate, and at a distance from those of young women or girls.
>
> As soon as they rise in the morning, they all repair to the same school-room, for an hour or two before

breakfast. A certain time is allowed of each day for recreation, in which the tutors are generally as much engaged as employed as while in the school. On Sundays they are exercised in moral and religious subjects during the forenoon.

Rumours were circulating for some time (before Francis Green wrote his book) that the methods adopted by Braidwood in teaching speech, especially in making pupils form positions of their tongues and lips to achieve correct sounds for letters and words, were both harmful and cruel. Nothing is known of the origin of these accusations and rumours of cruelty, but what can be perceived is that following Braidwood's success in attending to the speech impediments of non-deaf pupils, there occurred a sort of rush to Edinburgh by elocutionists and speech-therapists from all over Britain.

On page 145 of his book, Green wrote in defence of Braidwood's method:

A mistake or prejudice respecting the methods of teaching articulation, I find hath been imbibed by some, upon a supposition that harsh and severe methods were privately used, in order to enforce exertions contrary to their natural disposition and inclinations, and such rigid discipline as is sometimes practised upon persons unfortunately deprived of reason. This error, I am bound by a regard to truth, (and also in justice to the worthy characters of these gentlemen to confute: it is no less necessary, in order to obviate the discouraging effects of such an idea. Nothing can possibly be more remote from a true description of their methods, for the most kind and affectionate mode is practised, much more tender, ingratiating, and consistent with the true art of governing the human mind, and making learning a pleasure, than I ever saw at any other school: the behaviour of the pupils is the most convincing proof imaginable of this; they enter punctually the school-room, with a degree of eagerness, they really love their learning, not regarding it (as young persons in general do) as a hardship or imposition, but as an indulgence ...

Green also mentioned that the teachers had no fixed desk and seat in the school and they continually moved from one scholar to another. Green also noted in page 146 the affection the deaf pupils had for Thomas Braidwood:

> Such a remarkable affection and gratitude have these scholars for their teachers, that I knew an instance of a lady who was really apprehensive of some secret charm, by which her child's affection would be more strongly fixed on Mr Braidwood than herself.

Green's account of the pupil's affection for Braidwood tallied with that of Dr Johnson who visited the school ten years earlier in 1773 and he wrote that:

> This school I visited, and found some of the scholars waiting for their master, whom they are said to receive with smiling countenances and sparkling eyes, delighted with the hope of new ideas.

There was also the myth that Braidwood used a secret instrument, as if it had magical powers, to make deaf pupils speak. This myth originated in Francis Green's book in which he wrote on page 147:

> The only instrument made use of, except their own hands and fingers of the instructor, is (I believe) a small round piece of silver, of a few inches long, the size of a tobacco-pipe, flatted at one end, with a ball (as large as a marble) at the other; by means of these the tongue is gently placed, at first the various positions respectively of proper for forming the articulations of the different letters and syllables; until they acquire (as we all do, in learning speech) by habit, the proper method.

There was nothing magical about the silver spatula with a ball at the end. Twelve years earlier the author of the article on Dumbness (*Encyclopaedia Britannica*, vol.2, 1771) wrote that Braidwood *puts his finger in the pupil's mouth, depresses or elevates the tongue...* What had really happened was that Braidwood later realised the importance of the health and hygiene of his pupils and refrained from putting his finger into their mouths, using instead a specially made spatula which was easily cleaned after use.

Francis Green's son, Charles, was eight years old when he was sent to Braidwood's academy in February 1780. Charles was discovered deaf at around the age of six months. Green wrote:

> ... although sprightly, sensible, and quick of apprehension, yet, having been either born deaf, or having lost his hearing by sickness in earliest infancy, he could not at that time produce or distinguish vocal sounds, nor articulate at all, neither had he any idea of the meaning of words, either when spoken, in writing, or in print; and for want of hearing, would doubtless have remained as speechless as he was born.

As Green described, his son Charles entered Braidwood's school with no language, no speech, no reading ability and almost a void in his brain that was badly in need of being filled with knowledge. And how, one wondered, would Braidwood start with such a person. We all now know, thanks to Francis Green, that Braidwood taught Charles using sign as well as speech, for Green wrote in page 149:

> My first visit to him was in May 1781. It exceeds the power of words to convey any idea of the sensations experienced at this interview. The child, ambitious to manifest his acquisition, eagerly advanced, and addressed me, with a distinct salutation of speech. He also made several enquiries in short sentences. I then delivered him a letter from his sister (couched in the simplest terms) which he read so as to be understood; he accompanied many of the words, as he pronounced them, with proper gestures, significative of their meaning, such as in the sentence, "write a letter by papa:" on uttering the first word, he described the action of writing, by the motion of his right hand; the second by tapping the letter he held; the third by pointing to me.

Charles Green signed when he was reading the letter from his sister. Did not Dr Johnson mention in his 1773 visit about writing a question on the slate of one of the young ladies, consisting of three figures to be multiplied by two figures that she *quivered her fingers* upon looking at it? She was actually signing the numbers to be multiplied by another set of numbers, and calculating the answer. And did not Thomas Pennant mention in his 1772 work that *every idea was locked up, or appeared but in their eyes, or at their fingers ends*? Also, did not Hugo Arnot mention in his writing on his 1779 visit to the Braidwood Academy that *the boys could not only converse by the help of the artificial alphabet they learned to put their fingers onto certain positions*? Signing was always there with Braidwood since his association with Charles Shirreff and signing and fingerspelling always played vital roles in both language acquisition and educational development of deaf children under Braidwood's tuition and care.

Francis Green next visited his son in Edinburgh in September 1782 and penned:

> ... his improvements were very perceptible in speech, the construction of language, and in writing; he made a good beginning in arithmetic, and surprising progress in the arts of drawing and painting. I found him capable of not only comparing ideas, and drawing inferences, but expressing his sentiments with judgement. On my desiring him to attempt something he thought himself unequal to, I set him the example by doing it myself: upon which he shook his head, and, with a smile, replied (distinctly, viva voce) "You are a man, Sir. I am a boy."

> Observing, that he was inclined in company to converse with one of his school-fellows, by the tacit finger-language, I asked him, why he did not speak to him with his mouth? To this, his answer was as pertinent as it was concise, "He is deaf."

According to Green, deaf pupils signed to deaf pupils at Braidwood Academy. What this informs us is that despite small numbers, there was a thriving and growing deaf community within the school, with the signing deaf developing signs and sign language, and creating their own deaf community and culture.

Additional information supporting evidence on the subject of signing as used by the Braidwoodian pupils can be gleaned by reading The *Collected Works of Dugald Stewart, Vol. IV (Ed: Sir William Hamilton, Pub: Constable & Co. Edinburgh, 1854)*. In the section *Philosophy of the Human Mind: Continuation of Part Second [1826]*, pages 16 and 17 read:

> ... I remember to have heard Mr. Braidwood remark, that his dumb pupils, from whatever part of the country they came, agreed, in most instances, in expressing assent by holding up the thumb, and dissent by holding up the little finger. Admitting this to be a fact, (which I would not be understood to state upon my own personal knowledge) it can be explained only by supposing that these gestures are abbreviations of those signs by which assent and dissent are generally expressed in the language of nature; and, in truth, the process by which they were introduced may be easily conceived. For, the natural sign of assent is to throw the body open, by moving the hand from the breast with the palm towards the body, and the thumb uppermost. The natural sign of dissent is the same movement, with the back of the hand towards the body, and the little finger uppermost. The former conveys the idea of cordiality, of good humour, and of inviting frankness; the latter of dislike and aversion. If two dumb persons were left to converse together, it is reasonable to suppose that they would gradually abridge their natural signs for the sake of despatch, and would content themselves with *hinting* at those movements, which could be easily anticipated from the commencement; and in this manner might arise those apparent arbitrary marks of assent and dissent, which have just been mentioned.

These 'assent' and 'dissent' signs are still in present day use, and their application nowadays generally refer to signs for 'good' and 'bad' respectively, but they still represent signs for 'assent' and 'dissent.'

Good or Assent   Bad or Dissent

It is not only fascinating to trace these signs back to the Braidwood Academy in Edinburgh, but to know that Braidwood's pupils signed among each other in what was most obviously their preferred and predominant mode of communication.

It is an indisputable fact that the Braidwood Academy was the first residential school for the deaf in Britain, albeit a small privately owned and run institution. This academy sowed the seeds of both deaf culture and community in the years to come. Braidwoodian pupils were close to each other in daily existence during their schooldays and they obviously adapted to each other's communication needs and methods, while in the case of signs, developing and creating new forms of signs to overcome lengthy fingerspelling of words. Although deaf communities of Britain may have existed long before 1760, as noted, for example, by Richard Carew in his *Survey of Cornwall* (1580-1602), it is my opinion that one cannot dispute that the Braidwood Academy was the birthplace of Britain's deaf community and culture. The quality of education and happy environment provided by Braidwood produced an interesting comment from a regular visitor to the school, Francis Green. He was praising Braidwood and his method throughout the book, and having seen first-hand on two visits the working of the school, the teaching and also speaking to a number of pupils, he had nothing more to say but this:

> The effect of this instruction is, also, that instead of
> being the most "dull and solitary" of all human
> beings, they become remarkable cheerful and social.

A little more information on Braidwood's academy is revealed in a letter from Francis Green and read out by Mr Mitchell, the first principal of the Institution for Deaf-Mutes in Kentucky, USA, in "*a discourse pronounced by request of the Society for Instructing the Deaf and Dumb, in New York*, on the 24th of March, 1818." This letter referred to Green's visit to the school in 1781 and was taken from *The Education of*

64

Deaf Mutes: A Manual for Teachers by Thomas Arnold. (Pages 96-97. Wertheimer, Lea & Co., London, 1888.)

The first two paragraphs of the letter have been omitted here because they were mentioned earlier, and the rest of the letter went:

> I remained in Edinburgh six weeks, and every day I was a witness of the real progress of my son and the other scholars; every day I was rejoiced to find in them marked signs of their being endowed with intelligence and the power of speech, of which they had been previously deprived through some defect in their hearing. By this method of instruction deaf-mutes should no longer live without being useful to the state, or condemned to ignorance and public neglect, but have the ability to acquire much useful knowledge and of profiting by the advantages and pleasures of their social position.
>
> I have also seen and become acquainted with the adult scholars educated in the institution. One of them, a very intelligent young man and an agreeable companion, is head clerk at Leith Custom House. Another is pursuing his studies at the University, and I am certain that my son will be adept in the art of speaking.
>
> The energy and faculties of deaf-mutes vary in the same manner as in the hearing. I have remarked also in all the boarders a special liking for study and it is not improbable that some extraordinary talents may be developed by study, attaining to such a degree of perfection as to become envied by persons in possession of all their senses.
>
> Permit me to add a few words on Mr Braidwood's methods. He at first teaches his pupils to utter sounds and to articulate letters; he then gives the tongue and the lips the positions necessary to the formation of syllables. Lastly, by numerous graduated exercises he leads them to pronounce words and understand their meaning, either as

printed or written. If the scholars attentively follow the movements of the mouth, they can understand what is said without hearing.

Vox oculis subjecta, such is his device. The eyes of the scholars are fixed on the mouth, as a bird fascinated by a serpent nailed to its place.

Sometime in 1782, there was a clamour from a group of prominent people in London for the Braidwood Academy to move south to England. They stated that most of Braidwood's scholars came from England and it made sense to move down. King George III put up a grant of £100 sterling that would enable some poor children to be educated, as well as employing a number of trainee teachers. It seemed that this offer of help from the King was a consequence of Braidwood's petition to the Commissioners of the Annexed Estates in 1779. Francis Green wrote in page 181 outlining his proposal to perpetuate and extend the art of teaching the deaf:

To render this art universally useful, it is necessary for some ingenious young men should be instructed and qualified to assist, and succeed the present professors, and that a fund should be established under the direction of proper managers, to be applied to the purpose of educating those whose parents are altogether unable to defray such expence, and to assist others who can afford a part but not whole, by which means, all the deaf, however scattered, might be collected, and taught, and consequently rescued from certain ignorance, from idleness, and from want, as well as every defect in speech (however inconvenient and violent) rectified.

Messrs. Braidwood have repeatedly declared their readiness to undertake to qualify a sufficient number of young men for the execution of such a plan.

On page 183, Green wrote...

"I have been made acquainted with His Majesty having been graciously pleased conditionally to give 100l per annum, out of his private purse, for this purpose.

Dumbie House was advertised for sale in the *Caledonian Mercury* on Saturday 27 July 1782, indicating that Braidwood had made a decision to move to London at a much earlier time than most past historians were aware of. Braidwood next advertised the sale of his Abbey Hill property in the same newspaper on Monday 27 January 1783. In the advertisement, Braidwood mentioned *"removing his Academy to London at Whitsunday first."*

---

ia cheap and convenient lodging, may apply to William ????

TO BE LET OR SOLD,

THAT large LODGING or Dwelling-House of St LEONARD's, with garden, coach-house, stable, and hay loft, lying on the south back of the Canongate, lately possessed by Thomas Braidwood, Esquire.—There is an excellent pump-well ;—the premises are all in good repair, and may be entered to immediately.

For particulars, enquire at Andrew Milligan watch-case maker, Canongate head.

N. B. This subject is admirably well calculated for a candle and soap manufactory.

Caledonian Mercury, Saturday 27 July 1782.

The sale of both buildings pose an interesting question - was Dumbie House closed and the Braidwood Academy temporarily transferred to the Abbey Hill building before moving to Hackney?

TO BE SOLD.

THAT Large and Commodious HOUSE, with the ground and offices, at the Abbey Hill, possessed by Mr Braidwood, he being to remove his Academy to London at Whitsunday first.

The House consists of three Storeys, containing an elegant dining-room, and drawing-room, seven bed rooms, dressing-rooms, closets, &c. a large hall, lobby, and kitchen, a neat larder, milk house, and wine cellar. The kitchen is large, and completely fitted up, with grate, ovens, stoves, and all proper fixtures, and adjoining to the kitchen is a house, consisting of servants apartments, and an ale cellar, with catacombs.

There is a pumpwell, a large stone cistern, and a washhouse, remarkably neat, with a copper boiler, grate, and other necessary fixtures. There is a coach house, a large hay loft, a cow house, a stable with six stalls, a hen-house, &c.

The ground consists of about an acre and half, contains a good many fine fruit trees, and is remarkably pleasant in situation.

Applications may be made to Mr Braidwood, or Mr Laurence Inglis, writer in Edinburgh.

Caledonian Mercury, Monday 27 January 1783

Whatever happened that caused Braidwood to close his Edinburgh academy and move south may never be fully known, but move out he did. Thomas Braidwood took his wife Margaret, daughter Isabella and her husband John Braidwood with him to Hackney, a place on the eastern outskirts of London.

Nothing is known of his eldest daughter Margaret, and she was not with the family when they left Edinburgh for Hackney. Nothing was known about what happened to the King George III's offer of the £100 annual payment, but with this went another opportunity for the school to take on children of the poor, and perhaps the opening up of the Braidwood Academy to take on and train more teachers from outside of their immediate family.

There was a final twist in the saga of King George III's gift of £100. This sum was obtained by the Duke of Montagu in 1783 after Braidwood moved his school to Hackney. It appears that there was a condition attached to the money, and that condition was that the school remain in Scotland. In *The Book of the Old Edinburgh Club, Vol. XX, page 137 (1934)*, the author W. Forbes Gray wrote:

AN EIGHTEENTH CENTURY RIDING SCHOOL

... It was in these depressing circumstances that on 30th December, at a meeting of the managers in the Exchange Coffee House, Principal Robertson brought forward a scheme for the rehabilitation of the establishment. He stated that the Duke of Montagu had obtained £100 from the King to encourage an Edinburgh school for the deaf and dumb founded by Thomas Braidwood (the first regularly organised institution of the kind in Great Britain). But before the royal gift was bestowed, Braidwood gave up the school and removed to London. Robertson thereupon suggested to the Duke of Montagu that the £100 might be handed over to the Royal Academy to help to pay its debts. His Lordship favoured the idea, and in due course obtained the transfer of the money. Thus it came about that the £100 which was to have assisted Thomas Braidwood to teach the deaf and dumb in Edinburgh was diverted into the coffers of the riding school.

Motto of the Braidwood Academy – "The Voice governed by the Eye"
© 2014 Raymond Lee

This motto is often loosely translated as "Voice made Visible."

The date of arrival of the Braidwoods in Hackney can be pinpointed to April/May 1783. This can be seen in the Minute Book of the Presbyterian Dissenters' Meeting House which stood on the south-west corner of St Thomas' Square, fronting onto Mare Street. The records noted that Thomas Braidwood was admitted as a member of the church in May 1784. The rules of the church included a section stating that newcomers had to wait a year before becoming fully accepted as a church member.

Presbyterian Dissenters' Meeting House, St Thomas Square/Mare Street.
Photograph by courtesy of Hackney Archives Department.

On arrival in Hackney in 1783, the Braidwood family resided in Bowling Green House which was situated on the corner of Chatham Place and Retreat Place, north east of the junction of these and (from about 1808) facing the side of the Paragon. There is a copy of the Minutes of the Grand Committee of St Thomas' Hospital dated 30 July 1783 (GLRO H1/ST/A6/7 p.64) showing the following note:

> Agreed that Dr John Rawlinson, tenant
> under lease from the hospital of divers parcel
> of land with a Messuage called the Bowling
> Green House at Hackney be at liberty to let

the same to Mr Thomas Braidwood of Hackney for such part of Dr Rawlinson's remaining term therein as he shall think proper Dr Rawlinson continuing tenant to the hospital.

Thomas Braidwood and his family never bought a building for use as a private school, always taking to renting. Bowling Green House was rented for the sum of £90 per annum. Braidwood quickly changed the name of the building to Grove House and the school was put into operation as soon as the family settled and the building made fit to take in both day and residential pupils.

The illustration below gives the location and surround of the Braidwood Academy in the Grove House building around 1800.

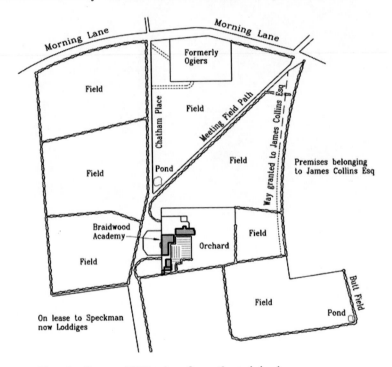

Sketch of area c1800 taken from the original survey map
H1/ST/E114/4, no.14
(Geoffrey Eagling 2001).

Grove House was very much larger than Dumbie House in Edinburgh; it was a large building with a large plot of land containing four

72

outbuildings within its boundary; there were two medium sized buildings, one large building and a sizeable shed for firewood or suchlike. The two medium outbuildings were used as a stable for horses and a brewhouse respectively. Unlike Dumbie House, Grove House had more than ample land used as playing fields, garden, an orchard and vegetable patches. The boundary of the building had fences along the west to east wall at the north side and the rest of the boundary was high and dense privy hedges. The front of the building had a dense gravel surface used as an approach from the road. There was a lawn between the house and the gravelled area.

Alain Holcroft's reconstruction of Grove House based on available images of the time and surviving photographs of 38 Chatham Place, (see page 74) which was demolished in the early part of the 1900's, is reproduced here:

The above photograph, taken in 1912, is the only known photograph of the front of the former Braidwood Academy for the Deaf and Dumb. At the time the picture was taken, the building was known as 38 Chatham Place. There were changes to the property and more houses were added to the surrounding area and to the left of the building. The photograph on the right is also the only known picture of the interior, that of the main staircase. This staircase was probably the only original feature then remaining from the days of Braidwood and his pupils.

Following a study of the above photograph and map of the area in 1800, an artist's impression of Grove House was created. See previous page.

Photographs by courtesy of Hackney Archives Department

Moving down from Edinburgh to Hackney, Braidwood retained a number of deaf pupils who were at the Edinburgh academy, and it is known that John Creasy and James Watt both continued their education at Hackney. The Minute Book of the Presbyterian Dissenters Meeting House recorded James Watt, from the Braidwood Academy becoming an occasional member on 6th March 1785. There were other deaf and hard-of-hearing pupils, but the vital pupil register was not, and could never, be found.

According to Deaflore, known deaf pupils at Hackney were:

John Creasy	James Watt	Jane Poole
Anne Walcott	Andrew Hay	Henry Fox
Mr Harris (Northampton)	Thomas Cooley	Charles A. Heathcote
Mr Flaxman	Thomas Arrowsmith	

The Braidwood Academy quickly established itself in Hackney and proceeded to flourish. The school was centralised at Grove House, and from available Land Tax Records in Hackney Archives, the whole of the Braidwood family resided at Grove House besides the residential deaf pupils. In 1784, a kinsman of Thomas Braidwood, Joseph Watson, joined the teaching staff, and began not only a long career as an instructor of the deaf but stood on the threshold of contributing enormously to the branching out and development of the art and science of educating the deaf.

The Land Tax Records stored in Hackney Archives are of great interest in that the movement of the Braidwood Academy and its family members can be tracked, and this goes some way in aiding the construction of their history in Hackney as can be seen below.

1784. Braidwood Academy flourishing at Grove House.
Arrival of Joseph Watson. John Braidwood born in June to John and Isabella Braidwood. He was christened on 10 July.

1785. Braidwood Academy flourishing at Grove House.

1786. Braidwood Academy flourishing at Grove House.
Henrietta Stewart born to John and Isabella Braidwood in January. She was christened on 5 February.

1787. Braidwood Academy flourishing at Grove House.
Thomas' wife Margaret, John and Isabella Braidwood became members of the Presbyterian Dissenters' Meeting House.

1788. Braidwood Academy flourishing at Grove House.
Elizabeth born to John and Isabella Braidwood in June. Christened on 25th July.
Joseph Watson became a member of the Presbyterian Dissenter's Meeting House.

1789. Braidwood Academy flourishing at Grove House.

1790. Braidwood Academy flourishing at Grove House.

1791. Braidwood Academy flourishing at Grove House. In late spring Margaret, Thomas' wife, passed away on 30th May at the age of 77 years.
Joseph Watson appeared to have left the Braidwood Academy in the summer on completion of his training as a teacher of the deaf. Watson went on to establish his own private school for the deaf in Bethnal Green.

After the death of Margaret Braidwood, the situation within the Braidwood family was never the same again - Isabella did not get on with her father after the death of his wife and it was from around that point onwards that they would be working together under uncomfortable circumstances since her husband John Braidwood had to continue with his teaching role in Grove House.

John Townsend   Henry Cox Mason

1792 was an important year for both Thomas Braidwood and Joseph Watson, who was at that time still running his own private school for the deaf in Bethnal Green independent of the Braidwood Academy. It appeared that Watson engaged one I. S. Woodman as an assistant teacher of the deaf under him. During the month of August of that year, Watson came into possession of a circular that was distributed widely by the Rev. John Townsend and the Rev. Henry Cox Mason as a part of their campaign to establish a charitable school for the deaf of poor families.

These two priests were inspired by Thomas Braidwood's former pupil, John Creasy, into establishing the first public school for the deaf. John Creasy was initially introduced to the Rev. John Townsend at his Jamaica Road Chapel at Southwark by his mother Mary Creasy, who mentioned having spent some £1,500 for John's ten year education at the Braidwood Academy, both at Edinburgh and Hackney. This vast sum included travelling, boarding and laundry costs as well as school outings and visits to places of interest. She mentioned that she was concerned about the absence of education for the deaf children of poor families and she urged Townsend to take action, which he did in partnership with Mason and they were backed by the wealthy banker Henry Thornton. After reading this circular, Watson stepped forward and offered his services as the head teacher of the planned school. It was said, through both Deaflore and hints from Watson's own book *The Instruction of the Deaf and Dumb (1806)*, that Watson consulted and spoke about it with Braidwood. What was said between them will never be known, but the outcome was positive in that Watson took up the post as a head instructor to the planned school which went on to open its door and take on the first six pupils on Wednesday 14th November 1792.

Braidwood apparently giving his blessing to Joseph Watson to accept the position of head teacher and manage the newly founded Asylum for the Deaf and Dumb Children of the Poor in Bermondsey, south London, led to further friction with his daughter Isabella, who probably saw the establishment of the new school as hindrance to, or in competition with, the Braidwood academy. The situation got so bad to the extent that Isabella, with her family in tow, moved out of Grove House and into a newly-built and magnificent house in Hackney Terrace (right) which was some twenty minutes' walk away south from the Presbyterian Dissenters' Meeting House. From then onwards, John Braidwood had to commute to work at Grove House which was some thirty-five Photograph - Raymond Lee 1993

77

minutes' walk from his new home, the Braidwood academy being some fifteen minutes walk north of the Presbyterian Dissenters' Meeting House.

In spite of the Braidwood family upheavals, there was a general consensus that the founding of the London Asylum for the Deaf and Dumb Children of the Poor did actually fulfil Thomas Braidwood's desire to have such a school formed, bearing in mind Braidwood's past appeals to train teachers of the deaf at his Edinburgh academy; the engagement of Joseph Watson as the head teacher with Thomas' blessing was a sign of his intention to see the new school established. Some past writers on the subject of British deaf history acknowledged this and one of them, Thomas Arnold, wrote on page 98 of his *Education of Deaf Mutes: A Manual for Teachers* (Wertheimer, Lea & Co., London, 1888) that...

> More generous than Baker, he prepared the way for
> founding the first public school in England in 1792,
> about thirty years after that of l'Épée in Paris, and
> fourteen years after that of Heinicke at Leipzig, and
> lived to see it prosper.

1793. The Braidwood Academy continued to flourish despite the situation between father and daughter.
Isabella gave birth to a third son, William, on 11th March.

That year turned out to be a very dark period for Isabella. The family rift manifested itself when Thomas Braidwood, then at the age of 78 years, married a 45 year old widow, Frances Betty Ravenscroft; the marriage was by licence and took place on 27th April at St John's Church, Hackney. This marriage went a long way to drive a wedge between father and daughter. It was believed that John Braidwood was conducting his classes in a room or an area of the building separate from Thomas Braidwood, effectively running his own school within the Braidwood academy at Grove House. There is currently no hard direct evidence to support this split, but indirect evidence supporting this separation emerged in a letter to *The Gentleman's Magazine* in 1798 (Vol. LXVIII). This letter from D. H. appeared to confirm the fact of the situation concerning the split between Thomas and his daughter Isabella.

The marriage between Braidwood and Ravenscroft was also reported in *The Scots Magazine* (Vol. 55, page 256):

At St. John's church, Hackney, Thomas
Braidwood, Esq., formerly of St. Leonard's
Hill, to Mrs Ravenscroft, widow of Mr Samuel
Ravenscroft, attorney at law, London.

1794.   No change in situation with the exception that William
Braidwood passed away on 13th August at the age of 17
months.

1795-7. No change - the school continued to function.

1798.   Dr Rawlinson sold the Grove House property to the Trustees
of St Thomas' hospital. Thomas Braidwood remained in the
property as a tenant and continued to run his school.

In September, John Braidwood became ill at his Hackney Terrace home
with pulmonary complaint. After a short illness, he passed away on the
24th of the same month at the age of 42 years. He was buried in the St.
Thomas Square burial ground.

The Gentleman's Magazine (Vol. LXVIII, 1798, p.908, Part Two - October)
published an obituary:

At Hackney-terrace, Mr John Braidwood, formerly
of Edinburgh and both there and at Hackney for
many years, an uncommonly eminent instructor of
the deaf and dumb. He was the son of Mr B. of
Edinburgh, professor of the same useful art, of
whose first academy at Edinburgh, see Pennant's
"Tour of Scotland 1772, Part II", p.256 - we doubt
not but one of his grateful pupils will favour us
with some farther particulars of so useful a member
of society.

There was a response in *The Gentleman's Magazine* of the same volume
on page 1032:

December 7th.

Mr John Braidwood was not son, but distantly
related to Mr B. also of Hackney, and married to
his daughter, by whom he has left several children.
He died after a few days illness and was a worthy
character and wonderfully successful in his arduous
and difficult undertaking. His father-in-law and he

were formerly concerned together, but had for a considerable number of years been unconnected. His widow, with the assistance of her son, a very sober and discreet lad, means to carry on the profession for which she is as qualified as her husband.

D. H.

1799   That year saw Isabella taking a huge leap and she made a break away from her father. She rented a large property situated between London Lane and West Street on the west side of Mare Street and it was rented for the sum of £150 per year. She conducted her own school, running the establishment entirely separate from her father. This building was later known as Pembroke House. Interestingly, historians always assumed that there was only one Braidwood Academy, but in truth there were two Braidwood academies in existence.

The location of Pembroke House on Mare Street is denoted by the white arrow on the 1831 map on the next page - there were two separate buildings, which over the years might have merged into a single building.

Photograph - courtesy of Hackney Archives Department

The picture above, taken in 1870, shows the surgeon's house in the forefront on the left (white building) and Pembroke House to the right of it. At the time the picture was taken, Pembroke House was a lunatic asylum providing care for the psychiatric casualties of the East India Company Service. It opened under Dr George Rees in 1818 and it was

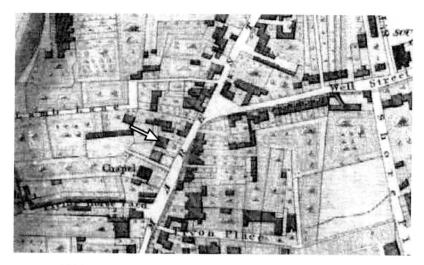
1831 Map - courtesy of Hackney Archives Department

closed down in 1870 under the superintendence of Dr William Williams, a former assistant of Dr Rees, and transferred to Ealing. Pembroke House no longer stands; it was redeveloped as Bayford Street. The writer has not yet been successful in obtaining a good and clear photograph of Pembroke House to date. However, Alain Holcroft's impression of the building (see below) would be how the building may have looked around Isabella Braidwood's time before her Institution moved out in 1810. In the 1870 picture a projected outbuilding to the right of Pembroke House is visible and this was not

shown in the 1831 plan. This outbuilding appears to have been added after 1810; it could have been built for the lunatic asylum's needs.

The relocation to Pembroke House, the breaking away from her father at Grove House and the upsurge in taking on further pupils were bold moves made by Isabella when one considers that she was working with her 17 year old son Thomas and 15 year old son John, leaving aside her 13 year old daughter Henrietta and 11 year old Elizabeth. And to make her task all the more arduous, she used the oral only approach in opposition to her father's combined system method.

Furthermore, Isabella completed driving the wedge between herself and her father by naming her new establishment the *Braidwood Institution for the Deaf and Dumb and for Removing Impediments in Speech* in opposition to her father's Braidwood Academy for the Deaf and Dumb; in that way she was creating her own identity and line of teaching method. Isabella did not appear to advocate signs in both the classroom and within her school, although she was not totally against fingerspelling. Correction of speech impediments appeared to become a strong point within her school and she began to receive hearing people who needed such therapy and lessons.

1800 Isabella's son Thomas Braidwood admitted as a member of the
      Presbyterian Dissenters Meeting House on June 1st.

Isabella's Institution appeared to progress well and the number of students seemed to be around 20 strong, which was probably slightly more than those who attended Grove House under her father Thomas. In 1802 a writer and educational reformer, Sarah Trimmer, in her *Guardian of Education (Vol. 1 no. 7, November 1802)* reviewed a book entitled *Julius; or the Deaf and Dumb Orphan* which was based on an original French play on the Abbé l'Épée. This play was adapted from a book by Jean Nicolas Bouilly. At the end of the review, Mrs Trimmer added a footnote:

> Amongst the numberless public Charities for which
> this nation is eminently distinguished, there is one
> for the maintenance and instruction of Deaf and
> Dumb children, which has afforded relief to many
> poor families; but from the annual report of the
> institution, which is published in the newspapers,
> it appears that a very small proportion of the

candidates, who offer to fill up the vacancies, can be admitted, on account of the fund not being sufficiently large to extend the benefits of the instructions. There is also at Hackney a school for the instruction of children in the higher classes of life, who are born under the same unhappy circumstances, formerly kept by a Mr Braidwood, and now carried on, we believe, by his widow; in which young ladies and gentlemen, naturally defective in the organs of speech and hearing, are not only taught to articulate distinctly, so as to be able to make themselves understood, but are even brought to a great degree of proficiency in the study of languages, and other branches of liberal education. This school, if it continues what it was in Mr Braidwood's time, is well worthy of the attention, not only of those parents whose children are disabled from receiving instructions in the common way, or who have any kind of impediment of speech, but of every person who can take a benevolent pleasure in seeing natural infirmities assisted, and the happiness of their fellow-creatures promoted.

Was the move a success, one might ask? Noting from both Mrs Trimmer's comments in *The Guardian of Education* and the Land Tax records, Isabella's Pembroke House school continued to do well and it also ran in parallel with Thomas Braidwood's Grove House academy and this was confirmed by *Kelly's Directory of 1804* which listed both Thomas Braidwood of Grove House and Isabella Braidwood of Mare Street as running their own respective schools.

More is learned of Braidwood's Institution through Dr Alexander Crombie's contribution to *The Monthly Magazine* (December 1801). Dr Crombie wrote a letter about the instruction of the deaf which is all too familiar with present day readers. There is a small part of his letter that is of interest and which contributes enormously to the picture of the standard of education offered by the Braidwood Academy:

> ... In this country, the art of instructing the deaf and dumb has been cultivated by Mr. Braidwood with considerable success. This gentleman's plan of

education differs, I understand, from that which was adopted by the venerable Abbé. The latter began with a communication of ideas, associating them with appropriate visible signs; the former adopts the common elementary mode of instruction, commencing with the alphabetical characters, as denoting certain conformations of the organs. Of the success accompanying this mode of instruction, the writer had this season, during a short stay in Margate, the most ample evidence in the pupils of Mrs. J. Braidwood, who, with her sons, superintends a most respectable seminary at Hackney for teaching the deaf and dumb.

To one of her pupils, I proposed in writing the following questions, the answers to which he wrote with surprising promptitude, and, for his years, with wonderful neatness:

What is your name?   - Thomas Pooley.
How old are you?   - I am eight years old.
Where were you born? - I was born in Dublin.
What is Grammar?   - Grammar is a collection of rules for speaking or writing any language correctly.
How long have you been at school?   - Two years.
How many months are there in a year?
                    - There are twelve months in a year.
How many weeks are there in a year?
                    -There are fifty-two weeks in a year.
Where is your school? - At Hackney.
Who teaches you?   - Mrs. Braidwood and her sons.
What is the sum of five and seven?
                    - Five and seven is twelve.

I then desired him to name the parts of speech, and to write 23 in letters, which he did with great readiness. I likewise prescribed to him two questions in arithmetic, one in addition and the other in subtraction, which he solved very correctly. To a young girl, who had been a pupil of Mrs. Braidwood about eighteen months, I proposed the question - What is my name? pronouncing the words as articulately as possible. She answered distinctly - Doctor Crombie.

I had also the pleasure of seeing a letter to Mrs. Braidwood from a gentleman, who was born deaf and dumb, of which it is but justice to say, that its grammatical accuracy forms by much the least part of its merit. This gentleman, though deaf, understands the oral language of others, and converses, I am informed, with surprising facility. He transacts the business of the two departments in a respectable public office under government, and has already appeared before the public as an author.

I may say with truth that I never received higher gratification than in examining the young pupils of Mrs. Braidwood; and, if these observations will furnish amusement to your readers, and serve to render this useful seminary more generally known, the intention of the writer will be fully answered.

From Dr Crombie's letter, we learn that the Braidwoodian pupils were on an outing to Margate for a short stay. This throws light on the fact that all boarding pupils were often taken on educational and leisure outings besides visiting places of interest as a part of their school fees package.

There is also a need for correction in this letter. Dr Crombie got the name Thomas Pooley wrong; the young boy was in fact the deaf artist Thomas Cooley.

Dr Crombie mentioned the pleasure of reading a letter from a deaf gentleman. What is most striking is his comment that this deaf gentleman *"... Understands the oral language of the others, and converses, I am informed, with surprising facility."* A question arises here - who did he understand this from? The answer is none other than Isabella Braidwood, who was most likely up to some mischief by lying to promote her school. The deaf gentleman referred to was none other than the great John Philp Wood, a man and former pupil of Thomas Braidwood, who was totally incapable of speech and lipreading. This was confirmed when the Scottish author and poet Sir Walter Scott penned in his Journal dated 27 June 1830... *"Honest John, my old friend, dined with us. I only regret I cannot understand him, as he has very powerful and much more curious information."* They both communicated in writing. It is obvious that Isabella was resorting to false claims to promote her

Pembroke House School, taking both attention and reputation away from the academy her father Thomas was running at Grove House.

1804   John Braidwood admitted as a member of the Presbyterian Dissenters' Meeting House on 13 May.

Both the Grove House academy and the Mare Street institution were noted in *Holden's Triennial Directory 1805-1807 (Vol 2. Part 1)* which listed the following:

> Braidwood Mr Thos.   Grove House, Hackney Is.
> Braidwood Mrs John   Mare Street,   Hackney Is.

1805   John Braidwood, then 21 years old, rented a small property in the St Thomas Square area for the sum of £50 per annum. This indicates that he might have been living away from his mother in 18 Hackney Terrace, which was still being rented by Isabella along with Pembroke House at that time. Did John's new-found freedom introduce him to the pleasures of life outside of work, especially to drink?
Henrietta Stewart and Elizabeth Braidwood admitted as members of the Presbyterian Dissenters' Meeting House in March.

1806 saw the passing of Thomas Braidwood. He died at Grove House on 24th October. An obituary in *The Times* dated Tuesday October 28th read:

> On Friday evening at Grove-house, Hackney, in
> the 91st year of his life; Thomas Braidwood Esq.,
> formerly of Edinburgh. He was most distinguished
> for the discovery of the art and successful method
> of instructing the deaf and dumb.

Thomas was interred in the churchyard behind the Presbyterian Dissenters' Meeting House. He was laid in the same plot as his wife Margaret, John Braidwood and William Braidwood.

The passing of Thomas Braidwood seemed to have caused anxiety for Isabella and her academy. The London Asylum for the Deaf and Dumb was going well and it was also expanding at a good pace around that time and the school's head teacher Joseph Watson was taking on private pupils with much success. Further to that, Watson was using not only his deaf pupils like William Hunter as teachers of the deaf

Braidwood family gravestone in St Thomas Square cemetery, 1993.
This gravestone was uprooted from its original plot and rested against the
boundary wall.

Photograph - Raymond Lee April 1993.

within the London Asylum for the Deaf and Dumb, but employing
former Braidwoodian pupils like John Creasy to instruct his private
pupils. Watson also used Creasy to train some of his Asylum pupils to
become teachers of the deaf. The number of pupils admitted to the
London Asylum was growing annually, although there were many who
were not admitted on grounds of lack of available funds.

Adding further to Isabella Braidwood's anxiety was the fact that Telfair
College for the Deaf and Dumb was still operating in the opulent area
of Knightsbridge in London. It was located on the south side of
Knightsbridge, east of Sloane Street near Hyde Park Corner. The
building in which the college was based was the largest house of a row
of eight houses and it was the former home of the Countess of
Salisbury. This college, which was initially a private academy for the
correction of speech defects and pronunciation before styling itself as
College for the Deaf and Dumb, moved to London from Edinburgh in
1779, four years before the Braidwood Academy moved to Hackney.
The Braidwood Institution on Mare Street had been increasing fees

steadily over the few years prior to Thomas' death and even some well-to-do families found themselves priced out of sending their deaf children to Isabella. In an effort to bolster the reputation of the Mare Street institution, Isabella took out an advertisement in *The Times* on 18 December 1806:

> INSTITUTION for the DEAF and DUMB, and for removing IMPEDIMENTS in SPEECH; conducted by Mrs. BRAIDWOOD and her Sons in Mare-street, Hackney.
>
> In consequence of the recent death of Mr. Braidwood, her late father, Mrs. Braidwood and her Sons, inducted by the advice of their most respected friends, take the liberty to lay before the Public a short account of their Academy for the Instruction of the Deaf and Dumb. Towards the close of the sixteenth century the first traces of this most useful and invaluable art were discovered. From that period to the middle of the last century, the improvements in it were very slow and gradual; when the Abbé de l'Épée in France and Mr. Braidwood, assisted by his son-in-law, Mr. John Braidwood, in Scotland, carried it to a high degree of utility and perfection. Much, however, as the plan of the illustrious Abbé merits the praise and gratitude of mankind, that of Mr. Braidwood, in the opinion of all competent judges, who have witnessed its advantages, justly claim a superiority. The former taught his pupils to communicate their ideas by appropriate visible signs, with astonishing precision and accuracy; but the latter, as in the rudiments of general education, began with the letters of the Alphabet, and brought them to pronounce and to articulate, by a method, adapted to the defective organ, particularly his own. The consequence of this curious and excellent system is, that his Pupils are enabled to support a conversation in a manner almost equal to that of other men, whose powers of Speech and Hearing are perfect; and that unhappy portion of our fellow-creatures, which otherwise would be incapable of any intellectual improvement, of any social enjoyment, and of the delights of

colloquial intercourse, are enabled to read and understand history, to study the sciences, to acquire all the polite and ornamental accomplishments, to engage in professional employments, and to appear in the world with cheerfulness, satisfaction and advantage. — Mrs. Braidwood having, from her earliest youth, been instructed by her father in this arduous, but truly beneficial art, and having also assisted her husband, the late Mr. J. Braidwood, who rendered himself so deservedly eminent by his distinguished skill, in this mode of education, continues to conduct the academy, assisted by her Sons: and she flatters herself, that the existing patronage which she has long experienced from the highest classes of society, and the present flourishing state of her Seminary, will convince the Public of its importance and merits, better than the amplest details, or the most laboured descriptions.

1807 John Braidwood moved to a smaller and cheaper house, renting it for £15 per annum, a huge drop from the £50 per annum he used to rent for his first house two years previously. This new building was situated on the east side of Mare Street and a few houses to the north of St Thomas Square.

The Braidwood Institution was still functioning, although they seemed to have slightly fewer pupils.

Further insight into the skill of Thomas Braidwood was revealed in a lengthy article to *The Monthly Magazine* dated June 1 1807 (vol. 23). A contributor named A. Mann, who hailed from Purfleet in Surrey, had an article dated May 12 published. Of interest to the Braidwood history is a small section from his article:

> ... I have heard, however, of a very fine young man, the natural son of a late great statesman by a lady of quality, having been shut up in a madhouse without the benefit of any such privilege; although his preceptor, the late Mr. T. Braidwood, was, I am well informed by persons intimately connected with the family of that gentleman, of opinion he was far from labouring under any mental derangement or inability whatever. I have not heard whether his imprisonment was the act of his

father with whom he was known not to agree perfectly in political opinions, nor if he be at present in existence; but certain it is, that no mention was made of him in that great man's will, nor in the subsequent arrangement made for the benefit of the widow and a daughter. He must, then, be no more. Peace to the ashes of the dead!

The above is one of the earliest reports showing how a learned teacher of the deaf can detect the mental capabilities of deaf persons and distinguish the difference between normal deaf persons and those suffering from mental illness of various forms.

Weeden Butler

The Gentleman's Magazine (Vol. 77, 1807 issue) that year provided interesting letters from three contributors, and this appeared to have instigated the beginning of the downfall of the Braidwood era in Hackney. From what can be gleaned, Isabella's excessive claims that deaf children could be highly educated were put into doubt by some writers, and she was seemingly "caught out" by those who knew such pupils that were referred to. Weeden Butler, despite his good intentions and altruism towards the deaf, must have wondered if he was being taken advantage of by Isabella Braidwood.

An extract from Weeden Butler's letter to *The Gentleman's Magazine*: on page 36 read:

MR URBAN,   *Cheyne Walk, Chelsea*
                                          Jan. 20

... Mr Thomas Braidwood, I am informed, was born in Scotland, in the year 1715; and died at Grove House, Hackney, Middlesex, on 24th Oct 1806. He finished his education at the College of Edinburgh, and was afterwards assistant in the Grammar School at Hamilton. After this, he opened a school in Edinburgh for the instruction of young men in geometry, mathematics, &c.

In the year 1760, a boy named Charles Sherriff, born deaf, was fortunately placed under Mr. B's care; but without any idea being entertained on the part of the parent or Mr. B. of the possibility of teaching the child anything besides plain writing. From very attentively noticing the situation of the poor boy, however, Mr. B. conceived the hope of teaching him to articulate; compassion simulated his patient exertions; and, in a few years, he enabled him to speak and understand language. Mr Sherriff is now in the East Indies, in a very flourishing way of business as a painter. The following lines appeared in some of the London news-papers, about the end of the year 1768; they were written by Mr. Sherriff, without assistance or amendment, and constitute, I think, a pleasing little specimen of the degree of advancement in original composition, to which the naturally Deaf are sometimes capable of arriving.

LINES.

On seeing Garrick act, by a deaf pupil of Mr. Braidwood.

When Britain's Roscius on the stage appears,
Who charms all eyes, and (I am told) all ears,
With ease the various passions I can trace,
Clearly reflected from that wond'rous face;
Whilst true conception, with just action join'd,
Strongly impress each image on my mind;
What need of sounds, when plainly I decry
Th' expressive featured, and the speaking eye?
That eye whose bright and penetrating ray
Doth Shakespeare's meaning to my soul convey;
Best commentator on great Shakespeare's text!
When Garrick acts, no passage seems perplex'd.

It is necessary to remark that, although Mr. Braidwood was not the first teacher who practiced the Art, yet he was the inventor of his own ingenious method; as, till Mr. Sherriff had very far advanced in education, he (Mr. B.) was wholly unacquainted with previous discoveries. The rapid addition of fresh pupils, and the wonderful extent of his practice, which he sedulously improved, amply attests his skill. Indeed, with the openness of sterling genius, he often candidly acknowledge that, in consequences of new discoveries made in the course of teaching, his final success very greatly exceeded what was at first the object of his soundest and most sanguine expectations.

About the year 1770, Mr. B. Senior, took his kinsman, Mr. John Braidwood as a co-adjuror or partner. This very amiable and indefatigable was born in 1756; and in 1782, married the daughter of his venerable near relation and associate: he died at Hackney of a pulmonary complaint, on the 24th Sept, 1798, leaving his widow with four children, viz. two sons and two daughters.

Having, from her earliest youth, been instructed by her father in this astonishing ART, and having constantly assisted her husband after their separation from that venerable character, who latterly declined the toil of business, Mrs. B. continues to conduct the ACADEMY in Mare-street, Hackney, with an augmenting success; being carefully aided by her sons, Messrs. Thomas and John Braidwood.

On Monday the 29th Dec. 1806, Mr. Urban, I myself visited this noble Institution for both sexes, and was most highly gratified with the examination of a fine youth of thirteen years of age, who was born deaf. He wrote, ciphered and conversed *viva voce,* before a large company, with utmost fluency and readiness. After the merited eulogies of Mr. Arnot, in his "History of Edinburgh"; of Dr Johnson, in his "Journey to the Hebrides"; of Lord Monboddo, in his "Origin and Progress of Language"; of Mr. Pennant, in his "Tour through Scotland"; and of Mr. Green, in his work "Vox oculis subjecta"; elaborate praise from a humbler pen, Sir, would prove equally vain and foolish. The long-established reputation of the

Braidwoods is founded on a rock; their labours are approved by their country; their reward is, assuredly, with the Most High...

Weeden Butler, Jun

It appears that Isabella Braidwood did not do her homework on the origin of the lines to Garrick which she attributed to Shirreff, and consequently her claim that Shirreff wrote the poem himself for the stage actor David Garrick backfired badly; it did more harm to the reputation of the Braidwood Institution than one initially thought. The situation was not really going well for Isabella barely a year after her father's death. There was no need for Isabella to make unfounded boasts to further the school, and such actions were both foolish and uncalled for, because the reputation of the Braidwood Institution alone up to that time was worth more than words or publicity.

The next letter was published on page 130 of the same issue of *The Gentleman's Magazine*, contributed by Medicus. His letter was lengthy and the only relevant part was the first paragraph which read:

Mr. URBAN   Feb. 7

In p.36, I perused a compendious letter on the deaf and dumb. Mr. Butler calls the subject affecting, and I think he has treated it in an affecting manner. To his warm panegyric on Braidwood, the founder of the first regular academy for these children, I certainly cannot with propriety object; although I deem it but right to apprize him and your readers, that, owing to an increase in her charges of late years, the advantages of Widow Braidwood's Establishment at Hackney, can now only be enjoyed by the sons and daughters of Opulence. The Poor, however, need not despair; a Charity named the ASYLUM was instituted A.D. 1792, in the Grange-road, Bermondsey, whither they are invited to send their deaf little ones of both sexes; and where, as a most striking example of the success attending it, William Hunter, an ingenious young man, himself born deaf and dumb, constantly assists Watson, the master, in instructing others.

93

The contribution from Medicus confirmed that the Braidwood Institution had been increasing fees to the stage that the institution was becoming expensive and those on a certain wealth scale just below the opulent were increasingly unable to meet their children's tuition and boarding fees. Medicus was referring to the Pembroke House institution on Mare Street, not the Grove House Academy, which did not exist at that time after the death of Thomas Braidwood the previous year. Another thing worth noting is the mention of William Hunter, a deaf charity pupil of Joseph Watson who was working as an assistant teacher.

Next, a contributor from Cambridge joined in the debate and wrote a very lengthy but interesting article to *The Gentleman's Magazine* in response to Weeden Butler's letter (pages 305-306). The Cambridge contributor's response appeared to have ended Weeden Butler's involvement with the education of the deaf:

Mr. URBAN,

Cambridge,
Feb. 21

In your January Magazine, p.38, I read Weeden Butler's letter on the superiority of Mr. Braidwood's method of instructing the deaf and dumb, to that of the Abbé L' Epée, as he taught them to speak (besides every other attainment they acquired with the Abbé). That he had been so happily successful with some of his pupils I can very readily believe; and I am happy to find Mrs. Trimmer, in her excellent work of the Guardian of Education, confirms this belief (*Vide vol. I, p.489*). Mrs. T. says there is a school at Hackney for the instruction of children born deaf and dumb, in the higher classes of life, formerly kept by a Mr. Braidwood, but now carried on by his widow, in which young ladies and gentlemen naturally defective in the organs of speech and hearing, are not only taught to articulate distinctly, so as to be able to make themselves understood, but are even brought to a great degree of proficiency in the study of languages and other branches of liberal education. As that lady is so acquainted with, and so qualified to inspect and speak of education in all

94

its variety of branches, I think it highly probable that the assertion in this note, that "the deaf and dumb are taught to articulate distinctly", was from personal knowledge. Mrs. Trimmer's authority must be incontestable; and so would Mr. Butler's, if, he spoke from personal knowledge. But as it is not the case, (although I entertain the highest opinion of his abilities and the benevolence of his intentions), he must excuse me for saying, I think him unfortunate in the instance he has given in the person of Mr. Charles Sherriff. I was well acquainted with that gentleman some years since, both at Bath and Brighton; but I own I have frequently tried, but always ineffectually, to understand him. His attempts at speech ever appeared to me like broken sounds, murmured in sleep, but much less distinct; and they were also extremely harsh and grating to the ear, so much so, that not only my own family, but every person whom I have ever seen in his company expressed their hope that Mr. Sherriff would not attempt to speak. A gentleman of this University assures me, precisely the same wish was expressed here; were it necessary, more than an hundred inhabitants of Cambridge would acknowledge they never could understand a single sentence of Mr. Sherriff's. I remember but one exception, which was in the person of a beautiful and amiable woman, to whom Mr. S. was attached, who assured me she could sometimes distinguish a word or two in a sentence. She considered him as so amiable and interesting a character that she declared she would have married him, if she had a competent fortune and better health, but she feared being an incumbrance rather than a comfort to him. He has this lady's portrait in miniature, in the character of Mary Queen of Scots. I am sorry it is not in my power to corroborate Mr. Butler's account of Mr. Sherriff being able to articulate; but Mr. S's talents in miniature-painting are held in such just estimation, that the circumstance, Mr. Urban, must be known to many of your readers. I feared Mr. Braidwood and family might suffer in the public opinion, if the test of speaking to be understood rested with Mr. Sherriff. Many of their pupils, I doubt not, far excel him in that respect; indeed, I used to imagine there was some defect in his palate. For so far even in thought from wishing to detract from Mr. Braidwood's truly well-earned fame, I only wish it to be founded on a firmer basis, in a more fortunate instance of some other pupil. I am happy to bear my testimony to Mr. Charles Sherriff's other attainments. His excellence in miniature-painting is too well known to need a comment. He reads (very possibly writes) in the French language; his manners are such as mark the gentleman. In company, by observing the motion of the lips, he was seldom at a loss for the subject of the discourse. If a sentence escaped him, by the time the second word was written he caught the meaning of the whole. His replies were remarkable for their terseness and elegance; it used to give me great pleasure to obtain his opinion of books, as I found him a man of superior understanding, and highly cultivated mind. And, what was more to his praise, I always understood he had greatly assisted his father, who lost some 20 to 30,000l in Fordyce's Banking-house. Mr. S. went to the East Indies a few years since, and, I have been informed, he realised a very handsome fortune, and retired to private life. I will not venture to vouch for the truth of this report, though I sincerely wish it may be correct; as I cannot recollect from whom I received my information. I must also take the liberty of assuring Mr. Butler that I think he must have been greatly misinformed with respect to the lines addressed to Mr. Garrick, which he inserted in his letter in p.36, having been written by Mr. S. I was always assured they were written by Caleb Whiteford, Esq. (unknown to Mr. S.) to facilitate his introduction to that admirable Actor, for which he expressed an ardent wish. The circumstance, as I have ever heard it related, was, that it was observed Mr. Sherriff never took a book with him when Garrick performed, and for which he was requested to declare his reason; his answer was, "that Garrick's countenance portrayed every passion so strongly, from its rise to its termination, that he did not require a book, as Garrick was the completest comment on Shakespeare's text." I have frequently heard the lines mentioned in large companies before Mr. Whiteford's friends, but never heard a doubt expressed on the occasion; they were constantly attributed to Mr. Whiteford. I have seen this opinion more than once in print, and can quote an instance; in the Public Characters for 1801 and 1802, p.392, under that of Mr. Whiteford. The circumstance is thus related: "Mr. Whiteford was glad of every opportunity of paying a handsome compliment to his friend David; and the following circumstance furnished him with a favourable occasion. A young artist of the name of Sherriff had come from Edinburgh to obtain employment as a miniature-painter; there were several circumstances which contributed to interest Mr. Whiteford in his favour; he was very ingenious, sensible, worthy young man, and by the labours of his pencil supported an aged father, who had failed in trade. Young Sherriff was deaf and dumb from his birth, but had been taught to read and write, and was particularly fond of Shakespeare's plays; whenever any of them were acted, he was sure to be in the pit, especially if Garrick performed, whom he admired the most, because he understood him the best. This young man was extremely desirous of being introduced to Garrick, and applied to Mr. W. for that purpose. In order to raise the curiosity of that celebrated performer, Mr. W. wrote the verses (quoted in your Magazine) in the name of the artist, expressing his feelings on seeing him in some of Shakespeare's principal characters. Garrick had been flattered by poets of all sorts; but to make the deaf and dumb speak his praise was something new, and therefore he was very much struck with it, and extremely desirous of seeing the young artist, whom Mr. W. accordingly introduced to him, and the scene that ensued was said to be a most curious one indeed.

A.

Caleb Whiteford (left) should be spelled Whitefoord. That aside, this letter reveals what people thought of Charles Shirreff apart from his voice! Many a deaf person will understand why Shirreff's voice sounded harsh and awful; and that will be because, after a regime of being constantly supervised and monitored to speak properly at school, there is no one in the outside world to take over the role of the teacher and the speech monitor, and the voice deteriorates. That was what happened to Shirreff and also to a good number of deaf people. If the "hundreds" of people in Cambridge who knew Shirreff did not want him to talk, why did they all not learn to fingerspell or sign?

Shirreff's personality and character, however, appeared to appeal to many people and also that he was a very well-liked person whose opinion and views were valued. This was indeed a tribute to the education he received under Thomas Braidwood, besides a statement on the quality of tuition imparted by Braidwood.

Weeden Butler never again contributed another letter in support of the Braidwood Institution to *The Gentleman's Magazine*. He must have felt both let down and misinformed by Isabella Braidwood about Shirreff's lines to Garrick.

The final of the quartet of letters was published on page 307 just following the above letter. It was contributed by a writer under the name of Iapis, and only the first two paragraphs are of interest:

Mr. URBAN,   Hackney, April 1.

I had the pleasure many years ago of knowing Mr. John Braidwood, who died in 1798; and can with great satisfaction add my testimony to that of Mr. Butler, p.38. He was, indeed, "a very amiable and indefatigable man," of a delicate frame of body. Medicus, p.130, candidly allows the undisputable title of the Braidwood family; but seems very unnecessarily to institute a comparison between the advantages of attending the ACADEMY in Mare-street, Hackney, and the ASYLUM in the Grange-road, Bermondsey.

As this short letter, Sir, is not meant to promote warmth of discussion, you will, I am persuaded, gladly excuse my unwillingness to prove by dint of lengthened argument, the right of the Braidwoods to claim pecuniary compensations for unceasing labours. I may, however, perhaps, be permitted to observe, en passant, that their charges appear to me fair, liberal and considerate; varying most materially, as the difficulties of the several cases vary. The parents of the youngest children, I believe, in general pay least.

Iapis.

This writer thought the Braidwoods' charges were fair as opposed to that of Medicus. Was it because he knew more of the Braidwood Institution and what they had to offer in terms of value for money compared with other educational establishments? This is a possibility that has to be taken into account, even though we all may never find any more information than what we have already about the Braidwood Institution.

1808   John Braidwood relinquished his rented property and moved into his original property which he first rented in 1805. However, the Land Tax record noted that the rent was paid by "Widow Braidwood".
Isabella was paying £140 per annum rent for both Pembroke House and John Braidwood's house, and also paying rent for the Hackney Terrace house.

1809   John Braidwood was noted as returning to live with Isabella at the Hackney Terrace house for a while before departing for Edinburgh, and the Institution was functioning at Pembroke House.
Henrietta Stewart Braidwood passed away on September 29, aged 23 years. She died after a short illness, the nature of which had never been recorded.

Around late 1809 Isabella Braidwood received an invitation from a group of people in Edinburgh to consider taking up the post of founder head teacher of the planned Edinburgh Institution for the Instruction of the Deaf and Dumb. She passed the invitation to her son John to consider employment as head teacher of the school. It is possible that Isabella Braidwood saw this as an opportunity not only for her son

John to gain employment elsewhere, but also for her to remove him from the vicinity of Hackney. There is indirect evidence from Isabella's Will that John Braidwood's alcoholism was both causing her much anxiety and becoming too well-known for both Isabella's liking and the reputation of her school; this evidence can also be drawn from the Land Tax records between 1805 and 1809 above, the moving of properties, the separation from the family, and Isabella moving her son back into a respectable property and paying the rent for him. She was most likely taking action to preserve the reputation of her institution. In any event, the committee of the proposed school for the deaf in Edinburgh took on John, giving him a generous remuneration package. John was off to Edinburgh towards the end of the year to participate in the preparations for the opening of the new school in 1810. At Edinburgh, John resided at 7 George Street.

Joseph Watson published his *Instruction of the Deaf and Dumb, Or A Theoretical and Practical View of the* Means *By Which They Are Taught To Speak And Understand A Language; containing Hints For The Correction Of Impediments In Speech.* (Darton and Harvey, London).

Watson's book may be considered as a full exposition of the Braidwoodian Method, later known as the Combined System; Watson used speaking, writing, reading, drawing, fingerspelling and natural signs as means of instruction. His book sold well and received rave reviews in the newspapers and magazines of the day.

1810 The Braidwood Institution continued at Pembroke House with Isabella, her son Thomas and daughter Elizabeth managing the school. The Edinburgh Institution for the Deaf and Dumb officially opened in a little building at 8 Union Street in the New Town with John Braidwood as its head teacher.

The Edinburgh school went well for the first few months. One of the earliest pupils at the school was Walter Geikie. His father, Archibald Geikie, had to pay 9 guineas per quarter for his tuition, which was a hefty fee in those days. Walter Geikie was previously instructed at home by his father and he was, at the time of enrolment into the Edinburgh Institution, educationally advanced. The school's committee initially offered Archibald Geikie the post of head teacher, but he turned it down before they offered the post to John Braidwood. John Braidwood noted how well educated Geikie was and he soon made him a monitor (a sort of assistant teacher in all but name). Soon afterwards and towards the end of the year, John Braidwood started to miss most classes, telling Walter to take over every time. His alcoholism appeared to take the better of him and the school was not being run as professionally and effectively as it should have been. Walter Geikie stayed for three quarters before being pulled out by his father.

1811   The Braidwood Institution was no longer in Pembroke House, Mare Street. It moved further south to Cambridge Heath by the canal. The exact name of the building was never known, but it is generally called Barclay House. It is believed that the move took place in the latter half of 1810.

Barclay House was a slightly smaller building than Pembroke House although it looked deceptively large, and it was situated on quite a large plot of land, opposite the present day canal located at the corner of Sheep Lane and Andrews Road in Hackney. The building is located by the white arrow in the 1831 map of Hackney below.

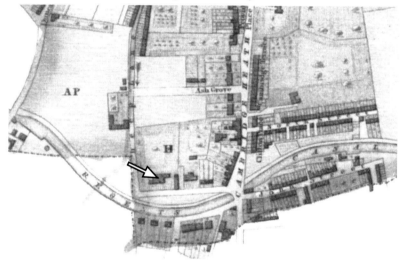

Map - courtesy of Hackney Archives Department

The Land Tax Records have a gap exactly co-extensive with Braidwood's occupation of the Cambridge Heath premises, and the other tax records are patchy between 1810 and 1830. The Poor Rates shows Thomas Braidwood in occupation of the only large house at Cambridge Heath in 1812 (P/J/P221 - Hackney Archives). It is valued at £110 along with two other small patches of land, each valued at £3. The local "census" of 1811 strangely, and perhaps erroneously, called Braidwood "William" when it should have been Thomas. However, it recorded the household as consisting of 12 males and 15 females, of which 20 were pupils and the rest staff, including the Braidwoods. This building later became known as Barclay House and after that Heath House. There is no available picture of the building.

John Braidwood's increasingly regular absences from the Edinburgh Institution classes began to cause alarm among the committee members. To make matters worse, John Braidwood was increasingly using his pupil, Walter Geikie, as a mentor to cover for his frequent absences. In the Easter of 1811, one of the committee members, James Farquhar Gordon, chanced to meet a Congregational minister named Robert Kinniburgh, who had recently resigned from Dunkeld Church. This chance encounter led to Kinniburgh being employed in May as an assistant teacher to train under John Braidwood. This employment of Kinniburgh did not please the wretched alcoholic and barely two months later in July, John Braidwood abruptly left the school. It was said through Deaflore that both his shameful alcoholic condition and personal debts through gambling were becoming too well known and Braidwood had no choice but to flee both the school and Edinburgh. He had acquired a nickname of "Alky John". Soon after leaving the Edinburgh Institution, his whereabouts were unknown.

Following John Braidwood's departure, the Edinburgh Institution for the Deaf and Dumb closed for business and the committee's anger was vented on the Braidwoods in Hackney for the behaviour of John Braidwood. The assistant teacher, Robert Kinniburgh, was taken on by John's brother Thomas Braidwood to train as a teacher of the deaf, seemingly to compensate for the mess and distress that John caused. There was no charge for his training, but because he was trained gratuitously, both Isabella and Thomas Braidwood put him on a seven year bond at a cost of £1000 not to reveal or pass on by way of teaching their method to any person without both the permission and knowledge of the Braidwood Institution. Kinniburgh accepted this condition and he wrote (in *The Scottish Congregational Magazine 1852*):

> I was then sent to the Academy for the deaf and dumb in Hackney, near London, at the head of which was Mr Braidwood's brother (Thomas); and there I remained the few months required to obtain the knowledge of the great outlines of the system of teaching the deaf and dumb...

At the end of Kinniburgh's training, the Edinburgh Institution reopened in December of the same year with ten pupils, and the school grew. This school under Kinniburgh produced some fine pupils who became leading figures in deaf history. [It must be stated here that this school was not the Braidwood School as some historians named it. Its only Braidwoodian connection was the disgraced alcoholic John Braidwood and nothing more. The school had always been known as the Edinburgh Institution for the Instruction of the Deaf and Dumb.]

Isabella Braidwood became increasingly domineering and ambitious in her endeavours to expand her business, which was her school. Despite receiving a tidy sum from her father Thomas' will, Isabella appeared to have spent it all on making the Braidwood Institution a luxurious establishment to impress the wealthy. It was a gamble that was doomed. There was another element that was to lead to lsabella's troubles - her reluctance to share teaching methods and this put people off.

1812   The Braidwood Institution continued in Barclay House. The number of pupils did not increase and this caused concern.

Charles Shirreff, Thomas Braidwood's first pupil, visited Isabella who sat for a portrait. This portrait was exhibited at the Royal Academy in the summer.
John Braidwood arrived in America in February.

1813   The Braidwood Institution at Barclay House was not going well. Pupil numbers were on the decline for the first time. The institution came to the end of its Hackney era in December.

1813 was also the year that the Braidwood Institution proper came to its end. Isabella saw everything around her come crashing down. There were no more inflows of pupils of the wealthy classes. Existing pupils were pulled out due to their parents tightening their spending, and in some cases placing their children much more cheaply in the private pupils section in the schools such as that of Joseph Watson in the Old Kent Road Asylum and in the private school of I. S. Woodman in Kilburn. Early in the year, Isabella made desperate appeals for children to be sent to her school, and one such example was printed in the Public Advertiser:

A Gentleman, whose Grandson has been from the age of four to that of nine years under the care and tuition of the Widow BRAIDWOOD and SON, at Hackney, is well satisfied of their proficiency in the difficult science of instructing Children who are unhappily subjected to the privation of Hearing, and, until properly instructed, also of Speech. He is convinced of the maternal tenderness evinced towards all the Children under the care of the deserving family before mentioned; and as she is the immediate descendant of the original Teacher and liberal-minded Promulgator of this useful Art, the Advertiser, in justice to Mrs. Braidwood and her son, feels it his duty thus to convey his sentiments to the Public, more especially as there are at present period a few Vacancies in this Institution, where Persons may place their unfortunate Children to the best advantage, and upon the most reasonable terms.

The Advertiser will, upon receipt of a line, (post-paid) and addressed to A. Z., Turks Head Coffee-house, Strand, willingly give such farther information as may be required.

There was another occurrence in that year that was to end the Braidwood era in Hackney. A gentleman banker by the name of James Woolley came to visit Thomas Braidwood at his school. He introduced himself as the treasurer of the newly-founded Institution for the Education of Deaf and Dumb Children in Birmingham. He invited Thomas to become the teacher of the new school. Let the First Report of the Committee to the Annual General Meeting of the Institution on January 28, 1814 take up the following:

— From what then passed, arose a correspondence between your Committee and Mr. Braidwood, which terminated in an invitation to that Gentleman, to undertake the management of your intended School. Your Committee were not deterred from making this offer, by the prospect of incurring much greater expence than you had at first contemplated; they regarded Mr. Braidwood's acknowledged skill in the art which had been in the possession of his family for two generations; and they thought that if, by his means, they could introduce it, in an advanced state, into your School, which would thus acquire at once a distinguished character, they should much better fulfil your intentions, than by the more frugal appointment of an inexperienced person, who must undertake the same task under great disadvantages, and perhaps with great uncertainty of success.

Some difficulties in Mr. Braidwood's acceptance of their offer arose from his connexion with his own School; but these being gradually removed, in the beginning of the present year he came down to Birmingham, and on the 11th of this month, actually opened the School, with a few of the Children, who are already beginning, under his direction, to articulate the sounds of language.

Things were taking a turn for the worse for Isabella, who was witnessing her world crumbling around her. The circumstances for the Braidwoods became so bad that she had to accept her situation, that her school was no more. There were rumours circulating at that time that the Braidwoods were unable to pay their creditors in the form of loans and outstanding trade and suppliers' accounts. Next, there was an advertisement appearing in several local newspapers of the day which threw interesting light on the situation of the Braidwood Institution and also gave an insight into Isabella Braidwood's ambitions. The announcement in the newspapers read:

Hackney, one mile from Shoreditch Church. Lease of a Capital Residence, Gardens, Pleasure Grounds, and Land, Furniture and Effects. By Mr. Robins, on the Premises, Cambridge Heath, near the Turnpike, Hackney, on MONDAY, Dec 6, at Twelve, for the benefit of the Creditors of Mrs. And Mr. Braidwood.

The valuable lease of a capital substantial Family RESIDENCE, seated on a Lawn, enclosed from the road by iron folding gates; consisting of a spacious entrance paved hall, large dining parlour, drawing room, breakfast room, store room and five roomy airy bed chambers on the first story, and six on the upper story, handsome principal and secondary staircases, excellent offers in the basement, a large

105

paved yard, with folding gates to the road, roomy stabling, coach-houses, brew-house, and outbuildings, good kitchen gardens, pleasure grounds and land, all walled round, the whole near three acres; upwards of 17 years unexpired of the lease, at a low rent.

Also on that and the following Day, will be sold by Auction, the next Household Furniture, fine-toned piano-forte, plate linen china, books and effect; the Furniture comprises 22 4-post, tent, and other bedsteads, with dinner furniture, good bedding, well -made cabinet work of all descriptions, carpets, pier and other glasses, good kitchen requisites, garden tools, brewing utensils, casks, and various effects. The House may be viewed to the time of sale; the Furniture on Friday and Saturday preceding. Particulars and Catalogues may be had on the Premises; at the Mermaid, Hackney; Garraway's of Messers. Saxon and Watkins, Solicitors, No. 5, Pump-court, Temple; and of Mr. Robins, Warwick-street, Golden-square.

This advertisement confirmed that the Hackney era came to an end at the end of November 1813. Two weeks after the auction on 6 December, there appeared an advertisement in the *Morning Chronicle* dated Monday 20th December:

The DEAF AND DUMB TAUGHT TO SPEAK - Mr. I. S. Woodman begs leave to acquaint his friends and Public that TWO VACANCIES remain in his Establishment for that unfortunate class of persons, situated at Kilburn, near London, where a continuance of his exertions, directed by scientific principles, and extended by successful experience, may be confidently relied on. Mr. W. also undertakes the removal of Impediments in Speech, whether the results of a natural defect, or contracted by bad habit. The health and morals of younger pupils are objects of particular concern.

N.B. School will recommence on Monday the 10th of January 1814.

An obscure newspaper article is said to have stated that this Mr I. S. Woodman was trained alongside Joseph Watson at Grove House by Thomas Braidwood, before joining Watson at his private school in Bethnal Green. Woodman established his own school for the deaf when Watson closed his Bethnal Green school to take up the headship of the newly formed London Asylum in November 1792. This source is in either the Hackney Archives or the Southwark Archives.

While Thomas Braidwood took up his post as the head teacher of the General Institution for the Instruction of Deaf and Dumb in Birmingham on Tuesday 11 January 1814, Isabella and her daughter Elizabeth headed for Holborn in London. The Land Tax Records for the Parish of St. George the Martyr (Holborn) showed Isabella Braidwood renting a property owned by John Hogarth for the sum of £50 per annum. This property was 7 Great Ormond Street and it was in these premises that Isabella and Elizabeth established their Seminary for Young Deaf Children. They ran their seminary in Holborn until sometime in 1816, from which time the Braidwoods were no longer situated in in London. Nothing can be unearthed about the Great Ormond Street seminary and Holborn Archives department does not have even a single shred of information on this venture by Isabella and Elizabeth.

Meanwhile in Birmingham, Thomas Braidwood was conducting the day school in the town with fourteen children, consisting of seven girls and seven boys at the beginning. There were a series of fundraising events organised by the committee of the General Institution for the Instruction of Deaf and Dumb Children. During the course of one of the numerous fundraising events, the committee were fortunate to secure a very large building which belonged to Lord Calthorpe and he leased the building on favourable terms to the committee, which in turn was able to transfer the school from the town into a country setting in Edgbaston, a suburban area of Birmingham, by the end of 1814. From that time on, the school became a residential school.

7 Great Ormond Street, (left door)
Photograph taken in 2007
by Raymond Lee.

The *Fourth Report of the Committee of the General Institution for the Instruction of Deaf and Dumb Children* published a list of ladies who were requested to act as a committee for the purpose of superintending the management and employment of the girls at the school. There were fifteen names, and one of these was Mrs. Braidwood.

Isabella and Elizabeth Braidwood had moved from Holborn to Edgbaston, taking up residence in a property known as The Mount, situated by the Worcester Canal in an affluent part of the area - her house is as denoted by the white arrow on the plan below. It was not far from the Edgbaston School where her son Thomas was working.

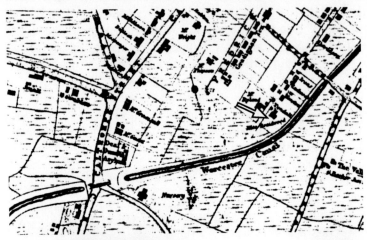

The Mount which Isabella rented still survives at present — above.
Photograph and plan by courtesy of Marcus Green.

While Thomas Braidwood was running the school, Isabella took on limited numbers of young girls or deaf children of both sexes in her seminary. It appears that the seminary was not as successful as she hoped. There were a number of newspapers outside Birmingham advertising her seminary. It does not appear that they had many children from the Birmingham area. One advertisement can be seen below:

Salisbury and Winchester Journal

Monday, June 22, 1818

DEAF and DUMB — MRS. ISABELLA BRAIDWOOD, the Daughter of Mr. Thomas Braidwood *(the original Instructor of the Deaf and Dumb in Edinburgh)* and Widow of the late Mr. John Braidwood, of Hackney, begs leave to state, that with the assistance of her Daughter, she continues to instruct a limited number of young Ladies or Children of either sex, who are deaf, or who labour under impediments in speech. The Mount, Edgbaston, near Birmingham.

The Highfields, former home and private school of Thomas Braidwood, Headmaster of the Edgbaston General Institution for the Instruction of Deaf and Dumb Children.   (Photograph - A. J. Boyce Collection)

Nothing is known about Isabella and her seminary. Thomas Braidwood appeared to have been initially residing at the Edgbaston General Institution for the Instruction of Deaf and Dumb Children. He later lived in a house not far from the school known as The Highfields. It was from this house that Thomas ran a private school for deaf pupils of the wealthy class. Like The Mount, this house still stands to the present day.

Next, there appeared an obituary in Arris's Birmingham Gazette on 9 August 1819 announcing...

> Braidwood. Mrs. Isabella, wife of John, of The Mount, Edgbaston, Mother of Braidwood, Instructor at the General Institute for the Deaf and Dumb. Died 1st Aug. 1819.

Isabella was interred in the catacombs of Christ Church, New Street, Birmingham on 5 August 1819. The situation left her daughter Elizabeth to continue running the seminary at the Mount.

The Gentleman's Magazine (Nov. 1819) carried an obituary on Isabella Braidwood.

> Aug. 1. At Edgbaston, in her 57th year, Isabella, relict of Mr. John Braidwood, of Hackney, and mother of Mr. Braidwood, instructor of the Deaf and Dumb at Birmingham. Mr. Thomas Braidwood, of Edinburgh, the father of this lady, was the first who in this country systematically attempted this arduous yet interesting pursuit (see our vol. LXVIII. 1032, LXXVII. 38, 206); and, after the most persevering application, may, in effect, be said to have given - hearing to the deaf and speech to the dumb. In 1760, the year, we believe, preceding that in which the justly-celebrated D. L'Epee first conceived his benevolent designs, Mr. Braidwood directed his active mind to this important art, an art he then conceived to be original, and the most successful realisation of which he was permitted to witness, and to bequeath to his family and to posterity. Mr. B. in 1783, removed from Edinburgh to Hackney, when, in conjunction with his son in law, Mr. John

Braidwood, he continued for many years to pursue his profession.

Most unexpectedly, at an early age, bereft of her husband, the first wish of Mrs. Braidwood was to perpetuate, through her family, the art which she had seen so beneficially exercised by her father. The connection of her son with the General Institution induced the removal of his parent and her surviving daughter to the vicinity of Birmingham. For the zealous fulfilment of every duty connected with her profession, few could be more peculiarly gifted than Mrs. Braidwood. Of an active mind; in disposition, gentle, kind, and endearing; in intellect well-endowed and ever bent on imparting to her pupils a knowledge of the sacred truths of the Gospel — she was eminently qualified to engage the attention, and command the love and confidence of all entrusted to her care.

Miss Braidwood continues the Seminary at Edgbaston, in the same manner as when under the direction of her deceased mother.

The General Institution for the Instruction of the Deaf and Dumb, according to the school's annual reports, was going well and the committee and the subscribers expressed their satisfaction with the work Thomas Braidwood was doing.

The quality of education the pupils were receiving was of an excellent standard and a large proportion of the children exceeded the committee's expectations in written English. The committee were so impressed with the deaf pupils' written English that they printed specimens of their work in the Annual Reports from 1821 onwards, but this ended with the 1824 Annual Report. (Some samples are shown in Appendix 2.)

Since the demise of his mother Isabella Braidwood, Thomas made it clear that he wanted to assist his sister Elizabeth with the seminary, and consequently, according to page 6 of the *Seventh Report of the Committee to the General Meeting on October 27, 1819*, he declared that he intended to leave his post as soon as a replacement was found. Braidwood, however, mentioned that he would postpone his retirement until a suitable successor could be found, and also that he would impart full knowledge of his mode of teaching to that successor. It was noted in this report that Braidwood would devote six hours every day to the school until his successor became fully qualified. Thomas moved out of his Highfields abode and resided with his sister at The Mount.

The *Gentleman's Magazine* (Nov. 1819, pages 452-3) carried an article:

> Oct. 27. At a general Meeting of the Subscribers to the Deaf and Dumb Institution, Birmingham, Mr. Thos. Braidwood (see our last number p.377), the Master of the asylum, having respectfully signified his intention to retire, in order to superintend his Sister's Establishment at Edgbaston, and to devote his whole time to private pupils; but having at the same time (with a liberality which reflected on him the highest honour) professed his readiness to remain until he should have imparted to his successor a knowledge of the mode of instruction sufficient to enable the latter to undertake the arduous office: — in testimony of their full approbation of Mr. Braidwood's conscientious and zealous services, the Governors unanimously voted to that gentleman a piece of plate of silver of the value of 20l, to be adorned with a suitable inscription.

The *Eighth Report of the Committee to the General Meeting on October 7, 1820,* reported that an assistant to Thomas Braidwood was found, but after a trial of a few months he found himself compelled to resign. During that year, Thomas Braidwood corresponded with Dr Orpen of Dublin and several other men connected with the education of the deaf, for their assistance and advice in obtaining a suitable assistant. His endeavours met with no success.

Early in 1817 Braidwood and his three private pupils boarded a coach at Leeds to head back to Birmingham after visiting some place where they presented a demonstration of the pupils' educational prowess. They were joined by a young man who was heading for London seeking employment. During the coach ride, this young man was fascinated by the way the three deaf children communicated using both signing and fingerspelling. His curiosity led him into a conversation with Thomas. He introduced himself as Henry Brothers Bingham and he mentioned he was seeking employment, but did not know exactly what he wanted to do. When the coach arrived at Birmingham, Braidwood offered Bingham a position as his assistant teacher and also to be trained with the view to take over his place once he had passed his training. Bingham had no hesitation in accepting the invitation and he did not continue his journey to London. He was put to work with Braidwood's private pupils for 4 years as a part of his training before being promoted to Assistant Teacher in the charity school in 1821.

The *Ninth Report of the Committee to the General Meeting on October 17, 1821,* mentioned that the school "had been fortunate enough to find in Mr Bingham, a young man, who appears, from his assiduity, gentleness and patience, well qualified to learn and afterwards practice the art, and who in the meantime, being resident in the school, is exercising by his constant presence, that moral government and control, of which deaf and dumb children stand so peculiarly in need."

The tenth, eleventh and twelfth annual reports expressed the committee's gratitude and pleasure in the work carried out by both Braidwood and Bingham, who had by that time completed three years' training as an assistant under Thomas.

Early in 1825, Thomas Braidwood became ill and he died on 27 April of the same year. His death was sudden and took many people by surprise. There was no reason given for his death. *Arris's Birmingham Gazette* ran a simple obituary:

> Braidwood, Thomas. Instructor of the Deaf and
> Dumb Institute, Edgbaston, died 27th April.

Thomas Braidwood was only 42 years old and this left Elizabeth Braidwood as the surviving member of the Braidwood family. On 4 May 1825, like his mother Isabella, Thomas' body was buried in the catacombs of Christ Church, New Street, Edgbaston.

Following the death of Thomas Braidwood, the General Institution for the Instruction of the Deaf and Dumb was thrown into turmoil. A small section of the committee members grouped together to demand the introduction of a different method to be adopted, that of sign only instead of the Braidwoodian method. They were influenced by a former teacher of the Asylum for the Deaf and Dumb at Hartford in Connecticut, USA. This teacher, the Rev. William Woodbridge, was travelling through Britain on his way to Switzerland and he happened to meet some members of the committee and, one way or the other, influenced them that the Hartford use of signs was the "best". Woodbridge, a frail and sickly man, even visited the Edgbaston school as an observer and he still came out with the possibly prejudiced opinion that the American way was the best.

Henry Brothers Bingham, Braidwood's anticipated successor, continued to run the school for a while as a caretaker. However, when the committee finally gave in to a number of its members' pressure and agreed to take on board the Rev. Woodbridge's opinion and do away with the Braidwoodian method in 1826, Bingham did not hesitate to relinquish his post soon after the committee's employment of a Swiss, Louis du Puget. The reason for Bingham's resignation was that he was unable to support the new regime under Puget. This new head teacher had no experience in the education of the deaf and also he did not know anything about signs. He underwent a three month crash course under Dr Orpen at the Claremont Institution for the Deaf in Dublin before taking up his post at Edgbaston. Oddly, Puget was not even taught signs during his crash course, and that led to an infamous event in Deaf history, which was drastically covered up by all concerned (See Appendix 3.)

The General Institution for the Instruction of the Deaf and Dumb had lost a fine teacher in Henry Brothers Bingham, who went on to become the headmaster of the West of England Institution for the Deaf and Dumb at Exeter in 1826 and then in 1834, the Old Trafford Institution for the Deaf in Manchester, before establishing a private school for the deaf in Rugby.

Elizabeth Braidwood was courted by a son of Edward Armfield, a wealthy proprietor of a plated and gilt button factory, Armfield & Son, based at 9-10 Newhall Street and Bath Row, Birmingham. This man, Richard Armfield, was some ten years younger than Elizabeth. Shortly after her brother Thomas Braidwood's death, Elizabeth closed her seminary and moved to London with Richard, where they married at St. Bride's, Fleet Street, on 23 July 1825.

Many historians assumed that the Braidwood dynasty ended when Elizabeth married Richard Armfield, but this is far from the truth. The President of the British Deaf History Society, Anthony J. Boyce, unearthed a small advertisement in the *Caledonian Mercury* dated 12

March 1858 in which Elizabeth Armfield was advertising her private school for the Deaf and Dumb and Children of Weak Intellect in Notting Hill, West London. She was running this private school with her daughter Elizabeth and "competent masters." At that time, Elizabeth, the granddaughter of Thomas Braidwood, was seventy years old and her daughter Elizabeth was twenty-eight years old.

Richard Armfield was a button manufacturer and merchant, he ran his business from a warehouse located at no.9 Cateaton Street (now Gresham Street). The business, which included living quarters, continued in 9 Cateaton Street until around 1839 when it moved to 18 King Street, Cheapside, until 1842. They had two children, a son and a daughter named Richard Braidwood Armfield, who was baptised on 1 October 1828 and Elizabeth Armfield, who was baptised on 22 October 1830. They were all recorded in the 1841 Census Return. After that, it was believed that the family moved to live in the Islington area. Richard Armfield was later declared bankrupt in 1843 and not long afterwards he died in 1845.

For interest purposes, Christ Church, New Street, Edgbaston, had 630 catacombs in four vaults under the church apart from its 139 burial plots. Each vault was twenty yards long and laid out so that the bodies faced towards the east. Isabella Braidwood was listed as Internment number 3, and Thomas Braidwood was listed as Internment number 15, both of them were very early internments of the vaults. Due to the population leaving the city centre for the suburbs, the numbers attending the church dwindled and it was closed in 1897. The church was soon after demolished.

On news of the closure of the church, relatives were informed and many took coffins away for burials in churches and family vaults in other cemeteries. The remainder, including the Braidwoods, were removed to Warstone Lane, where they were re-interred in the catacombs there. Both Isabella and Thomas are not listed on the main burial register at Warstone Lane as it was a "transfer."

A list of people transferred from Christ Church to Warstone Lane is given in the 1900 *History of Christchurch and Warstone Lane* supplied by Brian Southwell and copies of two pages from this publication are reproduced on the next page. It was also reported that all bodies interred in Christ Church were dug up under cover of darkness in the early hours of the morning.

39

Interment No.

9.—BEILBY, JAMES HENRY, died Nov., 1865, ætat 69.   123

Of the firm of Beilby, Knott, and Beilby, who are described in Wrightson's Directory of 1823 as Manufacturers of marble, coloured and fancy paper, of Brook House, Bordesley, and wholesale booksellers, medicine vendors, etc., of *Aris's Birmingham Gazette* Office, 95, High Street.
See Inscription.

10.—BENNETT, JOSEPH, died March, 1827, ætat 27   22

He was a builder and contractor in partnership with his Brother John. He built St. Peter's Church in Dale End.

  ,,   JOHN, died June, 1836, ætat 43.   57

He built the Grammar School in New Street.
See Inscription.

  ,,   HANNAH, died March, 1854, ætat 47. 102

11.—BILLINGTON, SARAH, died Dec., 1851, ætat 67. 97

  ,,   EDWARD, died August, 1857, ætat 78   109

He was a butcher, of 5, Congreave Street, and in the Warwickshire Yeomanry.

12.—BROWN, ANNIE LUCAS, died 1871, ætat 82. 132

Sister to Jane W. Wickenden (No. 53).
See Inscription.

13.—BRAIDWOOD, ISABELLA, died 1819, ætat 57   3

  ,,   THOMAS, died 27th April, 1825 ætat 42   15

He had a private school at Hackney, London, for the Instruction of the Deaf and Dumb, being assisted by his Mother, Mrs. Isabella Braidwood.
He came of a family of Teachers of the deaf and dumb, for his Grandfather and Father had an Academy at Edinburgh

40

Interment No.

which was for deaf and dumb children whose parents could afford to pay for the instruction, and also for those people to whom they gave instruction gratuitously.
He was engaged by the Committee of the Deaf and Dumb Institution as their first Teacher, and came to Birmingham in January, 1814, and on the 11th of the same month he opened the school with a few children who began under his direction to articulate the sounds of the language. To Mr. James Woolley, Banker of Birmingham (see James Woolley, No. 55), Treasurer of this Institution, is the credit due of introducing this worthy man to the Committee of the Deaf and Dumb Institution. His Mother, who accompanied him, died in 1819, aged 57. His circumstances being altered by her death, he gave notice to terminate his engagement, at the same time offering to stay on till his successor was appointed, and to teach him the secret of the art of his family in instructing the children, till he should be qualified to instruct them. He also kept a private school for the Deaf and Dumb in Edgbaston. He was a man full of patience, kindness, zeal, tact, and talent, which endeared him to all with whom he came in contact. For nearly eleven years he held the appointment of Instructor to this Institution.
(Culled from the Reports of the Institution, kindly lent by Walter Charlton, Esq., Secretary).

14.—BLYTH, WILLIAM HENRY, died 1835, ætat 1½. 51

He was probably the son of Frederick Blyth, factor and merchant, of 44, Ann Street, in 1833.

15.—COPE, FREDERICK, an infant, died 5th Nov., 1825.

  ,,   JOHN, an infant, died 30th March, 1831.

These infants were found when the church was pulled down underneath the floorway of one of the vaults.

  ,,   MARY, died 1856, ætat 65.   104

  ,,   SARAH, died 1856, ætat 32.   105

  ,,   CHARLES HENRY, died 1863, ætat 7½. 112

A Tamworth family. Sarah died at Holywell, Flintshire. Charles Henry was her Father and Mary her Mother. He was a wine and spirit merchant, at 101, High Street, in 1830. He lived at Sparkhill.

Both Thomas and Isabella Braidwood were reinterred in Warstone Lane catacombs on 22 February 1899, Thomas being entry no. 53278 and Isabella entry no. 53282. The majority of the reinterred from Christ Church are listed as catacomb 11, but all have individual catacomb number against their names. It is probable that catacomb 11 is a vault or corridor number, and the individual numbers are the actual position numbers of the coffins. Thomas is listed in catacomb no. 61 and Isabella in catacomb no. 66.

Warstone Lane cemetery catacombs (All photographs
reproduced by courtesy of Brian Southwell, secretary of
Friends of Key Hill and Warstone Lane Cemeteries)

5 - JOHN BRAIDWOOD IN AMERICA

The best account of John Braidwood in America was written by Alexander Graham Bell in a series of articles entitled *Historical Notes* which were printed in *The Association Review* during 1900. (*The Association Review* was, and still is, the official organ of The American Association to Promote the Teaching of Speech to the Deaf. This organisation merged with the Volta Bureau in 1908. From 1956, The American Association to Promote the Teaching of Speech to the Deaf became known as the Alexander Graham Bell Association.) It is my opinion that no researcher can better what Bell had written unless new evidence emerges that was not previously known. With this in mind Bell's account is fully reprinted here.

The author has dutifully copied everything here, word for word from the original publication and any errors are as copied from the original. Any comments and notes in this account are not those of the author, but Bell's own words.

HISTORICAL NOTES – Chapter IV, June 1900

COL. WM. BOLLING AND JOHN BRAIDWOOD.

Col. Wm. Bolling (right, b. 1777, d. 1845), of Bolling Hall, in Goochland County, Virginia, had from his boyhood been interested in the deaf, because his brothers John and Thomas, and his sister Mary were deaf from birth; and in 1799 his interest was still further increased by the discovery that his own son, William Albert, was also deaf from birth.

The question of this boy's education soon became to him a perplexing problem. There was no school for the deaf in America; and the most feasible plan seemed to be to send him to the Braidwood School in England. Col. Bolling, however, was averse to entrusting his deaf child to the care of strangers in crossing the Atlantic, and parental affection pleaded for delay: so he delayed – and delayed – and in 1809 another deaf child appeared in his family, his little daughter Mary.

This, of course, increased his anxiety; and we may imagine with what pleasure and interest he received in March 1812, a letter from his friend,

Hon. James Pleasants, Member of Congress from his District in Virginia, communicating the intelligence that John Braidwood, an accomplished teacher of the Deaf and Dumb, and grandson of the celebrated Thomas Braidwood of Edinburgh, was in America. Col. Bolling at once set himself in communication with John Braidwood, and the following is a copy of his first letter:

Bolling Hall, March 17, 1812.

Sir:

Under cover of a Letter from Mr. James Pleasants Jr. I received yesterday yours of the 5th inst. announcing your arrival in this country with the view of establishing an institution for the instruction of the deaf and dumb. The unfortunate situation of my son has disagreeable reflections in my mind. The want of some friend with whom he had been in the habit of associating and who would feel disposed to go with him to a foreign country, added to the meek and affectionate disposition he possesses, have deterred me from a separation which would have been so distressing to all parties. These obstacles to his Education are I trust removed by your arrival. I invite you therefore to my House for the purpose of communicating with each other more fully than can be done by Letter, on an affair which is to me of so much importance. It may not perhaps be disagreeable to you to spend some time in a private Family previous to the necessary arrangements you will have to make for a permanent establishment, towards the accomplishment of which the deep interest I feel on the subject will ensure to you every aid in my power. To my Friend Mr. Pleasants I refer you for any information you may wish to have respecting my situation in life &c. who has kindly offered to facilitate any communications between us, and should you determine to visit me, I will with much pleasure meet you in Richmond, prepared to conduct you to my house, at any time after the 25th of next month until that period my engagements are such that I might probably not have it in my power to do so. My brother Thomas and Sister Mary are living at present with my mother at Cobbs, about 50 miles distant from me, they were in good health when I heard from them last and no doubt will be overjoyed at the possibility of seeing you. Your letter to my sister will be forwarded by the first conveyance.

I am Respectfully
Yr. Obt.St.
Wm. Bolling
Mr. John Braidwood,
Washington City,
Care of J. Pleasants, Jr., Esq.

In response to this letter, Braidwood visited Col. Bolling in May 1812, and explained to him his plans. He proposed, he said, to open an Institution for the Deaf and Dumb in Baltimore, Md., similar to the one established in Edinburgh by his grandfather and father (Messrs. Thos. And John Braidwood); and he secured the promise of William Albert Bolling as a pupil. He undoubtedly had a full talk with the boy's parents concerning his education, and advised them what they could do at home to promote his instruction pending the opening of the proposed school - probably urging upon them the importance of making him write daily.

Col. Bolling accompanied him as far as Richmond on his return from Bolling Hall, and parted from him with the understanding that Braidwood would write to him from time to time to let him know how his plans were progressing, and notify him when to bring his son to Baltimore.

By June 1812, Braidwood's plans had so far matured that he advertised for pupils in the *Richmond Enquirer, The Argus* and probably in other papers – stating that his school would be open on the first of July.

The following is one of his advertisements:

BRAIDWOOD'S ADVERTISEMENT OF HIS
PROPOSED
BALTIMORE SCHOOL

INSTITUTION for the Deaf and Dumb and for the Removing of Impediments of Speech. Mr. J. Braidwood has the honor to acquaint the public that in consequence of repeated applications from persons of the highest respectability, many of whom had visited the Institution for the education of the Deaf and Dumb, originally established at Edinburgh in 1760, by the late Messrs. Thomas and John Braidwood, and since carried on by their descendants in the vicinity of London. He visited this country with a view to establish a similar Institution in the United States; calculated to restore to society an unfortunate class of our fellow-creatures, who from being deprived of the Education they are so capable of receiving, are excluded from the knowledge of everything except the immediate objects of sense.

Children who have been born Deaf, or those who have lost their hearing by accident or disease are taught to speak and read distinctly, to write and understand accurately the principles of Language; they are also instructed in Arithmetic, Geography with the use of the Globes, and every branch of Education that may be necessary to qualify them for any situation in life. Those put under Mr Braidwood's tuition for the removal of Impediments in speech are at the same time instructed in every part of Education & Science that may be required.

Mr. Braidwood having made arrangements with several families who have Children requiring his instructions in the city of Baltimore, on the first of July next. Those therefore who may wish further information are requested to address him in that City.

May 29.

(From the *Richmond Enquirer*, June 2, 1812.)

Col. Bolling had expected to place his son with Braidwood in the Baltimore School as soon as the arrangements for its opening had been completed; but, not hearing from Braidwood by the first of July – the advertised date of the opening – he became somewhat anxious about the matter. Day after day passed and still no word from Braidwood; and so on the ninth of August, Col. Bolling sent him the following letter:

Bolling Hall, 9th August, 1812.

Dear Sir,

I have with much anxiety been expecting a letter from you for two months past, have sent regularly to the Post Office, but have not been favoured with a line since our separation in Richmond. I was informed by Mr. Pleasants since his return from Congress that you have been in Washington some short time previous to its adjournment and mentioned your wish to write me thro' him, but said he did not receive any letter to forward. I had made all the necessary arrangements to have carried my son to Baltimore at the time appointed, and seeing your advertisement appear in the Virginia Argus late in June in which the same time was mentioned as the probable period of your commencement I made no doubt I should hear particularly from you. Being disappointed in this expectation I, of course, declined leaving home until I should. I have intended for some time to make the present communication to inquire what your prospects and intentions are respecting the commencement of your institution, but have delayed it under the continued hope that the next mail would bring me a letter. I hope when this gets to hand you will write me fully on the subject. Albert and myself have just returned from a visit to his grandmother, with which he was much pleased. He continues to write daily and improves considerably. My family are all well and join me in sincere wishes for your health and prosperity.

Yours respectfully,
W. BOLLING.

Mr. John Braidwood, Baltimore.

To this note, Col. Bolling received no answer; but on August 20, a letter arrived from Braidwood written from the *New York jail*! – the contents of which may be inferred from the colonel's reply:

Bolling Hall, August 22nd, 1812.

My dear Sir:

Your letter from New York has filled me with astonishment and concern. It refers to two others, the one from Baltimore and the other from Philadelphia, in which you made a tender of your services as a private tutor in my family to my son and other children. Neither of these letters have ever been received by me, and all the distressed occurrences which have since happened to you has been the consequence of their failure: But, why, dear Sir, did you wait for an answer to such a proposal, or why think it necessary to write at all? Had you returned here, instead of taking your unfortunate trip to the north, you would have been most joyfully and gratefully received and all your subsequent sufferings avoided.

I will now suggest to you the plan which is most advisable for your relief. Write immediately to the person to whom the debt, for which you are confined, is due (whose name or address you did not communicate to me) and inform him that I will meet him or his agent with you at any appointed time in Richmond prepared to discharge it. If he should doubt my responsibility let him refer me to any correspondent he may have in Richmond and I will thro' that correspondent give him every necessary assurance. This appears to me to be the only plan I can adopt for your relief. The uncertainty of our Post Offices are such that I cannot risk remitting the money and the situation of my family and affairs at this time precludes my going in person so great a distance from them. I only got home yesterday from a trip of near a fortnight to Cobbs, where I was suddenly and unexpectedly called to visit my mother who has been most dangerously ill, but I thank God was on the recovery when I left her to return to my family. Your letter had gotten to hand the day before and I found my wife in great distress on your account.

I will by the next mail forward a duplicate of this in case it should miscarry and shall anxiously await your further communications in the hope that the arrangements I have suggested may meet the approbation of all the parties concerned. Nothing could be more congenial than to have you fixed here as a member of our family from whom we should calculate such advantages to our children from your professional attendance and every effort on our part would be exerted to relieve your mind from its present depression.

Believe me most sincerely your friend,
W. BOLLING.
Mr. J. Braidwood,
New York.

Further details concerning the events that led up to Braidwood's incarceration in the New York jail are contained in a communication from Col. William Bolling to the Rev. Joseph D. Tyler, written from Bolling Hall on the 10th of December, 1841, and published in the *Southern Churchman* on Friday March 18, 1842, Vol. VIII, No. 8.

LETTER OF 1841 (FIRST EXTRACT)

whole of my money was squandered — had gotten in debt — Braidwood fled to New York, where he was pursued, arrested for debt, and committed to jail. In his miserable situation he applied to me for relief. He said he was arrested for that nobleman's debt, for which he was in no wise liable, yet before he could be released it would be necessary for me to establish a credit in some responsible house there, for the sum of $400, to discharge the judgement, should one be obtained against him, and that $200 more would be required to pay his jail fees, and defray his expenses to my house — which, In the spring of 1812, John Braidwood

127

(grandson of my brother's preceptor) arrived in the city of Washington. The late Gov. Pleasants of this County, then a Member of the House of Representatives from this District, knowing the situation of my family, immediately informed me thereof; by my solicitation Braidwood visited me in the month of May in this year. His plan was to rent a suitable house in Baltimore, hire servants, and procure everything necessary to board all his pupils. War having been declared by the United States against Great Britain, he was thereby, as he said, cut off from receiving remittances from London (the fact was he had no funds) that several gentlemen in Philadelphia and Baltimore had engaged scholars to him (which was not a fact) and each had promised to advance to him $600, to enable him to establish his institution. I accompanied him to Richmond on his return, and placed that sum in his hands, with the understanding when we parted, that his institution would open on the 1st July following; and that in the meantime he would write me every week or ten days. I heard nothing from him till the month of October following when I received a letter from him, dated in jail in New York.

He had associated himself in Richmond, with a young Englishman, recently arrived, who imposed himself on the public as the son of a nobleman. They went on together to Washington, Baltimore, Philadelphia, &c., moving in high style, until the if I would do, he would return, take charge of my son, and remain with me until I should be compensated for those advances.

Contrary to the advice and opinion of all my friends, I determined to make one more effort to obtain his services — negotiated the credit as required, and remitted the money to him. Judgement was recovered against him and the money paid — but he complied with his promise — returned in November (1812), took charge of

128

my son, was faithful and diligent; exhibiting unequivocal evidence of his qualifications in his profession, &c.

We must remember that the letter from which the above has been quoted, was written nearly thirty years after the events narrated. The sequence of events is probably correct; but comparison with more nearly contemporaneous documents reveals the fact that there are errors of date. For example: Col. Bolling's note of August 22, 1812, is proof that Braidwood's letter from New York jail was received in August, not "October" 1812; and a letter to the Marshal of Virginia, March 20, 1813, shows that Braidwood commenced his labors at Bolling Hall in October, 1812, not "November."

THE BOLLING HALL SCHOOL
(Oct. 1812 to Feb. 15, 1815)

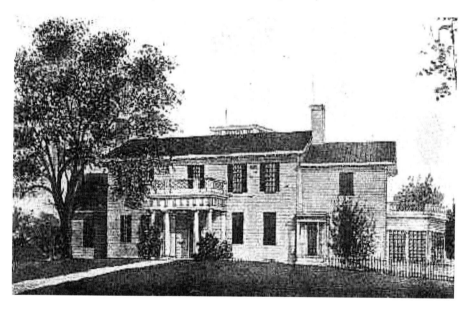

In October 1812, John Braidwood took up his residence in Bolling Hall, Goochland Co., Va., (above) where he became private tutor to the Bolling family. Among his pupils were William Albert Bolling (deaf and dumb) then thirteen years of age, Mary Bolling (deaf and dumb) about three years of age, and their hearing sister and brother, Anne Meade and Thomas. This was established at Bolling Hall, a little private family-school for the children of Col. Bolling, in charge of Mr. Braidwood.

Col. Bolling seems to have been much pleased with the progress made by his son William Albert; and, in March 1813, made application to the Marshal of Virginia to permit John Braidwood though a subject of the king of England, to remain at his house, and continue the instruction of his deaf son.

The following is the full text of this letter:

Bolling Hall, March 20, 1813.

Sir:—

Mr. John Braidwood, a subject of the King of England, is at this time residing with me. His profession is that of a teacher of the deaf and dumb, and having a son in that unfortunate situation, he is and has been since October last pursuing his professional avocations as private tutor in my family. He arrived in the U. States in the month of February, 1812, and it was his first intention to have commenced a public school for teaching the Deaf-and-Dumb to speak, in Baltimore. The declaration of war and other intervening circumstances induced him to alter that intention and to remain with me for some years. In conformity with the requisitions of our Government he reported himself to the Marshal of Maryland during his residence in Baltimore and until lately I was uncertain whether it was necessary he should report himself again. He, however, went to Richmond a few weeks since and applied for that purpose repeatedly at your office without finding it open. At length he saw your Deputy in the Farmers Bank who told him he might at any convenient time do it by letter, which he has done this day. This communication, therefore, is made in compliance with your request in the Enquirer of the 16th inst.

Mr. Braidwood was personally acquainted with Col. Monroe, now Secretary of State, during his Embassy to London, and since in Washington City where he spent the greater part of the winter of his arrival, from whom and the President he received

130

every assurance of safety in his remaining here — as they no doubt considered his Instructions might be of the utmost importance to many unfortunate beings who otherwise would be doomed to a life of Ignorance, Idleness and Misery. I trust, therefore, there will be no occasion for removing him from my house where my unfortunate son is making rapid progress in his education. He is a gentleman of liberal education and sentiments, and not in the smallest degree inclined to have any interference in the events of the present times. Could I think there was any possibility of his being any injury in any respect to my country now engaged in a just and necessary conflict with his, no private consideration could prevent my saying so, but being entirely convinced of the contrary, I trust there will be no objection to his remaining here.

Being personally unknown to you, I would beg leave to refer you to Mr. William Robertson, the Clerk of the Council, who might give you some further particulars that might be satisfactory to you on this subject. Mr. Ryland Randolph, Mr. Rutherford, and many other citizens of Richmond are likewise well acquainted with me.

I am very respectfully
Yr. Obt. Servt.

W. BOLLING
Andrew Moore, Esq.,
Marshal of Virginia,
Richmond.

It is obvious that this application was successful, and that Braidwood was permitted to remain; for the Bolling Hall School continued in existence as a family school for two and a half years, when the applications for admission from parents of deaf children, and other circumstances, led to its removal to Cobbs, Va., and its conversion into a public institution for the education of the deaf and dumb.

In his letter of 1841, from which quotations have already been made, Col. Bolling says:

LETTER OF 1841 (SECOND EXTRACT).

Braidwood (in October 1812) took charge of my son, was faithful and diligent; exhibiting unequivocal evidence of his qualifications in his profession, and admitted my son's extraordinary capacity to receive instruction, whose progress was truly gratifying, until the following summer, when being in command of the troop of cavalry of this country, I was ordered to Norfolk, where I remained six months in military service: From this time he began to relax, and on my return had almost abandoned his duties. Aware of my dependence on him I forbore to remonstrate, hoping, as was the case for some time, that my presence would produce an amendment in his conduct. My mother died during my absence, and I became possessed of Cobbs, the old family mansion. This was a large, convenient, comfortable building, in every respect suitable for an Institution in the line of his profession. It not being convenient to me to convert my own residence into a boarding house, and not being disposed to discriminate, I had refused all applications for pupils, which was painful to one like myself who could so fully sympathize with parents who had children similarly unfortunate as my son. Braidwood, being an alien, and Cobbs situated on the Tide Water, I obtained permission from Mr. Monroe, then Secretary of State, for him to reside there. I gave him possession of the house, its furniture, servants, stocked nearly as my mother had left them. Here he expressed, and I thought felt, unbounded gratitude to me, for placing him in a situation to make his own fortune, and render incalculable benefit to many unfortunate Deaf-Mutes. &c.

BRAIDWOOD'S ADVERTISEMENT OF HIS PROPOSED SCHOOL AT COBBS, VA.

The following advertisement announcing that Braidwood's Institution "will commence at Cobbs, near Petersburg, Va., on the first of March next" is copied from the *Richmond Enquirer* of February 15, 1815:

BRAIDWOOD'S INSTITUTION
For the Education of the Deaf and Dumb
And for Removing
IMPEDIMENTS IN SPEECH

Children who have been born deaf, or those who have lost their hearing by accident of disease, are taught to Speak and Read distinctly, to write, and understand accurately the principles of Language — they are also instructed in Arithmetic, Geography and the use of the Globes, and every branch of education necessary to render them useful and intelligent members of society.

Those attending the Institution for the removal of Impediments in Speech, are instructed in such parts of Education & Science, as do not immediately interfere with the objects of their attendance.

The Public are respectfully informed that the above Institution will commence at Cobbs, near Petersburg, Va., on the first of March next, under the tuition of Mr. J. Braidwood, a descendant of the late Messrs. Thos. and John Braidwood, of Edinburgh & London, the inventors and successful patrons of an art which is calculated to render the most unfortunate class of our fellow-creatures happy — useful and intelligent members of the community.

The mansion-House at Cobbs is very commodious, and possesses every desirable requisite for the establishment — the situation and vicinity are remarkably healthy.

Information as to the terms of the Institution are to be obtained till the 15th Feb. by letter addressed to Mr. Braidwood, at Capt. Wm. Bolling's, Goochland, Va., after which date applications may be made at the Institution, where Mr. Braidwood will then have taken up his residence, preparatory to its commencement.

Feb. 11.

(To be continued)

BRAIDWOOD'S INSTITUTION FOR THE EDUCATION
OF THE DEAF AND DUMB, AT COBBS, VA.
(1815, March 1, to Summer of 1816)

The official permit to Braidwood to reside at Cobbs, rendered necessary by its situation upon tide-water, was authorized on the 19th of December, 1814, by the following letter from the Commissary General of Prisoners to the Marshal of Virginia:

Office of Commissary General of Prisoners,
Washington, December 19th, 1814.

Sir:

Mr. J. Braidwood, a British subject, now at Captain Bolling's, in Goochland County, and who came to this country something more than two years ago, and has since exercised his profession in a private family, as Teacher to the Dumb, is desirous, with the assistance of his friends, to establish himself for the purpose of dispensing more generally the advantages of his art, at Cobbs, the late residence of Mrs. Bolling in Chesterfield County, between Richmond and Petersburg; — and not only from the character of Mr. Braidwood, as represented by gentlemen who know him well, and who can be entirely relied on, being such that no evil consequence is to be apprehended from the indulgence, — but from its being an object worthy the attention of Government to facilitate by all proper means, the exercise of an Art so interesting to humanity as that possessed by Mr. Braidwood; it has been determined to grant the permission asked by him.

You will be pleased on reception of this letter, to furnish him with the requisite passports in the usual form, to go and reside at Cobbs, as before mentioned.

I have the honor to be

Sir,
Your most obedient servant

J. MASON
Andrew Moore, Esq.,
Marshal of Virginia (Richmond).

THE OPENING OF THE INSTITUTION (1815)

The necessary formalities having been complied with and advertisements announcing the opening of the proposed school having been inserted in the newspapers, "Braidwood's Institution for the Deaf and Dumb" was duly opened at Cobbs (above) on the first of March 1815.

The opportunity of Braidwood's life had come at last. It had been his ambition to found in America an Institution like that which had been so successfully carried on by his grandfather and father in Edinburgh, Scotland. But his Baltimore plans in 1812 had come to an untimely end through his own misconduct. Led away by an unfortunate propensity for drink, he had squandered in riotous living, in less than three months, the six hundred dollars advanced to him in Richmond by Col. Bolling for his son's education; and he had only been rescued from a debtor's prison by the continued generosity of Col. Bolling, who advanced an additional six hundred dollars to get him out of jail.

Filled with gratitude for this relief, he has done his best to work out his redemption, and repay the Colonel for these advances. For two and a half years he had remained at Bolling Hall as private tutor to Wm. Albert and the other children of Col. Bolling; and, although occasional lapses of conduct had occurred, his efforts were in the main successful; and Col. Bolling was satisfied with his son's progress under instruction.

He had demonstrated his ability as an instructor of the deaf, and other parents of deaf children were anxious to secure his services. And now, on the first of March, 1815, Braidwood was placed by Col. Bolling in a position to accommodate a larger number of pupils, and to make a new start in life, under the best auspices.

The family mansion at Cobbs (above) was admirably adapted for his purpose; and, with the prestige of his family name, and his own personal success at Bolling Hall, he might reasonably hope to accomplish in America all that his family had done in Great Britain.

With the exception of the Almshouse Class in New York (which did not last long), his own school at Bolling Hall had been the first of its kind in the United States; and the new school opened in Cobbs was the first public institution for the education of the deaf and dumb in America. There was no other school for the deaf in existence in the country, and everything seemed favorable to success.

If he could only conquer his unfortunate habits of life — his future was assured. He felt very grateful to Col. Bolling for all he had done, and threw himself in his work at Cobbs with courage and energy, and with a determination to avoid the temptations that had led to his downfall in the past.

The plantation known as "Cobbs", in Chesterfield County, Va., was situated on the north side of the Appomattox River, about ten miles from the city of Petersburg, and within sight of its tall spires and chimneys. It was one of the many beautiful country seats owned and occupied by wealthy Virginian planters which in the old times crowned the heights and picturesque promontories on both sides of the Appomattox. The estate had passed into the hands of Col. William Bolling upon the death of his mother; his deaf brother and sister, Thomas and Mary Bolling, had joined his own family at Bolling Hall, thus leaving the Cobbs estate unoccupied, save for the negroes and their overseer.

Col. Bolling placed at Braidwood's disposal all the buildings, furniture, farming utensils, servants, and stock of all kinds, so that he was at once enabled to open the house as a boarding school; and here, according to Col. Bolling, "he took charge of four or five young gentlemen at $500 per annum." (Letter of 1841).

THE PUPILS

The names of some of these scholars have been handed down to us by William Albert Bolling — himself the first pupil — in a manuscript school-book now owned by the Volta Bureau.

George Lee Tuberville, stepson of the Rev. Wm. Maffit of Salona, was one of them. John Hancock and John M. Scott were others.

These names have also been recalled as those of pupils by the mother of Col. Halliday of Genito, Va. Her father, Hon. Wm. Green Poindexter, a well-known lawyer in his day, was an intimate friend of Col. Wm. Bolling, with whom he roomed in Richmond at a time when he was senator, and Col. Bolling member of the House of Delegates from Goochland District. It seems that Mr. Poindexter was able to do Mr. Braidwood some kindness — he may possibly have been his legal adviser — and his daughter heard a good deal of Braidwood in her youth. In a recent note to Mrs. A. C. Pratt, Col. Halliday says:

> I cannot ascertain from my mother's aged recollections and knowledge of the number of Mr. Braidwood's pupils at Cobbs, but during that period there was with him George Lee Tuberville — a young man named Scott from Pittsburgh, Penn. — and one named Hancock from Charlotte County, Va.

The last named young man, John Hancock, had two brothers younger than himself who were deaf and dumb — Anthony and Martin. Prof. Chamberlayne, a teacher in the Staunton Institution, writes (1900, April 21):

> John and Anthony were Braidwood's pupils at Cobbs.

This seems very probable; although, as yet, we have no contemporaneous evidence that Anthony was a pupil there.

Prof. Chamberlayne was also authority for the statement that —

St. George, or St. George Tucker, was Anthony
Hancock's school-mate at Cobbs; he was a nephew
of John Randolph of Roanoke.

St. George Tucker Randolph (deaf and dumb) was a cousin of Wm.
Albert Bolling, and we would therefore naturally expect to find him at
Cobbs. Wm. Albert Bolling however makes no mention of him there;
and John Randolph of Roanoke, uncle of St. George, in a letter written
in 1814, mentions his nephew as at that date hopelessly insane (see
Garland's *Life of John Randolph*). It is hardly likely therefore that he
could have been a pupil at Cobbs.

The advertisement of Braidwood's Institution seems to have
been extensively circulated. One of his pupils (Scott) came from
Pennsylvania; and the Volta Bureau possesses copies of answers to the
advertisement from persons residing in Maryland and Massachusetts.

Mr. Otis Withington answered it from Taunton, Mass., under date
1815, February 19, making enquiries concerning terms, etc., on behalf
of his deaf daughter, then three years and seven months old. There is no
evidence that she was admitted; nor do we find any trace of little Mary
Bolling (sister of Wm. Albert) at the Cobbs School. From the statement
of Col. Bolling, quoted above, it is probable that only boys were
received.

The pupils certainly known to have been there were four in number,
viz.: Wm. Albert Bolling, George Lee Tuberville, John Hancock and
John M. Scott.

MR. THOMAS BOLLING.

Mr. Thomas Bolling, the deaf brother of Col. Wm. Bolling, was also at
Cobbs a good deal of the time, judging from the frequent references to
him contained in the manuscript school-book of his nephew, Wm.
Albert. For example — (Extract from school exercise):

> Where did you dine yesterday?
> At Capt. John Stratton's.
> Did you walk or ride to Capt. Stratton?
> Walk.
> Who went with you?
> Mr. Braidwood, my uncle Mr. Bolling, Mr.
> Tuberville, Mr. Hancock, and Mr. Scott.

Mr. Thomas Bolling had been educated in Edinburgh, Scotland, by the Messrs. Thomas and John Braidwood, grandfather and father of our Mr. Braidwood. He entered their Academy in 1775 and remained until 1783, when the school was moved to Hackney, near London. Some account of him has already been given in Chapter 1 (REVIEW II, 36-40).

Mr. Thomas Bolling's home had been in Cobbs up to the time of his mother's death in 1813; and it is probable that he returned there in 1815 upon the opening of the Braidwood Institution and re-occupied his old quarters in the family mansion.

It would doubtless be agreeable to him to reside with Braidwood, and meet the deaf pupils of the school; and, on the other hand, it would be an advantage to Braidwood to have him there. He was a highly educated deaf gentlemen — a good speech-reader and able himself to speak in a perfectly intelligible manner — a good example of what could be accomplished by the Braidwood system. Being perfectly familiar with the Braidwood method of instruction, he might also, on occasion, be called upon to act as assistant to Braidwood in the instruction of his pupils.

All this however is surmise — the fact simply being that he is alluded to very frequently in the school exercise book as companion of the pupils. The following extracts from this book may be of interest:

> Do you wish to understand language better?
> I wish very much to understand language better.
> Why?
> Because I wish to understand what people say to
> me, and to be able to ask what I want, and tell
> what I think.
> Do you wish to speak and read better?
> I wish very much to speak and read better.

The old school exercise book from which the above quotations have been made becomes of fascinating interest when we realize it belonged to Wm. Albert Bolling, the first American deaf-mute to receive an education in his own country; and that it reveals, at least in part, the Braidwood method of instruction. Under these circumstances a few extracts showing the character of the earlier school exercises may be of interest:

SPECIMENS OF EARLY SCHOOL EXERCISES

The nearest approach to a vocabulary consists in a long list of expressions like the following — headed by the letters "J. B." (John Braidwood):

> J. B.
> An idle boy
> An ugly bat
> A fat cow
> A mad dog
> A large rat
> A tall man
> A white hat
> Etc., etc.

Then these expressions appear again in amplified form. For example:

> An idle boy, he is lazy, whip him, bring a whip.
> An ugly bat, take your gun and shoot him, I cannot shoot him.
> A fat cow, milk her, she gives much milk.
> A mad dog, he will bite you — Kill him — shoot him.
> A large rat — rats are bad, rats steal, set a trap to catch rats.
> A tall man — he is a tall man, you are a short man — I am not a tall man.
> A white hat for summer — a black hat for winter.
> Etc., etc.

A great many of the exercises consisted of conversation (probably oral) reduced to writing in the book. In some cases both questions and answers are noted as in the specimens already quoted above. In others, the answers alone are recorded — and these reveal a methodical plan of questioning whereby Braidwood drew out his pupils' knowledge and led him naturally from one subject to another. For example:

> A shoemaker is a person who makes shoes.
> Shoes are a covering for the feet.
> Shoes are made of leather.
> Leather is tanned hides.
> Hides are the skins of animals.

I wear 2 shoes at one time.
Two shoes are called a pair of shoes.
I have only one pair of shoes at present.
They are old.
A cobbler is a person who mends shoes.
To mend shoes is to repair them when they fail.
A tailor is a person who makes clothes.
Clothes are made of cloth.
All kinds of cloth may be comprehended under 4, viz.
Silk, cotton, woolen and flax-linen.
Silk cloth is made of silk.
Silk is thread made by silk worms.
A worm is an insect or an animal.
Cotton-cloth is made of cotton thread.
Cotton is the down of a tree.
Cotton thread is spun.
Women spin cotton.
Woolen cloth is made of woolen thread.
Woolen thread is made of wool.
Wool is spun into thread.
Women spin wool.
Wool is the fleece of sheep.
Linen cloth is made of flax or linen thread.
Linen thread is made of flax or lint.
Flax or lint is the herb or plant of which linen is made.
Etc., etc.

An autograph letter from John Braidwood to Capt. Pollard of the ship Middlesex has been discovered by Col. Holladay among the papers of his grandfather, Mr. Poindexter; and the hand-writing shows that the list of phrases in the old exercise book headed by the letters "J. B." was written by John Braidwood himself.

THE BRAIDWOOD CREST

A wax impression of a seal was also discovered by Col. Holladay showing the Braidwood crest as described by Francis Green in his letter of 1781:

> Consonant to this is the motto he hath adopted, 'Vox oculis subjecta.' His crest is a bird charmed by a serpent.

Although the impress of the seal is rather faint, all the details are perfectly discernible under a powerful glass, and, as may be seen by the accompanying cut, correspond exactly with the description quoted:

LETTER TO BRAIDWOOD FROM HIS MOTHER IN ENGLAND
(1815)

Among the Poindexter papers is a letter to John Braidwood from his mother in England, dated 1815, October 4, from London, — No. 7 Great Ormond Street, — from which the following is extracted:

> We were very much surprised and rather alarmed lately by the application of a Mr. Gallaydett from Connecticut, he informed your brother that he had been sent over by some gentlemen who wished to form an Institution for Deaf and Dumb and he wished to receive instruction in our art. Having flattered ourselves that you were long ere this establishment, we have felt much at a loss to acct. for this event, and trusting that you are in life and in the practice of your profession we have judged it proper to have no concern with him, but we have recommended his making application to you.

This refers of course to the Rev. Thomas Hopkins Gallaudet, who was then in Great Britain trying to obtain knowledge of the Braidwood method of instruction preparatory to opening a school for the deaf in Hartford, Conn. (which was done in 1817).

The Braidwood family seem to have been at a loss to account for the fact that Gallaudet should have deemed it necessary to cross the Atlantic to learn the Braidwood method when he knew that John Braidwood was right at hand on Virginian soil. Not understanding the condition of affairs in America, they feared that, in aiding Gallaudet, they might be injuring their own relative in Virginia, and helping to establish a rival   institution.

GALLAUDET'S LETTERS CONCERNING BRAIDWOOD (1815)

It is hardly likely that Braidwood was a good correspondent, and his family in England evidently knew but little of him. Gallaudet wrote to Cogswell (1815, August 15):

> The mother of Mr. Braidwood who is in America, will be much obliged by any information you can give me respecting him. Do take some pains to do this, I wish to oblige her, and write all you know of him, be it good, bad or indifferent.

(Life of T. H. Gallaudet by E. M. Gallaudet, 1888, p. 72.)

In another letter to Dr Cogswell from Edinburgh, — 1815, September 22, — Gallaudet says:

> Mr. Kinniburgh, the instructor of the school in this place for the deaf and dumb, received his first instruction in his Art from Mr. Thomas Braidwood, the grandson of the original Mr. Braidwood, to whom he bound himself not to communicate any information respecting the subject to any individual for seven years. Four years of this period has expired. I have been corresponding with Mr. Thomas Braidwood on this subject, in hopes that I might prevail on him to release Mr. Kinniburgh so far as his bond might refer to America. But Mr. Braidwood is not to be moved. This morning I received a positive refusal to my application. The reason for this which Mr. B. assigned is, that his brother, Mr. Jno. B. is in our country — the same gentleman of whom we heard as being in Virginia. The truth is, he left this place a few years since in disgrace. He was solicited to undertake the superintendence of a public school for the deaf and dumb. He conducted so badly and contracted so many debts that he was obliged to abscond. What dependence can be placed on such a character?

(Life of T. H. Gallaudet by E. M. Gallaudet, 1888, p. 77)

John Braidwood, however, at this time was doing well in Virginia. The Institution at Cobbs was in full operation and seemed to give promise of becoming a permanent Institution. It safely weathered the first year of its existence; and the following is one of the advertisements that heralded the beginning of the second year:

BRAIDWOOD'S ADVERTISEMENT ANNOUNCING THE OPENING OF THE SECOND YEAR OF THE SCHOOL (1816)

INSTITUTION For the Education of the Deaf and Dumb and for Removing IMPEDIMENTS in SPEECH

Established at Cobbs, near Petersburg, Va., conducted by Mr. J. Braidwood, a descendant of the late Messrs. Thomas and John Braidwood of Edinburgh and London.

Children who have been born deaf, or those who have lost their hearing by accident of disease, are taught to Speak and Read distinctly, to write, and understand accurately the principles of Language — they are also instructed in Arithmetic, Geography and the use of the Globes, and every branch of Education necessary to render them useful and intelligent members of Society.

Those attending the Institution for the Removal of Impediments in Speech, arising from deficiencies and mal-conformation of the organic system, constitutional debility or habitual imitation, &c., may receive instruction, if required, in such parts of education and science as might not immediately interfere with the object of their attendance.

The public are respectfully informed that the above Institution was commenced at Cobbs in March last, since which several pupils have been received under the tuition of the professor; and the most satisfactory testimony can be obtained of the progress of the students, by personal, or written application to the Honorable James Pleasants, M. C., Washington; the Rev. Wm. Maffit, Salona, near Georgetown, Potomac; Capt. Wm. Bolling, Goochland, Va., or at the Institution.

January 9.

144

(The advertisement was copied from the Petersburg, Va., *Republican*, 1816, February 9. The advertisement also appeared in the issues of February 13, 16, 20, 25.)

We know very little about the second year of the school. It was certainly in existence on the twenty-second of May, 1816, when the Rev. Wm. Maffit, stepfather of Braidwood's pupil, George Lee Tuberville, wrote the following letter, which was found by Col. Holladay, among the papers of his grandfather, Mr. Poindexter.

LETTER FROM REV. WM. MAFFIT (1816)

Salona, May 22d, 1816.

To John Braidwood, Esq.,
Cobbs, near Petersburg, Va.,

Dear Sir:

Colo. Cox of Geo-Town informed me that you had drawn on me for six hundred and forty or fifty dollars. I am really distressed on account of my inability to honor your draft at this time. In consequence of Banks calling in their paper there is utmost distress in this part of the country. If I could borrow the above sum I would most cheerfully; but that is impossible in the present state of our currency. When I had the pleasure of writing you last I believe I informed you that it was probable I could advance the sum you wanted early in the month of June. I am now in daily expectation of a visit from a gentleman who has the management of my property in Westmoreland; and who wrote me lately that he had no doubt of being able to bring me all the money I had requested. As soon as he shall arrive I will write you and I trust he will enable me to meet your wishes. Please to present me affectionately to George and believe me

Dear Sir to be very sincerely your
Well wisher and Hbl. Servt.

Wm. MAFFIT.

Early in 1816 Braidwood found himself in financial straits; and the above letter shows that he had difficulty in collecting the money due him for the instruction of pupils. Debt was a serious matter in those days, as he had found out to his cost in 1812. He owed considerable money to the merchants of Petersburg, Va., and was unable to pay; disheartened and discouraged; he left the Institution and went to Richmond, Va., where, no doubt, he sought the counsel of his legal friend, Mr. Poindexter. Without money to properly meet his weekly expenses, and harassed by his creditors, Braidwood forestalled any further action of the Courts by leaving the State of Virginia, in the autumn of 1816, and journeying North. Nothing more was heard of him in Virginia until the following year (1817), when he returned to Richmond "penniless, friendless, and scarcely decently clad," and besought once more the assistance of Col. Wm. Bolling.

In reference to the Cobbs School Col. Bolling says:

LETTER OF 1841 (THIRD EXTRACT).

Braidwood being an alien and Cobbs situated on the Tide Water, I obtained permission from Mr. Monroe, then Secretary of State, for him to reside there. I gave him possession of the house, its furniture, servants, stocked nearly as my mother left them. Here he expressed, and I thought I felt, unbounded   gratitude to me, for placing him in a situation to make his own fortune, and render incalculable benefit to many deaf mutes.

Here he took charge of four or five young gentlemen at $500 each per annum, and here, like his commencement at my house, he for some time conducted himself and his institution to the entire satisfaction of all concerned. At length, having become generally acquainted in the neighborhood and in Petersburg (ten miles distant), he relapsed into his former habits of neglect, dissipation and extravagance, he became largely indebted to the merchants of that place, and suddenly abandoned the institution and fled to the North; — did nothing — and in 1818 returned to Richmond, penniless, friendless, and scarcely decently clad — again he

146

applied to me, and again I went to his relief by forming a connection between the Rev. Mr. Kirkpatrick, then residing in Manchester, and himself. &c., &c.

(To be continued)

APPENDIX H.

BRAIDWOOD IMPORTUNED TO OPEN A PUBLIC INSTITUTION.

The following extracts from letters written by John Braidwood show that during the time he was fulfilling his engagement at Bolling Hall, he was frequently importuned to open a public institution.

Under date of August 28, 1813, Braidwood writes:

> In a former letter I promised to make you acquainted with the particulars of my conversation with Mr. Samuel Branch, which I now fulfil with pleasure. He said his call upon me was at the request of Mr. Hancock of Charlotte, and two other friends, one resident in Pittsylvania, the other in Georgia, to obtain information as to my intentions of residence in this country, being led to hope (from the notice which appeared from me in the papers of June 1812) that I purposed ere long forming an establishment for the reception of the many unfortunate children who depended upon receiving an education at my hands. That he was authorized by Mr. Hancock and friends to say that they were ready to place their children, six number, under my care at any moment, and disposed to meet any terms I might suggest with liberality. He observed that he felt it his duty to urge me to extend to such claimants benefits which I was called upon to give to as many as lay in my power, adding that Mr. Hancock had determined to incur any expense for their education and was on the eve of sending the children to my family in England when my advertisement in the Enquirer arrested his attention, — pleased with my communications, he determined to place them with me in Baltimore last November, had I settled there.

And again under date of September 2, 1813, Braidwood writes:

> I met with General Moore at the Court House some few days ago, — Mr. Anderson introduced me to him, at my request. He expressed much satisfaction at meeting with me having been for some time desirous to learn something about my important art, and fulfil a commission delegated to him by a family who reside in the neighbourhood of Staunton, who have a little girl of eight years of age born deaf. They are in affluent circumstances and their proposals to me most liberally made.

APPENDIX I.

BRAIDWOOD'S LETTER TO CAPT. POLLARD.

To Captain Pollard, Ship Middlesex, Bermuda Hundred, by Billy.
Cobbs, Saturday Morning.

Dear Sir:

You will much oblige me by the loan of your boat today to bring a gentleman down to the point who has some tobacco (sat Ninety Hogsheads) to ship for London. Most probably should you find it convenient and agreeable to come up, you may obtain them on freight.

I shall be most happy to see you at dinner and hope nothing may disappoint me in seeing you. I was sorry you hurried away so early on Wednesday morning, I expected you would have breakfasted with me.

Mr. Bolling and the boys desired to be remembered by you and hope you will not fail to be our kind Captain today in which desire I beg leave to add the assurance of yours very truly, in hast,

P.S.   Tomorrow being Sunday make your arrangements to return this evening with me and spend the day tomorrow at Bachelor's Hall.

J. B.

APPENDIX K.

BRAIDWOOD IN THE EDINBURGH INSTITUTION (1810).

In a sketch of Walter Geikie, Esq., deaf and dumb, (see *Annals*, VII, pp. 232-233), his brother, Rev. Archibald Geikie, relates that his father met with some success in teaching his deaf son, and that Robt. Cathcart, Esq., became interested in the matter, and interested many benevolent gentlemen in a scheme to open an institution for the education of the deaf in Edinburgh (opened 1810). He says:

> Funds were liberally provided and my father was requested to take charge of it. * * * Unfortunately he rated his capabilities too humbly and declined the offer on the ground that he could not properly or with advantage to the class for whom the institution was designed, accept of it. * * * On his refusal, Mr. Braidwood was invited from London, and about, I think, 1810, that gentleman came to Edinburgh on his own terms; i.e., he was to receive liberal salary, and to charge for those pupils whose parents were in circumstances to pay, such price as he thought reasonable, a limited number being admitted to gratuitous instruction.

> My brother was one of the first pupils enrolled, and the fee charged was nine guineas, or $38 a quarter; this extravagant charge was paid during three quarters, at the end of which Mr. Braidwood abruptly left Edinburgh and the Institution was abruptly brought to a standstill. My brother was a day scholar, attending so many hours, and returning home in the afternoon; he however received little or no instruction; as during the time Mr. B. employed him as a teacher under him, taking little or no interest in the business himself.

BRAIDWOOD AT RICHMOND, VA. (1816)
(Takes the stage for the North.)

The following letter from Edward Hallam at Richmond, Va., is addressed to Dr Mason Cogswell, Hartford, Connecticut. The original manuscript is on file at the rooms of the Connecticut Historical Society, Hartford, Conn. A copy of it has been obtained through the courtesy of Mr. Albert C. Bates, the librarian of the Society:

Richmond, Octr. 6, 1816.

Dear Sir:

I rec'd your very friendly letter by Mrs. Jones, also a letter directed to Mr. Braidwood. — I made immediate enquiry for Mr. Braidwood and was inform'd tha' he had abandoned his school or rather he had been discharged from it. — And that Capt. Bowling, his principal patron, had taken his son home, and that Mr. Braidwood had come to Richmond, and was at the Bell Tavern. I without delay went to the Bell, and was inform'd he had been there but had gone to the Swann Tavern, I enquir'd for him at the Swann, and was told he had taken the stage for the North and left his Bills unpaid at both places. — I am apprehensive he has given himself up to dissipation, a great pity Indeed. That a man so abundantly capable of doing so much good should throw himself away, or should yield himself up to dissipation and vicious habits, — no doubt has ever been entertained here of his incompenentancy. Evident proof has been evinced of his being duly qualified. — It is possible when he feels very sencible, the spur of necessity, — that he may find his way to Hartford. — I wish he may. It is possible he may yet be reclaim'd, he is quite a young man, a suitable degree of restraint, together with the Benefit of Example, may possibly restore him to regular habits. — While in Virginia, he has been under no restraint, more than a loose contract might impose, and no one near him to attend to the fulfilment. — Whenever I heard from him, I will forward your letter, unless otherwise advis'd. — I receive with much pleasure your favourable anticipations of my son John. — It would afford me inexpressible satisfaction should they soon be realized. — His brother James visited Rich'd during the Vacation, on his return to New York he inform'd me, that he had agreeably to my directions, remitted his brother Six Hundred Dollars, which will enable my son John to attend the Medical lectures at New Haven this winter. — I hope, and trust, he will avail himself of every opportunity for improvement. Both his age and Size, lead me to expect that at no very distant period he will be capable of providing for himself. — In behalf of my experienced son, I must solicit a continuance of your friendly advice and admonitions. — and believe me to be with Sentiments of Respect and Esteem yours very Sincerely,

ED. HALLAM.

HISTORICAL NOTES – Chapter VI, October 1900

THE MANCHESTER SCHOOL (VA.)
(1817 – 1819)

We have very little information concerning Braidwood's wanderings between the autumn of 1816 and the Spring of 1817. During this period he probably —

> … made his way to New York and collected a few deaf mutes, to form a school in that city, which, however, was soon broke up like those in Virginia, by his own misconduct. — (Hist. N. Y. Inst., pub. by Volta Bureau.)

When, early in 1817, he returned to Virginia, "penniless, friendless, and scarcely decently clad," Col. Bolling once more came to his relief.

There had never been any question as to Braidwood's ability as a teacher; but after the experience of the past, it did not seem wise to give

151

him again the exclusive control of a school. If, however, he could be associated with some man of reliable habits who could be made responsible for the welfare of the pupils, he might do well — at least for a time! And if he could be induced to impart to his associate knowledge of his method of teaching so as to qualify him to become an instructor of the deaf, Wm. Albert Bolling and other pupils would not suffer should Braidwood again fall from grace, and the school would have some chance of becoming a permanent Institution.

No doubt this last consideration had some weight with Col. Bolling in determining him to come again to the assistance of Braidwood; for Col. Bolling was a man of broad and liberal views — a philanthropist and a patriot — and, of course, a Virginian with Virginian pride. Through his agency the first public school for the education of the deaf ever opened in America had been planted upon Virginian soil — and should it be allowed to die?

Beginning in 1812 as a private school at Bolling Hall, it had been transferred to Cobbs in 1815 and opened to the public. Until the summer or autumn of 1816, it had been in successful operation there; and though for several months it had been suspended, Braidwood had now returned, and the pupils were still available.

THE REV. JOHN KIRKPATRICK AND HIS CLASSICAL SCHOOL.

Now it so happened that at this time there was in successful operation in Manchester, Virginia, — just across the James river from Richmond, — a classical school for young ladies and gentlemen carried on by the Rev. John Kirkpatrick, a gentleman known personally to Col. Bolling as a man of culture, ability, and excellent character.

Mr. Kirkpatrick had been drafted into the army during the war with Great Britain, and was in Norfolk, Va., acting as Secretary to the General Porter, at the time Col. Bolling was stationed there in charge of a troop of cavalry.

Mr. Kirkpatrick was highly respected by all who knew him, and his school was patronized by the best families in Manchester and Richmond.

The school occupied the lower floor of the Masonic Building in

Manchester — a brick building of two stories — the largest in the town (see photograph below). The rooms on the upper floor were reserved for the exclusive use of the Masonic fraternity; but the lower floor, excepting when wanted for banqueting purposes, was rented to Mr. Kirkpatrick. Here, on week days, he conducted his school, and on Sundays preached and superintended a Sabbath School. There were two rooms — one of considerable size, and the other a small room suitable for special classes.

Col. Bolling proposed that the Braidwood Institution should be re-opened in connection with the Kirkpatrick school; that the deaf pupils should be boarded in the family of Mr. Kirkpatrick, who should be responsible for their welfare; and that Braidwood should qualify Kirkpatrick to become an instructor of the deaf.

THE MANCHESTER SCHOOL UNDER BRAIDWOOD AND KIRKPATRICK (1817-1818).

Col. Bolling's plan was carried into operation, and soon afterwards (June 20, 1817) an interesting article appeared in the *Richmond Enquirer* calling public attention to the school and appealing to the charitable and benevolent to support it. Indirect allusion was made to the school just opened in Hartford, Conn. (opened April 1817); and an effort was made to arouse local pride in the Institution established in the Commonwealth of Virginia.

> Parents of the deaf and dumb! An opportunity is here afforded of doing the best thing that can be done for your unfortunate children.
>
> Benevolent Virginians! If there should be in the neighbourhood of any of you, children of the poor who cannot hear or speak, you may gratify your benevolence by making contributions for their support and education. The cheapest luxury in the world is the luxury of doing good. 'It is more blessed to give than to receive,' etc. (The full text of this article is given in Appendix N.)

On the first of July, 1817, the following advertisement, relating to the school, appeared in the local newspapers (Copied from the *Richmond Enquirer* of July 1st, 1817):

INSTITUTION for the education of the DEAF and DUMB established in Manchester conducted by MR. BRAIDWOOD, in association with the REV. MR. KIRKPATRICK.

MR. BRAIDWOOD, Professor of the Art of instructing the Deaf and Dumb, according to the system invented by the late Mr. Thomas Braidwood of Edinburgh and London, respectfully informs the Citizens of Virginia and the adjoining States, that he has lately associated himself with the Rev. Mr. Kirkpatrick of this place; to whom he has engaged to communicate and has commenced teaching the knowledge of his profession. Mr. Braidwood would further inform all whom it may concern, that during his stay in Virginia, he intends instructing to such an extent, as the time will permit, all children who may be placed under his tuition, of the following description in the undermentioned attainments; Children born Deaf, or those who may have lost their hearing from accident or disease, will be taught to speak and read distinctly, to write and understand accurately the principles of the English Language. They will also be instructed in Arithmetic, Geography (with the use of the Globes) and every branch of education necessary to render them useful and intelligent members of society.

Respecting Mr. Braidwood's competency to instruct the Deaf and Dumb in any of the above mentioned attainments the most satisfactory testimonials, both by certificate and by experiment, can be produced. His stay in Virginia, it is expected, will be but temporary, yet of such continuance as will afford him an opportunity of rendering important service to such Pupils as may be immediately placed under his tuition and also of communicating to Mr. Kirkpatrick that knowledge of his profession, as will efficiently qualify him to manage and complete the Education of such children, after Mr. Braidwood's departure from the State.

The terms of Tuition may be ascertained on application to Mr. Braidwood and although they must in a measure be graduated according to the pecuniary ability of applicants, yet he is persuaded that the moderation of his charge will be acknowledged by all.

Board and Lodgings may be obtained in the family of Mr. Kirkpatrick on the following terms — Pupils under the age of 12 years $40 — those over that age $50 per scholastic quarter (twelve weeks) payable in advance. The sum will include every article pertaining to Board. etc., with the exception of a Bed which must be furnished by the pupil.

Accommodation may also be had in several other respectable families.

Manchester, June 24th.

The statement that Mr. Braidwood's stay in Virginia — "it is expected will be but temporary" — requires some explanation. We cannot for a moment suppose that he would permit public attention to be directed to an expectation of this sort, if it was based simply upon distrust of his ability to perform his duties for any great length of time. There must be some other explanation of which we are not informed.

Perhaps he had reason to expect a call from Hartford or New York? Dr Cogswell had written to him in 1812 and the Hartford School had now come into operation. The New York Institution, although not yet ready for the reception of pupils, had effected an organization, and the Directors were looking for a man acquainted with the Braidwood system to take charge of the school. They had written to England for a teacher; and judging from the attitude of the Braidwood family towards Gallaudet in 1815 the Directors were probably referred to John Braidwood in Virginia. The New York Institution was not opened until 1818, and at that date of the advertisement (June 24, 1817) it is probable that Braidwood was in correspondence with gentlemen in New York, and looked upon himself as a likely candidate for the principalship of the New York Institution. All this would naturally lead him to anticipate that his stay in Virginia might be but temporary.

However this may be, the Braidwood Institution was reopened in Manchester, Va., in accordance with the terms of the above advertisement.

The Masonic Hall, Manchester.
Picture taken on 19 December 1900. The white placard below the front side window points to the initial burial place of John Braidwood before his body was removed prior to demolition of the building.

THE PUPILS (1817-1818)

It is a little difficult to ascertain from Wm. Albert's schoolbook the number of pupils present at the opening of the Institution. Wm. Albert Bolling, John Hancock, and Katherine McNutt were certainly there then; and Virginia Weisiger was present during the year.

George Lee Tuberville was probably one of the early pupils; and it is possible that John M. Scott may have attended too.

Visitors were frequent; and the following appreciative letter concerning the pupils and their progress appeared in the *Richmond Enquirer* Sept. 19, 1817:

> To the Editor of the Enquirer:
>
> Permit me, though a stranger, to inform you of the extreme gratification I experienced a few days since, in visiting an institution lately established in Manchester, for the Education of the Deaf and Dumb conducted by Mr. Braidwood in association with the Rev. Mr. Kirkpatrick, an eminent clergyman of that village, who has sometime been engaged in the education of youth.

156

Astonishing to relate I saw persons born deaf and dumb, of   different ages, who have already made considerable progress articulation and knowledge of words &c. One in particular, a young man whom I have known for several years, who was a disregarded member of society and only served to add to the burthens of his parents in this life, can now read, write and speak intelligibly, thereby becoming a blessing to his parents — and he will, no doubt, when he has finished his education, be a useful and intelligent member of society.

To interest my fellow-citizens in the support of this institution, is the object of my addressing you.

A VIRGINIAN.

The *Richmond Enquirer* continued to keep the education of the deaf before the public, by publishing, 1817, Oct. 31, an account (copied from a London paper) of the public exhibition at Aberdeen, Scotland, of pupils of Mr. Kinniburgh's school; followed, 1818, February 3, by an account of the pupils in the school for the deaf in Groningen, Holland.

NOTES FROM WM. ALBERT'S SCHOOL-BOOK

In connection with Braidwood's stipulation to impart to Kirkpatrick knowledge of his profession, it is interesting to observe that exercises appear in Wm. Albert's school-book on p. 64 which are headed by the letters "J. K." (John Kirkpatrick); and these are immediately followed on p.65 by other exercises headed "J. B." (John Braidwood):

A cold hand — go to the fire warm your hands; a cotton plant — cotton grows in a warm country — my Papa plants cotton at home—.

My Papa plants tobacco — it grows on my papa's land, some tobacco grows little, some grows large, the black people hoe the tobacco and plow it: — the tobacco grows large — the black people pull off the ground leaves; they top it, pull off the suckers and worms — the tobacco grows ripe, they spilt the stalk and cut it and lay it on the ground — When the tobacco gets soft by the sun, the black people put it in a cart and haul it to the tobacco house —

put it on sticks, hang it on a scaffold, and when the tobacco turns yellow, they take it into the house, hang it up, and put fire under it, until the tobacco is cured. When the tobacco is cured they take it down and cover it with husks or straw, then they strip it and wrap it up in bundles — put it in a hogshead, prize it close, then Papa puts it in the wagon, sends it to Lynchburg or Richmond, sells it, gets the money and comes home.

I often think of my Papa and my Mama. I think of them many times every day — I often wish to see my Mama—.

J. B.

This is a hot day — harvest will soon begin. The heat of the sun will soon make the wheat ready to cut — my Papa sows much wheat — I saw my Papa yesterday — my Papa told me he would begin to cut wheat in in eight or ten day — the black people cut the wheat with scythes —

A fine horse — how old is he? I wish to buy your horse — well you sell your horse? A gig horse he trots well, he is quiet in harness — will you sell him?

Yesterday was Sunday — I went to meeting, — yesterday I saw many ladies and gentlemen at meeting. I went to meeting in the morning and after dinner — There was a storm yesterday the wind blew very hard I saw much rain fall I saw much lightening I felt the thunder — I saw at meeting where the storm began — A lady was much frightened — The sugar cane grows in both the East and West Indies. This is a pretty tree: there are several kinds of willow.

We find occasional items in the written exercises which furnishes glimpses of the life in the school-rooms and playgrounds:

The large school room on the ground floor of the Masonic Building.
Picture taken on 17 December 1900.

Kirkpatrick's grand-daughter in the small school room on the ground
floor of the Masonic Building.
Picture taken on 19 December 1900.

> Mr. Harris sent a little girl into this room — She is a bad girl and will not mind her book —. Mr. Harris has taken her in his school again. She has come back again.

Mr. James S. Harris was Mr. Kirkpatrick's assistant in the classical school.

> This morning John Hancock caught Mrs. McRae's little black boy Peter and brought him into the porch. Mr. Harris took him and put him in the closet and shut the door. Mr. Harris then went and Got a rod and went into the closet and whipped Peter for throwing stones. Peter promised he would not throw any more stones, and Mr. Harris told him to put on his clothes and go home and be a good boy.

> W. A. Bolling.

Here we have a glimpse of a little negro slave (probably owned by Colin McRae, Esq,) throwing stones, when one of the deaf pupils caught him, and handed him over to the rude justice of the school-master Harris.

Until about the close of the year 1817, Braidwood's conduct in the Manchester School had been satisfactory; but early in 1818 his old deplorable habits began again to assert themselves. Before the middle of March (1818) his "irregularities" had become so frequent and annoying that Kirkpatrick dissolved connection with him and carried on the school alone.

In May 1818, a new pupil, Miss Jane C. Davenport — "naturally deaf and dumb" — appeared in the school. Where Mr. Braidwood was at this time we do not know; but, about a month later, he seems to have been present when Mr. Duval visited the school and noted the progress made by Miss Davenport under the sole instruction of Kirkpatrick.

Wm. Albert writes (p. 71):

> Manchester, June 18, 1818.

> The morning after breakfast Mrs. Kirkpatrick and John Hancock rode about three miles into the country, they rode in a Gig, and took little Thomas

160

and a Servant with them. About eleven o' clock Mr. Duval of Richmond came into the School — he wanted to collect money from Mr. Kirkpatrick for the printing of a Newspaper. Mr. Kirkpatrick paid him $5. Mr. Duval then heard Miss Jane C. Davenport read, and appeared to be much surprised and pleased — this evening Mr. Braidwood has not come into school — he has to attend with the Free Masons of Manchester in Richmond in order to lay the corner stone of a Great Church. It is raining while I am writing this.

W. A. Bolling.

The last mention of John Braidwood in Wm. Albert's book (apparently written on Thursday June 25, 1818), occurs on page 77 as follows:

> It is five minutes past three o' clock.
> Mr. Braidwood had not come into school.

BOLLING'S LETTER OF 1841 (FOURTH EXTRACT).

Col. Bolling says:

> Again he (Braidwood) applied to me, and again I went to his relief by forming a connection between the Rev. Mr. Kirkpatrick, then residing in Manchester, and himself. I again sent my son to him, under the care of Mr. K., Braidwood stipulating to impart to Mr. K. the art of teaching deaf-mutes — they had two or three other pupils, and he conducted himself for about six months to the entire satisfaction of Mr. K., who I am assured, if he had pursued the profession had sufficiently qualified himself; but before the third quarter ended, Braidwood's conduct was such as to oblige Mr. K. to dissolve all further connection with him. After this he became a bar-keeper in a tavern in Manchester, a situation peculiarly adapted to indulgence in his unfortunate and inveterate propensities, where he died a victim to the bottle in the winter of 1819-20.

In conclusion, my dear Sir, I have only to add that this communication has been extended far beyond my intention when I commenced it — while I might say much more. I submit it to your discretion to make such use of it as may be desired in your proposed publication on the subject, either in extracts or otherwise, with authority to refer to me by name for all the facts which I have stated. With high esteem and friendly regard,

WILL – BOLLING.

MASONIC RECORDS RELATING TO BRAIDWOOD

Mr. Henry Maurice, Mayor of the city of Manchester, Va. — himself a Member of the Masonic Lodge No. 14 — has made a careful examination of the old Record Book belonging to that Lodge, for entries relating to John Braidwood, and reports the following discoveries:

> John Braidwood became a member of Masonic Lodge No. 14 of Manchester, Va., in 1817. The petition for his membership was presented to the Lodge at the September meeting, 1817, Sept. 6, and his initiation took place at the following meeting in October. John Braidwood visited the Lodge June 23, 1818; June 24, 1818; Sept. 24, 1819; June 24, 1820; July 1, 1820; and he died either on the 24th or 25thof October 1820, as he was buried by the Lodge on the 26th of October, 1820.

We are indebted to Mayor Maurice for the following copy of the last entry made in the Masonic Record Book relating to Braidwood:

> At a called meeting of Manchester Lodge No. 14, held in the Hall on Thursday the 26th October, A. L. 5820, A. D. 1820 — for the purpose of paying the last tribute of respect to their departed Brother, John Braidwood.
>
> Present.
>
> Whpfl. Richard O. Henderson, Master.
> Whpfl. P. M. James HendersonS.W. pro tem.

Bro. James Bander	J.W. pro tem
Whpfl. P. M. Richd. Booker	S.D. pro tem
Bro. William Angus	J.D. pro tem
Bro. Jno. Howlett	Treasurer pro tem
L. Addison	– visiting
Br. Tyler	Secy. pro tem
Bro. D. D. Baker	
Bro. Wm. Matthews	
Bro. Obed: Winfred	

Visiting Brethren.
Whpfl. P. M. Jno. Johnson of No. 14
Whpfl. Jno. Dove — Master of No. 19
Jas. B. Roddy of No. 10, Richd.
Jos. Viglinive — of No. 10
Zachariah Clarke of No. 10
Assist Jr. Deacon, J. B. Richardson of No. 19
Assist Sr. Dea. D. Hickey — No. 1 — Norfolk.
Edmd. Redford — 19 Richd.

The Whpfl. Master informed the lodge that we were called together to render our last duties to our departed brother — and after mentioning the form of the procession the lodge proceeded to the late residence of the decd. And accompanied his remains to the place of interment; where after the usual ceremony, his body was deposited in the grave; when the procession returned to the hall. The lodge was then adjourned.

Richard O. Henderson, Master.
Andrew L. Addison, Secy. Pro tem.

The place of interment was not mentioned; but, about the year 1875, Wm. Albert Bolling pointed out the grave to Mr. Edwin Cheatham, a deaf gentleman now living in Richmond, Va. It has thus been ascertained that Braidwood was buried in the Masonic lot in Manchester, Va., close to Old Mason's Hall, and right under one of the windows of the Kirkpatrick school.

He was laid to rest beside the old school building in which his labors for the deaf had been brought to a close.

APPENDIX N

PUBLIC APPEAL FOR THE SUPPORT OF THE MANCHESTER SCHOOL (1817)
(From the *Richmond Enquirer, June 20, 1817.*)

FOR THE INQUIRER

DEAF & DUMB

Few objects more calculated to excite pity, or more worthy of the attentions and exertions of an active benevolence, can be presented than children deprived of the sense of hearing, and the faculty of speech. With such an object are associated all the anxieties and sorrows of the parents, and the dreadful privations of the child, cut off from all that is most delightful in intercourse with its fellow creatures, and denied access to the varied stores of knowledge, which at once afford the capacity and pleasure of doing good. It is impossible to behold a human being in this deplorable situation, without earnestly wishing to afford relief. The ingenuity of benevolence has devised a plan, by which, what at first, and for a long time indeed, seemed hopeless, has been accomplished. The power of receiving and communicating ideas, and making improvement in almost every branch of knowledge, has been imparted. Among the benefactors of the deaf and dumb, Braidwood of Edinburgh, holds a very distinguished place; as will appear from the subjoined extract from Dr Johnson's Tour to the Hebrides.

The grandson of Braidwood is now in Manchester, and has recently formed a connection with the Rev. Mr. Kirkpatrick, who superintends a flourishing School in that place. It is understood, that the principal object of the association is, that Mr. Braidwood may communicate to Mr. Kirkpatrick a knowledge of the art of which his grandfather was the inventor:

and that the most unquestionable evidence of competency can be adduced. It is surely most delightful that we should have among us in Virginia, a man capable of affording instruction to the deaf and dumb; and it is gratifying to learn that a gentleman of Mr. Kirkpatrick's character and abilities has undertaken to qualify himself for this important office. While our brethren to the Northward and Eastward are signalizing their zeal and benevolence in support of an institution for the instruction of the *sourd-muets*, surely the people of Virginia will not regard with indifference, any efforts of benevolent individuals in behalf of such unfortunate children as may be among us.

The connection between the gentlemen mentioned above, is expected to continue until Mr. Kirkpatrick shall have fully acquired the art. To facilitate the attainment of this object, Mr. Braidwood will immediately receive pupils that may be entrusted to his care, to be instructed, in part, at least, in the presence of Mr. K. — Any children that may be sent for this purpose, will be boarded in the family of this Reverend gentleman, where, the writer of this is well assured, they will receive all kind of attentions which humanity and Christian benevolence can dictate. As to the terms of boarding, tuition, &c., these gentlemen will, no doubt, speedily publish information.

Parents of the deaf and dumb! An opportunity is here afforded of doing the best thing that can be done for your unfortunate children.

Benevolent Virginians! If there should be in the neighbourhood of any of you, children of the poor who cannot hear or speak, you may gratify your benevolence by making contributions for their support and education. The cheapest luxury in the world is the luxury of doing good. 'It is more blessed to give than to receive.'

165

From the last pages of Johnson's 'Journey to the Western Isles of Scotland.' 1773.

There is one subject of philosophical curiosity to be found in Edinburgh, which no other city has to shew; a college of the deaf and dumb, who are taught to speak, to read, to write, and to practice arithmetick, by a gentleman, whose name is Braidwood. The number which attends him is, I think, about twelve, which he brings together into a little school, and instructs according to their several degrees of proficiency.

I do not mean to mention the instruction of the deaf as new. Having been first practiced upon the son of a constable of Spain, it was afterwards cultivated with much emulation in England, by Wallis and Holder, and was latterly professed by Mr Baker, who once flattered me with hopes of seeing his method published. How far any former teachers have succeeded, it is not easy to know; the improvement of Mr Braidwood's pupils is wonderful. They not only speak, write and understand what is written, but if he that speaks looks towards them, and modifies his organs by distinct and full utterance, they know so well what is spoken, that is an expression scarcely figurative to say, they hear with the eye. That any have attained to the power mentioned by Burnet, of feeling sounds, by laying a hand on the speaker's mouth, I know not; but I have seen so much, that I can believe more; a single word, or a short sentence, I think, may possibly be so distinguished.

It will readily be supposed by those that consider this subject, that Mr Braidwood's scholars spell accurately. Orthography is vitiated among such as learn first to speak, and then to write, by imperfect notions of the relations between letters and vocal utterance; but to those students every character is of equal importance; for letters are to them not symbols of names, but of things; when they write they do not represent a sound, but delineate a form.

This school I visited, and found some of the scholars waiting for their master, whom they are said to receive at his entrance with smiling countenances and sparkling eyes, delighted with the hope of new ideas. One of the young Ladies had her slate before her, on which I wrote a question consisting of three figures, to be multiplied by two figures. She looked upon it, and quivering her fingers in a manner which I thought very pretty, but of which I know not whether it was art or play, multiplied the sum regularly in two lines, observing the decimal place; but did not add the two lines together, probably disdaining so easy an operation. I pointed at the place where the sum total should stand, and she noted it with such expedition as seemed to shew that she had it only to write.

It was pleasing to see one of the most desperate of human calamities capable of so much help: whatever enlarges hope, will exalt courage; after having seen the deaf taught arithmetick, who would be afraid to cultivate the *Hebrides*?

APPENDIX 0

LETTER FROM EDWARD HALLAM
TO DR. COGSWELL
(1818, March 10.)

Richmond, March 10, 1818.

Dear Sir:

Your letter would sooner have been answered had I possessed the information required. Upon Enquiry, I learn (from the most authentic Sources) that the connexion — between Braidwood, and

Mr. Kirkpatrick, was dissolved on account of the irregularities of Mr. Braidwood that during the connexion Mr. Kirkpatrick attended particularly to the art of teaching the deaf and dumb to speak or articulate, that he thinks himself in possession of that requisite. But with a View of perfecting himself in those Branches of the art in which he considers himself deficient it is his purpose to visit the Institution at Hartford; Mr. Kirkpatrick is a native of North Carolina, a Young man probably about thirty, after becoming piouse, with a View to his profession, the ministry of the gospel, he went through the Usual course at Hampden Sydney College, he is a man of great natural abilities, of persevering industry, of extreme warmth of feelings benevolence and Kindness of disposition. — for some time previous to his connexion with Braidwood he kept a school in Manchester, his family consist of a wife and one child:—

I feel much pleasure in saying my family enjoy uninterrupted good health, they beg to be respectfully remembered to You, and family, and friends generally in Hartford. With Sentiments of sincere wishes for your Happiness, I remain your very Sincerely,
Ed. Hallam.

(Letter addressed to Doc. Mason F. Cogswell, Hartford, Connecticut. Original on file at Yale University Library, New Haven, Conn.)

Further reference to John Braidwood and the New York School.

———————

APPENDIX P.

BRAIDWOOD'S NEW YORK SCHOOL
(Winter of 1816?)

(From *Niles Weekly Register*, Baltimore, Maryland, 1817, Jan. 4, vol. XI, p.298.)

DEAF AND DUMB

We have been long desirous of giving a detailed account of a very interesting institution about to be established in Connecticutt for the instruction of the deaf and dumb, and of the intelligent and highly accomplished Mr. Le Clerc, the proposed principal, of the school, himself a deaf and dumb man, who writes as fluently, and conveys his ideas on any subject submitted to him, as clearly as any person whatever. He has exhibited his talents in this way in several of our cities, for the purpose of raising funds to assist in the beneficient undertaking, and appears to have succeeded to the extent of his wishes.

Mr. Le Clerc is a pupil of the Abbe Sicard. He writes English well, though he did not commence the study of the language until June last; shewing a proficiency in acquiring it that is, perhaps, without many rivals.

But a Mr. *Braidwood*, now in New York, carries the instruction of the deaf and dumb still further — he not only teaches them to write and understand accurately the principles of language, "but to *speak* and read distinctly" — instructs them in "arithmetic, geography, the use of the globes, and every branch of education necessary to render them useful and intelligent members of society." An account of the original institution of Mr. *Braidwood* is inserted in vol. II of the *Weekly Register*, page 53.

As soon as the pressure of documents has past and room is allowed for Miscellany, we intend to notice these things at length — as well to aid the institutions, as to shew that this unfortunate class of persons are not so destitute of the means of happiness and comfort as is generally supposed.

[Great uncertainty exists as to the exact date of Braidwood's New York School.] The above article seems to indicate that it was in operation at the close of the year 1816, and this fits in with Braidwood's history so far as we have been able to unravel it. (See REVIEW Index to Vol. II.)

His time has been fully accounted for from the summer of 1812 until the autumn of 1816, when he left Virginia and took the stage "for the North." (Letter from Hallam to Cogswell, 1816, Oct. 6, REVIEW II. p.408). At this point in his career we lose sight of him for a few months — and it may well be that he went to New York and opened a school there, although the evidence, to my mind, is not conclusive. In the spring of 1817 he returned to Virginia "penniless, friendless, & scarcely decently clad," and Col. Bolling assisted him in opening a school in Manchester, Va., in conjunction with the Rev. John Kirkpatrick. This school had been in operation for some time before the appearance of the article about it in the *Richmond Enquirer*, published June 20, 1817 (REVIEW II, p.514). He retained his connection with the Manchester School until about the beginning of March, 1818, (letter from Hallam to Cogswell dated 1818, March 10, REVIEW II, 517). The New York Institution was opened in 1818, May 20 — and Braidwood's New York School was in operation before then. See *History of the New York Institution* published by the Volta Bureau, p.10, where the following passage occurs:

> In the course of his melancholy eccentricities he (Braidwood) made his way to New York, and collected a few deaf-mutes to form a school in that city, which, however, was soon broke up, like those in Virginia, by his own misconduct

> His undertaking in New York attracted the attention, among others, of Dr Samuel Ackerly, afterward one of the earliest and most efficient friends of the New York Institution, &c.

Whatever may have been the exact date of Braidwood's New York School, all references indicate that it lasted only for a short period of time, and it may not, therefore, have been in existence on the 14th of January, 1817, when Clerc wrote to Cogswell the letter quoted in *Appendix* 36 — in which case Clerc was right in supposing that, at that date, there was no school for the deaf in the United States. The Hartford school had not then been opened; and the New York Institution was still *in embryo*.

— A. G. B.]

(End of Alexander Graham Bell's historical account.)

170

6 - MISCELLANEOUS SOURCES and RESEARCH NOTES

In the following pages documents and illustrations associated with Braidwood have been included as a part of the package on the history of Thomas Braidwood and his family. These material may turn out to be useful sources for future researchers who wish to take up the Braidwood history in order to complete the whole picture. The first three documents in the following pages were transcribed by the author from original sources.

Below is a detail from 1820 map:

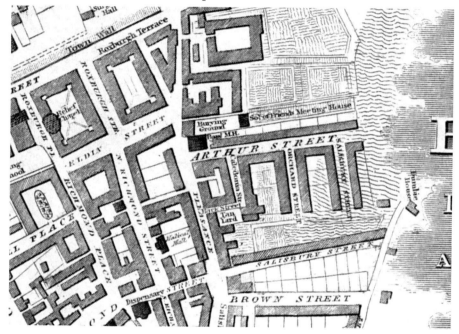

Reproduced with kind permission of Edinburgh City Library.
Section of John Wood's 1820 map of Edinburgh.

Dumbie House is seen on the far right of the map in the valley between Arthur Street and Salisbury Street. Following Braidwood's relocation to England, the school's nickname 'Dumbie House', endured. From around 1820 onwards the road running past Dumbie House from St Leonard's to the Canongate began to appear on maps as 'Dumbie Dykes' – the latter part of this name referring to the walls which bordered the King's Park. Within a few short years Dumbiedykes would be used exclusively to describe the entire district. Dumbie House was later renamed Craigside House, in reference to the nearby crags which towered over it. Craigside House was demolished in 1942.

Contract of Feu
Betwixt
Dame Elizabeth Nicolson
And Thomas Carnegy Eq
and
Thomas Braidwood

14th 16th February 1767

It is contracted, agreed, and ended betwixt Dame Elizabeth Carnegy
alias Nicolson, Relict of the deceased Sir James Nicolson, of that ilk
Baronet, and Thomas Carnegy Esquire of Craigs, her nephew, and
apparent heir Heritable proprietors of the piece of ground
aftermentioned on the one part, and Thomas Braidwood, Writing
master in Edinburgh on the other part, in manner following, that is to
say whereas the said Dame Elizabeth Nicolson having some time ago
made out a plan of Nicolson park lying in the south side of the city wall
of Edinburgh without the Potterrow Part and on the east of the
Potterrow Street in the parish of Saint Cuthbert's and sheriffdom of
Edinburgh; In terms of which plan the said Lady Nicolson feued out
several Plots and parcels of the said Park with the power and privilege
of a Road or Causeway of thirty feet wide going through the said park
from south to North entering from the Grass causeway street on the
west of John Mars' house, and then dividing into two branches both
terminating on the Road going alongst the south side of the said City
wall; one of the said branches going to the East and the other to the
west of Nicolson House, and which road or Causeway was to be called
Nicolson Street; and there was likewise another road of the same
wideness going through the said Park from East to West, entering from
the road at the Backrow through the Lousy Lane, and so going
westward by the north end of the Earl of Glencairn's House, and there
was farther marked out in the said plan a space for a foot road of five
feet wide, along each side of the said street either to be causewayed or
laid with pavement, as the majority of the Feuars should think most
proper, and thereafter by an agreement Registrate in in the Sheriff court
book of Edinburgh the sixteenth day of January seventeen hundred and
sixty five years, entered into among the Feuars from the said Lady
Nicolson, and approven of by her.

It was agreed that the foresaid Roads or Streets should be widened from
thirty feet to fourty feet, except as to the branches on each side of
Nicolson House which was to be widened only to thirty five feet, and

172

that of the foot-roads should be widened from five feet to seven feet, and now seeing that the said Thomas Braidwood has agreed to take a feu of a part of one of the Plots in the said Park marked in the said Plan with the letter S and has made payment to the said Dame Elizabeth Nicolson of the sum of Eight pounds, one shilling and eight pence sterling of Grossum or entry-money, with the sum of eight pounds, nine shillings and two pence sterling, as the price of four perches and twenty six yards of land, English measure, as his proportion of the ground of the said original road of thirty feet wide allowed by the said Lady Nicolson to be purchased in by her respective Feuars, and agreed to by the said parties, and of both which sums the said Dame Elizabeth Nicolson hereby grants the receipt, renouncing all objections to the contrary therefore, and for the yearly Feu duty aftermentioned, and with and under the burdens and provisions underwritten, the said Dame Elizabeth Nicolson and Thomas Carnegy for their respective Interests of liferent and fee by these presents, sells, alienates and dispones, and in Feu, Farm and heritage for ever, Letts and Demitts to the said Thomas Braidwood, his heirs and assignees whatsoever and heritably and inedeemably all and whole the North side of that Plot or piece of ground marked with the letter S in the said plan containing thirty two perches, and ten yards English land measure or thereby, being part of Nicolson Park, and measuring on the east side fifty three feet four inches, on the south side one hundred fifty three feet eight inches, and on the west side along Nicolson Street fifty three feet four inches, and on the north side one hundred fifty two feet ten inches, and Bounded as follows, to wit, By the hedge separating the ground feued by Lady Nicolson to John Robertson, Mason in Edinburgh, on the east by the remainder of the said Plot S not yet feued out on the South, By the New road called Nicolson Street, on the west, and by the mutual stone Dyke separating the piece of ground hereby feued, from ground feued to the late Baillie James Hutton on the north parts, as the said piece of ground was lately measured and lined out by John Lawrie, Land surveyor, and agreed by both the said parties, Declaring, Nonetheless, that there is already laid off, and contained in the foresaid measurement twelve feet of ground along the west end of the piece of ground hereby feued, which with twelve feet opposite thereto laid off by the other Feuars widens or enlarges the foresaid coach road from thirty feet to forty feet wide, and the foot-roads on both sides of the coach roads from five to seven feet each in Breadth, as the same is presently lined out of the dimensions foresaid, with free Ish and entry by all Roads already made or to lie hereafter made, by the Feuars and Heritors of Nicolson Park in common with them.

173

Together with the Teinds of the said piece of ground, and all right on title which the said Dame Elizabeth Nicolson and Thomas Carnegy has or can pretend to the same all lying in the same parish of Saint Cuthbert's, and Sheriffdom of Edinburgh; In the which piece of ground above disponed Teinds and pertinents of the same the said Dame Elizabeth Nicolson and Thomas Carnegy Bind and Oblige them, their heirs, and successors to Insist and Sease the said Thomas Braidwood and his foresaids upon their own proper Charges and expences, to be holden of, and under the said Dame Elizabeth Nicolson, and Thomas Carnegie, their heirs and successors in feu farm and heritage for payment to the said Dame Elizabeth Nicolson during all the days and years of her life, and failing her by death, to the said Thomas Carnegy, his heirs or assignees of the sum of four pounds sixteen shillings and eleven pence halfpenny sterling yearly of Feu duty, and doubling the same the first year of the entry of each heir or singular successor to the said piece of ground, and with and under the Burdens and provisions in the precept of Seisine after written, and also the said Dame Elizabeth Nicolson and Thomas Carnegy for their respective rights of liferent and in name of [bess], and for the name of reparation of Church and Church yeard Dykes, and other burdens of that nature conform to the valued rent which is hereby declared to be twenty six pounds Scots, or thereby, each acre, and moreover, in case any casualty of superiority shall happen to fall into the hands of the said Dame Elizabeth Nicolson, and Thomas Carnegy, or their foresaids, as superiors of the ground above disponed, they bind and oblige them, and their foresaids to Dispone the same Like as now as if the same had already fallen into their hands. They per verba de praesenti dispones and makes over the same to the said Thomas Braidwood and his foresaids for payment of five shillings sterling so often as the same shall happen to fall out and the said Dame Elizabeth Nicolson, and Thomas Carnegy, for their respective interests of Fee and liferent, as said is, Bind and oblige them and their foresaids to [warrand] the piece of ground above disponed, and this Feu contract, with the infeftments to follow hereupon to the said Thomas Braidwood and his foresaids, at all hands, and against all deadly as law will, Excepting the [Temois], maills and duties which they and their foresaids are only to [warrand] from fact and deed allenarly; For the which causes and on the other part the said Thomas Braidwood Binds and obliges him, his Heirs, or successors to content and pay to the said Dame Elizabeth Nicolson in liferent and to the said Thomas Carnegy his heirs or assignees in fee the foresaid sum of four pounds sixteen shillings and eleven pence halfpenny sterling, as the agreed Feu duty for the said piece of ground above disponed, and that yearly, and each year at two terms in the year, Lambas* and

174

Candlemass, by equal portions; beginning the first term's payment thereof at the term of Lambas* next one thousand, seven hundred, and sixty seven, for the current half year, and the next term's payment at Candlemass thereafter, seventeen hundred and sixty eight, for the first year, and so forth yearly and termly, in all time coming with a fifth part more of a penalty for each term's faillie and annual rent of the said Feu duty from the respective terms of payment till paid; and also to pay the double of the said Feu duty the first year of the entry of each heir or singular successor as vassals therein, upon payment whereof, the said Dame Elizabeth Nicolson, and Thomas Varnegy and his foresaids shall be bound to enter and receive them as well heirs, and singular successors, as vassals without any other compensation or good deed whatsoever any law or custom to the contrary notwithstanding. And also the said Thomas Braidwood Binds and obliges him, and his foresaids, to pay the same respective public burdens above specified, and to fulfil and perform the whole other burdens, provisions, and conditions before and after written; and both the said parties consent to the Registration hereof, and the precept of Seisine afterwritten in the Books of Council and Session, or others competent to have the strength of a Decreet interponed hereto, That letters of Homing on six days charge, and all other execution necessary may pass, and be direct thereon as Effeirs, and for that effect they constitute.

Their Primo and moreover to the end the said Thomas Braidwood and his foresaids may be infeft and seised in the said Plott or piece of ground before disponed with the Teinds and pertinents of the same to be holden as said is; The said Dame Elizabeth Nicolson and Thomas Carnegy desires and requires you their Baillies in that part conjunctly and severally hereby specially constitute That on sight hereof ye pass to the ground of the said piece of land above disponed, and there give and deliver heritable state and Sasine, actual, real, and corporal possession to the said Thomas Braidwood and his foresaids of all and whole the north part of the foresaid Plott or piece of ground marked S in the said plan and containing thirty two perches ten yards of land or thereby (with the deduction aforesaid) above disponed with the Teinds and pertinents of the same lying and bounded as aforesaid, and that by deliverance of Earth and Stone of the ground of the said lands, and an handful of corn and shaw, or grass and stubble for the said Teinds to him or them, or to his or their certain Attorney, or Attorneys in their names, bearers hereof. But always with and under the conditions, burdens and provisions before and after mentioned, To wit, That the said Thomas Braidwood and his foresaids shall be obliged within the space of six years after his entry to erect and build upon his own proper charges and expenses a handsome dwelling house upon some part of the said piece of ground, at the distance of eight feet from the said new road called Nicolson Street as the same is presently formed and lined out. Secundo. That he shall not erect any buildings whatever upon the said twelve feet in breadth along the west end of the said piece of ground already laid off for widening the said road, five feet whereof is thrown into the said Thirty feet coach-road, and the remaining seven feet is made [is made] into a foot-road and shall be Bound and Obliged to Dispone and convey to the other Feuars in Nicolson park, the said twelve feet in breadth, along the west side of the said piece of ground, as the majority of the Feuars shall direct, they always being obliged to convey and make over to him as much of the grounds opposite to their respective Plotts as will be sufficient to keep the said coach road of Nicolson street forty feet wide from the Cross road leading through the said Park, from east to west, till the road separate into two branches on the east and west sides of Nicolson House, as it presently is, and the two foot roads opposite thereto, to continue seven foot wide each, as they are at present, and as makes the east and west branches of the said road opposite Nicolson House thirty five feet wide for the Coach road and seven feet wide for the foot path, as the said roads are at present. It being agreed, that there is no foot road to be made upon the sides of the said two branches next to the ground about Nicolson House. Tertio. That the said Thomas Braidwood and his foresaids shall be obliged instantly to pay his proportion of the expence of forming and making the whole principal roads in Nicolson Park before mentioned with the expence of furnishing and leading the materials fit for that purpose, and the making the said foot roads, and common syvers along the said high roads conform to the extent of the said piece of ground or as the majority of the Feuars shall direct, the said whole other Feuars being always obliged to pay in proportion thereto. Quarto. That the said Thomas Braidwood and his foresaids shall not erect any houses or buildings of any kind upon the foresaid piece of ground within eight feet of the said road on the west side thereof reserving power to him or them to enclose the same with a stone wall not exceeding eight feet high above the foot road with pillars for gates of any reasonable height; and also with power and liberty to build vaults under the said eight feet or under the said foot road provided he or they do not alter the swell, nor do any damages to the said foot road. Quinto. That the said Thomas Braidwood and his foresaids shall be obliged to inclose the said piece of ground on the west, without encroaching upon any part of the foot road above described, all upon his own expences and charges; and shall be bound and obliged to pay the just and equal half of the expence of the stone Dyke lately built by Patrick Jamieson, mason on the north side, and shall be obliged to pay the whole of the expence of a stone Dyke on the south side, betwixt his ground and the remainder of the said Plott S till such a time as the said Dame Elizabeth Nicolson and Thomas Carnegy shall Feu out the same, when the Feuar or Feuars shall be obliged to pay the half of the said expence. Sexto .That the said Thomas Braidwood and his foresaids shall not allow any shops or yards for masons, wrights, coopers, smiths, weavers, candlemakers, Crackling houses, nauseous chymical preparations, or other noxious or noisy manufactories whatsoever, which may occasion disturbance to any of the neighbouring Feuars, to be erected, placed, or kept within any part of the said piece of ground hereby feued, nor shall shall it be in the power of the said Thomas Braidwood and his foresaids to keep or lay any dunghills upon the said roads, or before the front of the house or houses to be erected by him or them upon the said piece of ground. Septimo. It is hereby expressly agreed by both the said parties, that it shall not be lawfull, nor in the power of the said Thomas Braidwood or his foresaids to subdivide and alienate the piece of ground above disponed, or the houses one or more to be built thereon, either by subfeuing or otherways, so as the Feu duty of any of the subdivisions or subfeus shall be under the sum of three pounds sterling yearly, and that the said Dame Elizabeth Nicolson and Thomas Carnegy and their foresaids shall not be bound to enter and receive the heirs and singular successors voluntarly, or legal as vassals in any such subdivisions in parcels whereof the Feu duty shall not be at least three pounds sterling yearly any law or custom to the contrary notwithstanding. Declaring always, that notwithstanding of such subdivisions or subfeus, the whole house to be built on the said piece of ground or any part thereof shall be liable in payment of the said yearly Feu duty above written, aye and while the same be completely paid up. Octavo. That all and each of the conditions, obligations, restrictions, burdens and servitudes aforesaid shall be holden and repute as real burdens and servitudes affecting the foresaid piece of ground, and that all and each of them shall be insert in the infeftments to follow hereupon, repeated in all the after conveyances of the same and infeftments following thereupon, and that the said Thomas Braidwood and his foresaids shall be holden obliged to implement and fulfil the same in all time coming; Declaring always that the said Thomas Braidwood and his foresaids shall be bound and obliged to observe and fulfil the whole other regulations and conditions made or to be made by the said Dame Elizabeth Nicolson and Thomas Carnegy and their foresaid Feuars in Nicolson park or the majority of them, and that it shall be not only in the power of the said Dame Elizabeth Nicolson and Thomas Carnegy, and their foresaids, but also to the said Thomas Braidwood and his foresaids, and to all the neighbouring Feuars in said park each of them their heirs and successors mutually to insist and pursue each other for Implement and performance of the several respective Conditions, obligations, restrictions, burdens and servitudes aforesaid, with and under the burdens thereof and each of them this Feu contract is granted, and to conform to the other Feu rights already made and granted by the said Lady Nicolson and Thomas Carnegy and accepted of, and no otherwise and whereas several matters may fall out to be determined by the majority of the Feuars, it is hereby covenanted and agreed to that the proprietor or proprietors of each piece of ground distinguished as Plott in the plan signed by the said Lady Nicolson and Thomas Carnegy and their Feuars shall only have one vote in any determination. And this in no ways ye leave undone, for doing whereof the said Dame Elizabeth Nicolson and Thomas Carnegy commits to you their full and unrevockable power by this their precept of Sasine. In Witness whereof, these presents are written upon this and the eleven preceding pages of stomp paper by Charles Innes, Writer in Edinburgh, and subscribed by the said parties as follows to witt, by the said Dame Elizabeth Nicolson at Nicolson House, the fourteenth day of February one thousand seven hundred and sixty seven years before these witness Thomas Walker writer in Edinburgh, and Alexander Inglis servant to the said Thomas Carnegy, and by the said Thomas Carnegy and Thomas Braidwood, the sixteenth day of the said month of February, place and year aforesaid. Before these witnesses Mr Baillie Blenshal sadler in Edinburgh and James Macpherson architect and mason in the Dean, and the said Thomas Walker inserter of the dates, witness names and designations to the subscriptions of the said Thomas Carnegy and Thomas Braidwood.

National Records of Scotland G081/302

Note:

There is an interesting reference in this document to Thomas Carnegy having a manservant named Alexander Inglis. One of Thomas Braidwood's pupils was Alexander Inglis and a question has been raised whether that deaf Braidwoodian pupil was the son of the Alexander Inglis mentioned in the document, and if so, whether his education had been financed by either Thomas Carnegy or Lady Nicolson.

CAUTIONARY

William Inglis, pursuer   William Bethune, defender

June 26 1796

Cautioner — Claim of relief against a new Cautioner who interposed, alone, by a separate missive, at a distance of time, on account of a change in the situation of one of the original cautioners, — refused.

In 1773, Alexander Simpson obtained a cash credit for L300 from the Bank of Scotland, on a bond granted by him, and by Thomas Braidwood and James Loch, who bound, conjunctly and severally with him, in the usual form.

In 1785, Braidwood went to permanently reside in England; and in consequence of a demand made on the occasion by the Bank, whose rules required two cautioners resident in Scotland. Simpson obtained a missive, as follows, in January1788, from Mr Bethune of Blebe:— "Sir, as Mr Thomas Braidwood, teacher of languages, at St Leonards, at present in England, is bound to the Bank of Scotland in a bond of credit for L300 sterling, jointly with Mr James loch, writer to the Signet, and Mr Alexander Simpson, merchant tailor in Edinburgh, and a cash accompt therein, in the name of the said Alexander Simpson, I hereby oblige myself, jointly and severally with the said Mr Braidwood, for the payment of the contents of the said bond to you or your successors in office, for behoof of the Bankers. I am, &c."

This missive was lodged with James Spence, the Treasurer of the Bank, to whom it was addressed, and was marked by him on the back, William Bethune, Edinburgh, 19th January, 1786, in corroboration of Alexander Simpson's bond of credit.

Simpson continued to operate on the cash account for a series of years, as before; but he, at last, stopped payment, after exhausting credit. The Bank got a payment of L97 out of the effects of Mr Loch, who had also died insolvent; and the balance was paid by Mr William Inglis, as attorney for Braidwood, on an assignation from the Bank, towards effectuating his relief. On this title, Mr Inglis brought a process before the Lords against Mr Bethune, in which he concluded for relief of one half of what he had paid to the Bank.

The Lord Ordinary (Craig) assoilzied the defender, "in respect of the missive letter, libelled on, was long posterior to the bond of credit by

Thomas Braidwood and the other obligants to the Bank of Scotland, and does not appear to have been granted for the relief of Mr Braidwood in that obligation, but merely as an additional security to the Bank, the creditor."

In a reclaiming petition for the pursuer, he referred to the case of Murray v. the Creditors of Maxwell, 15th December 1722, and that of Smeaton v. Miller, 15th Nov. 1792, as having finally settled the general rule of a proportional relief among co-cautioners, whether bound in several and successive bonds, or at one time and in one bond only. He also maintained that it made no difference in point of principle, whether the principal debtor gave bond along with a new cautioner, as in the above mentioned cases, or whether the cautioner became bound, as in this instance, in a separate bond or missive, by himself alone. True, Erskine's authority was on the other side; but Erskine had not treated this matter with his usual accuracy.

The Court thought that the principle of the decision in Smeaton and Miller, did not apply to the circumstance of this case, and refused the petition.

There seems to be room here for a difference of opinion. It was owing to Mr Bethune's missive that Simpson's cash account was allowed to continue; and Bethune interfered for that very purpose. If he had declined, the transaction would have been closed, and the balance paid in June 1786, when all the cautioners were still solvent; and Braidwood would thus have been called on for his own proportion only. See the case of Lennox &c. v. Campbell, 18th May, 1815, where the new cautioner, taken by the Bank on the death of one of the original cautioners was found liable in relief pro rata. It is true that, in that instance, the new cautioner, though bound in a separate and posterior writing, granted by him only, had obliged himself, conjunctly and severally, with all the obligants of the original bond. But it may be questioned whether this is a substantial ground of distinction.

Decisions of the court of session
1781 – 1822 pages 87-88
Collected by David Hume

Wm. Blackwood & Sons, Edinburgh
& Thomas Cadell, London   1839

Braidwood v. Brown

My Lords Geo. Shows your Lordships' Servitor Mr Thomas Braidwood Teacher at St Leonards near Edinburgh That by each dated the 6th of June 1772 years entered into between William Brown of Harehope on the one part and me on the other part he set to me and my Heirs assignees or Subtenants all and haill that part of the Lands of Harehope with Houses Biggings yeards and pertinents of the same lying within the Parish of Eddlestone & Shire of Peebles as sometime possessed by James Rammage tenant thereof, And that for the space of nine years from and after the term of Whitsunday 1772 as to the Pasture of said Lands and as to the arable Lands against the separation of that year's crop from the Ground and from thencefurth to be peaceably laboured & possessed by him and his foresaids during the saidspace and bound himself in absolute warrandice of the Tack for which causes I became bound to pay him a rent of L120 sterling which very much higher than any Farmer in the County have offered to give, Or than the farm ever yielded. But I had the prospect of indemnifying myself by improvements of the farm and more extensive plowing as it is both a Sheep and labouring farm, consisting of above six hundred acres of ground and not above fifty acres thereof unarable, in which your Lordships see I am noways restricted in any part of the tack, my copy of which is produced.

This farm Mr Brown and the Neighbourhood well knows that I had no other motives of taking it than to enable a Friend who was reduced to low Circumstances and had a numerous family of small children. Accordingly I entered to Possession by draining and drying wet grounds, manuring others and to make them fit for labouring and had always two Plows on the farm since my entry and at some few times three — And as the next crop 1781 is my last in virtue of said tack I thought myself well entitled to indemnify myself as much as possible by plowing more this season than formerly in virtue of the tack which bears no restriction, limitation or mode of labouring or manuring the farm. But altho' the former improvements and plowing of Grounds not apparently laboured before, particularly a great part of what Mr Brown calls the Hogfence and a great part of the hill ground was all done under Mr Brown's eyes and with his approbation. Yet he has thought proper to change his mind and take umbrage at my plowing rather more extensively this season than formerly. In this spirit he presented a petition upon the 18th day of Decemr currt to the Sherriff of Peebles reciting a part of the tack and further setting furth to my great surprise, that for every year since my entry I only kept one plow for the arable

181

Land which was very inconsiderable as the ground was always (plerished) up and occupied as a Sheep farm. But this last year and which is the last of my tack, I reared up two plows which have been constantly employed in plowing the ground that was formerly in use to be lpowed and likewise in breaking up and tilling a considerable part of the hill & sheep Ground above the town that never was in tillage before, and upon which there is not the smallest vestige of ridge & (furr) and that I had brought a third plow from Scotstown & farm I possess in the neighbourhood and with that and the former two intend to carry on my tillage of these parts of his farm that never were in tillage and to break up and till the Hogfence of said farm for this current year's crops whereby the Petitioner must suffer considerable damages.

Therefore praying for an Interdict Geo. Upon advising this clamorous petition the Sherriff immediately pronounced the following interlocutor "Chappelhill 18th Decemr 1780. The Sherriff having considered the above Petition appoints the same to be served upon the said Thomas Braidwood or his Servants at the farm house of Harehope & ordains him to give in answers thereto within forty eight hours after such service and in the meantime Interdicts prohibits and discharges the said Thomas Braidwood, his Servants and all others in his name in the management of said farm from plowing or breaking up any part of the hill or sheep pasture ground that was never in tillage before, or any part of the Hogfence."

The Petition was accordingly served upon me and I put in answers thereto, the substance of which is above stated, and upon advising these the Sherriff pronounced the following interlocutor "Chappelhill 20th Decemr 1780. The Sherriff having considered the Petition for William Brown of Harehope with the foregoing answers thereto by Thomas Braidwood Defender and tack produced therewith finds that from the nature of a Sheep farm supported by the custom of the Country of the Defender is barr'd from lpowing or breaking up any part of the ground known by the name of the Hogfence or any part of the Hill and sheep pasture ground that never was in tillage. Therefore and in respect that the Defender has not instructed an allowance from the Petitioner to plow or break up any part of the farm of Harehope under the above description prohibits and discharges the said Thomas Braidwood Defender to do so during the currency of his lease of that farm."

By which Interlocutor I humbly apprehend the Sherriff has committed iniquity the cause ought either be advocated to your Lords or remitt with an Instruction as after mentioned for the following reasons. The tack is as broad and gives as unlimited powers over the farm and particularly to peaceably labour and possess the same without any limittation and restriction whatever, as ever occurred in any case. It was upon the faith of theses unlimitted powers that I agreed to give an exorbitant rent and it is extremely hard now upon a pretence of the custom of the Country, which is not the case, to be deprived of the Benefite of using any farm in the manner I think most conductive towards my own Idemnification pro tanto for a deep loser I must be at any rate. Besides this farm is not only a sheep pasture but also an arable farm and as such I took and covenanted for the High rent of it and if Mr Brown had it in view to deceive me into a high rent by a regular and formal Contract and then take the Benefite of the custom of the Country as to sheep farms, he ought not to be allowed to profite by his own fraud. But as already said this is not only a sheep farm but an arable farm which can be proved if necessary and as such was set to and taken by me, and accordingly I sowed a hundred Bolls last year on it and from fifty to a hundred every year before since my entry and do not intend to sow much more than a hundred Bolls next season nor to labour above twenty acres more than I formerly did which, when done, is but a small part of the arable land, and indeed if it was truely a sheep farm the custom of the Country can certainly be laid aside by two contracting parties on a special spot of Ground binding themselves in a legal and formal manner and in support of this doctrine I am advised, there are a number of decisions of your Lordships.

The Sherriff's Interlocutor bears as one of the rationes decidendi "That the Defender has not instructed an allowance from the Petitioner to plow or break up any part of the farm of Harehope under the above description." That is the Hogfence, the hill and Sheep Pasture ground. But the Sherriff is here in a very great mistake, for the allowance is legally instructed by the tack itself which bears no restriction or limitation but power to peaceably labour & possess. Besides Mr Brown the pursuer had as much cause of complaint if ever there was any from the Beginning of the tack as now. He recently saw me by my Servants draining wet grounds both in the ground called the Hogfence and hill, for it was in these places I began my operations in order to make them fit for tillage and could not miss to know my Intention. I also immediately after my entry to the Possession of the farm plowed up a part of what he calls the Hogfence and part of the Hill ground both arable and fit for tillage, and this I did under the eye & even by the particular direction of the Pursuer himself. This certainly homologated the allowance in the tack, if any Homologation was necessary.

Upon finding myself yearly losing by this unlucky tack I did four years ago and frequently since repeatedly offer to the pursuer to relinquish it with all my improvements and even to give him L150 sterling to accept renounciation of the tack, having already lost by the tack above L600 sterling. But every proposal he was pleased to reject and now wants maliciously deprive me of the proper benefit of my last year's possession in which the Sherriff seems too much to countenance him. But I humbly apprehend I have an unquestionable right to continue my plowing especially as the Grounds I am presently labouring are as proper for tillage and seems to promise good crops as any other in the neighbourhood, particularly there are two folds upon the side of the Hill which have been folded and teathed and is upon ground as plain as a bowling green and were intended to have been plowed up last year, But that was prevented by an almost continued frost from November to March. It would be absurd to say that these teathed folds are not fit for the plow, and indeed all the Grounds which was labouring or intended to labour when Interdicted have been teathed or drained and rendered fit arable ground wholly upon my Expence and would also have been plowed last year But for the frosts above mentioned. And it would certainly be peculiarly hard upon me this last year of the lease to prohibite me from taking the Benefite of my own Improvements.

Besides it is absurd to suggest that I would be so blind to my interest as to plow up any part of the pasture grounds and thereby starve my own sheep of which I have a very large stock on the Hill ground. Herefore I beseech your Lordships to advocate the foresaid cause, Or rather remit to the said Sherriff with an Instruction immediately to remove the Interdict and allow me to proceed in my labouring of the said farm as the season is far advanced According to Justice

(signed James Crawford Apud Edinr 25 December Seventeen hundred and eighty, marked by/ signed H. D. Ingles — Edinbr 25th December 1780 To see and answer against Thursday next and sists procedivie till Tuesday thereafter and to be intimated (signed Robert Bruce for Lord Stonefield). — Geo Laing NP

What is wrote on this and eleven preceding pages is a just and true copy of the Bill of Advocacy presented for Thomas Braidwood before designed and of the sist pronounced thereon by the Lord Hennell. I Notary public subscribing having duly collated and compared the same with the original at Edinburgh the twentyfifth day of December one thousand & seven hundred eighty years Before these witness John Mason, writer in Edinburgh, and David Scott merchant there.

Geo Laing N.P.

(signatures
David Scott witness
John Mason witness)

Peebles 28th December 1780.

Intimate the forgoing notarial copy of the Bill of Advocation and Deliver once thereon to William Little Writer in Peebles, Doer for William Brown of Harehope Esq. James Bartram, Messenger in Peebles being Procurator, James Cairns and Robert Ballantyre, Clerks to me Notary Publick witnesses.

John Robertson N.P.

(signatures
James Cairns witness
Robt Ballantyre witness)

(National Records of Scotland – CS271-40979-00014 Braidwood v. Brown Bill Advocation 1780)

Note:

The author has not been able to locate any account or document yielding the judgement on the case.

Braidwood's Institution
for the Deaf and Dumb
——— and for ———
Removing Impediments in Speech.
Originally established by the late Mr. Thos. Braidwood
At Edinburgh:
Now conducted by Mrs. Braidwood & Son.
at Hackney, near London.

Children who have been born Deaf, or those who have
lost their hearing by Accident or Disease are taught
to Speak and Read distinctly, to write and understand
accurately the principles of Language; they are also
instructed in Arithmetic, Geography, with the Use of
the Globes, together with the polite accomplishments of
Drawing, Dancing, and every Branch of Education
that may be necessary to qualify them for any situation
in Life.

——— Those put under their tuition for the removal
of Impediments in Speech, are at the same time
instructed in every other part of Education & Science
that may be required.

A flyer advertising the Braidwood Institution

Copy donated by the late Louis M. Balfour, USA.

ELIZABETH ARMFIELD AND HER DAUGHTER ELIZABETH

It was said through various family history notes on genealogical websites that Elizabeth Armfield came into possession of papers which indicated that the Braidwood family had a claim on 300 acres of land neat Little Falls, on the Potomac in Virginia, USA. (Note:- Little Falls seems to be an unincorporated area in Stafford County, Virginia, on the right bank of the Rappahannock river between Fredericksburg and Washington DC). This source came from an article in one 1903 New Zealand newspaper *Poverty Bay Herald*:

> A Gisborne Resident, Miss E. Higgins, has laid claim to a vast estate in the United States. The Poverty Bay Herald says: —"An estate of 300 acres near Little Falls, on the river Potomac, may not have been worth many dollars one hundred years ago, although on the outskirts of the capital town of a great and rising country. What was then open field is now a solidly-built part of the flourishing city of Washington, the seat of Government of nearly eighty million of people, and such a property must be of immense value in 1903. It is such an inheritance that Mrs Higgins is a claimant and is causing inquiries to be made in the United States with a view of establishing her rights. Briefly put, her claim is based on the fact that in 1806 the land was conveyed to her grandparents, Thomas and Isabella Braidwood, whose only daughter, a Mrs Armfield, was the mother of Mrs Higgins. About 1860 the daughter of Thomas Braidwood proceeded to America and proved her claim to the land. The estate was then of considerable value, being, as it was on the Washington side of the Potomac, and negotiations were entered into, with the proprietor of a bus service, which passed the property, for the sale of the land. The commencement of the Civil War broke off the negotiations and the two partners in the firm of lawyers with whom Mrs Armfield did her business left Washington, one, it is thought, proceeding south to join the Confederates. By the departure of the lawyers, Mrs Armfield lost her papers, which, so far, have not been recovered.

Inquiry has elicited the information that one died in 1862, but the whereabouts, if living, of the other have not been discovered. Investigation has shown that the only public records in connection with the property are those proving the conveyance to the Braidwoods, and further inquiries are being made to find by what title the present occupiers hold the land, and also to discover the whereabouts of the missing papers put into the custody of the legal firm. At present there is an electric power plant on the estate, run by the tram-way company, and among the buildings is included a college. The property is estimated to be worth millions of dollars, and, provided her claim can be sufficiently authenticated, Mrs Higgins has a windfall of immense value. Quite recently, by a missing friends' notice, which appeared in the Herald, Mrs Higgins was able to lay claim to a considerable sum of money left her by her aunt in England."

The above account was a follow-up to a small notice inserted in the 22 May 1902 edition of the same *Poverty Bay Herald* newspaper:

HIGGINS (ARMFIELD).

HENRY HIGGINS and Elizabeth, his wife (maiden name, Armfield), who some years since resided at Gisborne, or their representatives, are requested to communicate to their advantage with Messrs HEAD AND HILL, Solicitors, 3, Raymond Buildings, Gray's Inn, London, England.   953

From what can be gathered during research, Elizabeth Armfield the younger and Henry Higgins departed England for America in 1859. Henry Higgins was probably at that time a boyfriend of the younger Elizabeth. All we know about their time in America was given in the *Poverty Bay Herald* account already mentioned. We do not know whether Elizabeth was pregnant at the time of departing England, or she was already carrying a baby born out of wedlock. More research needs to be undertaken in that area to close the picture which is sketchy.

It appears that the younger Elizabeth Armfield and Henry Higgins proceeded to Boston, Massachusetts, where they might have married and settled down. They had four children, two boys and two girls. Of the four children, the firstborn Florence Henrietta Catherine Higgins was believed to have been born in Boston before the birth of their first son, Braidwood Thomas Higgins, who was born on 7 May 1862 at 30 Gouch Street, Boston. Of their two remaining children, Vernon Graham, was born in 1868 in San Francisco and the youngest daughter Lillie was born in Hawaii. From Hawaii, the Higgins family embarked the steamship Nevada bound for New Zealand, where arrived on 16 August 1871. The marriage of Elizabeth and Henry have yet to be confirmed as no registration can be found in either Britain or USA.

Henry Higgins was a teacher and he ran a private school in Ormond, Gisborne. He died in 1902 at the age of 70 years old and Elizabeth died on 17 December 1915. It was reported her age was 87, but according to her birth year of 1830, she was aged 85 at the time of her death. Her son Braidwood Thomas Higgins lived a long life and he died on 22 December 1954, aged 92 years old. His son, Braidwood Raymond Higgins, who was born on 26 April 1910, died in 1987.

As for Richard Braidwood Armfield, he travelled from England to the US, arriving in New York in 1851. His name was on the New York Passengers Lists for June 1851, and he arrived from England on the ship *Margaret Evans*. He was stated as 28 years old, but this was wrong. Richard might have lied or fiddled with his age as most people do in these days. He in reality was 23 years old at the time of his arrival in New York. It is of great interest to note that Richard left his mother and sister behind and this may indicate that he went to the US for a reason connected with the land matter, but no evidence is available to suggest this. What happened after his arrival is not known, and next there appeared a note from a firm of solicitors Sydney, Australia, in the Melbourne newspaper *The Argus* dated 11 June 1855:

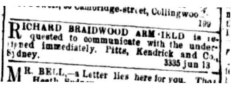

It appears that Richard Braidwood Armfield travelled to Australia from America and there is a New York Passengers List for August to September 1855 noting R B Armfield arriving on the ship *W. Lapscott*. His stated age was 28 years old, which would be correct because he was a month short of his actual 28th birthday. Another item of interest is that he stated his nationality as American, indicating that he had been given US citizenship since his initial arrival in the US in 1851. It is possible to match his arrival in the US in 1855 with the note in *The Argus* and Richard might have alerted his mother and sister in England about the land matter. Richard, however, did not seem to have done much about the land claim.

Next Richard was noted as having joined the Confederate Army when the US Civil War broke out. He was taken on as a Private in Waul's Texas Legion in 1861, and he later became a Sergeant, serving with the Texas Heavy Artillery Regiment under Waul. His military service came to an end in the following year when he was killed in battle in Holly Springs, Mississippi, on 24 October 1862. He was buried in Hillcrest cemetery.

The reason why the Armfield family came to the United States was to attend to the land claim matter and this seemed to have been forgotten for a long while until a query was made by a firm of lawyers, Cardozo Brothers of 96 Broadway, New York, into the whereabouts of Richard Braidwood Armfield in 1895.

Seven years after the query by the legal firm, Cardozo Brothers, the land claimant, Elizabeth Higgins, was finally contacted in New Zealand via the *Poverty Bay Herald.*

The Braidwood/Armfield claim on the land appears to have origins stretching back to the days of Colonel Thomas Bolling of Cobbs, Chesterfield County, Virginia. He had three children who were born deaf. They were John (b.31 January 1761), Mary (b.27 January 1765) and Thomas (b.1 July 1766). In 1771 Bolling send his son John to Edinburgh to attend the Braidwood Academy for the Deaf and Dumb which was founded in 1760 by Thomas Braidwood. Bolling received letters from his son and he was pleased with John's education and progress and as a consequence he sent Mary and Thomas to join John at the school in 1775. The duration of the education for each child was supposed to be 5 years, but due to the war between Britain and America, the three Bolling children were kept on and provided for by Braidwood until 1783, when it was deemed safe for the children to sail home.

There was a snag: Bolling never fully paid Braidwood for the education, board, clothing, necessities and upkeep of sorts for his three children between May 1777 and 9 April 1783, when the children were returned to America. As a result of Bolling's non-payment to settle the accounts, Braidwood put in a claim for monies owed and sued Thomas Bolling.

There exists in the Library of Virginia in Richmond, Virginia, copies of Colonel Thomas Bolling's papers referring to the Braidwood v. Bolling saga:

Thomas Braidwood v. Thomas Bolling
Federal Circuit Court, Ended Cases (unrestored), B-C, Box 39, 1797.

Thomas Braidwood was represented by an attorney whose office was probably based in Washington DC and there is no information available whether the monies recovered from Col. Thomas Bolling were sent to England, or used to purchase land in the US. The latter seems possible following Richard and Elizabeth Armfield's involvement with the land claim saga.

A note on the Braidwood v. Bolling legal situation is in Appendix 7.

The Last Will and Testament of Thomas Braidwood

In the Name of God, Amen. I Thomas Braidwood of the parish of St. John, Hackney, near London, being thro' the divine goodness at this time of sound and perfect mind and memory, do make this my last will and testament in manner following viz: first, I will that all my just debts and funeral expenses be fully paid. Secondly as by a deed bearing date the twenty sixth day of April one thousand seven hundred and ninety three I settled upon my dear wife Frances Betty Braidwood the annual sum of fifty pounds sterling to be paid her after my decease during her life. I will that it be said as the word bears I also hereby desire and direct my executors to sell all my household goods and chattels as soon as convenient and out of that sum they may bring to pay my said wife sixty pounds over and above the said word and to lay out the Remainder in the purchase of stock in out of funds public where stock must go to the Rest and Residue of my estate and all the Rest and Residue of my estate whether consisting of sons mortgage bonds or other securities of relative matter or kind soever or wheresoever situated I give and bequeath unto my executors & executrix named or the survivors of them, and to the executors and executrix of the survivors in trust for the following uses intents and purposes viz; that they constantly divide all the interests and profits of the said rest and residue of my said estate into six equal shares an pay to my daughter Elizabeth Ward, wife of Mr William Ward, surgeon in Durham, during her life for the behoof of herself and her two daughters Margaret and Catherine at her sole discretion, two of those said shares and her receipt shall be a sufficient discharge but should she die or become the wife of a future husband during the minority of her said daughters, the shares shall be applied to the education and maintenance of the said daughters till they shall attain the age of twenty one years or otherwise for their advantage according to the discretion of my executors and when they shall attain that age they have their mother's share paid into their own hands and their receipt shall be a good marriage. Should either of them die unmarried or without children, the survivor shall be her son and should both die unmarried or without children, then shall the children of the deceased John Braidwood be their heirs jointly. I also will that the remaining four of the said six equal shares be constantly paid to my daughter Isabella Braidwood, widow of John Braidwood, late of the parish of Hackney, deceased during her life for the behoof of herself and four children Thomas, John, Henrietta Stewart and Elizabeth, at her own discretion and her receipt shall be a sufficient discharge but should one die or marry during the minority of any of the said children, the said shares shall be thereinforth applied to their education and maintenance of the children till they attain the age of twenty one years and as they shall attain that age respectively, they shall have their shares paid into their own hands and should any of them die in minority or unmarried or without children, the share or shares of such child or children shall become the property in equal shares of those who survive and should they all die in minority, or unmarried or without children, then shall the said Elizabeth Ward's said children be those heirs equally and all the Rest and Residue of my said estate shall be equally divided among my grandchildren where they shall all have attained the age of twenty one years. Lastly I do hereby appoint George Dennis of Milk End Old Town in the parish of Stepney, Gentleman, and Samuel John Earle of the Strand, Engraver, executors of this my will. Revoking all four wills made by me, I declare this to be my last will and testament in writing whereof I the said Thomas Braidwood have set my hand and seal this 20th day of February 1799 in the thirty ninth year of the Reign of our sovereign Lord George third and in the year of our Lord one thousand seven hundred and ninety nine. (signed) Thomas Braidwood. Sealed, published and declared by the testator Thomas Braidwood as his last will and testament written with his own hand and signed by him in our presence — N.I.S. Croix — G. Powell.

I hereby direct that this paper may be taken as a Codicil to my will dated the twentieth day of February one thousand seven hundred and ninety nine. I give and bequeath to my dear wife Frances Betty Braidwood for her absolute use all the provisions at Hackney granted by loan from Jonathan Glover to William Hunt dated the 12th January 1792 and where I have demised to John Fagorty and William Bright (in lieu of their fifty pounds per annum settled upon her by me by deed dated 26th day of April 1793 during her life) to hold to my said wife for the new remainder of the time of thirty one years. Therein witness my hand this 10th day of March 1804 – (signed) Thomas Braidwood. Signed in the presence of us C. Parsons — H. Hibberd — Witnesses.

A Codicil to my Will whereas my two grandchildren Margaret and Catherine Ward are now amply provided for by the death of their father's uncle Mr Ward of Norton, my will and pleasure now is and I do hereby give and bequeath that proportion of my estate given to my said Grand Children by my Will unto my daughter Isabella Braidwood that interest thereof to be enjoyed by her during her Life and at her decease the said property is to be divided amongst her four Children Thomas, John, Henrietta Stewart and Elizabeth Braidwood in equal shares and I do further give and bequeath unto my wife Mrs Frances Betty Braidwood the sum of ten pounds per annum during her life in addition to the sum of fifty pounds already given to her as stated in my last will and I do hereby appoint my Grandson Thomas Braidwood to be one of my executors conjointly with those gentlemen nominated in my said last will as witness my hand and seal this 22nd day of October 1805 – (signed) *Thomas Braidwood* — signed, sealed and delivered in the presence of James Delegal — Mercer Roberts.

This Will was proved at London with two Codicils the twenty second day of April in the Year of Our Lord one thousand eight hundred and seven before the Worshipful Samuel Pearce Parson Doctor of Laws and Surrogate of the highest honourable Sir William Wynne Surrogate Doctor of Laws, Master Keeper or Commissary of the Prerogative Court of Canterbury lawfully constituted by the oaths of George Dennis and Samuel John Earle, the executors named in the said Will and Thomas Braidwood the grandson of the deceased and the executor named in the second Codicil to whom administration was granted of all and singular the Goods, Chattels and Credits of the said deceased, they having been first sworn duly to administer.

The Last Will and Testament of Isabella Braidwood

This is the last Will and Testament of me Isabella Braidwood of Great Ormond Street in the county of Middx, widow. I wish my just debts and my funeral and testamentary expenses to be first paid. I give to my son Thomas Braidwood five guineas for a mourning Ring as a testimony of my affection for him. I give the like sum for the like purpose to my son John Braidwood and I particularly desire that he may be informed that this bequest to him was left by his own affectionate mother as a proof of her own forgiveness for the anxieties he has unfortunately occasioned her and as an assurance of her tender regard towards him which will last whilst she has the power of affection. I give and bequeath all the rest and residue of my property and estate goods, chattels and effects of what nature or whatsoever and whichsoever may be unto my daughter Elizabeth Braidwood. To hold to her her executors' advice and assigns absolutely forever. I appoint George Phillips Towry of Somerset House esqr and Daniel Garrett of Gower Street, Bedford Sqr esqr and my said daughter executors and executrix of this my will. In writing whereof I have hereunto set my hand & seal this twenty eighth day of January 1815. Isabella Braidwood signed, sealed, published and declared by the said Isabella Braidwood as and for her last will and testament in the presence of us who at her request have hereunto subscribed our names as witnesses.

Chas Watkins, 5 Pump Court, Temple.
Hannah Manvers Stratton, 7 Ormond Street.

Isabella Braidwood of Nº 7 Great Ormond Street do request and desire that my daughter Elizabeth Braidwood of the same place may not consider Daniel Garrett esqr of Gower Street as an executor but that anyone she may wish to act with herself and our faithful friend & benefactor G. P. Towry esqr of Somerset Place.

(signed) Isabella Braidwood
March 3rd 1816.

20th day of December 1820

Appeared personally John Gordon of Birmingham in the county of Warwick, banker, and Thomas Braidwood of Edgbaston near Birmingham aforesaid gentleman and jointly made oath as follows, that they know and were well acquainted with Isabella Braidwood, late of Great Ormond Street in the county of Middlesex, widow before and at the time of her oath, and also with her manner & character of handwriting and subscription having frequently seen her write and subscribe her name, and having now carefully viewed and perusing the paper writing hereunto annexed purporting to be and containing a Codicil to the last will and testament of the said deceased, the said codicil being in the words following "I Isabella Braidwood of No 7 Great Ormond St. do request and desire that my daughter Elizth Braidwood may not consider Daniel Garratt Esq as an executor but choose any one she may wish to act with her and our faithful friend and benefactor G. P. Towry Esq. of Somerset Place." They this day do depose that they do verily and in their conscientious believe the whole body sizes and contents of the said Codicil to be all of the proper hand writing of the said deceased. (signed) John Gordon. Thomas Braidwood.

Same day the said John Gordon and Thomas Braidwood were duly sworn to the truth of this affidavit before me John Darwall, Commissioner.

Proved at London with a Codicil 11 July 1822 before the Judge by the oath of Elizabeth Braidwood, spinster, the daughter and surviving executor to whom administration was granted having both first sworn Commission duly to administer.

An Extract from Bingham's *Essays by the Deaf and Dumb*

Henry Brothers Bingham was probably the last outsider to work as a teacher of the Deaf under the Braidwood family. He was engaged by Thomas Braidwood, Isabella's son, as a trainee teacher with his private pupils. Being close to Braidwood and sharing intimate conversations, it is clear from Bingham's account in the Introduction in his book that the accurate date of the opening of the Braidwood Academy was at the beginning of 1760 - see below:

but nothing of any moment was accomplished until Mr. Braidwood, of Edinburgh, in the beginning of the year 1760, opened an establishment for this afflicted portion of our fellow creatures, from which have sprung all the present institutions of the kind in Great Britain and Ireland.

At the latter part of the same year (1760), the Abbe de l'Epeé also opened a school for the deaf and dumb; and each of these philanthropists carried on their respective establishments for the space of five years, without being conscious of the existence of a competitor in any part of the world.

It would be presumptuous in me to attempt to speak of the merits of these great and good men; suffice it to say, that Arnot, in his history of Edinburgh, Dr. Johnson, in his tour to the Hebrides, Lord Monboddo, in his origin and progress of language, and Pennant, in his tour through Scotland, have each individually made most honourable mention of the former, and France has erected a national monument to the

MONUMENTAL INSCRIPTION

GRAVESTONE No. 16

St Thomas Square Cemetery

Mrs Margaret Braidwood
Died May 30th 1791
Aged 77 years.

Also William Braidwood, son of
John and Isabella Braidwood &
Grandson of the above died 13th August 1794
Aged 17 months and 2 days.

Likewise Mr John Braidwood
Father of the above Wm. Braidwood
Departed this life 24th September 1798
Aged 42 years.

Also Mr Thomas Braidwood
Husband of the above Mrs M. Braidwood
Died Oct. 23rd 1806 in the 91st year of his age.

Likewise
Henrietta Stewart Braidwood
Daughter of John and Isabella Braidwood
Died Sept. 27th 1809 in the 23rd. Year of her age.

The Braidwoodian Pupils

It was no easy task trying to track down the pupils of both the Braidwood Academy and the Braidwood Institution. An extremely large number of pupils were deaf. It is very well known that Thomas Braidwood did take on a good number of hearing and hard-of-hearing people with severe speech impediments and, where found, they are included here. Only forty-six pupils have been identified and they are found to have been at either the Braidwood Academy or the Braidwood Institution and they are listed as follows, along with sources:

Charles Shirreff	(*Gentleman's Magazine* & various sources)
John Douglas	(*Gentleman's Magazine*)
Francis H. Mackenzie	(Seaforth Muniments, Colonial Office Records, W. R. Roe's *Peeps into the Deaf World* – 1917)
Robert Burns	(*Blackwood's Edinburgh Magazine*)
John Philip Wood	(*Gentleman's Magazine* & various sources)
Anna Colmer Rogers	(*Gentleman's Magazine* & Dorset History Centre)
Mary Rogers	(*Gentleman's Magazine* & Dorset History Centre)
Elizabeth Metcalfe	(*Gentleman's Magazine* & Shropshire Archives)
John Bolling	(*The Association Review*, Vol. 2, 1900)
Mary Bolling	(*The Association Review*, Vol. 2, 1900)
Thomas Bolling Jnr	(*The Association Review*, Vol. 2, 1900)
John Goodricke	(W. R. Roe's *Peeps into the Deaf World* – 1917 & various sources)
Charles Green	(*Vox oculis subjecta* – 1783)
Archibald Douglas	(*Caledonian Mercury*, Monday 14 September 1789)
Alexander Inglis	(Deaflore)
Henry Fox	(*Recollections of Table Talk of Samuel Rogers* - 1856)
Thomas Cooley	(David Breslin)
Jane Poole	(Court of Probate Proceedings & Shropshire Archives)
Anne Walcott	(Deaflore and Walcott Papers - Shropshire Archives)
John Creasy	(Various sources & Deaflore)
Sarah Dashwood	(*Notes and Queries* – Feb 1974 & Shropshire Archives)
Mary Brunton	(*Newcastle Courant*, p.2, Sat 19 September 1772)

James Watt	(Presbyterian Dissenters Meeting House Minute Book – Hackney Archives & Deaflore)
Charlotte Carter	(Papers of Redbourne Hall, Lincolnshire Archives)
Lister Sagar	(Bookseller's Inventory – for sale: 1777 letter printed on Internet - 2008)
Margaret Gibson	(*Edgbaston Institution Annual Report*, p56, 1823)
Isabella Gibson	(Ditto)
Mr Harris	(Deaflore & Thomas Arrowsmith's painting)
Mr Flaxman	(Deaflore & Thomas Arrowsmith's painting)
Thomas Arrowsmith	(Deaflore & Thomas Arrowsmith's painting)
James Woodfall, son of George Woodfall	(Public Advertiser)
Ann Barksdale	(Alexander Hewat's 1820 letter to G. Edwards)
Unidentified Mole-catcher	(Deaflore & *Edinburgh Messenger* no. 8, 1844)
Miss Graham of Airth Castle	(W. R. Roe's *Peeps into the Deaf World* – 1917)
Anne Burnett Craigie	(W. R. Roe's *Peeps into the Deaf World* – 1917)
Richard Edensor	(W. R. Roe's *Peeps into the Deaf World* – 1917)
John Heathcote	(Heathcote Family Account – Warren & Son, 1899)
Charles B. A. Heathcote	(Heathcote Family Account – Warren & Son, 1899)
Andrew Hay	(W. R. Roe's *Peeps into the Deaf World* – 1917)
Son of Sir Alexander Keith	(W. R. Roe's *Peeps into the Deaf World* – 1917)
Pelham Maitland	(*Gentleman's Magazine* & Heriot's Hospital Records)
St. George Randolph	(*The Association Review, Vol. 2, 1900*)
Girl from Shepton Mallet	(*Gentleman's Magazine*)
Student at Edinburgh University	(*Vox oculis subjecta* - 1783)
Dudley Ryder, Viscount Sandon	(*House of Commons 1820-1832, VI* – D. R. Fisher)
Daughter of R. F.	*Monthly Review, LXIX, 1783, pages 526-527.*

There were more pupils but both the lack of school records kept by the Braidwood family and the disgraceful failure of past writers to show respect to deaf children and deaf adults by not naming them using their full names in their articles and reports contributed to the dearth of the list of pupils. Deaflore had it that there were Braidwoodian pupils named Harris and Flaxman, both of whom were well acquainted with Thomas Arrowsmith, and Arrowsmith himself was said to have been a pupil at Braidwood Academy. However, like hearing oral history that had never been written, these names will have to be just that – sources from Deaflore. If academia accepts the oral histories of the hearing as valid and had them written down, then hitherto unwritten sources from Deaflore will likewise have to be accepted and written down unless evidence to the contrary can be found to challenge these sources – hence the names listed here. Of the above list, those listed below are unknown and very little or no further information on them can be found:

Richard Edensor, the girl from Shepton Mallet, James Woodfall (1802-1820), the son of the editor of Public Advertiser, daughter of R.F., Mr Harris, Mr Flaxman, a student at Edinburgh university, John Douglas (Braidwood's second pupil who commenced in October 1763), James Watt, Alexander Inglis and the son of Sir Alexander Keith.

For the rest of the pupils information was obtained and is included in the following pages. It is hoped that the information, no matter how sparse, will provide a good base for future researchers should they become interested in continuing the research into the history of Braidwood and/or his pupils.

Unidentified mole catcher

Edinburgh Messenger VIII   Tuesday 23 July 1844:

> The first taught mute your correspondent ever saw was in Perthshire, above or almost 50 years ago. This person was under the tuition of a Mr Braidwood but how long I cannot say. He was very smart and amazingly quick with his slate pencil. He supported himself by mole-catching and owing to his dexterity and success he was much employed. After realizing a little money in that way, he got married, and took up a

large inn on the banks of the river Spey. A friend of his told me that he had a letter from him which he stated among other things, that he had a fine son, and added, with glowing parental feeling, "He can speak."

Anna Colmer Rogers and Mary Rogers

Both sisters were daughters of the Rev Richard Colmer Rogers, the son of the Rev Richard Rogers. He was born in Sutton, Dorset, and apart from studying at Oxford for qualifications and ordination, he spent his whole very circumscribed life in small thinly populated Dorset villages around Blandford Forum. He was curate at Shroton and from there he went on to hold multiple livings consecutively and concurrently till he died at Child Okeford in March 1812. He did nothing of note beyond retaining a church register for 19 years after leaving the church.

He married Eliza Henville at Abbotsbury on 8 March 1757 before he was ordained. Eliza was to become better known as Elizabeth.

Anna Colmer Rogers was born deaf at Abbotsbury and she was baptised on 24 October 1758. She started at Braidwood's Academy in late May/early June 1767 with her younger sister. There is a burial record in the Shroton Registers of Ann Rogers, daughter of RC and Elizabeth at Edinburgh for 17 October 1767. This indicates she died at the age of nine years while still a pupil at the Braidwood Academy at Dumbie House, and she had only been at the school for no more than 5 months. It is believed, although not proven, that Anna was badly affected by the cold climate in Edinburgh as she was used to the warmer conditions in Dorset.

Mary Rogers was born deaf at Child Okeford on 6 Jan 1762, and her age had always been mixed up by various visiting writers. John Hepburn wrote in *The Scots Magazine* (28 July 1767) that...

> *Two ladies, one of nine and the other of seven, daughters of the Rev. Mr. Rogers of Shroton...*

In fact, the younger daughter, Mary, was 5 years 6 months old at that time! She was nearly 11 years old at the time of Thomas Pennant's visit to the Braidwood Academy during his tour of Scotland. Mary must have looked older than her actual age.

Very little is known of Mary but according to unnamed newspaper cutting in the author's possession, Mary left the Braidwood Academy in the summer of 1776 at the age of fourteen to reside with her parents at Child Okeford. It was said that she fitted in very well with the local community and became very popular. Other than that, all that is known is there is a church record showing that she was buried at Child Okeford on 14 June 1810.

Robert Burns

Blackwood's Edinburgh Magazine Vol. 12, 1822, page 302, Death:

> Nov. 1. At Hamilton, *Robert Burns, Esq.*, of Westport, Bothwell. This gentleman was the fourth pupil of the celebrated Mr Braidwood of the Edinburgh Deaf and Dumb Institution when, at an early period in life, he made such astonishing proficiency, that he felt but very little inconvenience from the want of hearing, being naturally a genius of great perception. So sensible was the deceased of the advantage he derived from the Deaf and Dumb Institution of Edinburgh, that he has left £100 for its support.

[The writer who contributed the above obituary needs to be corrected; Robert Burns was pupil at the Braidwood Academy, not at the Edinburgh Deaf and Dumb Institution which was run by Robert Kinniburgh.]

Robert Burns (1754-1822) was born deaf at Westport, Bothwell, Lanarkshire. In Roe's *Peeps into the Deaf World,* Burns mentioned that he remembered the day when Dr Samuel Johnson visited the school; he patted young Burns on the head and told him he was a good boy whilst Mr Boswell was in attendance, taking notes. On leaving the Braidwood Academy, Burns never seemed to have taken on a career or a profession; he was apparently a very wealthy man and lived the life of an *Esquire*, a gentleman.

At the age of 46, Burns married one Margaret Nisbet in Edinburgh on 8 December 1800. He was listed as "Esquire" on the marriage register.

Pelham Maitland

Nothing is known about Pelham Maitland except for the minutes of a meeting of the Governors of Heriot's Hospital which took place on 15 February 1773. He was the first known and recorded poor deaf person to be educated free of charge by Thomas Braidwood. Heriot's Hospital contributed a sum of £10 annually for Maitland's needs such as clothing and food.

Initially Pelham, a son of a poor shoemaker Obrian Maitland, was accepted on 19 October 1772 for an education in Heriot's Hospital. When it was discovered that Pelham could neither follow nor keep pace with other pupils, the governors decided to place him at the Braidwood Academy and Thomas Braidwood generously accepted his admission for free education. (see copy of Heriot's Hospital minutes dated 15 February 1773 on the next page.)

Andrew Hay

Andrew Hay was born deaf in 1764, the son of a Banff-born merchant, James Hay. Between 1770 and 1772, he began his education at the Braidwood Academy. Upon leaving school, Andrew Hay set himself up as a freelance painter and decorator. Although he lived permanently at 20 Dublin Street, Edinburgh, he traded from 12 Clyde Street, Edinburgh. His business thrived and was very profitable. Among his work contracts, Andrew was awarded the tender to decorate the new Edinburgh Deaf and Dumb Institution premises at Chessel's Court in the southern part of the historic Royal Mile for the sum of £62-17-6d. Andrew was a regular subscriber to the Edinburgh Deaf and Dumb Institution, supporting the school in every way he could.

Andrew never married and died on 5 August 1844 at the age of 80 years, He was interred within the Thomas Innes of Montielle plot in the 4th division of the graveyard at Greyfriars Churchyard in Edinburgh. Andrew Hay is remembered as one of Britain's earliest deaf businessmen.

15th February 1773

found to be sound and free of Scrophula,
but deaf and dumb are of opinion that
it is improper that a Boy in these
circumstances should be brought into
the House, but Because of his peculiar
Situation, and as Mr. Braidwood who
has shown so extraordinary a skill in
that way has agreed to teach the Boy
to read and write gratis (they authorize
the Treasurer of the Hospital to pay
to the said Pelham Maitland the Sum of
Ten pound Ster! yearly by such pro-
-portions as he shall Judge reasonable
for maintaining him out of the House
and that in full for maintainance educa-
-tion and Cloathing and every thing else
he can demand of the Hospital excepting
an apprentice fee when he shall be bound
out to a master in the same way as the
other Boys of the Hospital

Copy of page 259 of the minutes of meeting of governors of Heriot's Hospital
agreeing to send Pelham Maitland to the Braidwood Academy.

Courtesy of George Heriot's Trust, Edinburgh

207

Lister Sagar

Bookseller: C. R. Johnson Rare Book Collections (London) — advertised for sale the following on the internet in 2008:
Bookseller Inventory No. 450-48
Price £450 + £3.35 Shipping
For Sale - Letter signed to his father Richard Sagar of Colne, Lancashire.

Edinburgh, 30 June, 1777.

I got here yesterday morning by 8 o'clock and found my brother in perfect health. He seems to be very happy in his present situation, having gained the esteem of the whole family by his good behaviour, in so much that they have never had the occasion to find fault with him since he came. His degree of hearing is so small that they are obliged to teach him by the motion of the lips, consequently his proficiency in speaking is not so great as I expected, yet he is greatly improved for the time in understanding how to give an answer to anything I ask him in writing, in so much that in a few months longer he will be able to compose a Letter himself or to answer one that's wrote on any common subject, so as to render him capable of transacting the Business of a Counting House, which, undoubtedly, will be worth all the trouble and expense.

I only repent we did not send him 5 or 6 years sooner, which, if we had done, I make no doubt but he would have learned to speak fluently too, but now I rather doubt whether it will be possible to teach him to converse intelligibly with a stranger, but if he gets capable to convey his Ideas in writing (it will be a great blessing) and I make no doubt but he will do this in a short time. For Mr Braidwood and his assistants, I believe, have taken a deal of pains with him, as all of them seem to discover a great liking for him.

William Sagar

Lister Sagar was born in May 1759 in Great Marsden, Colne, Lancashire. He was the son of the wealthy merchant Richard Sagar and his wife Sally, and a brother to William Sagar (1751-1809) who was deeply involved in the spread of Methodism with John Wesley.

At the time of the 1777 letter, Lister was over 18 years of age. The content of the letter appears to indicate that the family initially did not send him to school or pay for him to receive specialised individualised education and they left it too late in the day to repair the damage by the time they sent him to Braidwood's Academy.

John Bolling, Mary Bolling and Thomas Bolling

All information below was taken from Alexander Graham Bell's *Historical Notes* in *The Association Review*, Vol. 2, 1900, unless otherwise stated.

John, Mary and Thomas Bolling Jnr. were the children of Major Thomas Bolling, of Cobbs, Chesterfield County, Virginia in America. They were all deaf from birth, or earliest infancy. The eldest, John Bolling who was born on 31 Jan 1761, was sent to the Braidwood Academy in Edinburgh in 1771, becoming the first American deaf person to receive an education. Mary, who was born on 27 Jan 1765, and Thomas Jnr., who was born on 1 July 1766, followed in 1775. Mary, known as Polly among her family members, was the first deaf American female to receive an education.

John Bolling

The three Bolling children received a good well-rounded education under the tuition of John Braidwood at the Braidwood Academy. They all remained at the school during the War of Independence between Britain and Colonial America and they all returned to America in July 1783. The quality and standard of education the three children received impressed their father and hearing brother, Col. William Bolling, who wrote a letter to one Joseph D. Tyler in December 1841 (published in the *Southern Churchman* on 18 March 1842, Vol. III, No. 8) saying:

> "John, the oldest, was sent by my father in the year
> 1771 to Edinburgh, and placed under the care and

tuition of John Braidwood; Thomas and Mary followed him in 1775; they all remained at his school during the Revolutionary War, and all returned to Cobbs, in Chesterfield Co., Va., the then residence of my father, in July 1783.

"John died about three months after his return. Thomas' acquirements were most extraordinary; he was a ready penman, of nice discriminating judgement, of scrupulous integrity in all his transactions, his intelligence and tact in communication such as to attract the attention, entertain and amuse every company in which he associated, with the manners of the most polished gentleman. His articulation so perfect, that his family, his friends, and the servants understood him in conversation , or in reading aloud, as well as they could any other person; and he possessed the faculty of modulating his voice from a low whisper to a loud call. No person would understand him at first; every one would more or less perfectly in proportion to the time they were together and the desire felt to do so. My sister's acquirements were equal to his, though her voice was not so pleasant; yet she was cheerful, intelligent, entertaining and industrious. She died in 1826; my brother in 1836, in the seventieth year of his age."

On page 270 of *The Association Review* Vol. 2, 1900, two letters from John Bolling were published. The first, written when John was 10 years old in 1771:

My dear Mamma:

I am very well and very happy, because I can speak, and read. My Uncle and Aunt are very kind to me; they give me many fine things. I hope this will find you all well.

I am, my dear mamma,
Your most loving son,

JOHN BOLLING.
St. Leonards, 26th November 1771.

John wrote another letter to his mother in March 1775 when he was fourteen years old and it showed not only a remarkable command and standard of English, but the development and maturity of the boy. The letter was written not long before his sister Mary and younger brother Thomas joined him at his school in that year:

> My dear Mamma: Your kind letter made me very happy, as I had got none for a Long Time. I was wishing very much to know how yourself, my good Papa, Brothers, Sisters, and all friends were. I wrote often. I was very sorry to be told by your kind Letter that my Uncle Gay is so in bad health. I am very sorry that my Sister Polly has met with such a Misfortune, but hope she will soon get the better of it, and retain the use of her Leg, so as to be able to come over here with my dear Brother Tom. I will be very kind to them, and do them all the service I can. I have been long expecting to see them, and shall be glad how soon they come. I am obliged to Mr. McKenzie for his good report of me. I thank you kindly for the care you are pleased to say that is taken of my mare and colts. Pray give my love to my Uncle and Aunt Buchanan, and tell them I always remember their kindness, and shall always be glad to hear of their welfare. I am much obliged to you for the Ruffles you sent me, and desire my best thanks to Miss Deans for the trouble she took in sewing and hemming them so prettily for me. I had no need of them to make me think of you, as I often think with pleasure, of the happiness I shall enjoy with you all when I come home. I had no Letter from Mrs. Hyndman since she went to Bath, but I expect one soon. Mr. Brisbain and Mr. Lindsay have not called for me yet. I wrote to my Papa the day before I received your Letter. Please give my duty to my dear Papa, love to my Brothers & Sisters and kind Compliments to all friends. Mrs. and the two Misses Braidwood and all friends desire their kind Compliments.
>
> I am leaving to draw and my Master says I do very well.

I am, dear mamma, your most loving son,

JOHN BOLLING
St. Leonards, 2nd March 1775.
Mrs. Bolling,   At Cobbs, Virginia.

There exists a copy of letter from William Bolling to Thomas Braidwood dated October 1783. An extract from this letter reads:

"My children all arrived at Hampton [Virginia] very well on 7th July, after a ten weeks passage, where I met them, and got home with them, on the 14th since which [we] have experienced a great deal of horror. They were all taken sick soon after getting home, and [we] have had the misfortune to loose [sic] my poor Dear Son Jon. He was taken with a Bilious Fever on 29th Agst. and struggled with his disorder with as much patience as ever a poor soul did, 'till the 11th October at which time he expired."

Bilious Fever is now an obsolete term for gynogenic infection. It appears that John actually suffered from Pyaemia, which is defined as blood poisoning by pus-forming bacteria which are emitted from an abscess. This condition sometimes leads to formation of numerous abscesses which may be fatal.

The following obituary notice of Thomas Bolling Jnr., written by his nephew, Judge Robertson, appeared in the *Richmond Enquirer*, on the 18th of February 1836:

"Died at Gaymont, the residence of John H. Bernard, Esq., on the 11th ult., Mr. Thomas Bolling, son of Thomas Bolling of Cobbs, in the sixty-ninth year of his age. To him nature in her providence denied the sense of hearing — and of consequence the gift of speech; and with them the thousand privileges and blessings that come of unrestrained social converse, and of the myriad sounds of created things. Yet thus disabled, her compensating gifts, seconded by favourable circumstances, conspired greatly to qualify these disadvantages, and to render him a very remarkable man.

"Placed at an early age under the tuition of the celebrated Braidwood, of Edinburgh, his naturally fine understanding was rapidly developed. He read with pleasure, especially such books as treated of life or described natural scenery — composed and wrote in a particular yet clear and graphic style, and achieved in attaining an artificial faculty of speech, almost equal to the natural (if I may so speak) the most signal triumph over constitutional infirmity that probably has ever been accomplished by a Mute.

"Uniting to these achievements, great vivacity of disposition, polished and graceful manners, unequalled powers of imitation, and almost intuitive perception of the meaning of the others, he was the admiration and wonder of strangers, and the delight of an extensive connection and friends. They will long deplore a loss that no time can supply."

After the death of Thomas Bolling Jnr., a paper was found among his effects, written by himself, purporting to be his last Will and Testament. This, although not witnessed, was admitted to probate upon satisfactory identification of the handwriting. A copy of the will, with attached certificates, is preserved in the Volta Bureau; and by the courtesy of the Hon. John Hitz (Supt.) these documents are reproduced here:

WILL OF THOMAS BOLLING (Jr), WRITTEN BY HIMSELF

"I, Thomas Bolling, son of the late Thomas Bolling of Cobbs, in Chesterfield Co., do make and publish this my last Will and Testament.

"First: I do hereby annul and cancel as fully and entirely as if the same had ever been written, all and every former will or writing that I may before this have signed, and I do hereby particularly cancel a will, or deed, which was brought to me many years since by Cousin Mr. David Meade Randolph, who prevailed and persuaded me to sign it. I have wrote to get this

213

back, but cannot get it. This makes me much unhappy. It has been long my wish to leave my Legacy to my nephew, William Albert Bolling, as it was always the intention of my sister Polly, to leave her legacy to our niece, Mary Bolling. I am now told her wish is disputed, and a law suit made to take it from her. Therefore, I now declare it my will that all the property that I may die possessed of, be the same in any bank stock, or money, in the hands of any of my relations, or other persons, and be the amount thereof what it may, shall be at my death paid into the hands of and received by my brother, Col. William Bolling, of Goochland Co., to be held by him as trustee for the benefit of my dear nephew, William Albert Bolling, his son, and his heirs forever, as my brother William is acquainted with the management of business, which my dear nephew, William Albert Bolling, his son, is not from the unfortunate circumstance of his being as well as myself and my dear sister Polly, born deaf and dumb. I do hereby by this my last Will and Testament, give and bequeath the whole and every part of the property and estate I may die possessed of, to my nephew, William Albert Bolling, and his heirs forever. I have about eighty-six shares in the banks, bought with the five thousand dollars that was in the hands of Capt. William Murray, of Grove Brook, in Amelia County, and four thousand dollars that was in Mr. David Meade Randolph's hands, and paid by my dear brother William Bolling. My nephew, Mr. John Robertson, trustee for me, receives the interest of my bank shares half yearly, and passes it to me.

"All these, my bank shares, and all other property, to be at my death, paid unto and received by my dear brother, William Bolling, as above, or his executor, or administrators, as trustee for the sole use and benefit of my dear nephew, William Albert Bolling, and his heirs forever. And I do hereby revoke, annul, and cancel any former will, deed or writing to the contrary, which may have been signed by me. And I do appoint

214

my dear brother, Col. William Bolling, Executor of this my last Will and Testament. The above written in my own hand, I do now sign and seal this thirteenth day of October, in the year of our Lord, one thousand eight hundred and twenty seven.

Th. BOLLING [SEAL]"

ACCOMPANYING CERTIFICATES

"At a General Court of Virginia, held at the Capitol, in the city of Richmond, on the 28th day of June 1837, this writing purporting to be the last Will and Testament of Thomas Bolling, late of Cobbs, deceased, was presented to the court by William Bolling, the Executor therein named; and there being no subscribing witnesses thereto, James B. Ferguson, Blair Bolling and Charles S. Gay, being sworn, severally deposed that they are well acquainted with the handwriting of the said Thomas Bolling, deceased, and verily believe that the said writing with the signature thereto, is wholly written with the decedent's own hand. And, at a General Court, held at the Capitol aforesaid, the twenty sixth day of June 1838, the said writing was ordered to be recorded as the true last Will and Testament of the said Thomas Bolling, deceased, and on the motion of the said William Bolling, the executor named in the said last Will and Testament, who made oath thereto, and together with George Woodson Payne, and Blair Bolling, his sureties (the first named of whom justified on oath as to his sufficiency), entered into and acknowledged a bond in the penalty of twenty-four thousand dollars, conditioned as the law directs, certificate is granted the said William Bolling for obtaining a probate of the said last Will and Testament in due form.

Teste

N. P. HOWARD, Clk.

"A Copy
Teste

Eustace Robinson, Clerk of the Circuit Court of the City of Richmond, and as such, according to law, keeper of the records of the late General Court of Virginia."

Thomas Bolling's last Will and Testament, written by him and without assistance from many people, is a lasting testimony to the standard and quality of education he received at the Braidwood Academy.

Mary Bolling died unmarried on 12 April 1826, ten years before her brother Thomas.

Charles Green

The fourth deaf American to attend Braidwood's Academy was Charles Green, who was born in 1772. He was the surviving son of Francis Green (1742-1809) who married his cousin Susanna. They had five children, of which two died in infancy and the other two died in accidents. Green wrote in *Vox oculis subjecta* that Charles was discovered deaf at around the age of six months and also that having been either born deaf , or having lost his hearing by sickness in earliest infancy, Charles could not at that time produce or distinguish any idea of the meaning of words whether spoken, written or in print. He also could not speak at all.

At the time of the war between Britain and Colonial America, Francis Green expressed his loyalty to Britain and he left Boston when it was evacuated by the rebels under General Howe. In 1775 his wife Susanna died. Green was always on the move around that time – in 1776 he was in Halifax, Nova Scotia, and in 1777 he was in New York, where he lost one of his sons in an accident. In 1778 Green was proscribed and banished. In 1779, he sent his son Charles to Edinburgh where he commenced his schooling in February 1780. Francis Green left America for England in 1780. The rest is as described in his seminal work *Vox oculis subjecta*, published in 1783. Charles was able to speak, sign, read and write in a short time after arriving at the Braidwood Academy, where he stayed for nearly six years. He returned home to Halifax in 1786. In the following year on 29 August 1787, Charles drowned while out shooting at Cole Harbour near Halifax.

Sarah Dashwood-King

The little girl who charmed and delighted Dr Samuel Johnson during his visit to the Braidwood Academy "... *quivering her fingers in a manner which I thought very pretty, but of which I know not whether it was art or play, multiplied the sum regularly in two lines, observing the decimal place...*" She came from a famous family based in West Wycombe. If Dr Johnson bothered to query her identity, he would have written something more about her and the academy. Her identity was not discovered until many years later when one Ralph E. Jenkins from Philadelphia, USA, contributed an article published in pages 59 to 60 in the February 1974 issue of *Notes and Queries*. Jenkins acquired a copy of the first edition of *Journey to the Hebrides* which once belonged to William Ambler, Recorder of the city of Durham and there was a date inscribed 1775 on the front free endpaper. In the book, beside Johnson's phrase "One of the young ladies..." Ambler put an asterisk and noted that the young lady was "*Miss Dashwood niece to the late Lord Le Despencer, as Mr Braidwood informed me.*" Ambler signed the note with his initials, apparently thinking it important enough to deserve authentication.

The late Lord Le Despencer was Sir Francis Dashwood. Baronet, of West Wycombe, Postmaster General, Chancellor of the Exchequer, and organiser of the "Knights of St Francis" at Medmenham Abbey — misnamed by tradition the Hellfire Club. Sir Francis assumed the title of 15th Baron Le Despencer in 1763 and died in 1781. Sir Francis also created the Hellfire Caves in West Wycombe by providing employment to the villagers in digging for materials for the new main road between West Wycombe and High Wycombe. After the completion of the main road, Sir Francis went on to build the Dashwood Mausoleum in 1765, using chalk and flint from the caves.

Sir Francis had two half-brothers; the elder Charles died unmarried in 1740. The younger, Sir John Dashwood-King, born in 1716, was a member of the inner circle at Medmenham Abbey and assumed the baronetcy after the death of Sir Francis.

Sarah Dashwood-King was the daughter of Sir John Dashwood-King by his marriage with Sarah Moore in 1761. Sarah Dashwood, as she is known among deaf historians, descended from an illustrious family lineage — she was fifth in direct descent from Anne Milton, sister of the great poet.

As was customary in all rich families from royalty down to the landed gentry, there were Walcot-Dashwood marriage settlements recorded from the sixteenth century. Settlements were arranged between father and prospective son-in-law. These "judicious marriages" could help a landowner extend his property and thus have more income from tenants and crops. Sir John Dashwood-King made a deal with the Rev. John Walcot of Bitterley. This settlement resulted in Sir John giving away his deaf daughter Sarah in marriage to her cousin the Rev. John Walcot, the son of Charles Walcot and Anne Levett.

Sarah Dashwood came with a large dowry and she married the Rev. John Walcot on 2 December 1788. Their marriage produced one son and three daughters viz: Sarah (b.1793), Charles Walcot (b.1794), Mary (bap.9 June 1795) and Catherine (bap.28 August 1797).

The Rev. John Walcot came into vast sums of money by his marriage to Sarah, but he spent his fortune, fell into debt and suffered great financial problems. John's situation was dire through his profligacy, his hunting and shooting hobbies, his hound-breeding, his horse and dog trading and the numerous servants involved. He was pursued by creditors and he once had to flee his home. The Dashwoods had to intervene, investigate and they eventually re-settled the whole Walcot-Dashwood agreement and financially restored stability.

Sarah Dashwood had a servant (and perhaps a number of servants) who were able to sign and therefore presented no problem in communication. She also had the company of friends like Elizabeth Metcalfe, Jane Poole and Ann Walcot, all Braidwoodian pupils. There may be a possibility that there were more Braidwoodian pupils from the area that have not yet been discovered. Sarah died on 22 March 1834 and the Rev. John Walcot followed on 23 November in the same year.

Elizabeth Metcalfe

Elizabeth Metcalfe was the only child of James Metcalfe and Mary Blakeway who married in the church of St. Michael and All Angels in the sparsely populated All Stretton on 1 July 1749. Elizabeth was baptised on 24 September 1755 by the curate Richard Wilding. James was a landowner and had a large estate from which he made good income.

Elizabeth was born deaf and she was sent to the Braidwood Academy in Edinburgh at the end of June 1767 when she was 12 years old. Within a month it was reported that her newly-acquired speech and pronunciation were excellent and could be distinctly understood. A year or so later Thomas Braidwood reported on her progress to her father, who replied that he could not believe what was reported – that she was able to speak, lipread, read and write. James Metcalfe dispatched two relatives to Edinburgh to verify Braidwood's claim and they reported back that it was true. Elizabeth wrote letters to her father, who looked on them as forgeries. James Metcalfe died in 1769, still suspicious of his daughter's achievements, which were later verified by Elizabeth's mother as true.

James Metcalfe left his entire estate to Elizabeth in his will and he appointed his wife her guardian as long as she remained a widow. After leaving the Braidwood Academy, it appeared that Elizabeth spent her life around the Church Stretton region, remaining at home, never having married despite her fabulous wealth. When Elizabeth was 57 years old, her mother passed away on 10 July 1812 at the age of 80. Not much is known about Elizabeth until the latter part of her life. Directory entries for Elizabeth in the various extant directories are few, but there is one in *Robson's Directory* for 1840 where she is listed under "Gentry." In 1839, business activities were growing in the town of Church Stretton and it was decided to pull down the old Market Hall, which was initially built in 1617, and replace it with a larger structure. Subscription lists were opened and persons were invited to contribute. Miss Metcalfe's first contribution was for £5.0.0. Names on this list were written in the collector's hand, but a year later the subscribers wrote their signatures themselves. Elizabeth, then 85 years old, wrote in a surprisingly clear hand as shown below.

Elizabeth Metcalfe's signature on Subscription list 1839.
Photo: Doreen E. Woodford. October 1997.

Elizabeth lived long enough to appear in the 1841 Census Return where she is shown living in the centre of the town of Church Stretton close to the Market Hall with two servants, Susannah Kyle aged 60 and Mary

219

Evans aged 23. Both the servants were remembered in Elizabeth's will which was proved in the Prerogative Court of Canterbury on 29 December 1841. Elizabeth died on 27 November 1841 at the age of 86 years. In the vestry of St Lawrence church, Church Stretton, hangs a board listing various charitable bequests to benefit the poor of the parish. This board shows Elizabeth having left in 1841 a sum of £100. These bequests were amalgamated by a charity Commission Scheme in 1907. Her bequest by then had increased to £108.5.1d and generated a year's interest of £2.4.0d. This matter also appears in her will.

MISS·E·METCALFE
bequeathed, 1841, to the Minister & Church Wardens of this parish the sum of 100£ the interest whereof to be paid, by them every new years day, unto and amongst the poor of the parish.

Part of Benefaction Board showing Elizabeth Metcalfe.
The church of St Lawrence, Church Stretton.
Photo: Doreen E. Woodford. October 1997.

Anne Walcot

Anne Walcot was born in Stoke St. Milborough, Shropshire, in 1792. Of her parents, Major William Walcot of the Moor married Catherine, daughter of his guardian the Rev. Charles Walcot, on 16 October 1788 at Bitterley. Whether Anne was born deaf or acquired deafness at an early age had not been recorded. It is believed that Anne attended the Braidwood Academy in Hackney in 1798 at the earliest.

In 1818 Anne Walcot married her cousin Charles Walcot (1795-1875), who later became Rector of Hopton Wafers in 1820. They had four sons — Charles, Charles Thomas, William Henry and Robert. On 24 August 1824, both Anne and her new-born son Robert, were recorded dead and on 26 August they were buried in the same coffin at Bitterley. Anne lived a very short and uneventful life, dead at the age of 32 years following complications in connection with the birth of her last son.

220

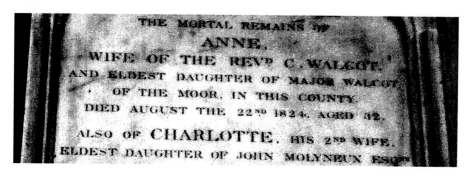

Part of the Walcot memorial tablet in the church of St Mary, Bitterley.
Photo: Doreen E. Woodford. November 1997.

Jane Poole

Very little is actually known about Jane Poole and the information on this deaf Braidwoodian pupil came mainly from David Buxton's contribution in the *Quarterly Review of Deaf Mute Education*, 1886 and a number of court case reports. It is known that she was born deaf in Ludlow in the county of Salop in July 1781 and she was christened on 1 August of the same year. She was the 6th daughter of James Poole and Ann Cooper who married on 28 July 1771 at Market Drayton. She had one brother and five sisters. Of her siblings, her sisters Mary Ann and the youngest sister Caroline were to play prominent roles in her life and death over family wills and finances. Jane attended the Braidwood Academy in Hackney at a young age. It was while at school that Jane acquired fingerspelling skills, becoming a very versatile dactylologist, using a mode of communication that would stand her in good stead in the last 20 years of her life. Upon leaving school, she lived a life of a spinster and she was an immensely wealthy person and in later years she became a constant sponsor of the Liverpool School for the Deaf which was then based at Oxford Street, East Liverpool. In the *Post Office Directory for 1856* she was listed under "Gentry" as Miss Poole of Broad Street, Ludlow. When she was about 60 years old, blindness crept in and she gradually became totally blind and lived as a deafblind person until her death on 10 April 1860.

Before she died and whilst deaf-blind, Jane wrote her last Will and Testament through fingerspelling via the use of interpreters. Her will was disputed upon her death by her widowed younger sister Caroline and this set the scene for a famous court case. The events surrounding the court case were outlined in Raymond Lee's article on Jane Poole which was published as a *Supplement* to volume 1, issue 1 of the British Deaf History Society's *Deaf History Journal* for April 1997. This article is reprinted here with reports of the court cases added and several alterations to the original publication to reflect latest facts unearthed during recent research in completing the work on Jane Poole.

Introduction

In the case of writing wills, the fact that a person suffered from a condition of being deaf and dumb did not, and still does not, affect that person's testamentary capacity in English Law: in fact, there never existed a law which debarred Deaf persons from writing their own wills. A totally illiterate deaf person was, and still is in the present day, permitted to make a will through a sign language interpreter or trusted friends and legal representatives, and the emphasis is on the word, *trusted*. In a predominately hearing world the wills of deaf people, literate or not, were sometimes regarded with suspicion due to hearing people's poor understanding and concept of deafness, and of what it was like to be Deaf. In the 18th and 19th centuries, Deaf people were looked down on with disdain at almost all levels of society in Britain. So little were hearing people's understanding and faith in Deaf people's intellectual abilities that they demanded Deaf people produce sufficient evidence to show that they understood their own actions and that they really comprehended the language of the testament. This terrible attitude of hearing people caused not only Deaf people but also hearing people to wrongly assume that a law stating that deaf people cannot write their own wills was in force - in reality, legal authorities made no attempt to dispel this impression and the wealthy saw this to their advantage, applying for powers of administration which gave them ample opportunities to create circumstances enabling them to gradually siphon off Deaf people's monies into their own coffers.

The research into the lives of four Salopian female pupils of the famous Braidwood Academy for the Deaf and Dumb yielded a tale of Jane Poole and her will battles, both when she was alive - and dead.

Society's Attitude Towards the Deaf.

In the 18th and 19th centuries, recorded accounts existed of society's attitudes towards the Deaf and many of these attitudes exposed how little hearing people really understood the Deaf. The attitudes revealed that hearing people's concept of what it was like to be deaf were based

222

purely on their own personal envisions and conjectures which, as usual, were eventually to be proved totally wrong. For the Deaf, society's negative attitude was both a general and nationwide problem and such attitudes made life hard and unbearable for the Deaf. Two examples are quoted here to furnish a clear picture of that attitude.

1. Francis Green - *Vox Oculis Subjecta*. (1783). p9 & 10.

> Whenever we meet a person (although an entire stranger) in this unhappy predicament, or reflect on the melancholy situation of such as were born *deaf*, and remain (consequently) *dumb*, does not our sensibility receive a shock, which is too violent and complicated to admit of description?

> -- Excluded from the knowledge of everything except the immediate objects of sense, apparently doomed to ignorance, idleness and uselessness, a burden to their friends and to society, incapable in such a state of that social intercourse and communication of mind, which constitute the most pleasing and rational enjoyment of intellectual beings, without distinct ideas of moral obligation, of their duty to God, or the nature and end of their existence; what pitiable animals are men in such circumstances, and how little superior to brutes!

> The mind flies off with pain, if not with horror, from the affecting idea.

2. Rev. Rann Kennedy - *Lines written by himself and spoken by the celebrated actress of the period, Mrs Edwin,* after a "play of the Deaf and Dumb" before the Duke of Devonshire for the benefit of the Institution at Edgbaston on 27 August 1814.

> If ye spectators of our Drama's plot
> Have sympathised with the injur'd Julio's lot,
> And if your breasts have hail'd with glad applause
> The warm asserter of his righteous cause,
> In them behold yourselves that hither come
> As generous Patrons of the Deaf and Dumb,
> Outcasts by birth, that still want in vain
> Rights dearer far than Julio's lost domain,

That unacquainted with creation's plan,
Might never feel the dignity of man,
Yet wear his form, while sunk in mental death,
They walk the earth mere vehicles of breath.

When the Thomas Braidwood managed to teach the Deaf to read, write, speak, sign, and understand a language, hearing people initially looked upon his work and achievement with suspicion due to their deep -rooted belief that the Deaf were no better than a "hearing idiot," or to use the Rev. Kennedy's words "they walk the earth mere vehicles of breath." To society at large, educating the Deaf was something of a novelty. Braidwood's very first pupil, Charles Shirreff (admitted 1760 and left in 1767), failed to produce speech like any normal hearing person, mainly due to his inability to hear his own voice and therefore comprehend sounds, and to make amends for this Braidwood taught him the French language. Shirreff then became fluent in reading and writing in French. No one could believe or accept that a Deaf person could master a foreign language and it was not until April 1807 when someone from Cambridge who knew Shirreff very well wrote to *The Gentlemen's Magazine* and grudgingly admitted "*he reads (and possibly writes) in the French language*" that society eventually became ready to accept that they were wrong to harbour a misleading concept of deafness and of the state of being Deaf. This was one of the earliest seeds of change. In these very early days, hearing people could not bring themselves to accept that deaf people could be educated, that they possessed an intelligence that was the equal of any person and also that they were capable of communication via writing and signs as well as lipreading and speech. Deaf people were simply victims of hearing people's poor and vain attitudes towards them and this is an undeniable fact.

Jane Poole's World.

Jane Poole was born deaf and dumb in Ludlow in the county of Salop in July 1781. She was the youngest of six children of James Poole and Ann Cooper who married on 28th July 1771 at Market Drayton in the county of Salop. Very little is known of Jane's siblings, Mary Ann (c. 25 Sept. 1773), Elizabeth (d. 26 Sept. 1774), Frances (c. 11 Sept. 1776), James (c.17 Feb. 1778), Elizabeth (c. 28 Aug. 1779) and Caroline (b.1788). Her sister, Caroline, was to play a major role in her life. Very little is known of Jane's parents. It has been established that her father died when Jane was very young and also that her family were wealthy.

The county of Salop contained numerous wealthy landowners scattered around the place and their families and relations were never short of a penny. These landed gentries tended to be generous to the poor, the unfortunate and the disabled as evidence exists to show that they contributed towards charities established to assist these people. However, growing evidence is now being gathered to show that some of the wealthy families exercised a kind of cruelty towards the deaf and dumb within their own family. Cruel, in that the family looked upon deafness as a terrible stigma and members of the family had no wish to be seen with the deaf relative. This happened to Jane Poole.

Ann Poole, Jane's mother, shunted Jane out of the family when she was barely six years old and Jane's two maiden aunts, Elizabeth and Frances, took her into their care. This was a common practice in these days and this kind of treatment was not confined only to deaf persons, but to disabled persons of all kinds in general. The practice, "boarding out with an income", may not have been as bad in these times' way of life, but it nevertheless deprived children of the love and care that could only be best provided by a close-knit immediate family life. Disabled persons who were boarded out by their families were known as *annuitants* (Woodford, 1996). In the case of Jane Poole, it is doubtful whether her two maiden aunts were paid for her keep, as they were most probably more than happy to care for a member of family, taking into account the fact that they had no children of their own. There came a day when a male member of the maiden aunts' family passed away and he left a vast sum of money to Jane and the maiden aunts set up a trust fund on her behalf to manage her newly-found wealth. The bequest was wisely used to send Jane to the Braidwood Academy for the Deaf and Dumb at Grove House in Hackney in the county of Middlesex. The fee for her education was believed to have been initially £110 per annum when Jane commenced her education in 1787 and it rose to £150 per annum in 1791 and remained constant until her last year around 1792 - 1793.

Although Jane was not the only member of her own family to inherit from her uncle's will, this somehow infuriated her sister Caroline and this set the tone for Jane's future and her life was to be made as miserable as could be by her sister. Very little is known at present research stages about how Jane spend her young life after leaving Braidwood Academy but it is known that she acquainted herself with Anne Walcot of Bitterley who was also Deaf and a former pupil of Braidwood Academy, which they both attended albeit at different periods. Ann Walcot married the Rev. Charles Walcot whilst Jane was never to marry, remaining a spinster until her death. Jane was also well acquainted with other Braidwoodian pupils, Elizabeth Metcalfe and Sarah Dashwood. There were also Deaf people in various towns around Salop and they met each other from time to time, but many appeared to meet on infrequent basis due to being scattered around the county and the poor transport facilities.

In 1826, Jane's surviving maiden aunt died and Jane took possession of her fortune from the trust set up on her behalf. To alleviate loneliness, she engaged one Elizabeth Russell as a servant. Elizabeth Russell had previously been a maid to Anne Walcot and was versatile in the manual alphabet. Jane and Elizabeth went to live with Jane's mother and sister Caroline at Hennor House near Leominster, Herefordshire. Jane appeared to cope well with her jealous sister for she stayed with them for nearly seven years until 1833 when her mother died. By that time, Caroline had married and Jane returned to Ludlow and lived there with her servant Elizabeth and her daughter Ann Russell.

The First Will Battle.

Jane's life appeared to have been marred by a series of misfortunes. In 1841 when she was 60 years old, she completely lost sight in both eyes and became deaf and blind. In spite of this, Jane was fluent at fingerspelling and used this as her main mode of communication: both her servants were proficient in the manual alphabet, and this went a long way to ease the pain of Jane's new-found visual disability considerably. In her blindness, Jane entrusted herself to her faithful servant, Elizabeth Russell, to write and sign letters on her behalf; Jane communicated by her fingers and Elizabeth then wrote according to her dictation and signed the letters herself. In that way, Jane was able to continue to conduct her life and business "independently".

Jane had one wealthy cousin, a Mr Benjamin Biddulph, who was connected with the banking firm of *Cox and Biddulph* and he managed her business transactions for many years. In 1849 upon his death, Biddulph left large sums of money to be shared equally between six benefactors of which the three sisters, Jane, Mary Ann and Caroline who was known by her married name of Caroline Stevenson were to received £7,000 each. Next, we read of the court case which took place on April 19 and 24 1852, a report given here:

In the Matter of the Trusts of the Estate of
Benjamin Biddulph, deceased;

And in the Matter of the Trusts of Jane Poole,
A Person deaf, dumb and blind;

and

In the Matter of The Act for the Relief of Trustees

The above-named Jane Poole presented her petition in the above matters; from statements in which the following are collected:—

Benjamin Biddulph, deceased, departed this life in the month of June 1849, leaving Penelope Gordon, widow, Harriet Woodyatt, widow, Frances Middleton, widow, Caroline Stevenson, widow, Mary Anne Poole, and the petitioner, his next of kin, him surviving. Administration of the estate and effects of the deceased were granted to the said Caroline Stevenson.

By decree dated 12th of July 1851, in a cause in which Mary Anne Poole and the petitioner, by their next friend Charles Benjamin Stevenson, the son of Mrs. Stevenson, were plaintiffs, and Mrs. Stevenson was defendant, the petitioner had become entitled to one-eighth of the residuary personal estate of the deceased, after certain payments agreed to be made thereout in the first instance; and in respect of such one-eighth the sum 7000*l.* was, under the provisions of the Trustee Act, 1850, paid by Mrs. Stevenson, as the administratrix, into the Bank of England, to the account of the Accountant-General of the Court of Chancery, "In the Matter of the Trusts of Jane Poole, a person deaf, dumb and blind," meaning the petitioner, who was born deaf and dumb, and who had become blind about nine years since.

After the payment by Mrs. Stevenson, and on the 15th of July 1851, Mr. Charles Benjamin Stevenson, as the next friend of the petitioner, presented a petition in her name in the above matters, on which an order was made by the Vice-Chancellor Knight Bruce on the 9th of August, 1851; by which it was ordered, that the 7000*l.* cash in the Bank on the credit of the matter intitled "In the Matter of the Trusts of

Jane Poole, a person deaf, dumb, and blind," should be laid out in the name of the Accountant-General, in the purchase of the Bank 3*l.* per cent. Annuities, in trust in the matter, subject to the further order of the Court. And it was ordered, that, out of the dividends to accrue on these Bank Annuities, when purchased, the sum of 100*l.* per annum, half yearly, should be paid to Mrs. Stevenson during the life of the petitioner, or until the further order of the Court, she undertaking to apply the same towards the maintenance of the petitioner; and it was ordered, that the residue of the dividends to accrue upon these Bank Annuities should, with all accumulations, be laid out in the purchase of like Bank Annuities to the like account, subject to the further order of the Court. This sum of 7000*l.* was, pursuant to the order, invested by the said Accountant-General in the purchase of the sum of 7235*l.* 2s. 10d. Bank 3*l.* per cent. Annuities; and these Annuities, with the sum of 56*l.* 16s. 5d. cash, being the residue of the dividends which accrued due thereon on the 5th of January 1852, after the receipt by Mrs. Stevenson of the sum of 50*l.*, by the order directed to be paid to her, were, at the date of the petition, standing in Court in trust in the matter, intitled "In the Matter of the Trusts of Jane Poole, a person deaf, dumb, and blind."

The present petition alleged that the petition of the 15th of July, 1851, had been presented, and that the order had been obtained, without the knowledge of, or any previous communication with, the petitioner; and that it was an unauthorised interference with the property and concerns of the petitioner, and had occasioned to the petitioner extreme annoyance and considerable pecuniary embarrassment; and the petition proceeded to set forth, that the petitioner, during the life of the inestate Benjamin Biddulph, who was a trustee for the petitioner of certain sums of stock and other property, had been in the receipt of, and had the entire control over, her own income and monies; and that Mrs. Stevenson had never been in the receipt of the income or monies, except during the period which had elapsed since the decease of Mr.

Biddulph, and in the character of his legal personal representative; and that Mrs. Stevenson had refused to pay into the hands of the petitioner, and upon her receipt, the monies which she had received on her behalf; and that, by reason and in consequence of such refusal, the petitioner had been compelled, for her necessary expenses, to realise a portion of her funded property; and that she was indebted for rent and servants' wages, and otherwise for expenses of her maintenance and establishment, in considerable sum; and the petitioner was advised that she was entitled to have, and that she was desirous of having, the uncontrolled dominion over her own property.

The petition prayed that the order of the 9th of August, 1851, might be discharged, and that the petition, upon which the same had been made, might be dismissed, and for a taxation of the petitioner's costs occasioned by that order, and of and incidental to the present application; and that the same might be raised by the sale of a competent part of the sum of 7235l. 2s. 10d., Bank 3l. Per cent. Annuities, standing in trust in the above matter; and that the residue of these annuities, with the said sum of 56l. 2s. 10d. cash, together with any further dividends which might accrue due on these annuities, might be transferred and paid to the petitioner; and that Mrs. Stevenson might be ordered to pay to the petitioner the sum of 50l. received by her under the order of the 9th of august, 1851.

Miss Poole's knowledge of business, and competency to manage her own affairs, subject only to her infirmities, were not questioned.

Mr. Bacon and Mr. Amphlett appeared in support of the petition.

Mr. Malins and Mr. Charles Hall objected, that the petitioner, being deaf, dumb and blind, was not a person competent to present a petition without the intervention of a next friend.

Mr. Osborne appeared for other parties.

The Vice-Chancellor said, that there was nothing that shewd that the petitioner was of unsound mind; and therefore it did not appear to him to be necessary that the petitioner should appear by a next friend. He thought it not likely that he should be disposed to part with so large a fund, and he should require the petition to be amended.

The petition was then amended according to the direction of the Court.

By the petition, as amended, it was prayed that the order of the 9th of August, 1851, might be discharged; and that the petition, upon which the same had been made, might be dismissed; and that the sum of 7235*l.* 2s. 10d., Bank 3*l.* per Cent. Annuities, standing in trust "In the Matter of the Trusts of Jane Poole, a person deaf, dumb, and blind," might be carried over by the Accountant-General to the account of the petitioner; and that the said sum of 56*l.* 16s. 5d. cash, And also the dividends thereafter to accrue due from time to time on the said Bank Annuities, when so carried over, might be paid to Thomas Dunne, of Burcher Hall, in the county of Hereford, Esq., and the petitioner's solicitor George Pleydell Wilton, or either of them, on behalf of the petitioner, until the further order of the Court; and that Mrs. Stevenson might be ordered to pay to Messrs. Dunne and Wilton, or either of them, the said sum of 50*l.* received under the order of the 9th of August, 1851.

The amended petition was mentioned this day by Mr. Bacon and Mr. Amphlett; Mr. Malins and Mr. Charles Hall appearing for Mrs. And Mr. C. B. Stevenson.

Mr. Elderton appeared for Messrs. Dunne and Wilton; and Mr. Osborne for other parties.

The Vice-Chancellor said, he should allow and order the past and future income to be paid to Messrs. Dunne and Wilton, the persons named by the petitioner to receive it, on their undertaking to account.

The order, after directing the taxation of Mrs. Stevenson's costs, charges and expenses, proceeded:

This Court doth order —

That it be referred to the Taxing Master of this Court in rotation, to tax the said Caroline Stevenson her costs of paying into Court the sum of 7000*l.*, in the petition mentioned, and of this application, including therein all reasonable charges and expenses properly incurred in relation to the said trust fund; And it is ordered, that such costs, charges and expenses, when so taxed, be retained by the said Caroline Stevenson out of any monies that may have come to her hands; [and after setting forth an undertaking by her, by her counsel, to account for and pay to Messrs. Dunne and Wilton the sums already received and thereafter to be received by her on the petitioner's account, after deducting her costs, proceeded thus:]—It is ordered, that the 7235*l.* 2s. 10d. Bank 3*l.* per Cent Annuities, standing in the name of the Accountant-General of this Court, "In the Matter of the Trusts of Jane Poole, a person deaf, dumb, and blind," be carried over, in trust in the same matter, to an account to be intitled, "The Account of the said Jane Poole;" and he is to declare the trust thereof accordingly, subject to the further order of this Court; And it is ordered, that the dividends from time to time to accrue due on the said Bank Annuities, previous to and when so carried over, and also the sum of 56*l.* 16s. 5d. cash in the Bank, on the credit of the said matter, be paid to the said Thomas Dunne and George Pleydell Wilton, or either of them, on behalf of the petitioner Jane Poole, until the further order of this Court; the said Thomas Dunne and George Pleydell Wilton, by their counsel, undertaking to apply all monies to be received by them or either of them under this order, for the benefit of the said Jane Poole, and to account for the same as this Court shall direct; and for the purposes aforesaid the said Accountant-General is to draw on the Bank, &c.."

231

Written statement in connection with the 1851 case
by the Rev. Charles Walcot, son of Sarah Dashwood
20 October 1851

Image reproduced with kind permission of
Shropshire Archives © - ref: 151/4144

Jane's Last Will and Testament.

A year after her successful battle against her sister to have her
inheritance from Benjamin Biddulph transferred into her own name,
Jane felt compelled to protect her wealth and assets, taking into account
her distrust of her sister Caroline and she set about to make her own
will. She made a point of not informing her sisters of her intention to
write her own will since she either knew or sensed that she would be
greatly discouraged to do so and also that Caroline would most likely
take steps, probably in the legal sense, to prevent her from writing her
own will. Jane was also aware that her will might be challenged but her
stubbornness and determination drove her on to exercise her right to
decide how her own wealth was to be disposed of upon her death. She
informed George Pleydell Wilton of her desire to write her will. After
careful consideration, taking into account legal difficulties which might
arise due to her deafness, Mr Wilton advised her to ensure that only
trustworthy persons should help her and that these persons should be
proficient in sign language. In response to Wilton's advice, Jane called
for the two children of her late friend, Ann Walcot. Jane had known the
Reverend Charles Thomas Walcot and his sister Sarah Price (who was

married to Robert Bell-Price) since they were both born, and they both excelled in communicating on the fingers as well as the deaf and dumb language of the gestural form. On 11 October 1852, the Rev. Mr Walcot and his sister Mrs Price visited Jane at her home in 29 Broad Street, Ludlow, and saw her alone. They ascertained her wishes as to the disposal of her property and wrote a memorandum of the conversation.

The following week on 18 October, the Rev. Charles Walcot and his sister Sarah again visited Jane for another interview. They both took further instructions respecting the appointment of the executors and of residuary legatees and made another note of what was discussed. The Rev. Walcot sent the instructions to Mr Wilton in London and a Will was drawn up in accordance with Jane's instructions and it read as follows:

The Last Will and Testament of Jane Poole

This is the last will of me, *Jane Poole*, Spinster of Ludlow in the County of Salop. I give several legacies to the following: To Mrs Dunne, the wife of Thomas Dunne, esquire of Burcher Hall the sum of one thousand pounds; to Mr Wilton the sum of one thousand pounds; to the Reverend Charles Walcot the sum of five hundred pounds; to my niece Isabella Fitzgerald the sum of one thousand pounds; to my niece Caroline Harrison the sum of one thousand pounds; to my niece Constance Dundas the sum of one thousand pounds; to my nephew Charles Benjamin Stevenson the sum of seventeen hundred pounds; to my maid Elizabeth Russell the sum of five hundred pounds and all my furniture and linen; to my maid Ann Russell the sum of five hundred pounds and all my books. I give unto my Executors the sum of one hundred pounds upon trust to pay the same out of my personal estate to the Treasurer of the School for the Deaf and Dumb, Oxford Street, East Liverpool, which sum one hundred pounds I desire may be applied for the Charity Fund. I give and desire the rest of my personal estate and real estate, if any, unto my said nephew and nieces to be divided equally between them. I appoint the said Thomas Dunne and Mr Wilton as executors of this my will.

Signed by me this thirtieth day of November one thousand eight hundred and fifty two - *Jane Poole.*

The contents of this paper-writing were communicated to the above named Jane Poole by speaking the same word for word on her fingers and she repeated the same word for word on her fingers, and being fully understood by her it was signed by her as her last will and testament in the presence of us, present at the same time who at her request in her presence and in the person of each other have hereunto our names as attesting witnesses:

Sarah Price of Bitterley. Widow.
David Buxton of Liverpool, Principal of the Liverpool School for the Deaf and Dumb.

After much work and assisted by sign language interpretation by David Buxton, the head of the Liverpool School for the Deaf, the will was formally signed and sealed on 30 November in front of several witnesses and the will was taken for safekeeping by Mr Wilton and the matter became forgotten until Jane Poole passed away on 10 April 1860 at her home in 29 Broad Street, Ludlow. She was 78 years old. George Pleydell Wilton took to reading her last will and testament to those present after Jane's funeral, and this somehow aroused anger in Caroline Stevenson. She made an immediate and vehement objection to the will, saying she had never heard of, or known of, its existence. (The total sum left initially amounted to £12,000 but the final figure was £14,000 when everything was finally settled in 1862).

Caroline Stevenson proceeded to complain that her sister, being deaf, dumb and blind, was totally incapable of writing such a will and she claimed Jane did not understand the contents of her own will. She opposed it vociferously even though her three daughters and only son were the main beneficiaries of Jane's will and that they were also the residuary legatees. Spiteful as ever, and perhaps humiliated in the realisation that Jane was more than capable of managing her own affairs in spite of society's poor opinion of the deaf, Caroline took legal measures to block the probate of the will and the only course for settlement was a hearing in the court of probate. Caroline was supremely confident of having her late sister's will declared null and void, and perhaps winning powers of administration which would enable her to dispose of it as she saw fit, and she apparently set about to achieve that end.

Oct 20. 1851.

A conversation held by speaking with the fingers with the [?]
Jane Poole at her house in [?].

Do you know any thing of a suit in chancery about Mr.
Biddulphs money, & that the money is placed in chancery
now? — Yes

Did you ever consent that your nephew should act
for you, — answer, never —

Do you wish your nephew to manage your affairs
answer No —

— Do you wish your nephew Charles Stephenson to
[?] for you — answer. No Mr. Dunne

How long since you were at Church answer Last Sunday week

Can you tell me what Day of the month it is —
[?] were the sixteenth — but upon my telling her
it was not, she calculated on her fingers & then said [?]
[?] too late[?]

[?] month is it — answer October

Written communication between George Pleydell Wilton
and Jane Poole via Walcot's interpreting in connection
with the 1851 case

Image reproduced with kind permission of
Shropshire Archives © - ref: 151/4144

The trial was held before Sir Cresswell Cresswell, the first Judge of the
Court of Probate, and a special jury over a year after Jane Poole's death
and it was instigated by George Pleydell Wilton as plaintiff against
Jane's sister, Caroline Stevenson. David Buxton delivered an account of
the situation and the case at the Court of Probate in Westminster Hall
which took place on Thursday 2 May and Friday 3 May 1861. Buxton's

account of 12 December 1861, which was read to a meeting of the Historic Society of Lancashire on the same day, is reprinted here, with some additions from the author.

In the Spring of the present year an entirely new question arose in one of the High Courts of English Judicature. On the 2nd of May, 1861, in the Court of Probate at Westminster, before Sir Cresswell Cresswell and a Special Jury, the case of Wilton v. Stevenson came on for hearing. Mr. Bovill, Q.C., M.P., and other counsel were for the plaintiff: Mr. Sergeant Pigott, M.P., and other learned gentlemen appeared for the defendant. Mr. George Pleydell Wilton, as surviving executor under the will of the late Miss Jane Poole of Ludlow, had applied for probate of the will; this was opposed by Caroline Stevenson, the defendant, and hence the trial. Defendant objected, to the will which was propounded, that the Testatrix, her sister, was not of testamentary capacity, and therefore the will was invalid. The facts were these. Miss Poole was born deaf and dumb and, at the age of sixty years, became blind also. In 1852, nine years afterwards, she made her will, and the novel question which the court had now to try was, whether a person deaf and dumb from her birth, and blind for nearly ten years, was capable, in the seventieth year of her age, of understanding her own affairs, and competent to make a will.

David Buxton

Concerning the mental competency of the blind there is no question. Communications *viva voce* are as common to them as ourselves. With respect to the deaf and dumb, who, in the absence of hearing, are to be addressed through the eye, the law requires certain proofs of ability to understand, and to be understood by, those who are versed in their peculiar mode of communication. This, however, is common to all legal proceedings in which they may be concerned — e.g., as witnesses or accused—and is not peculiar to the question of competency to make a will. As a class they are not under any disability: but circumstances may raise the question as to the mental capacity of any individual mute as of any other person, and this question of fact can only be settled by an enquiry of precisely the same nature as would be resorted to in any other case. But when we come to regard the position of one who is blind, as well as deaf and dumb,—who having had to depend solely upon the eye as a substitute for the ear, is bereft of sight as well as hearing, the case then assumes an exceptional character — happily most exceptional — and on the first consideration of the matter perhaps the question of competency may seem decided, or rather put aside altogether, by the enormous difficulty, or as some may think, impossibility, of holding adequate communication with a mind imprisoned in the darkness and the silence of such fearful solitude.

We use the terms "blind" and "deaf and dumb" very familiarly — so familiarly, that when we recognise the condition they describe, we never pause to consider the characteristics which belong to it. The deaf person, being deprived of hearing, relies upon the sight: the blind, without the function of the eye, relies upon the hearing. But when these two afflictions meet in the same person, the sufferer has not merely one loss added to another, but he is deprived of that very alternative sense which in ordinary cases is the resource and compensation of the other. And it is impossible fully to understand and to realize the condition we have now to consider, unless we compare it with our own. In this very matter of bequeathing property, (1) some persons make their own wills. Now Miss Poole could not do that, because she was blind and could not see a written character. (2) Others give directions as to their will; but she could not do that, because she was dumb. Or, (3) they answer questions put to them to ascertain their wishes; yet this, too, was denied to her, for she was deaf, and could not hear a question put. And finally (4) every testator can see, and read, the draft of the will when completed; but she could not do that either, for, in her blindness, she could not tell whether a paper in her hand was written upon all over, or was a perfect blank. It is impossible to conceive a condition of more helpless dependence than this: and thence probably arose the thought that a human being, so dependent upon others, could not possess that independence of thought and action, necessary to make such a will as the law would hold to be a valid instrument.

And now you see the difficulty. Here was a person who could not write her own wishes, nor read them when written by another, and who could neither speak or be spoken to. If you spoke to her, she could not hear; if you wrote, she could not see; and if she made signs to you, you could not understand her. This is the exact state of the case. How the difficulty was met and overcome; how the will was framed and executed; how it was impeached and tried, and, in the end, triumphantly sustained, are the matters which, in conformity with a suggestion made to me soon after the trial, I have undertaken now to detail to this Society.

My acquaintance with the late Miss Jane Poole commenced in the month of January 1852.

Shortly before my appointment to my present office (as head teacher of the Liverpool School for the Deaf) in 1851, enquiries had been made at the Institution in London with which I was then connected, to ascertain if any official of that Institution was capable, and would be willing, to hold an interview with a lady deaf, dumb and blind, so as to pronounce an opinion upon her competency to understand the nature of her own property, and to have the management of her own affairs. The late Mr. Watson, Principal of the London Asylum, mentioned my name to the gentleman making the enquiry, and recommended me for the task. For some months the matter remained in abeyance, but on a second application, by another friend of the lady, in January, 1852, he again referred the enquirer to me, though I had then left London and come to reside in Liverpool. The result was a visit to Ludlow on the 17th January, 1852, when I had two interviews with the lady, in the presence of gentlemen who became, with myself, witnesses in the Court of Probate in May last. The object of that enquiry was to discover how far she knew the extent of her own property and was acquainted with the nature of it, and, further, whether she was willing that it should remain under the control of relatives who had assumed the right to manage it for her, or whether she wished it to be placed under her own control.

In the prosecution of this enquiry it was inevitable that I should form a definite and strong opinion as to the mental capacity of one capable of answering all the questions which arose in such an investigation, in spite of the extraordinary difficulties caused by her accumulated afflictions. The questions proposed were suggested by Mr. Wilton, her solicitor; conveyed to her by myself, and her answers repeated aloud by me: the whole thing being taken down in writing by Mr. Wilton. The questions and answers thus recorded were embodied in an affidavit, which set forth the particulars of her age, early life and education, personal knowledge of the parties connected with her property, and her feelings towards them, and the exact expression of her wishes with respect to the management of a sum of £7000 left her by a deceased relative, and of other moneys to which she was previously entitled. To this was added my own opinion as to her mental capacity, with the grounds upon which that opinion was based. In due course, the court of chancery was moved to withdraw from the relatives of Miss Poole the charge of her property, and to vest it in herself. On this, the solicitor of her relatives applied to me to visit her again, on their behalf. I at once declined to do so. The final result of the application was to establish beyond a doubt that miss Poole's mental capacity was adequate for directing the management of her own affairs; and under the direction of the court, the £7000 involved in the enquiry were re-invested, the whole income arising therefrom being made payable to trustees chosen by Miss Poole herself, to act on her behalf.

A few months afterwards — at the close of the same year 1852 — I was informed that Miss Poole had given directions for the preparation of her will, and that my aid was absolutely required, and my judgement of her fitness and capacity necessary. It was considered that with such physical infirmities to contend against, too much caution could not be used in the preparation of such an instrument.

I have not yet described the mode of communication which the numerous afflictions of this lady rendered necessary. It was, of course, the same on all occasions, but the importance of the transaction, the weighty interests involved, and all the impressive circumstances surrounding the final execution of the will, — which have left an impression on my own mind and a pictured scene in my own memory which can never be effaced, — seem to point this out as the proper occasion for explaining the mode of communication between myself and the testatrix.

I have said that the scene which I am now striving to recall was a very impressive one. Not only the occasion, and the place, but the time itself tended to make it so.

None of us can have forgotten that memorable week when the greatest of modern heroes was laid, amid the regrets of an empire, and the homage of the world, in his last resting place under the dome of St. Paul's. That gloomy November morning — that imposing array — all the outward pomp and circumstance of war, with all its spirit gone, — armed men by thousands, all trained and marshalled to obey the voice which never should be heard again; now trooping on in mournful silence, and now to the still more mournful wail of military music — consciously stricken with humbleness and awe in the presence of that mortal Foe against whom courage is vain, and battle hopeless; before those unerring shaft we one and all must fall:— all this we can remember, and that wonderful crowd, living and moving, but hushed — led thither by one impulse, influenced by one feeling, attracted by one object,—countless thousands of living men and women drawn around to one point, and that point — Death; an old man's honoured ashes carried to their last abode. Such a centre to such a circle was never seen before in the whole world's history, and may never be seen again.

It was on the last day of the same week that the transactions occurred of which I am about to speak. The funeral of the Duke of Wellington was the one subject in every man's thoughts, and on every man's lips; and as one always reads of the death of another great military commander, Oliver Cromwell, in connexion with the terrific storm which occurred on the day of his death, so the extraordinary weather which prevailed at the time I am speaking of became associated with the event of the great Duke's funeral. The heavy rains had flooded the meadows and swollen then rivers throughout the country; bridges had been washed away, low-lying houses inundated, railway-traffic suspended, and the rising waters had spread injury and panic far and wide. Of all this there were numerous traces on every hand. The line between Shrewsbury and Ludlow had only been made fit for the resumption of ordinary traffic a few hours before I got there, and the rain was pouring down still.

On such a day, then, and at such a time, I found myself once more, and for the last time, within that old-fashioned house, in the old-fashioned town of Ludlow, in which Miss Poole lived. She rose on being told I was present, took my hand and shook it heartily, and on being asked, said she remembered my former visit very well.

All the persons who were present became witnesses at the trial. They were either personal friends of the lady, or professional and official gentlemen hose attendance had been obtained (as the judge long afterwards described it) as a guarantee for the openness and justice of the proceedings. Of this latter class were [the Rev. Mr Phillips] the rector of Ludlow; [Mr Henry Hodges] her medical attendant; [Mr. Robert Anderson] her legal adviser; and the intimate personal friends being a clergyman [Charles Walcot] and his sister [Sarah Price], who had known Miss Poole all their lives, she having been in early life the schoolfellow, and afterwards the neighbour and frequent visitor of their mother, a lady deaf and dumb, — which latter circumstance had made them readily conversant with the mode of communication to be employed in the case just before us.

There were two copies of the will. One which I shall describe as No.1, lay before Miss Poole and me; the other, No.2, was in the hands of the professional gentleman who had drawn it up.

Now, most persons know that nearly all of the letters of the manual alphabet used in this country are made by using both hands. In ordinary spelling, I make the letters with one hand upon the other. In this case, I made them with one of my hands upon one of hers. C, which is formed with the right hand only, I traced, whenever it occurred, with the point of my forefinger on the palm of her hand. In this manner, my communications were made to her — she replying in the ordinary way, spelling with both hands, but sometimes making signs, and occasionally accompanying the words she spelled, or the signs she used, with intelligible efforts at articulation.

In this manner, I read over the contents of Will No.1, clause by clause; and in order to satisfy those whom I may call the official spectators, that its meaning was understood, and that it conveyed Miss Poole's own wishes, the following plan was adopted: — I, sitting on her left hand, spelled over to her, without uttering a word, a clause in the will, and then stopped. She, turning to the lady on her right, told her (in manual language, of course) what I had just said. That lady (the daughter of Miss Poole's schoolfellow, already mentioned) repeated aloud what has just been silently said to her, and the company assembled saw that it was identical with the text of the document No.2, which the solicitor held in his hands. In this way, we went through the entire contents of the will. She paused at the technical words — "devise," and "executors," for instance—with a determination to master them, and asked me to repeat them if she did not readily apprehend them. Then, when she got the word correctly, she spelled it over to herself, slowly and elaborately, afterwards reverting to her own more familiar expression for conveying the same sense; and the identity of meaning was to me a manifest proof that the phraseology of the will was fully expressive of her own wishes. In one instance she corrected me by saying that a certain bequest was "one hundred," not "one thousand" pounds. She named with great precision all the legatees, and the amount of bequest to each, repeating some of these particulars several times with unfaltering accuracy (spelling the words letter by letter), in such a manner as was conclusive, not only of her competency to make a will, but of the fact that its provisions were emphatically the expression of her own strong wishes and purpose. It was to me peculiarly gratifying to find she had not forgotten the institution with which I am connected. Her own words were, "I give 'the poor deaf and dumb at school at Liverpool, one hundred pounds'," and she dwelt upon the phrase, "the poor deaf and dumb" with a degree of sympathy which we can, perhaps, but imperfectly conceive. When all was done, she said it was "all right" and put out her hand for the pen with which she was to affix her signature. I handed it to her, and when she had placed it in the proper position, she felt the point, thereby measuring the requisite distance, and ascertaining if it was furnished with ink; and then, she who had never seen a written character for nine years, —

being at that time sixty years of age, and now nearly seventy— wrote her name in full, boldly and very legibly, and, with the exception of the signature inclining upwards, exactly as any one else might have done. It was a striking and suggestive sight. It shewed a human mind unextinguished and inextinguishable under an accumulation of afflictions — deafness, blindness and old age — which one would have thought were more than sufficient to crush out every glimmer of vitality.

These were the facts to which I was called to bear witness at the trial. Evidence was also given by those best acquainted with her life and habits, as to her systemic manner of keeping her own moneys, even when she could no longer keep her accounts. On two occasions, when she was applied to by the Rector and the Mayor for her assistance to some local object, she rose and fetched from some part of the house, two sovereigns in one case, and a five pound note in the other. She would even go shopping, buying what she required, with the aid of her attendants, and herself paying for what was bought. Some of her early school-books were put in evidence, and her own books of account, in which she noted down her regular disbursements and household expenses in after life, but previously, of courses, to the time when she became blind.

It was interesting to observe from where I sat in court the effect of the evidence on the minds of the jury. After those witnesses had been examined who were present at the execution of the will, and while the plaintiff was giving his testimony, it became evident that the cause was won. An attempt was made to stop the case. One of the Jury said it was useless to occupy their time any longer. Mr. Sergeant Pigott [for Caroline Stevenson] replied that only one side had yet been heard. The judge said it was not for him to pronounce an opinion, but it was very clear that very strong evidence was required to answer that which had already been given. However, the trial went on, but presently, as the corroborative testimony accumulated, and no point was made by the other side, the impatience of the jury broke out again, and a proposal was made by the defendant's counsel to compromise the case. This was unsatisfactory, and the cause again went on until five o'clock, when the court rose, adjoining the further hearing until the next day. As we came out into Westminster Hall, the members of the House of Commons were thronging down to the great debate on Mr. Horsfall's motion upon the Tea Duties.

Next morning we were again in court, and no sooner had the jury taken their places, and the judge his seat upon the bench, than Mr. Sergeant Pigott rose and said that, after the evidence which had been given on the previous day, and the significant observations of the jury, the defendant had determined to withdraw from all further opposition. He added, that the fact of the existence of the will had never been known to the defendant until after the death of the testatrix, and the evidence in support of it, and the manner of its execution, had come upon her quite by surprise. It will have been gathered from what has been said previously, that the sisters were not on good terms — that Miss Poole believed her sister endeavoured to injure her, and she resented it accordingly — not an amiable feeling certainly, but scarcely a fact to be appealed to as proof of imbecility of mind. And yet, while the poor lady bore gratefully in mind those who had been truly her friends, she did not allow her resentment to lead her to forget the real claims of relationship, for the bulk of her property was, after all, left to this very sister's children.

And now, before I conclude, you must allow me to point to the moral of my story. It is very short and simple, but very obvious, and essentially practical. It is this. How vastly, how immeasurably important must education be to the deaf and dumb. For every one, education does much—for some persons more than for others — but for the deaf-mute it does absolutely everything.

This afflicted lady received her education in the very first School for the deaf and dumb (a private one) which was ever opened in England. An assistant in that establishment became the first principal of the London Asylum: and an assistant in that asylum became the principal of your own Institution here in Liverpool, in which capacity he was the means of obtaining justice and securing comfort for this injured lady in her melancholy condition of deafness, blindness and old age. When she was a young child, requiring education, there was not a single public institution in this country capable of affording it to such as she. Yet now Schools for the deaf and dumb are to be found in every populous district of the kingdom. There are upwards of two hundred in Europe and America, whereas a century ago there was not one. The local Institution, whose officer I am, has not been established forty years, yet it has done incalculable good. It never turns a single eligible applicant away, though to do this has lately been enlarged at very considerable cost, a part of which, I am sorry to say, still remains as a debt and an embarrassment to its free action.

And now, education which in this lady's youth was a novelty and an experiment — only just placed within the reach of any, and they the wealthy few — is attainable by every one requiring it. Thanks to the generous hearts and hands in Liverpool there is not a single deaf and dumb child, however poor and friendless, who may not enjoy the blessing to which she owed so much, ay, everything. For it was this — education — which enabled her to claim her rights, to defeat injustice, to enjoy her own, to practice forgiveness at the last towards those who injured her, and to cultivate and gratify her natural sympathies with those afflicted like herself. It was by this that the native powers of her mind were cultivated; that she grew up in the enjoyment of the pleasures of life, and trained to perform its duties; and, when to the silence of sixty years was added the darkness of twenty more, she could still. With quick intelligence, and cheerfulness of spirit unimpaired, hold on her course until her summons came — until she was admitted into that new and higher life where we shall all be delivered *"from the body of this death"* and *"where the eyes of the Blind shall be opened, and the ears of the Deaf shall be unstopped, and the tongue of the Dumb shall sing."*

Jane Poole's will was proved on 31 May 1861; she left around £12,000. It was re-sworn in January 1862, her estate finally totalled just under £14,000.

Publicity of the case was reported in only three newspapers of the day - *Liverpool Daily Post* (Tuesday May 7th), *Eddowes' Shrewsbury Journal* (Wednesday May 8th) and *Shrewsbury Chronicle* (Thursday May 9th) and then total silence.

Next in 1863, John Geale of Yately, Berkshire, who was deaf and dumb and illiterate left a will which was executed by putting his mark to it. An objection was raised and the Judge of the court of probate, Sir J.P. Wilde refused probate of John Geale's will on the ground that there was no sufficient evidence of the testator's understanding and assenting to its provisions. The Judge also doubted the validity of certain signs used in communication via sign language... but that is another story.

Anne Burnett Craigie

Anne Burnett was born deaf on 21 March 1789 to a wealthy legal advocate and proprietor William Burnett (1731-1811) and his wife

Anne Rust of Brucklebogg, Kincardine. William Burnett was a younger brother of James Burnett, best known as Lord Monboddo (1714-1799) and he was fortunate to be given great advice about the placement of his deaf daughter Anne regarding her education. Monboddo pointed his finger in one direction - the Braidwood Academy for the Deaf and Dumb in Hackney. Monboddo was qualified to give advice as he wrote about Thomas Braidwood and his academy in his *On The Origin and Progress of Language* (6 volumes, Edinburgh and London, J. Balfour and T. Cadell, 1773–1792). Lord Monboddo was a strong advocate of the method of instruction employed by Thomas Braidwood.

William Burnett

Nothing much is known about Anne and her life with the exception that she married a Banff -born surgeon, Jonathan Craigie, on February 15 1810 (*Scots Magazine, Vol.72, p236*). The marriage produced one son, William Burnett Craigie, who was baptised on 9 December 1810 at St. Nicholas, Aberdeen. Jonathan Craigie died in 1812, aged 32 years old, in Edinburgh and was buried on 19 April 1812. There is an interesting tale behind Anne's marriage and what her father had secured for her future from a short article translated from a lengthy court proceedings by Peter Jackson, of the British Deaf History Society...

James Burnett,
Lord Monboddo

One of Thomas Braidwood's pupils Anne Burnett, a member of the wealthy family Burnetts of Ley, which had considerable estates in Aberdeenshire and whilst still a child and unmarried, Anne was bestowed Linton House (now a listed building) together with lands surrounding it (the Linton Mains) as an inheritance. The incomes from these lands ten miles west of Aberdeen were considerable and made Anne a desirable catch for any suitor.

Anne Burnett was apparently well-educated at Braidwood's Academy, and was considered capable of acting for herself, and entered into a marriage with a gentleman surgeon named Jonathan Craigie. At that time, any property owned by a bride entering into a marriage became the property of the husband, but at the insistence of her family, Anne Burnett Craigie (as she became known) entered into a postnuptial contract of marriage where her estate at Linton and the sum of 10,000*l* were bound up in trust which protected her assets in the event of her husband predeceasing her and entitling her to the net proceeds of rents from the estate and the interest on the sum of 10,000*l*.

Jonathan Craigie died in 1812, leaving Anne a widow with a young child, William Burnett Craigie who was aged 2 at the time of his father's death.

William Burnett Craigie married in 1836, and his mother wished to make over the Linton estate to him, his wife and heirs of that marriage in return for an annuity of 400*l* which would be a charge on the estate as long as she lived. She petitioned in lawsuit through the Scottish Court of Session to discharge the trustees from the postnuptial contract, and to allow her to dispose of the estate and fund of 10,000*l* in accordance with her wishes to provide for her son and his heirs.

The three judges sitting on the action brought by Mrs. Burnett Craigie and her son agreed that notwithstanding the fact she was deaf and dumb, she was perfectly capable of making a decision regarding the discharge of the postnuptial contract and found that she was fully entitled to put an end to the original trust.

Anne was said to have passed away in 1846.

Miss Graham of Airth Castle

W. R. Roe (1848-1920), the headmaster of Derby School for the Deaf, wrote a number of books on the deaf and one of these, *Peeps into the Deaf World* (Bembrose & Sons Ltd, Derby and London, 1917), yielded some names of Thomas Braidwood's former pupils between pages 356 and 358. In page 358, Roe mentioned "Miss Graham of Airth Castle."

A search was undertaken to find this "Miss Graham" and identify her. It was discovered that the Miss Graham in question belonged to the family of William Graham and his wife Anne Stirling. The marriage produced seven sons and seven daughters, out of which five sons died young. Of the daughters:

Anne (1762-1836) married in 1781 to David Erskine.
Mary (1763 -?) married in 1781 to John Stirling.

Elizabeth and Christian (both born in 1764) were twins: the latter died unmarried in 1848-49, whereas the former married in 1794 to James Dundas.
Jean (1770-1850).
Wilhelmina (1773 - ?) married in 1791 to D. H. MacDowall.

Since Roe mentioned "Miss Graham" it indicated that the deaf lady in question never married; one is left with a choice between Christian and Jean, and despite an extensive search among the Graham family for the mention of deafness in the family, nothing was found. It appears that "deaf" was a taboo to the family and its mention was thoroughly eliminated. It is the author's inkling that the person who attended the Braidwood Academy was Jean Graham.

Ann Barksdale

Ann Barksdale (c.1774-1790). This Braidwoodian pupil was recently unearthed as a result of a letter published on the internet by Alan William Hewat:

11 May 1997

Alexander's 1820 letter to George Edwards

George Edwards
Charleston
So. Carolina

Carolina Coffee House
Sept. 28th 1820

On the death of his wife (formerly Mrs Barksdale) Alexander wrote to G. Edwards, her relation in Charleston, showing much affection still for SC (courtesy of Victoria Dunlop).

[MS#79 CLS. Rev. Dr Hewat's letter presented by George Edwards Esquire to Charleston L. Society thro' Ogden Hammond. Autograph of Rev. Dr Alexander Hewat, Historian of So. Carolina.]

George Edwards
Charleston
So. Carolina

Carolina Coffee House
Sept. 28th 1820

Dr Hewat presents his best respects to Mr & Mrs
Edwards, and having an excellent opportunity sends
them by the Bearer two miniature pictures which
belong to the good family of Barksdale. From what he
often heard during Mrs Hewat's lifetime he has reason
to conclude they will be particularly acceptable to Mrs
Edwards of whom Mrs Hewat often spoke with much
affection. They will be handed to her by Mr Hall in
the same condition & in the Same Box in which they
were left by the Deceased; and She will be pleased to
accept of them in memorial of two dear and beautiful
relations. They both died in Flanders and were
brought to England & buried, to which place their
Mother at her request was also conveyed & buried
betwixt them in the same Tomb at Dover. I never saw
the children, having never met their Mother in
England till both were above three years & dead &
buried; tho' she belonged to my Parish before she was
first married; and Mr Barksdale I remember well, and
together with Mr & Mrs Gordon I approved of the
Choice she made. Mr Thomas Braidwood our English
Teacher of the Deaf & Dumb has oft expressed to me
his surprise at the degree of perfection to which the
child had attained in speaking; but her mother,
anxious for still greater proficiency, was advised to
carry her to another famous master in France, which
advice was to her matter of great lamentation till
Death. Farwell & God bless you & all friends in
Carolina.

With the above letter as the only source of information on the
Barksdale girl, an approach was made to the Kentish Family History
Society for assistance and the request was passed on to one of the
society's veteran and experienced researchers, Bill Beer, who went on
to establish and outline an interesting historical scenario...

Elizabeth Patterson (born circa 1744) migrated from England to South
Carolina. On 31 October 1765 she married a planter George Barksdale
at Lamprey in the Christ church parish. The priest conducting the
marriage was Alexander Hewat, who was born in Roxburgh, Scotland,

in 1739. Hewat went out to South Carolina as a Presbyterian preacher in 1763. The marriage produced three children, the first two being twin girls, one of whom was deaf and the other afflicted with palsy. The third was a boy named George. The deaf girl was named as Ann, and her twin sister's name is as yet not known.

The colonial war between Britain and America which began in 1775 led to a situation where Elizabeth and her children had to depart for England. George Barksdale, a British loyalist, removed to Charleston in 1780. Alexander Hewat, also a loyalist, was deported to England in 1777 and all his property was confiscated. In May 1780, George Barksdale's cattle were taken by the British army and during the occupation of Charleston the British troops took George's home in Charles Street to be used as a hospital and afterwards as a barrack. The house was much damaged. At the evacuation by the British, the house was restored, but George died soon in 1781, leaving his wife and children in England with nothing.

During the stay in England, Elizabeth placed her deaf daughter Ann at the Braidwood Academy under Thomas Braidwood. It is not known when Elizabeth and her children left South Carolina for England. Ann's placement at the school cannot be before 1779 because the minimum age for the child to be received into Braidwood Academy was five years old. As the 1820 letter from Hewat to Edwards stated, "Mr Thomas Braidwood our English Teacher of the Deaf & Dumb," the use of the word "English teacher" would indicate that Ann was at the Hackney school (1783) rather than the Edinburgh school. After a few years, according to Hewat in his letter, Elizabeth was advised to carry her to another famous master in France, namely the Abbe Charles-Michel de l'Épée (1712-1789) in his school in Paris. Again according to Hewat's 1820 letter, Ann's education in the Paris school was a disappointment compared with her education under Thomas Braidwood. It is assumed that Elizabeth and her children stayed in Boulogne, France, during Ann's stay at the Paris school. During that stay, the hearing half of the twins lost the use of her limbs through palsy. It is known that Elizabeth was in London in 1786-88; whether she left behind Ann as a boarder in the Paris school for the deaf or not is open to question. It is possible that Ann attended the school in 1789 as there is evidence of a letter from Elizabeth dated 1789 from Boulogne.

According to Hewat's letter, the twins died in Flanders and they were brought back to England by their mother and buried at St Mary the Virgin cemetery in Dover. There is a reference to Ann in an obituary:

"Barksdale, Ann, dau. of – B., formerly of So. Carolina. Mar. 1790, aet. 16." (*Musgrave's Obituaries Prior to 1800, Parts 1&2*).

Alexander Hewat met Elizabeth Barksdale in 1793 and they married at the church of St Mary, St Marylebone, London, on 16 September 1798 and both resided in New Road in the same borough. Elizabeth passed away and was buried on 25 April 1814, aged 70 years, in the same tomb as her children in St Mary the Virgin cemetery in Dover. The tragic story of the twins still remains a mystery and their deaths in Flanders are quite unusual but worth investigating further purely for interest alone.

Henry Fox

Henry Fox was the illegitimate son of the great British politician Charles James Fox and his mistress Elizabeth Armistead. Almost nothing is known of Henry Fox with the exception of a small account in pages 81 and 82 of the book *Recollections of the Table Talk of Samuel Rogers* (1856):

> "I once dined at Mr Stone's (at Hackney) with Fox, Sheridan, Talleyrand, Madame de Genlis, Pamela, and some other celebrated persons of the time. A natural son of Fox, a dumb boy (who was the very image of his father, and who died a few years after, when about the age of fifteen) was also there, having come for the occasion, from Braidwood's Academy. To him Fox almost entirely confined his attention, conversing with him by the fingers; and their eyes glistened as they looked at each other. Talleyrand remarked to me, "How strange it was, to dine in company with the first orator in Europe, and only see him talk with his fingers!"

Charlotte Carter

Charlotte Carter was the only child of the Rev. Robert Carter, who later changed his name to Carter-Thelwall shortly before his wife Charlotte (nee Nelthorpe) died on 8 March 1780. Charlotte, who was born on 20 April 1769, had severe speech defect, probably since birth. In 1772, Robert Carter engaged "a man from Wistow, who had the same defect in speech as Charlotte, yet speaking very intelligibly." It appeared that the Wistow man's attempts to correct Charlotte's speech defect were unsuccessful, as the Rev. Robert Carter sent her to Edinburgh in 1780, where she spent five months under Thomas Braidwood at his academy. Robert Carter noted in his account book – "to Mr. Braidwood for 5 months teaching Charlotte to speak and read without any Benefit at the rate of one guinea per hour and at his own school - £315." Charlotte was then eleven years old and it appeared that she also had reading problems on top of her speech impediments. There are to date no clues as to whether she was deaf or not.

Charlotte Carter
by Thomas Lawrence, 1789.
Reproduced with kind
permission of Tom Nelthorpe,
Scawby Estates, Lincs.

Charlotte married Lord William Beauclerk (1766-1825), who was descended "on the wrong side of the blanket" from King Charles II and Nell Gwynne. Beauclerk was a social climber and a land grabber, and it was suggested that his motive for marrying Charlotte was for purely selfish purposes. The marriage produced one child, William Robert Beauclerk, who died soon after birth. Charlotte died on 15 September 1797 a young age of 28, and Redbourne Hall and the land attached to it passed into Beauclerk's hands.

Not surprisingly, following Charlotte's death, Beauclerk went on to marry Maria Janetta Nelthorpe of the Little Grimsby branch of the Nelthorpe family and he got his hands on the Nelthorpe lands there as well.

John Creasy

The name John Creasy is very well known to those concerned with the early days of the history of the education of the Deaf in Britain, especially in connection with the founding of the first public school for the deaf – the London Asylum for Deaf and Dumb Children in Bermondsey, south London, in 1792.

Interestingly, no one has ever researched or written a book about this person, which in a number of ways is quite sad because his contribution to Deaf history, Deaf education and Deaf community was immense –

he was the first Deaf teacher, employed as writing and drawing master by both Thomas Braidwood and Joseph Watson in connection with private pupils. Not only that, according to the minutes of the Committee of the London Asylum for the Instruction of the Deaf and Dumb of the Poor, Creasy was later employed by the committee of that school in 1802 to train a number of Deaf pupils to become teachers of the Deaf – he was notably associated with the training of William Hunter, who became the first employed Deaf teacher at the London Asylum in June 1804. After that, two other pupils, John Hamilton and William White, were also trained by John Creasy to become teachers, following the footsteps of William Hunter.

An extract from the Minutes of the committee of the London Asylum for the Instruction of the Deaf and Dumb of the Poor - dated 12 April 1802, showing the payment to Mr Creasy for the tuition of William Hunter and the materials required.

Reprinted with kind permission of Royal School for the Deaf, Margate.

John Creasy was the son of John and Mary (nee Sully) Creasy of Deptford, who had three sons and a daughter. He was christened on 18 September 1774, and was the oldest of the four children. John went deaf in early infancy and was sent to the Braidwood Academy in Edinburgh around 1781. When the academy moved to Hackney, John continued his education there.

Creasy's mother Mary was a very caring person and she was determined that the gift of education should be made free and available to every Deaf child, rich or poor. Mary Creasy was a frequent visitor to the Jamaica Row Congregational Chapel in Bermondsey, south London. The minister at the chapel was a young man of 35 years named John Townsend and it was to this person that she came for help, bringing along her Deaf son John to meet him after the morning church service on Sunday 20 May 1792 and the rest is history, for within six months of meeting John Creasy the first public school for the education of the Deaf of the poor was opened in Fort Place, Bermondsey, on Wednesday 14 November with six pupils and Joseph Watson from the Braidwood Academy as the head teacher. (*Bermondsey 1792 – Raymond Lee & John A. Hay. Pub: 1993, National Union of the Deaf.*) John Townsend was impressed with John Creasy when he met and conversed with him.

Fort Place, Bermondsey, SE London.

It was a tribute to the education Creasy received from Thomas Braidwood that led to the Rev. John Townsend being inspired to take up the cause to establish a public school for the Deaf children of poor parents, and that school still survives at present as the Royal School for the Deaf, Margate.

After the death of Joseph Watson in 1829, Creasy continued as a teacher of private pupils for Watson's son and successor. He lived a long life and died when he was about the age of 85, believed to be in the late summer of 1858 in Greenwich.

John Heathcote

John Heathcote (1782-1851) was the second son of Sir John Edensor Heathcote and Anne Gresley. He was deaf and dumb and he attended the Braidwood Institution for the Deaf and Dumb under Isabella Braidwood in Mare Street, Hackney. He married Emma Tudor and they had nine children.

EDUCATION OF DEAF AND DUMB CHILDREN.
MR. AND MRS. JOHN HEATHCOTE.

AVAIL themselves of this method of communicating to the Public, and particularly to Parents and Guardians, that it is their intention to form an Establishment for the education of Deaf and Dumb Children, between the ages of eight and twelve years. For this undertaking, Mr. J. Heathcote presumes to advance his more than ordinary fitness; having himself from Infancy laboured under the infirmity in question, but having, with the superintendence of the late Mr. Thomas Braidwood, Teacher of Deaf and Dumb, at Hackney, near London, and with the further advantage of ten years tuition, under an amiable and accomplished Clergyman, not only acquired the power of speaking articulately and intelligibly; but also he trusts the means of teaching every thing usually expected in the early department of Education in this country. Mrs. John Heathcote being fully impressed with a consciousness of the great responsibility connected with the care and comfort of Pupils, under such circumstances, will not only undertake the superintendence of the domestic department, but will also be able to assist Mr. J. Heathcote very materially, in many of the preparatory steps; and neither zeal nor exertion will be wanting on her part, to consult as far as possible, the health and comfort entrusted to their care.

TERMS

Of the intended School for the education of Deaf and Dumb Children, at Green-dock Cottage, Lane-End, near Newcastle-under-Lyne, Staffordshire.

For Board and Lodging, with general Instruction, 100 guineas per annum.

Writing, Drawing and Washing, on the usual terms.

A quarter's notice to be given previous to the removal of any Pupil from the School, or in default thereof, the quarter to be charged.

N.B. The pupils to take their meals with, and to form, in all respects, a part of the family.

The situation of the house is airy, and well adapted to the object proposed.

A little information on him is available through old newspapers, but apart from that, there is nothing more. We learn that Heathcote and his wife were running a private school for the education of deaf children from the Leicester Journal dated Friday 24 February 1832 as shown on the previous page.

Charles Bowyer Adderley Heathcote

Charles (1797-1844) was a younger brother of John Heathcote; his mother Anne Gresley died almost immediately after giving birth to Charles and she left 10 children under the age of eighteen. A relative moved in to take over the household and raise the children.

Like his elder deaf brother John Heathcote years earlier, Charles attended the Braidwood Institution under Isabella Braidwood in Hackney. Nothing is practically known about Charles apart from the fact that he died unmarried in 1844.

St. George Randolph

St. George Randolph was the fifth American to attend the Braidwood Institution. He was born deaf in 1792 to Richard and Judith Randolph of Virginia. His father died in 1796. St. George Randolph, then eighteen years old, was sent to England in 1810 and taken into the care of James Monroe, then the US representative in Britain. It was Monroe who enlisted St. George Randolph at the Braidwood Institution in Hackney, where he spent almost two years before going on to France with Monroe. In France, he was sent to the St. Jacques School and was a pupil under Laurent Clerc, who reported that he was doing quite well. Of his stay at the Braidwood Institution, Monroe wrote to his uncle, "He has improved… but owing to his natural defects not as fast as he would otherwise do… the articulation cannot be made quite natural…" This indicates St. George Randolph may have been a slow learner, but it is more likely that the lack of constant and fluent signing employed in communication coupled with his late age may have been the cause. However, historical records contain reference to his quick temper and independence of spirit; and numerous genealogical notes list him as "deaf and dumb and crazy."

Randolph returned to America in 1814, and upon hearing of his younger brother Tudor's illness at Harvard College, he became deranged. It was said that from that day until his death on 4 December 1857 St. George Randolph never had a lucid interval, spending time in places like the Philadelphia Hospital for the Insane and also he spent about twenty years in a lunatic asylum in Baltimore. His brother Tudor went to England in 1814, but he died of pulmonary TB on 18 August 1815 in Cheltenham.

Archibald Douglas

Not much is known about this person and, along with the name that was passed down in Deaflore, the only source of information linking him to the Braidwood Academy came from the Scottish newspaper *Caledonian Mercury* dated Monday 14 September 1789. Archibald Douglas successfully applied for gun licence and was granted one on purchase of two guineas.

ADDITIONAL LIST.
GAME DUTY, COUNTY OF MID LOTHIAN.

LIST of Game Certificates, at Two Guineas each, issued by the Sheriff-clerk of the county of Mid-Lothian since the 13th of August 1789.

A

Anderson, Francis, Esq. of George Street
Anderson, Mr Peter, Currie
Anderson, Mr John, at Hatton

B

Bell, Mr William, junior, merchant, Leith
Bartlet, Capt. F. B. D. of Drummikill
Borthwick, John, Esq. of Crookston
Beveridge, William, Esq. writer to the signet
Belford, Captain William, 57th regiment
Bowes, the Right Hon. George, Edinburgh
Baird, Mr James, Exchequer

C

Crawford. Captain Charles, Queen's Dragoon Guards
Craigie, Robert, Esq. advocate
Clerk, Sir John, of Pennycuick, Bart.
Charteris, Henry William, Esq. Bruntsland
Cochran, Major Spencer, of the East India Company

D

Dupuis, Capt. Richard, of the Queen's Dragoon Guards
Dick, Sir William, of Prestonfield
Dundas, Robert, Esq. his Majesty's Solicitor General
Douglas, Archibald, Esq. Edinburgh, late pupil of Mr Braidwood
Dick, John, Esq. Salisbury Green

E

Evatt, Capt. Henry, Queen's Dragoon Guards
Eiston, John, Esq. Edinburgh

F

Fenwick, the Rev. Mr Robert, Leith
Fairfax, Capt. of his Majesty Navy, Burntisland
Forbes, the Right Hon. Andrew, Edinburgh
Farquharson, Francis, Esq. of Haughton

G

Margaret and Isabella Gibson

The source of these two Braidwoodian pupils came from page 56 of the *11th Report of the General Institution for the Instruction of the Deaf and Dumb Children at Edgbaston, 1823.* This little contribution of a reproduced school work by Jasper Gibson revealed Margaret Gibson as a pupil of the Braidwood Institution under Isabella and her son Thomas. Jasper's younger sister was a pupil of Isabella and her daughter Elizabeth at the Seminary for Young Deaf Children at the Mount, Edgbaston. This small account also revealed the popularity of Isabella Braidwood and how much she was loved.

56

I have four brothers and four sisters. My father's name is John Gibson ; my mother's name is Margaret Gibson. My brothers and sisters are named William, John, Henry, Thomas, Jane, Elizabeth, Isabella, Helen, and Julia Gibson. My sister Margaret is dead ; she was deaf; she was a very good girl;—I hope she will be happy for ever in heaven. Your mother and you taught her at Hackney. Hackney is in Middlesex. I never was at Hackney.—My sister Isabella is deaf. Your mother and your sister taught her at the Mount. She is at home now. Your mother was a very good woman;— we all loved her. I hope she is gone to heaven.—I hope my brother Thomas will come here very soon to learn his duty to God and man, to understand accounts, to speak, to read, and to write. I suppose he will be happy to come here very soon— he is deaf.—I hope you will teach him at Edgbaston.—I hope you and your sister are very well and happy. You live at Highfields—your sister lives at the Mount.

I am, respectfully,

Your obedient, and humble, and

Affectionate pupil,

JASPER GIBSON.

Thomas Cooley

Thomas Cooley was born in Sandymount Green, Dublin in 1795, the son of the lawyer William Cooley. He was born deaf and sent to the Braidwood Institution in Hackney around 1803 and he stayed there until 1811. After ending his education, Cooley studied art for portrait painting and sketching at the Royal Academy of Arts in London under the tuition of renowned painters such as William Turner, John Flaxman and Sir John Sloane. While studying art, he stayed as a private boarder in Isabella Braidwood's Mare Street institution.

About three or four years afterwards, Thomas returned to Dublin to commence his first work painting portraits of Lord Mayors, Aldermen and some wealthy families. He exhibited his works at the Royal Hibernian Academy (RHA).

Thomas Cooley continued to paint and exhibit his work at RHA exhibitions for numerous years and he became an associate member of the RHA in 1825 until he resigned to live and work in London where he continued his profession as a portrait painter; dozens of his works were exhibited at the Royal Academy Exhibitions from 1826 to 1840s.

Thomas Cooley - Self Portrait
Reproduced with kind permission of David Breslin

In 1845 Thomas returned to Dublin and resided with his aged father William in Sandymount for a short time. After William's death, Thomas settled on his own at 97 Harcourt Street. After a period of declining health, Thomas passed away on 20 June 1872 at the age of 77 and he was buried two days later in Mount Jerome, Harold's Cross, Dublin.

Mary Brunton

Mary Brunton was born deaf on 1 January 1761 in Newcastle-upon-Tyne. Her parents were a wealthy shoemaker Benjamin Brunton and his wife Mary Henderson. She had two sisters and one brother, all of whom were hearing. Nothing much is known about this deaf lady with the exception of two small mentions from the *Newcastle Courant* newspapers:

Saturday 1 October 1768

MR BRAIDWOOD, of Edinburgh, having already taught several Persons, who were deaf and dumb, to speak, read, and understand the grammatical Construction of the English Language, also to write and cypher; and being willing to extend his Practice in

258

the Art, hereby gives Notice, That he is ready to undertake the Instruction of an additional Number of Pupils to those at present under his Care. Mr Braidwood applied to the Rev. Dr Robertson, Principal of the University of Edinburgh, and other Persons of Distinction there, Who, after examining his deaf Pupils, gave their assertions to the Truth of the above in their Letters to several Gentlemen in London. And the following Gentlemen, who saw one of his principal Pupils, when he was lately in London, permitted their Names to be mentioned as being highly satisfied with the Progress they found he had made in Speaking, Reading, Writing, &c. viz. Sir John Pringle, Dr Wilbraham, Dr Hunter, Dr Watson, Dr Huck, Dr Franklin of Pennsylvania, Dr Orme, Dr Munro, and the Rev. Dr Gilford, at the British Museum.

N.B. Mr Braidwood has at present deaf Pupils from seven to twenty six Years of Age. He has also had considerable Success in correcting the Defects of Persons who stutter, or have any other Impediments in their Speech.

A daughter of Mr Benj Brunton, of Newcastle, who was deaf and dumb from her Birth, now seven and a Half Years old, has been under Mr Braidwood's Care and Instructions only seven Months, and has made astonishing Progress: She can already understand what is said to her by the Motion of the Lips, can return short Answers, and has lately wrote, with her own Hand, a Letter to her Father, which gave great Pleasure and Surprise to all who saw it —The Particulars of her Care may be learned by enquiring of the aforesaid Mr Brunton, Shoemaker, in Newcastle.

From the above newspaper article, it is easy to pinpoint that Mary Brunton started at the Braidwood Academy in March 1768 at the age of seven years and three months. The article indicated that it was Charles Shirreff whom the gentlemen from London saw at the British Museum, for he left the Braidwood Academy in 1767 and headed for London soon afterwards. It also comes as a surprise that 'Dr Franklin of Pennsylvania' was indeed Benjamin Franklin.

Four years after the newspaper article, another was published on Saturday 19 September 1772 in the same *Newcastle Courant*:

> A Gentleman of this town being at Edinburgh, waited upon Mr Braidwood, Teacher there, and catching hold of Lord Bacon's works, hit upon the following passage, which he requested Miss Brunton, (who was born deaf) daughter of Mr Benjamin Brunton of this town, to explain which she instantly did, in a manner we apprehend, both for the credit of the young Lady and Master, will be agreeable to the Public.—*Passage.* Lord Bacon has divided the whole of human knowledge into history, poetry, and philosophy; which are referred to the three powers of the mind, memory, imagination, and reason.—*The Explanation.* A noble man had parted the total or all of man's study on understanding, into an account of the life, manners, religion and customs, and so on, of any people or country, verse or metre, moral or natural knowledge; which are pointed to the three faculties of the soul or spirit, the faculty of remembering what is past, thought or conception, and right judgement.

The quality of instruction that Mary Brunton received under Thomas Braidwood can be summed up by reading the above newspaper article.

Dudley Ryder, Viscount Stanton

Dudley Ryder was born on 19 May 1798, the first son of the Earl of Harrowby and Lady Susan Leveson Gower. Although Dudley Ryder is described in Parliamentary biographies as having been instructed by Mrs Braidwood at her Braidwood Institution in Hackney between 1803 and 1806, there are no references to his being deaf. Earlier 1790-1820 volumes of *House of Commons Parliamentary Biographies* do refer to a serious childhood speech impediment which caused his father to send him to a succession of private schools and tutors, including the Braidwood Institution. The reference to Dudley attending Mrs Braidwood's school as a young boy probably came from his *Reminiscences by Dudley, 2nd Earl of Harrowby*, located at the Harrowby mss at Sandon Hall. Dudley Ryder died in 1882.

Thomas Arrowsmith

He was... blessed with a quick and comprehensive mind...
— Thomas Dodds

Thomas Arrowsmith was born deaf in Newent, Gloucestershire, the fourth of six children of Nathaniel and Elizabeth, nee Cook. According to available church records Thomas was christened on 23 January 1771. Thomas' early life was described in the book *The Art of Instructing the Infant Deaf and Dumb*, published in 1819. The author of that book was none other than Thomas' younger brother John Pauncefort Arrowsmith (christened 30 December 1772 in Newent).

According to the book, when Thomas was about four or five years old his mother took him to a local dame school and she demanded that her son be educated in spite of his deafness. When the schoolmistress expressed difficulties that would occur due to Thomas' deafness and lack of speech in a totally hearing environment within the school, Elizabeth Arrowsmith merely told the schoolmistress to teach her son to read and write, and take matters from there. It appears that Thomas did well at his local dame school and he was able to attain a good command of written English and also of the understanding of the language. His speech was nowhere as good as anyone hoped. Thomas stayed at the school until he was 11 years old, and John Pauncefort Arrowsmith's work

Thomas Arrowsmith—self portrait
(From J.P. Arrowsmith's 1819 book
The Art of Instructing the Infant Deaf and Dumb)

ended abruptly at that stage of Thomas' life, and another section was written about the Abbe de l'Epée and his systematic sign method...

Why did John Pauncefort Arrowsmith not continue with the second phase of Thomas' education after he left the dame school? There must surely be a reason for that — was Thomas' brother either disappointed with, or trying to hide facts concerning Thomas' next stage of education? There is an echo of Francis Green and his *Vox oculis subjecta* (1783) here; Green ended his work on Braidwood Academy and jumped onto the subject of l'Epée. It is not unreasonable to suggest that John Pauncefort Arrowsmith was disappointed perhaps with the method of communication that Thomas Braidwood employed in the next stage of his brother's education. What one has to bear in mind is the fact that John Pauncefort Arrowsmith's book was published in 1819, some thirty-seven years after his brother Thomas left the dame school in 1782. In between these two dates John Pauncefort Arrowsmith must have developed an opinion which he included in his work. According to John Pauncefort Arrowsmith, Thomas ended his dame school education in 1782, a year short of the Braidwood Academy moving from Edinburgh to Hackney, and it is possible that Thomas Arrowsmith was educated at the dame school until 1783 when his parents were in a position to send him to Hackney for the next phase of his education.

British Deaf historians have come to a common consensus that Thomas attended the Braidwood Academy located at the former Bowling Green House in Hackney and a number of factors points to this conclusion:

1. Thomas was well acquainted with a number of Braidwoodian pupils, particularly Creasy and Harris. He painted portraits of these two deaf Braidwoodian pupils, as well as of their fathers. The only way he would have been acquainted with Creasy and Harris would be at the Braidwood Academy.

2. John Pauncefort Arrowsmith was critical of the classroom environment in which his brother Thomas was educated in the second stage of his education and this can be perceived by reading his article published on pages 70-79 of the book *An Essay on the Deaf and Dumb* by John Harrison Curtis (Pub: Longman, Rees, Orme, Brown and Green, Paternoster Row, London. 1829). This Arrowsmith portion of the essay is reproduced in Appendix 4.

It seems that Thomas acquired the "deaf way" and deaf identity while at the Braidwood academy and this might be the reason why he turned out to be a disappointment to his brother John. John also expressed a great dislike of deaf children being educated apart from hearing children and he was a strong advocate of what is known at present mainstreaming system of education.

3. In 1827 Thomas Dodd of Manchester wrote of Thomas Arrowsmith in *The Connoisseur's Repertory*:

Thomas... was blessed with a quick and comprehensive mind and a natural turn towards attaining to a proficiency in the art of painting portraits and other subjects in miniature, in which practice he excels, and continues to do so in the present time. He first exhibited at Somerset House in 1792, with two subjects in miniature compass, Cain slaying Abel and Mary Magdalene conversing with Christ. In the following year he applied himself to portrait painting and exhibited two portraits of gentlemen. In 1795 he reappeared at Somerset House in a miniature of himself and of six others of different individuals. In 1796 he produced a portrait of a bishop, and that of an old man. In 1797 miniature portraits of Mr. Harris, Mr. Flaxman and Mr. Weston, also of himself, Mr. Harris Jnr. And Mr. Creasy Jnr., the two latter his associates, who were also alike defective in speech and hearing. In 1799 a miniature of Mr. Luke Fitzgerald. Mr. Arrowsmith now resides in Manchester where his talents are duly appreciated.

Thomas Dodd confirmed Arrowsmith's association with Harris and Creasy, and, along with Deaflore, this went some way to indicate Thomas' link with the Braidwood Academy for the second phase of his education.

Thomas entered the Royal Academy Schools in 1789 and became a pupil of Sir Joshua Reynolds, who was himself deaf and also the President of the Royal Academy. Thomas excelled as a miniature and portrait painter. He began exhibiting his work in the Royal Academy, which was based in Somerset House, in 1792 and his list of exhibitions were:

> *7 Charlotte Street, Pimlico*
> 1792 337 Cain and Abel
>   589 Mary Magdalen with Christ
>
> *2 Devonshire Street, Queen's Square*
> 1793 429 Portrait of a Gentleman (Alexander Small)
>   454 Portrait of a Gentleman

148 Drury Lane
1795 468 Miniature, Girl and Boy
      469 do. Himself and Four Others

274 Holborn
1796 547 Miniature, John Baker, Bishop of Hereford
      640 Miniature, An Old Man
148 Drury Lane
1797 1035 Miniature, Two Young Gentlemen
      1038 Miniature, Lady

79 Lower Grosvenor Street
1798 765 Miniatures, Frame with Mr. Harris, Mr.
           Flaxman and Mr Weston
      872 Miniatures, Himself, Mr. Harris, Jr., and
           Mr. Creasy, Jr.
1799 798 Miniature, Mr. Luke Fitzgerald

16 Elliott's Row
1800 831 Miniature, Gentleman
      929 Miniature, Lady

31 Coventry Street
1829 424, Mr. Singleton, Professor of Mechanism

In December 1796 the Royal Academy awarded its distinguished Annual Medal to Thomas in recognition of his merit and contribution to art, despite the fierce competition from other artists of greater renown. The President of the Royal Academy, B. West, presented the award and remarked that despite being deaf and dumb, Thomas "had long been considered among the first of his contemporaries, and whose very descriptive pencil at length enabled him to acquire the laurel against utmost efforts of his numerous competitors."

Thomas painted a large number of portraits which included quite a number of famous sitters such as the merchant William Durning, Carr Fenton, the banker Burrell of Liverpool, the Rev. Edward Green of Croft and the jockey Frank Buckle. Thomas, however, did not attain the same level of fame and renown as Charles Shirreff. What little is known of Thomas can be found in a series of contributions to *Notes and Queries* by the renowned deaf artist and antiquarian Frederick Lawrence Tavaré (1846-1930), who wrote a memoir of Thomas which was published in the *Deaf and Dumb World* for December 1885.

In *Notes and Queries* (8th S.I. April 16, 1892) Tavaré contributed the following:

> THOMAS ARROWSMITH (8th S. i. 168) — I sent a question concerning this painter to 'N & Q' 7th S. i. 249,but no reply was obtained. I saw a small oil painting of the famous David Lambert, weight 52st. 11lb. (14lb to the stone), at Mr. Pratt's in Hulme, which I should think has been an excellent likeness. It is carefully painted and beautiful. The subjoined is written on the back of the painting:—
>
> "Taken by T. Arrowsmith, an artist deaf and dumb, and presented by him to Mr Daniel Lambert as a token of respect, June 1808."
>
> The following query, which also elicited no reply is from 'Local Notes and Queries,' from the Manchester Guardian, 1875:—
>
> "688. T. Arrowsmith. — Could any of your numerous correspondents give me any clue to an artist of the name T. Arrowsmith, who has executed some splendid portrait paintings (dated 1806 to 1824) of persons in Rochdale and neighbourhood? Any information would be thankfully received by one who possesses an number of his exquisite paintings.
>
> JOHN JONES."

Left:
Frank Buckle, champion jockey
by Thomas Arrowsmith.

Photograph reproduced by courtesy of
Graham Budd Auctions.

I have been consulting a book (272 pages, 8vo., 1819) at the Manchester Public Reference Library, King Street. This work is entitled 'The Art of Instructing the Infant Deaf and Dumb' by John Pauncefort Arrowsmith, illustrated with copper plates, drawn and engraved by the author's brother Thomas, an artist born deaf and dumb, to which is annexed the method of educating mutes of a more mature age, which has been practised with so much success on the continent by the Abbé de l'Epée, London. The frontispiece is a portrait, in old fashioned attire, with a brush in the right hand, of Mr. Arrowsmith. He was a native of Newent, in the county of Gloucester. In a footnote is given a copy from the Bath and Cheltenham Gazette of January 14, 1818, of part of a letter, written by G. Chippendale, Esq., of Winwick, illustrative of the sense of feeling in Mr. Arrowsmith. J. P. Arrowsmith died at his house, Pembroke Garden, Liverpool, April 14, 1829, but I cannot tell the date of his brother's decease, who would be fifty-four years of age when ceasing to exhibit his works of art.

"Thomas Arrowsmith. — Deaf and dumb from his birth, which occurred about the year 1776, was nevertheless blessed with a quick and comprehensive mind and a natural turn towards attaining to a proficiency in the art of painting portraits and other subjects in miniature, in which practice he excels, and continues to do in the present time. He first exhibited at Somerset House in 1792 two subjects in miniature compass of Cain slaying Abel and Mary Magdalen conversing with Christ. In the following year he applied himself to portrait painting and exhibited two portraits of gentlemen. In 1795 he reappeared at Somerset House in a miniature of himself, and of six others of different individuals. In 1796 he produced the portrait of a bishop, and that of an old man. In 1797, miniature portraits of two young gentlemen, and that of a lady. In 1798, miniature portraits of

Mr. Flaxman, Mrs. Harris, and Mr. Weston; also of himself, Mr. Harris jun., and Mr. Creasy, jun., the two latter his associates, who were also alike defective in speech and hearing. In 1799, a miniature of Mr. Luke Fitzgerald. Mr. Arrowsmith now resides at Manchester, where his talents are duly appreciated."

FREDERICK LAWRENCE TAVARÉ
30 Rusholme Grove, Manchester.

The Connoisseur's Repertory — Part III. And Art, by Thomas Dodd of Manchester, afterwards London, about 1827, gave the following:—

> ... (Arrowsmith exhibited) in 1797 miniature portraits of Mr Flaxman, Mr Harris and Mr Weston; also of himself, Mr Harris Jun., and Mr Creasy, Jun., the two latter his associates, who were also alike defective in speech and hearing.

Between 1807 and 1810, Thomas Arrowsmith resided at 26 Piccadilly, Manchester, and this is confirmed by Dean's Manchester and Salford Directory for 1809 and it is known that after 1810 Thomas also resided in Liverpool , Manchester and Rochdale. It appears that Thomas took up a role of journeyman artist, travelling to various towns offering his services to those who could not be bothered to travel. Thomas was making tidy sums of money painting those who wished to have their portraits done. In tandem with Thomas' travels, his brother John Pauncefort also took to travelling all over England: he was an itinerary lawyer, visiting places where income could be made. The *Lancaster Gazette* of Saturday 7 May reported that on the 30th of May John Pauncefort Arrowsmith, of Manchester, attorney at law, married Miss Holt, third daughter of Mr Oliver Holt, of Underwood, Rochdale. This was Elizabeth Holt.

John Pauncefort Arrowsmith died on 14 April 1829 at his home in Pembroke Gardens, Liverpool, and his wife Elizabeth died on 18 September 1855 at Rochdale.

Around the Spring of 1812 Thomas returned to London and later it was recorded that he married Elizabeth Carpenter on 17 September 1812 at the church of St Mary's, St Marylebone, London. There are accounts which describe Elizabeth Carpenter as "illiterate." The veracity of this description of Elizabeth as illiterate was concluded from her mark on their marriage registration:

Registration of marriage between Thomas Arrowsmith and Elizabeth Carpenter—note the "X" mark of Elizabeth Carpenter.

Thomas' marriage to Elizabeth did not appear to make him settle down. He continued to travel around the country, visiting places like Edinburgh, Doncaster, Norwich and Worcester amongst several others. His name became very well known in various cities due to both his travels and the quality of his finished paintings. Despite his renown, very little is available about the man and his life.

A Gentleman 1810
Thomas Arrowsmith
© Woolley & Wallis
Salisbury Salerooms

There was a letter written by G. Chippendale of Winwick, near Warrington, which is of great interest, and fortunately Frederick Lawrence Tavaré sent in a copy of it in his *Notes & Queries* contribution printed in the 11 S. X. October 31, 1914 issue:

… Some particulars respecting this artist will, perhaps, be of interest:—

"My mother (says the author) had three children who lived to be educated besides him (Thomas Arrowsmith). In a few months after my brother's birth it was discovered that he could not hear, but in every other respect he was perfect and sensible."

268

One remarkable trait of the deaf artist was that he took the highest delight in music, and some evidences of this are quoted from a letter written by G. Chippendale of Winwick, near Warrington, to *The Bath and Cheltenham Gazette* of 14 Jan. 1818. See the footnote in this book, pp. 74-6.

Mr. Chippendale says:—

"Some years back, probably five or six, a young gentleman of the name of Arrowsmith, a member of the Royal Academy at Somerset House, of what degree I cannot remember, came down to this country, and resided some months in Warrington in the exercise of his profession as miniature and portrait painter. He was quite deaf, so as to be entirely dumb. He had been taught to write, and wrote an elegant hand, in which he was enabled to

Elizabeth Arrowsmith nee Carpenter, 1818
Painted by Thomas Arrowsmith.
Photograph of painting by courtesy of Pook & Pook Inc.

express his own ideas with facility; he was also able to read and understand the ideas of others expressed in writing. It will scarcely be credited that a person thus circumstanced should be fond of music, but this was the fact in the case of Arrowsmith. He was at a gentleman's Glee Club, of which I was president at that time, and as the glees were sung, he would place himself near some articles of wooden furniture or a partition, door or window-shutter, and would fix the extreme end of his finger-nails, which he kept rather long, upon the edge of the wood, or some projecting part of it, and there remain until the piece under performance was finished, all the while expressing, by the most significant gestures, the pleasure he experienced from the perception of the musical sounds. He was not so much pleased with a solo as with a pretty full clash of harmony, and if the music was not very good, or, I should rather say, if it was not correctly executed, he would shew no sensation of pleasure. But the most extraordinary circumstance in this case is, that he was most evidently delighted with those passages in which the composer displayed his science in modulating his different keys. When such passages happen to be executed with precision he could scarcely repress the emotions of pleasure he received within any bounds; for the delight he evinced seemed to border on ecstasy. This was expressed most remarkably at our Club when the glee was sung with which we often conclude. It is by Stevens, and begins with the words, 'Ye spotted snakes,' &c., from Shakespeare's 'Midsummer Night's Dream.' In the second stanza on the words 'Weaving spiders, come not here.' &c., there is some modulation of the kind above alluded to, and here Mr Arrowsmith would be in raptures, such as would not be exceeded by one who was in immediate possession of the sense of hearing. These facts are very extraordinary ones, and, that they are facts, can be proved by the evidence of six or eight gentlemen who were present, and by turns observed him accurately."

FRED. L. TAVARÉ

22, Trentham Street, Pendleton, Manchester.

Thomas' paintings were scattered all over the country and it appears that many ended up in private collections. Some of Thomas' missing or lesser known works can be identified from yet another contribution by Tavaré to the 11 S. X Nov. 14, 1914 issue of *Notes and Queries*. Extracted from page 395, a part of Tavaré's letter reads:

S.G. Aged 46, 1800
by Thomas Arrowsmith.

Photograph reproduced by courtesy of the British Deaf History Society

> On 11 Dec, 1884, when I was passing a shop of E. Ulph, an assumed name for Mr. Wilkinson, a dealer in antique furniture, china, brasses, &c., 17 Albert Street, Manchester, my attention was drawn to two lithographs in black antique frames. The inscription on these lithographs read thus:—

From a sketch by T. Arrowsmith,
Martha Blears
Of the Jolly Carter in Winton cum Barton, near Eccles, Lancashire, who narrowly escaped being assassinated on Monday 22nd May, 1826, after receiving several wounds by one of the McKeands, in particular one by a Whittle under the left eye, which fastened in the upper jaw so firm that it was an hour and half before it was extracted.
Printed by H. G. James, Manchester.

From a sketch by T. Arrowsmith,
Wm Higgins
Servant to J. Blears of the Jolly Carter in Winton cum Barton, near Eccles, Lancashire, who escaped being assassinated on Monday 22 May, 1826, by jumping out of bed, running and hiding himself in the hedge of the garden.
No. 1 printed by H. G. James, Manchester.

Mr. Ulph said the me: "I have the 'Jolly Carters' original signboard; it is on sale.' I live next door to the place, and am only showing for curiosity (not for sale) two lithographs in my window."

Alexander and Michael McKeand were hanged at Lancaster on 18 Aug. 1826, for the murder of Elizabeth Bates at "The Jolly Carters" on 22 May.

FRED. L. TAVARÉ.
22, Trentham Street, Pendleton, Manchester.

Immediately below Tavaré's contribution on the same page 395, there was a short letter printed:

One of my relations has an engraving or lithograph (I forget which) of the Rev. Giles Chippendale, who was for many years the curate of Winwick, on which is inscribed: "From a drawing by T. Arrowsmith, printed by C. Hullmandel." The Rev. Giles Chippendale died on 10 Oct., 1823, aged 63.

W. H. CHIPPENDALE, Col. Kirkby, Lonsdale.

In 1829, Thomas is known to have visited the Yorkshire Residential School for the Deaf in Doncaster and he entered his place of residence as London as shown in the school's Visitors book:

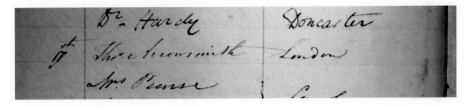

Thomas Arrowsmith's signature in the Visitor's Register Book of the Yorkshire Institute for the Deaf and Dumb, 1829.
Photograph by A. J. Boyce.

The place of Thomas' London residence was listed on the Royal Academy exhibitors' list as 31 Coventry Street, a short street running between Piccadilly Circus and Leicester Square.

During the 1820s and 1830s Thomas was still touring all over Britain, offering his services in miniature and portrait painting to members of the wealthy classes and this is verified by a series of newspaper announcements such as two adverts from the *Worcester Journal*

Thomas was living at Bury St Edmunds around 1832 and a small note in the *Stamford Mercury* dated Friday 23 November 1832 revealed that he had an accident in which he broke a rib when a coach overturned:

> Friday se'nnight, as the Cambridge coach was passing through Bottisham, the two leaders took fright, and the coach was, in consequence, overturned. The driver, Lamb, was bruised, and otherwise injured. Mr Arrowsmith, portrait painter of Bury St Edmunds, had a rib broken. The other passengers were but slightly injured.

George Augustus and Augustus John Child Villiers at Osterley Park
by Thomas Arrowsmith (painted c1815)

(Unable to locate original source - taken from
a photocopy left by the late Doreen E. Woodford.)

Although information on Thomas, his work and his travels have been gradually unearthed over years of research, there still remains the mystery of his wife Elizabeth and questions abound about her role in Thomas' life. Apart from the marriage record and one painting of her by her husband, nothing more is known about her. It should be said here that the fact that she was illiterate should not be taken to imply that she was not educationally normal. For someone to be accepted and married to a person of Thomas Arrowsmith's calibre, it appears that Elizabeth possessed normal intelligence, and also she was more than able to communicate and hold her own in conversations using signs.

Self Portrait of the artist
Thomas Arrowsmith

(Doreen E. Woodford Collection)

Thomas' death at the age of 69 at Oxford on 12 August 1839 was announced in the Obituary section of the *Hereford Journal* dated 21 August 1839:

> wife of Mr. Robert Young.—At Monmouth, on Friday, awfully sudden, Mr. Renell, skinner.—Aug. 12, Eleanor, wife of J. Best Esq. solicitor, Britannia-square, Worcester.—At Oxford, aged 69, Mr. Thomas Arrowsmith, well known as an eminent portrait painter.—On Monday, from the effects of a fall from his horse on the 4th inst. Wm. C. Brandram, Esq. of Gower-street and Size-lane, London, aged 51.—In London, Mr. Dowding, aged 62, formerly of Cradley, Herefordshire.

Thomas Arrowsmith

Charles Shirreff

Admire the painter…
— an unknown female admirer

In British Deaf history, the name Charles Shirreff will forever be associated with Thomas Braidwood in the same way as with other surdohistorical pair-associate names such as Thomas Gallaudet – Laurent Clerc; Abbé Sicard – Jean Massieu; Joseph Watson – John William Lowe and Henry Brothers Bingham – Arthur Henry Bather.

Charles Shirreff was born on 1 October 1749 in South Leith, Midlothian, Scotland. He was the son of a wealthy wine merchant Alexander Shirreff (b.1715) and his wife Agnes Young (b.1717) who resided in Bernard Street, South Leith. Charles was the youngest of Alexander's five sons – George (b.23 May 1741), James (b.26 May 1743), Alexander (b.1 March 1744) and John (b.12 June 1745). It is also recorded that Alexander Shirreff married again, presumably on the death of his wife Agnes, to Margaret Pitcairn. This marriage yielded two daughters, Mary, who was christened on 20 April 1759, and Alison, who was born on 18 February 1764.

Nothing much is known about Charles' early life before he was taken to Edinburgh to meet Thomas Braidwood. It was said that Charles went deaf at the age of three years. Charles was around ten and a half years old when he commenced his education under Thomas Braidwood, pinpointing the date to March 1760 at the very latest. We will never know what was agreed between Alexander Shirreff and Thomas Braidwood regarding Charles' education; for example, did Alexander desire that his son be proficient in speech? The reason why Alexander chose Thomas Braidwood of all teachers in Edinburgh has never been fully unearthed, but there is a clue. This clue is the nature of the private academy that Braidwood conducted – it was an academy for young gentlemen who were groomed to become educationally well-rounded especially in the Arts, English and mathematics; they were exercised to display etiquette and good manners at all times, and they were also trained to speak proper and correct. It is that last part which is of interest – Braidwood obviously held elocution lessons, speech therapy and corrections of stammering and speech impediments.

There is also a possibility that one of Alexander Shirreff's sons, or some of his acquaintances, attended the academy and this may have attracted Alexander to query if Braidwood could try and teach his deaf son Charles. All these comments mentioned here are pure speculation exploring the possibilities of how Thomas Braidwood began to get involved with the deaf based on reasonable construction of possible events.

Under Braidwood's tuition, Charles was taught to speak and to pronounce words as a part of his education. Lord Monboddo mentioned in page 179 of Volume 1 of *The Origin and Progress of Language (Edinburgh, 1773)* that Charles' speech was "good." Monboddo was being generous, perhaps taking into account the fact of how extremely difficult it was for a deaf person to acquire normal speech – and Charles' speech was more of the artificial speech that was typical of many deaf children under oralism.

Artificial speech can be both easily understood and maintained for as long as there is a teacher at hand to constantly monitor and correct proper pronunciation and voice levels. This was what happened to Shirreff during his schooldays with Braidwood. However, once Shirreff left the Braidwood Academy for the world outside, his speech and voice quality deteriorated due to the lack of monitoring.

Fingerspelling and signs played a very important part in Charles' education and these assisted him greatly. Not only was Charles proficient in English language, he also learned French under Braidwood and achieved a good level of fluency in both reading and writing modes. Shirreff developed into an excellent artist with an eye for portrait painting, and he became a very well-mannered young gentleman, oozing grace, charm and politeness. Braidwood took his pupils to the theatre on several occasions and Shirreff took a shine to David Garrick and his style of acting; not only that, Shirreff was also impressed by Garrick's interpretation of major characters in Shakespearean plays through his unique style, expression and brand of acting.

Upon leaving the Braidwood Academy probably before Christmas 1767, Shirreff took to painting as a profession and it is known that he left Edinburgh in early January 1768 for London. Shirreff was accompanied by his father, who had a good connections with persons of the higher class.

There exists a letter dated 17 January 1768, written by Horace Walpole to Sir David Dalrymple (published in a book entitled *The Letters of Horace Walpole, Earl of Orfon,* Volume V - ed. J Wright; pub: Samuel Bentley, London, 1840). In page 186, the letter read:

276

I will begin, Sir, with telling you that I have seen Mr Sherriff and his son. The father desired my opinion on sending his son to Italy. I own I could be no means advise it. Where a genius is indubitable and has already made much progress, the study of the antique and the works of the great masters may improve a young man extremely, and open lights to him which he might never discover of himself. But it is very different, sending a young man to Rome to try whether he has genius or not; which may be ascertained with infinitely less trouble and expense at home. Young Mr Sheriff has certainly a disposition to drawing; but that may not be genius. His misfortune may have made him embrace it as a resource in his melancholy hours. Labouring under the misfortune of deafness, his friends should consider to what unhappiness they may expose him. His family may have naturally applied to alleviate his misfortune, and to cultivate the parts they saw in him. But who, in so long a journey and at such distance, is to attend to him in the same affectionate manner? Can he shift for himself, especially without the language? Who will take the trouble at Rome of assisting him, instructing him, pointing out to him what he should study? Who will facilitate the means to him of gaining access to palaces, and churches, and obtain permission for him to work there? I felt so much for the distresses he must undergo that I could not see the benefits to accrue, and those eventual, as a compensation. Surely Sir, it were better to place him with some painter for a year or two. He does not seem to me to be grounded enough for such an expedition.

It appears that Charles' plan to follow the path of many artists of his day, notably Joshua Reynolds who was also deaf, had to be scuppered as he appeared to have received little encouragement from Horace Walpole. Through Alexander Shirreff's contacts, Charles moved around in the upper circles of society, rubbing shoulders with the rich, the famous and the influential elite. One of the earliest persons Shirreff befriended was the diplomatist Caleb Whitefoord (1734-1810) who had known Shirreff when he was at Edinburgh. Whitefoord wrote the famous Britain's Roscius poem and attributed the authorship to Shirreff to enable him to be introduced to David Garrick.

Caleb Whitefoord   David Garrick

There is an interesting anecdote in Arthur Murphy's *The Life of David Garrick* (1801, vol. II, pp. 181-186) in which the author mentioned he was dining with Shirreff and the latter's stepsister, Alison, who was the wife of John Heriot (1760-1833), the author and proprietor of *True Briton*. Murphy was told that by spelling his words in the air with his finger, he could converse with Shirreff, and found that the plan was answered.

> He put the following questions to him: 'Did you know Garrick?' 'Yes,' in an inarticulate sound. 'Did you ever see him act?' 'Yes.' 'Did you admire him?' 'Yes.' 'How could that be, when you could not hear him, and, of course, could not understand him?' The answer was unintelligible. Mr. and Mrs. Heriot were used to his manner; at their desire, the question was repeated, and the answer, when explained, astonished the whole company. Mr. Shirreff's reply was, Garrick's face was a language. To prove that it was so, Mr. Shirreff stood up after dinner, and, muttering uncouth sounds went through the part of Richard III by his deportment, by his action, and the most significant looks, distinguishing every scene and all the various situations of Richard from the beginning to his death in Bosworth Field. Hence a judgement may be formed of the actor who could play before the deaf and dumb, and make them capable. His face was a language!

Shirreff entered the Royal Academy Schools on 9 August 1769 at the age of nineteen and in the following year he took up shared lodgings with Thomas Burgess in Gloucester Street, Queen's Square, Bloomsbury. Burgess was a figure and portrait painter who studied at the St. Martin's Lane Academy and later kept an academy of his own in Maiden Lane. Shirreff exhibited at the Free Society of Artists between 1770 and 1773 and from 1771 at the Royal Academy. One of his early exhibits was a self-portrait in crayons. In 1772 Shirreff was awarded a silver medal for drawing but that year turned out to be a sad and trying year for young Charles.

In June 1772, a partner in one of the greatest banking firms in London, Neale, James, Fordyce and Down, Alexander Fordyce (1729-1789) was speculating in high risk stocks and funds in Change Alley (later known as Stock Exchange) and he had been initially successful in the past. However, in that month, Fordyce had been speculating by shorting East India Company stock on a massive scale and apparently using customer deposits to cover losses. On 10 June the Neal, James, Fordyce and Down Bank had to close while Fordyce himself fled to France with nearly £300,000 of money from his Ayr Bank. On 12 June, three other London banking firms with Scottish connections collapsed, and in the twelve days after Fordyce fled, twenty two significant banks, notably the Scottish Douglas, Heron & Co. known as the Ayr Bank, and many other smaller ones stopped payments, never to resume. In London the Bank of England was able to stabilise the situation, but attempts in London to save the situation in Scotland failed. The Scottish banks, especially those in Edinburgh, had mostly been borrowing from the Ayr Bank, partly to finance the building of the New Town. This crisis led to a liquidity calamity which affected not only London but the next most important banking centre in Europe, Amsterdam where the bank Clifford and Sons went bankrupt. This crisis was far-reaching; it worsened the relations between Britain and the thirteen colonies in America. The East India Company, already in serious financial difficulties around that time, was further weakened by the crisis, and in 1773 managed to persuade Parliament to pass the Tea Act, exempting it from the duty that all other importers in the colonies had to pay. The unpopularity of this led to the Boston Tea Party in Colonial America at the end of 1773.

Alexander Shirreff had invested a large amount of money between £20,000 and £30,000 (£1,274,000 and £1,911,000 in 2011 equivalent value) in Fordyce's Ayr Bank and following the collapse of that bank, Shirreff struggled to keep his business afloat, but he was hit by the fact that his business partner, Guthrie, wanted out. This resulted in Shirreff having to buy him out, raising whatever money he had through loans and sales of stock as shown in the advertisement in *Caledonian* Mercury dated 29 August 1772 below:

WINES to be SOLD.

THE Partnerſhip of SHIRREFF and GUTHRIE being diſſolved. their STOCK of WINES, conſiſting of Clarets, Port, and a great variety of White Wines, is to be diſpoſed of on the moſt reaſonable terms, at their cellars in Leith, where proper perſons will attend for that purpoſe.

Such as owe any accompt to the ſaid Shirreff and Guthrie, will pleaſe to pay the ſame to Alexander Shirreff of Craig-leith.

N. B. When the ſtock of ſaid Company is ſold off, the buſineſs will ſtill be continued under the firm of ALEXANDER SHIRREFF, SON, and COMPANY.

Alexander Shirreff's business was never to recover fully from the loss of his investment and in July 1775 he was forced to come to terms with the fact that he had to sell his entire business. Evidence of the collapse of his business was advertised in the *Caledonian Mercury* dated Saturday 15 July 1775 below:

NOTICE

To the CREDITORS of ALEXANDER SHIRREFF of Craigleith, Merchant in Leith.

Edinburgh, July 8. 1775.

AT Deſire of ſeveral of the Creditors of the ſaid Alexander Shirreff, the factor, in terms of the ſtatute anent inſolvent debtors, hereby requires the whole creditors of the ſaid Alexander Shirreff, to meet by themſelves, or their attornies or agents properly authoriſed by them, within the Exchange coffeehouſe, on Thurſday the 27th day of July current, at 12 o'clock, in order to conſider whether it is more for the intereſt of all concerned, that the perſonal eſtate of the ſaid Alexander Shirreff, at preſent under ſequeſtration before the Court of Seſſion, ſhould be veſted in a truſtee or truſtees, or continued under the management of the Court.

ALEXANDER ABERCROMBY.

Shirreff lost his entire investment and savings. For interest purposes, Alexander Fordyce returned to England later in 1772 and declared personal bankruptcy. In December 1772, Fordyce agreed a repayment scheme with his creditors; Alexander Shirreff did not recover very much out of the agreement. After Alexander Shirreff's sale of his wine business in the Port of Leith and payment to his creditors, his quality of life deteriorated, dropping a step at a time away from opulence as the years progressed. For reasons that have not yet been discovered, Alexander began to rely heavily on his deaf son Charles for support despite having four other sons and two daughters.

While in London, Charles Shirreff often moved around the capital, changing addresses quite frequently. In 1774, he resided at 35 Lambs Conduit Street near the Foundling Hospital, a children's home established for the education and maintenance of exposed and deserted young children; in 1776 he lived at 70 The Strand, and a little later at various addresses around the Covent Garden area until about 1788. Charles became a successful and well-established miniature painter, achieving parity not only with the established hearing miniaturists of his time, but with his deaf contemporaries such as Richard Crosse (1742-1810) and Sampson Togwood Roche (1749-1847). In 1786, Shirreff took on a Scot, Archibald Robertson (1765-1835), as a pupil in the art of miniature painting.

Exhibition records exist showing the kind of clients that Shirreff painted. Many sitters were often both of the noble class and of theatrical background like the actresses Elizabeth Hartley (1751-1824) and Sarah Siddons (1755-1831) and the actor John Philip Kemble (1757-1823). Shirreff gained high reputation for his work and there were at least two poems, one published in the London Courant (5 June 1781) and another published in a Scottish newspaper in 1786, both written in appreciation of Shirreff's excellence as a miniaturist.

In August 1778, Charles Shirreff applied for permission to travel to India and to take his father and step-sister Mary with him. He obtained the necessary sanction, but postponed the trip for a good number of years, possibly due to his father's ailing health.

On 5 June 1781, the *London Courant* published a poem of fifty-four lines "by a lady whom he shewed his collection, and who sat bye whilst he drew her husband"—

> Shirreff, learn thy wondrous gifts to prize
> Nor e'er arraign the Infinitely Wise.—
> What tho' no language can thy ear assail—
> The imitative signs as well prevail;
> And all you lose is but the drossy part
> Of conversation light, which soils the heart.
> Temptation wears no form so sly as words,
> Their subtle meaning like empoisoned swords;
> Where'er they strike, the venom rankling spreads,
> Betrays to vice—or into error leads.
>
> You with a look can steal each diff'rent face,
> And follow nature in her ev'ry grace;
> Or doth the eye in gentle softness roll,
> Or look of firmness speak the hero's soul;

Thy pencil equal to the task shall prove;
Here hit the taste, or there the passion move.
Thy mimic touch a Hartley's self can shew
In all the phrenzy of Elfrida's woe;
Where love, despair and various passions roll,
Conflicting tumults of the human soul:
If Eloise, a favour'd youth would charm,
Thou canst her tresses with new beauties arm.
When stain'd by thee the iv'ry I caress:
Admire the painter, and his skill confess:
For while I gaze upon a husband's face,
Thy pow'rs in ev'ry line my eye can trace.

Thomas Wilkes of Overseal,
Derbyshire

© V&A Museum London

Jane Dorothy Lambton
1790
Reproduced with kind permission
of Sotheby's London

Shirreff's fame spread far and wide and people were not only in admiration of his work, or of his capability of overcoming his handicap of deafness, communication and mixing with the hearing world, but of his character, his personality, his charm and his skill as a miniaturist. There were poems written in his praise which were published from time to time all over Britain. Another poem to Shirreff appeared in 1786, but it had been written several years before by "a clergyman of Scotland, whose character stands equally as an author, a philosopher and a man." It was published in a newspaper, and the clergyman, after alluding feelingly to Homer, Ossian and Milton, all of whom were blind, penned:-

"So you secure by nature's kindly power,
From all intrusions on the studious hour,
Shall rise to rival all those illustrious names,
Whose happy pencil general honour claims;
Shall be again what Raphael was before,
And wear the laurels which Apelles wore;
Shall vie with nature in the glorious strife,
'Till we mistake the likeness for the life:—
Thy works beholding, ages yet to come,
Shall wish their children to be deaf and dumb."

Shirreff continued to exhibit miniatures of individuals from the elite class of society – in 1784 he exhibited a miniature of the actress Miss Phillips at the Society for Promoting Painting and Design in Liverpool. His miniatures at the Royal Academy exhibition of 1786 were described as "superlatively elegant — his likeness of Mr. Whitefoord is his chef d'ouvre (sic)." In the same year Sarah Siddons wrote that Shirreff was more successful in her portrait than any other miniature painter. Shirreff's miniature of Doctor Howard was "allowed to be as good a likeness, and as well finished a picture as any at the Royal Exhibition." His portrait of Lady Elizabeth Stanley "from its exquisite taste and finishing, reflects credit upon the very improved state of the Fine Arts in this country." Shirreff also exhibited briefly at Brighton.

Between 1791 and 1794, Shirreff was residing at 10 Berners Street (between Mortimer Street and Oxford Street) and he exhibited another portrait of the actress Elizabeth Hartley. This portrait received great praise from the journals of the day. However, Shirreff departed London for Bath in that year and this surprised many people in view of the high reputation which he enjoyed in the Metropolis. In the 1795 Royal Academy exhibition, Shirreff distinguished himself highly and his miniature of Miss Wallis and Mr. Dimond in Romeo and Juliet was very large and *gives an interesting representation of the two unfortunate Lovers who are the subject of it. The scene is well imagined, and the likeness of both the performers faithful and spirited."*

Shirreff's works that were exhibited at the Royal Academy between 1771 and 1796 were:

At Mr Burgess's, Gloucester Street, Red Lion Square.
1771. 186 A portrait of himself; in crayons.

35, Lamb's Conduit Street, Foundling Hospital.
1774. 250 Portrait of a lady; miniature.
        281 Portrait of himself; miniature.
1775   93   Two portraits; miniatures.

At Mr Strachan's, 70, near the Adelphi, Strand.
1776. 283 Portrait of a gentleman; in miniature.
        284 A frame with five miniatures.

15, Salisbury Street, Strand.
1777. 325 A family; a miniature piece in water-colours.

At Mr Fentum's, 78, Salisbury Street, Strand.
1778. 253 Portrait of a child; full length, in miniature.

24, Southampton Street, Covent Garden.
1780. 232 Portrait of a lady.
        234 Fancy head.
        235 Portrait of a boy.
        261 Portrait of a gentleman.
1781. 344 A frame with portraits.
        345 Portrait of a gentleman.

10, Tavistock Row, Covent Garden.
1783. 219 An officer.
        313 Portrait of a lady. (Miss O.)
        321 Portrait of a lady.
        420 Portrait of a lady.
        443 Group of three ladies.

14, Tavistock Row, Covent Garden.
1784. 267 Portrait of a gentleman. (Mr. Shirreff.)
        275 Portrait of a gentleman. (Mr. Kemble.)
        281 Portrait of a lady. (Miss Phillips.)
1785. 310 Portraits of Mrs. Siddons and Mr. Kemble in the
            character of Tancred and Sigismunda.
1786. 290 Portrait of an aerial traveller.
1787. 290 Portrait of a gentleman (Caleb Whitefoord).

13, Tavistock Row, Covent Garden.
1788. 179 Portrait of a gentleman.

341 Portrait of a gentleman.
343 Portrait of a lady.
345 Portrait of a gentleman.
1789. 295 Portrait of a lady.
317 H.R.H. the Prince of Wales.
319 Portrait of an officer.
331 Portrait of a lady.
1790. 305 Portrait of a gentleman.
340 Portrait of a gentleman.
355 Portrait of an artist.
367 Portrait of a gentleman.

10, Berners Street.
1791. 277 A sleeping nymph.

Bath.
1794. 512 Two Bacchants.
525 Portrait of a lady (Mrs. Hartley).

527 Portrait of a lady.
536 Portrait of a Chinese
542 Portrait of a lady.
1795 550 Portrait of a young lady.
552 The Master of the Ceremonies, Bath {Mr. Tyson) .
562 Miss Wallis and Mr. Dimond in Romeo and Juliet.
1796 604 Portrait of a gentleman {Mr. Heriot).
625 Portrait of a lady {Mrs. Heriot).

Shirreff's stay in Bath did not last long, for late in 1795 Shirreff returned to London to attend to his dying father, who was living in Walworth. He also renewed his application to go to India and on 30 December he was granted permission to proceed to Bengal as a miniature painter. Two securities from Edward Perry and Francis Freeling (who was later to become H.M. Secretary of the Post Office) were approved on 11 May 1796. This time, Shirreff was travelling independently. His father Alexander passed away in June 1796 at the age of 88 years (*Gentleman's Magazine LXVI 1796, p.531*).

It is also interesting to note that there were individuals of the surname Shirreff in India at that time, but whether they were related to the artist is not known. Charles painted a portrait of one Mr. Shirreff in India and this person was believed to be either one of his close relatives or even one of his brothers and this was most probably the reason for Charles wishing to make the trip to India. In those days a visit to India was no small undertaking: the cost of the passage often amounted to several hundred pounds; the journey by sea always lasted over three months, and sometimes ten months or more depending on the conditions; many a good ship went down on the way, and not a few were captured by the French — this last fate befell the portrait painters Thomas Hickey and William Doughty.

Shirreff's decision to embark for India elicited another poetic outburst, which appeared on the *London Courant* on 27 May 1796:

> Artist, why from Albion's shore
> Wilt thou eager bend thy way?
> If to gain the tempting ore,
> British taste must bid thee to stay.
>
> Seek'st thou beauty? Surely here
> Venus and the Loves reside;
> British Damsels need not fear
> Charms o'er all the World beside.
>
> Worth Heroic to descry,
> Would'st thou cross the troublous Main? —
> Proudly turn thy Patriot eye
> On thy Country's warring train.
>
> Yet to India, Artist, sail,
> And if judgment there abide,
> India will thy talents hail,
> Cheering thee with bounteous pride.
>
> Then adieu, ingenious Friend,
> And if rough old Ocean prove,
> Doubt not Fortune will attend
> Him whom Taste and Virtue love.

Shirreff took his passage to India on the Lord Hawkesby, which reached Fort St. George, Madras, on 9 January 1797. Shirreff remained at Madras until 1800. During that period, Shirreff earned a tidy sum painting miniatures of members of the Civil Service and armed forces.

A Young Lady with
Powdered Wig   c1790

A Young Girl with
Red Hair   c1822

John Kilby

The photographs of the three
Shirreff miniatures on this page
are the copyright of Claudia Hill
@ Ellison Fine Art.

Robert Polhill

Photograph by courtesy of
Brightwells Ltd., Leominster

Junior Naval Officer, c1800

Photograph by courtesy of
The British Deaf History Society

Commander James Oswald

Photograph by courtesy of
Claudia Hill @ Ellison Fine Art

John Phillip Kemble and Mrs Siddons as "Tancred and Sigismunda"
By Caroline Watson, after Charles Shirreff's miniature.
Exhibited in 1785.

© V&A Museum London

After Madras, Shirreff moved to Calcutta, continuing to paint miniatures of notable persons and residents. It appeared that Shirreff resided in a house opposite the East India Company's Printing Office in Old Post Office Street and remained there until the end of 1804.

Shirreff doubtlessly visited various parts of the country, for after his return to England, he exhibited portraits of a Nabob of the Carnatic, a Rajah of Benares and two natives of Malabar and Bengal respectively and a native of Cawnpore. In 1803, he advertised in the Calcutta Gazette that he was selling at reduced prices a consignment of gems, cameos, &c. In April 1807, Shirreff contributed 100 rupees to a subscription for the relief of poor inhabitants of Madras. In the same newspaper for 24 December 1807, he announce that he was preparing to return to England by the next fleet, and proposed a raffle of his miniature of Bacchantes (40 tickets at 50 rupees apiece).

Shirreff also stated that his Finger Alphabet was in great forwardness and would be delivered to subscribers as soon as possible; meanwhile fresh subscriptions would be received at his house at 40 Durrumtollah Road. Shirreff made a fortune during his stay in India. No copy of his Finger Alphabet can be traced and it is believed that it was lost or stolen on the voyage back to England.

Shirreff did not leave Calcutta until 9 January 1809, boarding the Sir William Bensley, which landed at Gravesend on 16 July 1809.

Next, we find Shirreff marrying Mary Ann Brown at the church of St George in Hanover Square, London on 11 January 1810. Shirreff's profession was written on the marriage register as "Esquire". It is believed that his wife Mary Ann was either a sister or a close relation to the artist William Berry Brown, and she was over 33 years younger than Shirreff.

Shirreff continued to paint and exhibit his work. He painted portraits of his late teacher Thomas Braidwood's daughter Isabella in 1812 and Joseph Watson, the head of the London Asylum for the Instruction of the Deaf and Dumb, in 1814. The Royal Academy listed his exhibited work between 1810 and 1823:

> 58, Green Street, Grosvenor Square.
> 1810. 670 Portraits of Mr. Shirreff, late Nabob of the Carnatic, the present Rajah of Benares, a Malabar native, Dr. Kay of St. Helena, and a Bengal native.
> 1811. 556 Lord Eardley.

561 A Madras native of rank.
594 Portrait of a young lady.
616 Portrait of a young lady.

1812. 606 Mrs. Braidwood, teacher of deaf and dumb persons.
613 Portrait of a gentleman.
623 Mr. Barton of Calcutta.
633 Venus and Cupid.

1813. 483 Miss Murchison.
495 Portrait of a native of Cawnpore.
534 W. Brown, Esq.
535 G. Owen, Esq.

38, Cumberland Street.

1814. 400 Master Williams.
411 Mrs. Brown.
444 Dr Watson.
467 Portrait of a lady.

1815. 541 Portrait of a lady.
544 Portrait of a lady.
554 Portrait of a child.

1816. 617 A nymph.
639 Portrait of a lady.
737 Portrait of a lady.

1817. 698 Portrait of a young gentleman.
710 Hebe.
822 Portrait of a lady.

1818. 428 Portraits.
445 Peneus.

45, Upper John Street, Fitzroy Square.

1823. 718 Portrait of a gentleman.

What happened to Shirreff from 1823 onwards is not known. Numerous writers mentioned Shirreff having exhibited his work up to 1833 at the very latest, but it is likely that his work was exhibited posthumously after 1829. Shirreff wrote his last Will and Testament (see Appendix 5) on 13 December 1824. Shirreff passed away in his home in late October 1829 at the age of 80 and he was interred on 3 November 1829 at Paddington Green St Mary church. Shirreff's will was proved on 11 November 1829 and it was noted that his address was 15 Upper Frederick Street, Connaught Square, London. In his will, he left everything to his surviving wife Mary Ann Shirreff.

Entry on the St Mary register of burials noting that Shirreff was buried on 3 November 1829—and his last residence was Frederick Street, Paddington.

Paddington Green St Mary where Shirreff was interred.
(This church was demolished around the turn of the 20th century)

For a profoundly deaf person, Charles Shirreff achieved fame and renown, living a good life and he certainly enjoyed it to the full in an independent manner, thanks to the education he received from Thomas Braidwood. His miniatures were greatly valued by those who had the privilege to be painted by this deaf artist — they were regarded as little treasures that could be carried around in the same way as modern day photographs.

And there is an intriguing question that has to be asked: did Shirreff leave behind a great mystery — was he the miniaturist who painted the large unsigned oil portrait of Dr Joseph Watson that still hangs in the Royal School for the Deaf, Margate? It is possible that this painting was indeed the same painting that was exhibited at the 1814 Royal Academy event and was listed as exhibit number 444.

C. Shirreff

John Goodricke

*He was deaf and dumb and remained so all through his life,
but there was nothing the matter with either his eyesight or
his brain: he became an expert observer as well as a theorist.*
— Sir Patrick Moore

John Goodricke, the son of the British diplomat Henry Goodricke and his Dutch wife Levina Benjamina Sessler of Namur, Woldthuzen in Friesland, was born on 17 September 1764 in Groningen, Holland. Goodricke became deaf at around the age of 5 years old following a severe illness, believed to be scarlet fever. In 1772 at the age of eight, Goodricke was sent to the Braidwood Academy in Edinburgh, initially to obtain help with his speech and lipreading. It appeared that Goodricke had gained some moderate lipreading skills, but his speech was not good – his voice was more of a "deaf quality." Goodricke went on to excel as a pupil and progressed well in all subjects, using both the manual alphabet and written English with great ease. Mathematics became his favourite subject and his teacher, Thomas Braidwood, who was an excellent mathematician, was able to educate young Goodricke to a high standard.

Six years later in 1778, Goodricke's progress was so good that Braidwood was not able to help him any further. Perhaps on the recommendation of Braidwood, Goodricke's parents entered him into Warrington Academy in Warrington, Lancashire. John Goodricke was accepted in September 1778. This academy had no facility for either deaf or handicapped persons. The establishment was run by three tutors and Goodricke was assigned to a kind, gentle and accomplished man, the Reverend Dr William Enfield. The design of Warrington Academy was the liberal education of youth in general: students were prepared for commerce or the law, for physics or the ministry, besides discipline and good order.

Goodricke, listed in the academy's book as pupil number 322, was boarded in Academy House (later known as Enfield House). His main tutor, Dr Enfield, specialised in natural philosophy: arithmetic, algebra, trigonometry and geography were subjects high on the curriculum. Enfield's hobby was astronomy, a subject in which Goodricke became interested through sharing this interest with his tutor. Further to that, Enfield was also a specialist in elocution and he might have experienced very little problem in communicating with Goodricke, through both lipreading and writing. Due to his deafness

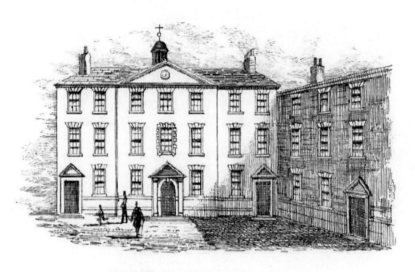

THE WARRINGTON ACADEMY, 1762.

Academy Court — Enfield House
where Goodricke was boarded.

and subsequent difficulties in following class, there is a possibility that Goodricke was taught on a one-to-one basis by Enfield on occasions when such an opportunity presented itself.

Warrington Academy was a dissenting academy established in 1757 in protest against the schools controlled by the clergy and it catered for the liberal and theological education of youths between the ages of 13 and 18 years. It appears that Goodricke did not fully complete his time at the academy, leaving in 1781 at the age of 16 years. No reason was given for Goodricke's early departure, but history indicated that between 1780 and 1782 when the academy was closed due to financial problems, there were disruptive hot-blooded young students, mainly from Ireland and also plantation owners' sons from Jamaica, St Kitts and Antigua causing havoc, exercising both rudeness and utter disregard to the tutors, especially the kindly and gentle Dr William Enfield, and they were also deliberately upsetting the general population of Warrington with their wild antics and utter contempt for respectful social behaviour. It is possible that Goodricke suffered insults from these students because of his deafness and his close association with William Enfield. Warrington Academy was officially dissolved in 1786.

During his stay at Warrington Academy, Goodricke developed an interest in the stars from the moment he was taught astronomy in the second year as a part of the mathematics curriculum. Goodricke's mathematics notebook is preserved in the Goodricke collection of the York City Archives. The notebook included various sketches, essays and comments on his astronomical observations, which include star and moon positions, various constellations, a record of a total lunar eclipse of 23 November 1779 and numerous calculations.

After leaving Warrington Academy early in 1781, Goodricke joined his family who were by then residing at Lendal in York. (The Goodricke family moved to York in 1776 after Henry Goodricke ended his term of diplomatic service abroad.) This house is known as the Treasurer's House (below).

The Goodricke family became acquainted with Nathaniel Pigott (1725-1804), a surveyor and an astronomer, whose family lived at 33 Bootham Place, York. The Goodricke and the Pigott family were distantly related. Pigott lived a vagrant life, wandering all over Britain and Europe with his family before settling in York in 1780. He had four children, but only two sons survived infancy – Edward Pigott (1753–1825) and Charles Gregory Pigott (d.1845). Nathaniel Pigott constructed a substantial well-equipped two-storey stone observatory in the garden at the rear of his house; he had obtained a model of the well-equipped Greenwich observatory of the noted astronomer William Herschel (1738-1822). Edward Pigott became friends with his cousin John Goodricke, both sharing their passion for astronomy and they later formed a historical partnership. Edward Pigott, however, was involved in astronomy for much longer than Goodricke: he was credited with the discovery of the Black Eye Galaxy in March 1779, a month before John Elert Bode and a year before Charles Messier.

In April 1781 Goodricke obtained and set up his new Dollond achromatic telescope in his house to observe the stars. Along with the telescope, Goodricke, later in July 1781, purchased and brought in one important accessory—a clock, which was specially made by one Mr Hartley for astronomical purposes. Goodricke systematically compared his clock with Pigott's excellent timepiece: each clock being read when the chimes of the last stroke of York Minster struck at 12.

Since Goodricke was deaf, he relied on the assistance of "some faithful persons" to listen to the chimes. This was deemed necessary as Goodricke was told that the York Minster clock made a little noise just before the chime and he felt it was of some importance to note it. Later the accuracy of the timing was so important that both Goodricke and Pigott had to allow for the difference due to Pigott's house being a greater distance away from York Minster than John's house which was a few hundred yards away. In his journal *Journey of the Going of my Clock*, his note for December 1782 read:

> As Mr Pigott is at greater distance from the Minster than I am, he must hear it somewhat later, therefore judge it necessary to make some allowance… where his clock is being set about half a mile from the Minster I always subtract one second from Mr P's time. My distance from the Minster is only a few yards, therefore no allowance.

Goodricke's journal became very important and all his observations and comments were dutifully recorded. On 16 November 1781 Goodricke made the first entry in his Journal of Astronomical Observations:

> Mr. E. Pigott told me that at 9 o'clock pm yesterday
> he discovered a Comet with a small nucleus & comma
> near the neck of Cygnus.

The relationship between Edward Pigott and John Goodricke was going strong, spirited and became a great astronomical alliance which appeared to have began initially that of instructor and pupil, but soon evolved into a close partnership: they often gave credit to each other in their personal journals. Interestingly, Pigott did mention in his personal correspondences to others, especially in a letter to the discoverer of the planet Uranus, William Herschel, that he had difficulty in conversing with Goodricke, and he also wrote that there were times he had no one to converse with despite Goodricke's presence. This indicated that it was near impossible for them to hold a conversation with each other during the night because of lack of light.

Perhaps through Pigott's encouragement and direction, Goodricke began to observe variable stars from a window in his home, Treasury House, and he started to note the star Algol (known as the Demon Star), also known as Beta Persei in the constellation Perseus. Goodricke found that Algol, usually a second magnitude object, had dropped to fourth magnitude and he entered in his Journal for 12 November 1872:

> This night I looked at β Persei & was much amazed to
> find its brightness altered — it now appears abt the 4th
> magnd ... I observed it diligently for abt an hour &
> upwards — I hardly believed that it changed its
> brightness because I never heard of any star varying so
> quick in its brightness — I thought it might perhaps be
> owing to an optical illusion or defect in my eyes or
> bad air but the sequel will shew that its change is true
> & that I was not mistaken.

Goodricke informed Pigott of his discovery. Both Goodricke and Pigott began to keep a close watch on Algol, attempting to discover reasons for the suddenness of Algol's variation in brightness and over a period of time they both began to note that the changes were regular. The observation on Algol continued until the end of the season when it could no longer be seen over the horizon at York. Goodricke did not only discover the first known short-period variable star but he also established an accurate estimation of its period: Goodricke's original value for Algol's period was 2 days, 20 hours and 45 minutes. In 1784, Goodricke revised this period to 2 days, 20 hours, 49 minutes and 9 seconds. Goodricke was not the first to notice the variability of β Persei (or Algol as it is commonly called): the Italian astronomer Geminiano Montanari recorded his observations in 1672 in Bologna. Goodricke was the first to establish that these light changes were periodic.

In a letter dated 12 May 1783, Goodricke informed the Rev. Anthony Shepherd, then Plumian professor of astronomy at Cambridge, of the results of his observations. His letter was read before the Royal Society on 15 May.

John Goodricke
by James Scouler.
This portrait is the property of the Royal Astronomical Society
and is reproduced with their kind permission.

Goodricke's observations generated considerable interest in astronomical circles and were immediately put into print. The council of the Royal Society awarded Goodricke one of the two Copley medals for 1783, the other going to Thomas Hutchins (1730-1789).

Goodricke continued observing the stars with Pigott and on the 10th of September 1784 both men made further discoveries. Firstly, Pigott discovered the fluctuating light of a yellow star named Eta Aquilae, a star lying in the constellation of Aquila: it was the first Delta Cepheid. Pigott noted that it was variable in brightness from night to night. Only hours later, Goodricke discovered that another star, Beta Lyrae, was a double star with an eclipse occurring a little more than every twelve days.

On 20 October 1784, Goodricke discovered the pulsating star, Delta Cephei in the constellation Cepheus: it was the second Delta Cephei Star, or Cepheid variable and he observed that Delta Cephei was variable in a similar way to Eta Aquilae. This star, Goodricke noted, showed a quick and sharp rise from minimum to maximum, and slowly declined to its minimum again.

Goodricke described the strange quality in fluctuations of brightness of Delta Cephei and this letter, his third to the Royal Society, was published in the Philosophical Transactions of the Royal Society in 1785. (Goodricke's papers published in the *Philosophical Transactions of the Royal Society* are *A Series of Observations On, and A Discovery of the Period of the Variation of Light of the Bright Star in the Head of Medusa, Called Algol*, 73, pt.2 (1783) 474-482; *On the Periods of the Changes of Light in the star Algol*, 74, (1784) 287-292; *Observations of a New Variable Star*, 75, (1785), 153-164; and *A Series of Observations on, and a Discovery of the Period of Variation of the Light of the Star Marked ∂ by Bayer, Near the Head of Cepheus*, 76, (1786), 48-61).

Towards the end of December 1785, Edward Pigott decided to pack up his telescope and travel to Europe, leaving Goodricke to continue with his observations on his own. Goodricke's work led Nathaniel Pigott to petition for Goodricke to become a Fellow of the Royal Society and a proposal citing Goodricke's work was made out and put forward with the signatures of ten Fellows. In recognition of his work, the Royal Society bestowed a Fellowship on Goodricke on 16 April 1786; the news of this highly esteemed award did not come to Goodricke's attention. Busy focusing himself in his night-time observations, Goodricke fell ill with pneumonia due to frequent exposure to the extremely cold night air and he died on 20 April 1786.

GB117 The Royal Society—Ref: EC/1786/01
Members' election for John Goodricke to be accepted for Fellowship 1786.

Reproduced with kind permission of the Royal Society.

His young life was whisked away just when he seemed to be entering a career as a promising astronomer. His friend Edward Pigott said of him upon being informed of his death:

> This worthy young man exists no more; he is not only regretted to many friends, but will prove a loss to astronomy, as the discoveries he so rapidly made evince.

John Goodricke's funeral was a low profile and private family affair and he was buried in the family vault in the churchyard of St John the

Baptist, Hunsingore, close to the 300 year old Goodricke family seat Ribson Hall. Goodricke's funeral was unreported nationwide despite his immense contribution not only to astronomy, but to the world. Interest in a deaf person like Goodricke was almost non-existent, save for those who knew and were associated with him. This lack of interest reflected people's attitude towards the deaf in those days, in a similar way they showed complete uninterest in Thomas Braidwood's offer to go public and train four teachers of the deaf some 17 years earlier.

It was much later that John Goodricke became remembered and respected when York named one of the University Halls of Residence after him – Goodricke College. In 1996 in Tucson, Arizona, a private astronomical observatory was built and it was named the Goodricke-Pigott Observatory. It was dedicated on 26 October 1996.

(Photograph - Raymond Lee 1997.)

John Goodricke's life was cut short tragically at the age of twenty-one and he should never be considered as handicapped, but a as deaf man who overcame his disadvantage in life to contribute great things.

John Philp Wood

Honest John, my old friend...
— Sir Walter Scott

John Philp Wood was born in a large house in the parish of Cramond, some five miles northwest of Edinburgh, on 9 March 1762 to John Wood and his wife Isobel, nee Philp. At about the age of three, young John became deaf and consequently dumb following an illness, which was believed to be scarlet fever.

Wood's father was a wealthy man, having amassed a fortune by trading in foreign lands. The family lived in a large mansion known as Cramond Regis, also called King's Cramond. It is believed that Wood was sent to the Braidwood Academy in 1768 or 1769, where he received an education from Thomas Braidwood, and this education was to stand Wood in good stead, setting out the course of his life in the days and years to come.

Upon becoming deaf, Wood completely lost his natural speech and he possessed an uncouth voice. In page 35 of the booklet Cramond (published by the Cramond Association, 1969) an "Anonymous Contemporary" described John:

> From the celebrated Braidwood He learns to utter such uncouth Sounds as are employed by Dumb Persons who have been instructed in that art of Speech. By his Mother (whose attentions to Him are unremitting) those sounds were commonly understood; but rarely so by Strangers, to whom they were extremely disagreeable.

> His quickness of comprehension was truly marvellous; and from the motion of the Mouth aided by a word or two described with the Fingers in the usual way He could generally understand what was said to Him. I have seen his Mother employ her Fingers nearly as fast as she spoke; and she would do the same while another Person was speaking. Hence he was able to understand pretty well the conversation which was passing in the room.

From that account, we know that Wood had the same kind of "deaf quality voice" as that of Charles Shirreff and John Goodricke and other numerous Braidwood pupils. Moreover, we know that John mainly employed fingerspelling and signs for communication and relied heavily on that mode with moderate lipreading ability thrown in — this points to evidence of the use of signs and fingerspelling as a vital part of the education and communication package employed by Thomas Braidwood.

As a pupil at the Braidwood Academy, Wood was very studious and took a very deep interest in history, especially of Edinburgh, its people and environs. He stayed at the school until 1778 when he was sixteen years old, leaving with an excellent standard of education and proficiency in a wide range of subjects including classics, Latin and mathematics, a subject which enabled him to obtain employment as a clerk to the Accountant of the Scottish Excise Office in Chessel's Court, Edinburgh.

The following year in 1779 Wood was transferred to the department of the Solicitor of Excise, again as a clerk and he remained in that position until 1785 when he was given a promotion and responsibility to keep and distribute auctioneers' bonds, besides the duty to register lawyers' opinions. Wood's career began to progress successfully and in 1797 he was again promoted. Wood returned to the Scottish Excise Office to become assistant accountant. After a further three years, he was again promoted as a fully-fledged accountant. In 1802, another promotion beckoned and Wood became the Over Deputy for signing licences.

Away from the steady climb of his career at the Excise Office, Wood's leisure time was taken up by his interest in historical and antiquarian lore. In 1791 he published his first literary work, *A Sketch of the Life of John Law of Lauriston, Comptroller General of the Finances of France*. It was an account of a Scotsman from the parish of Wood's birth, who founded the Bank of France. A murderer, a gambler, a duellist and a brilliant financier, John Law (1671-1729) fought a duel with Edward Wilson on 9 April 1694. Wilson had challenged Law to a duel over the affections of a woman named Elizabeth Villiers. After Law killed Wilson, he was tried and found guilty of murder and sentenced to death. His sentence was commuted to a fine, upon the ground that the

John Law of
Lauriston

offence only amounted to manslaughter. Wilson's brother appealed and had Law imprisoned, but Law managed to escape to Amsterdam. He spent ten years moving between France and the Netherlands, dealing in financial speculations. In 1720, Law was appointed by the regent Philippe d'Orléans to manage the French finances, which were in a mess due to the wars waged by Louis XIV. For the next few years Law sorted out the situation and was regarded as a saviour of France and he was courted by the highest, mightiest and greatest in France.

On 11 January 1791, Wood's work was honoured and he was awarded the Fellowship of The Society of the Antiquaries of Scotland, a unique achievement in the annals of Scottish deaf history, and no deaf persons after Wood came close to sharing the same achievement.

In 1794, Wood's book *The Antient and Modern State of the Parish of Cramond* was published and it immediately became a sensational hit. John Philp Wood became the first person ever to write a parochial history in Scotland, and his work set the benchmark that would be used in similar future works by others. John's book was also a precursor to the technique later employed by Sir John Sinclair for his monumental The Statistical Account of Scotland which was published in volumes between 1791 and 1799. It was the first statistical survey of any nation in history. Prior to the publication of the 1794 book, Wood's 1790 abstract on his parish of Cramond featured prominently in Sinclair's first volume. Wood's work was highly praised in the journals of the day – *The Gentleman's Magazine,* Vol. 65, 1795 had this to say:

> This publication, the first parochial history attempted in Scotland, upon the extensive and minute plan frequently followed in the southern part of the United Kingdom, is one of the most exact and elegant topographical works ever published, and is illustrated and ornamented with several plates...

Another respected publication, *The Critical Review, Or Annals of Literature, 1795* devoted 17 pages to Wood's seminal 1794 work and in the section for reviews during September 1794 in which Wood's book was mentioned, the reviewer opened —

> The author of this ingenious and entertaining little work, John Phillip Wood, Esq., is already known to our readers by his *Sketch of the Life of John Law,* here reprinted; and which, on its separate appearance, we

had occasion to mention with applause. Nor did the present work disappoint our expectations, being on the whole, one of the most exact and elegant topographical works ever published. It is illustrated and ornamented with several plates, which do honour to Scott the engraver.

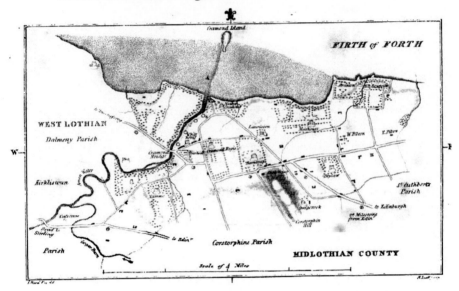

Map of the parish of Cramond from Wood's 1794 book

During his initial legwork work for the *Antient and Modern State of the Parish of Cramond,* Wood relied on the services of his mother and his good friend, the local doctor Robert Spotswood, who was also the treasurer of Cramond Kirk. Both the mother and the doctor were proficient in fingerspelling and signs and they acted as Wood's interpreters when accompanying him on his house to house trips where he needed to question the occupants to gather information for his book. Although the book was published in 1794, Wood had actually completed it by 1792.

Wood went some way during his research on the parish of Cramond to dispel the story of King James V granting his lands of Braehead to one Jack Howison, a tenant farmer, as a grateful gift for his bravery in rescuing the king, who was in disguise, from the ravaging and plundering gypsies in Cramond in the 1530s. Wood, meticulous and accurate as always, discovered that the Howison family had been landowners since 1745, many years before the reputed historical incident.

In 1792, Wood went on to cover a survey of the neighbouring parish of Corstorphine, but this work, along similar lines to that of the parish of Cramond, was not published. The transcriptions of this unpublished survey are kept in the Edinburgh Room of the Edinburgh Central library.

THE

ANTIENT AND MODERN STATE

OF THE

PARISH OF CRAMOND.

TO WHICH ARE ADDED,

BIOGRAPHICAL AND GENEALOGICAL COLLECTIONS,
RESPECTING SOME OF THE MOST CONSIDERABLE FAMILIES
AND INDIVIDUALS CONNECTED WITH THAT DISTRICT;

COMPREHENDING A SKETCH OF THE LIFE AND PROJECTS OF

JOHN LAW OF LAURISTON,

COMPTROLLER GENERAL OF THE FINANCES OF FRANCE.

————Τεμενος νεμομεσθα μεγα,————
Καλον, φυταλιης, και αρουρης πυροφοροιο.
'ΩΜ. Ιλ. Μ. 313.

EDINBURGH:

PRINTED BY JOHN PATERSON,

AND SOLD BY PETER HILL, AT THE CROSS.—ALSO BY B. WHITE AND SON,
FLEET-STREET, LONDON.

M,DCC,XCIV.

The Scottish Excise Office moved in 1794 to Dundas House in St. Andrew's Square in Edinburgh and Wood continued working there. Between 1794 and 1797, Wood resided in 9 North Castle Street and one of his neighbours at that time was Walter Scott, who struck up a friendship with Wood. Wood met and courted Marion Cadell, daughter of the distinguished family owners of the Cramond Iron Foundry. This Cadell family also owned a publishing company. On 2 July 1803,

Wood and Marion Cadell married and returned to Edinburgh, living in 92 Princes Street. Their marriage produced seven offsprings, three boys and four girls.

Wood's steady career climb reached its pinnacle when he became Auditor of Excise by a letter of appointment dated 2 July 1809. This letter was written from 10 Downing Street during the office of the Prime Minister, Spencer Percival. Wood's promotion was initially suggested and sponsored by Charles Hay, Lord Newton, the eminent Judge of the Court of Session. Hay's influence was powerful and elite members of the Excise Office and various authorities took up Hay's proposition. The Wood family then moved from their Princes Street home westwards to South Charlotte Street.

In 1810 a public meeting was held in Edinburgh to discuss the formation of a national school for deaf children in Scotland. This came about because there was no form of instruction for the deaf in Scotland since the departure of the Braidwood Academy in 1783. Only two schools were in practice in England at that time – the Braidwood Institution in Hackney which was run by Isabella Braidwood and her children, and the London Asylum for the Instruction of the Deaf and Dumb of the Poor. The meeting agreed to establish a school for the deaf in Edinburgh; the ball was set in motion by the appointment of James Farquhar Gordon, a writer of the Signet, and John Philp Wood as joint secretaries of the newly founded Edinburgh Institution for the Education of Deaf and Dumb Children. This school was formally established on 25 June 1810. The committee invited John Braidwood, a grandson of Thomas Braidwood, to become its head teacher. The school opened in a small room in 8 Union Street.

Wood had for some time taken an interest in genealogy, especially that concerning Scottish peers. He drew up a genealogical work on Scottish peers from 1707 to 1809 ready for publication. For one reason or another, Wood was persuaded to incorporate his collections with the original work of Sir Robert Douglas of Glenbervie, *The Peerage of Scotland* which was initially published in 1764. Wood submitted to this persuasion and combined his work with that of Douglas, along with editing, correcting and updating Douglas' original work. Wood's edition of *The Peerage of Scotland* in two volumes came out in 1813 and it won great praise and rave reviews. Following publication of the book, Wood gained recognition as Scotland's leading genealogist of his time. *The Gentleman's Magazine* of July 1813 described it in its Review of New Publications section *The Peerage of Scotland* as "a very splendid work."

THE

PEERAGE

OF

SCOTLAND:

CONTAINING AN

HISTORICAL AND GENEALOGICAL ACCOUNT

OF THE

𝕹𝖔𝖇𝖎𝖑𝖎𝖙𝖞 𝖔𝖋 𝖙𝖍𝖆𝖙 𝕶𝖎𝖓𝖌𝖉𝖔𝖒,

FROM

THEIR ORIGIN TO THE PRESENT GENERATION:

COLLECTED FROM

THE PUBLIC RECORDS, ANTIENT CHARTULARIES, THE CHARTERS AND OTHER WRITINGS OF THE
NOBILITY, WORKS OF OUR BEST HISTORIANS, &c.

BY SIR ROBERT DOUGLAS OF GLENBERVIE, BART.

SECOND EDITION.

REVISED AND CORRECTED, WITH A CONTINUATION TO THE PRESENT PERIOD,

BY JOHN PHILIP WOOD, Esq.

𝕎𝖎𝖙𝖍 𝕰𝖓𝖌𝖗𝖆𝖛𝖎𝖓𝖌𝖘 𝖔𝖋 𝖙𝖍𝖊 𝕬𝖗𝖒𝖘 𝖔𝖋 𝖙𝖍𝖊 𝕻𝖊𝖊𝖗𝖘.

VOLUME FIRST.

EDINBURGH:

PRINTED BY GEORGE RAMSAY AND COMPANY,
FOR ARCHIBALD CONSTABLE AND COMPANY, EDINBURGH:
LONGMAN, HURST, REES, ORME, AND BROWN; WHITE, COCHRANE,
AND CO.; JOHN MURRAY; AND RICHARD REES,
LONDON.

1813.

As a joint secretary of the Edinburgh Institution for the Education of Deaf and Dumb Children, Wood was extremely busy in his ex-gratis post despite his full time occupation as Auditor of Excise Office. John Braidwood, the head teacher, had abandoned his post, leaving the school in limbo. The committee protested to the Braidwoods and

309

expressed their anger that John Braidwood's behaviour had interrupted and deprived the deaf pupils of their education. Apparently an agreement was reached between the committee and the Braidwood Institution in Hackney that Robert Kinniburgh, a Methodist minister and a recently appointed assistant to John Braidwood, would be gratuitously trained in all aspects respecting the education of the deaf. However, because Kinniburgh was trained free of charge, he had to agree to accept a bond at a cost of £1000 for seven years not to reveal the methods employed to educate deaf children to any person without the permission or knowledge of the Braidwood Institution.

The school was re-opened after the completion of Kinniburgh's training and it was managed in rented premises. Since rental periods were of a very short term, the school moved around more often than it wanted. When the school reopened with Robert Kinniburgh as its head teacher, it was initially located at 54 Rose Street and not long after it moved from there onwards to 15 St James Square. It was then located at 57 Princes Street. In 1814, possibly through Wood's influence, the Edinburgh Institution for the Education of Deaf and Dumb Children finally found its permanent home at the very place where Wood used to work – Chessel's Court.

Wood's increasing public responsibilities as Auditor of Excise led him to leave his post as joint secretary of the school for the deaf in 1817. His association with the school, however, continued as the Edinburgh

Chessel's Court

Institution reports showed that he regularly paid an annual subscription of one guinea (roughly £40 annually in present day equivalent) to the school between 1815 and 1838.

Wood's versatility in the use of sign language and manual communication next saw him being approached for assistance by Robert Kinniburgh. Kinniburgh was asked by the police and the legal bodies in Glasgow to interpret on behalf of a deaf lady named Jean Campbell who was arrested on a charge of murdering her infant child. Although Kinniburgh was able to understand Jean Campbell during their conversations during the prosecution's interviews, there were a number of signs that made or caused Kinniburgh to feel that he had to employ a deaf person proper as a relay interpreter, and that was where Wood came in. This was the first known record of a deaf person in an interpreting situation associated with the law.

Jean Campbell, an uneducated deaf lady, was indicted in April 1817 for the murder of her own three years old child on 19 November 1816 by throwing it from the Saltmarket bridge into the Clyde, where the child drowned. Wood and Kinniburgh, as interpreters, were able to discover that Jean Campbell, despite her lack of education, was in no way "ignorant or incompetent" in the eyes of the law and also that she was able to stand trial. The Court of Justiciary convened on 17 July 1817 to decide whether Jean was able to stand trial or not. Wood gave a statement to the court. With Kinniburgh as an interpreter, Wood could only say to the judges that it appeared to him that Jean Campbell did not understand the nature and consequences of pleading guilty or not guilty. Wood remarked that at the same time, it appeared to him that she knew the distinction between right and wrong, so far as to consider herself liable to punishment if the death of the child was occasioned by her wilfully throwing it in the river; and that she had been imprisoned in consequence of the death of the child, which she stated was occasioned by its falling over the ledge of the bridge accidentally, in consequence of her gown or wrapper in which the child was, being loosened.

The court decided that Jean Campbell was fit to stand trial. Her trial was at Glasgow on 24 September 1817. With Kinniburgh as the interpreter, she pleaded not guilty. The trial concluded by finding not proven due to insufficient evidence to convict the defendant and she was freed.

In 1824, the Excise Office again moved to new premises in Bellevue House in Drummond Street, having sold Dundas House to the Royal

Bank of Scotland. In the same year, Wood brought out his fourth and final book, Memoirs of John Law of Lauriston. This was a much more detailed biography than that of the 1791 original; it covered the burst of the "Mississippi Bubble", an event which saw Law removed from his post by the regent Philippe d'Orléans when the French finances collapsed. Law escaped to Holland and eventually ended up penniless in exile in Venice, where he died of pneumonia.

Wood continued to correspond and contribute to various magazines of the day – such as *The Analytical Review, The Critical Review, The New Annual Register* and *The Gentleman's Magazine.* Wood also supplied most of the biographical

Silhouette of John Philp Wood, 1834 —Artist unknown.

notes on the writers of the poetry comprised in *The Muses' Welcome to King James* printed in John Nichols' *The Progresses of King James I* (1828).

Wood's career as Auditor of Excise attracted the note of many authorities. He was very meticulous in his work and he would not tolerate any mistakes, discrepancies and anything that was "out of line." Wood's work at the Excise Office also won approval from the government of the day with a letter sent to the Lords of the Treasury:

> We know and have full experience that Mr. Wood is an officer of great merit and possesses uncommon talents for accuracy and astuteness in business, and who in place of leaving the execution of his office to the deputy, as his predecessors were in use to do, discharges himself with the attention and anxious care for the interest of the Revenue, well deserving to be followed by every public officer.

This testimonial written by the Barons of the Court of the Exchequer in 1812 underlined how Wood earned the tag of "Honest" (as regarded by Walter Scott) for his sincere and diligent auditing. From the year of his appointment as auditor in 1809 until his retirement in 1832, when both the Scottish and English Excise offices amalgamated into a single British office based in London, Wood did thirty years work in twenty-two years, catching up with neglected audits that were incomplete for eight years before his appointment. On one occasion Wood discovered that some £36,000 was incorrectly written down as £12,000. Wood had to chase many people on numerous occasions to make them pay up their taxes and duties to balance the books. Wood also exposed practices of corruption and account fiddling within and outwith the Civil Service and put a stop to them. The Barons of the Court of the Exchequer also signified their approbation of Wood's conduct when he opposed the grant to the Commissioners of the Excise Office towards payments of their private expenses from the public purse.

In 1830, a group of deaf people led by a Dundee-born deaf man named Matthew Robert Burns (1798-1880) met in a single 22 feet by 13 feet room with one small window in Lady Stairs Close. This group participated in the world's first deaf-led church service. John Philp Wood was among those in the congregation which included Robert Tait, William Gray, Walter Geikie, Alexander Blackwood and James Heriot amongst those on a roll call of names notable in Deaf history.

Wood led an active social life and he was often a guest of people of renown, being invited to dinner or official occasions, besides socialising with members of the deaf community of Edinburgh and its neighbouring towns. Wood was a great friend of the Scottish poet and writer, Sir Walter Scott. Lockhart's *Memoirs of Scott* (1845), page 709 (taking an extract from Scott's Journal) described Scott's day with Francis Cadell, his publisher's brother in law at Cockenzie on 27 June 1830:

> Honest John, my old friend, dined with us. I only
> regret I cannot understand him, as he has a very
> powerful memory, and much curious information.

Wood was a guest of Cadell at the dinner of 'tiled whiting' (a dish of fish dried in the sun) with Scott and members of the Cadell's family.

John Philp Wood died on 25 October 1838 at his home in 8 South Charlotte Street, where he lived for 28 years. He was interred in St Cuthbert's churchyard.

Cecilia Robertson Edinburgh
81 John Philip Wood, aged 76 Died 1838, (aged 78)
82 Barbara Brown
83 Robert Kirkham, Died 9th Nov 1840 (aged 20)
84 William Gray, junr, Leith
85 James Neilson
86 John Pinkerton, Paisley, Died 1836
87 Mrs John Hardie, wife to No 62 Ramsay, Leith.
88 Frances Gordon, died 18 Novr aged 56 1864 husband of No 65
89 Alexander Thomson, father to No 281 & No 316
90 Agnes Bell
91 James Ritchie, died suddenly 4th June 1862 removed to No 38. married to Newcastle on Tyne No 42
92 John Reid, Hawick now Newcastle on Tyne
93 Charles Watson, Perth died 1st Aug 1854
94 Robert Newall, Hawick
95 Donald Ferguson, Comrie
96 Richard Heaviside, London

This Hall was 22 feet long by 13 x 14
feet wide, and had three windows.
Elders were first elected by
—the congregation in this meeting
place, and also the Edinburgh
Deaf and Dumb Benevolent
Society was instituted, at first privately

A page from the Edinburgh Deaf and Dumb Benevolent Society
Showing John Philp Wood as member number 81.

(Reproduced with kind permission of Deaf Action, Edinburgh)

Francis Humberston Mackenzie

Lord Seaforth's deafness was a merciful imposition to
lower him to the ordinary rate of capacity in society.
—Henry "Harry" Erskine

The story of Francis Humberston Mackenzie is a story of epic proportions and he deserves a book solely devoted to his life and deeds. We cannot do full justice to his life story here as the intention of this book is to give a brief outline of the Braidwoodian pupil's life and contributions. Mackenzie's story is also entwined with a touch of mysticism and fate that was foretold by a seer less than one hundred years before he was born and this prophecy is inseparable from Mackenzie's life.

According to Alexander Mackenzie's two published works, *History of the Mackenzies* (pub: 1879) and *Prophecies of the Brahan Seer* (pub: 1899). The Brahan Seer, Coinneach Odhar, was born Kenneth Mackenzie, at Baile-na-Cille, in the Parish of Uig and Island of Lewis, around the beginning of the 17th century. He lived at Loch Ussie near to Dingwall in Ross-shire and worked as a labourer on the Brahan estate, the seat of the Seaforth chieftains, from sometime around 1675. Odhar one day stumbled while out walking and found a small white stone with a hole in the middle, through which he would look and see visions. Over a period of time he foretold future events with such accuracy that it would be hard for the most sceptical scientist to dispute his gifts of prophecy.

News of Odhar's power came to Lord Mackenzie of Kintail, the second Earl of Seaforth and the powerful overlord of Brahan. Mackenzie sent for Odhar to test his gifts of prophecy. The seer then went to live at Brahan and worked as a labourer. Lord Mackenzie, however, soon died and he was succeeded by Kenneth, the third Earl of Seaforth. It would be that Seaforth clan that would bring doom to Coinneach Odhar... and in turn, be doomed by him.

The 3rd Earl of Seaforth was married to Isabella Mackenzie of the equally great Mackenzie family, and it was said that Isabella was a woman of no beauty. Seaforth was a close friend of King Charles II and was one day sent by King Charles to Paris on a diplomatic mission. This mission kept Seaforth out of contact with his wife for many weeks. Isabella became impatient when she had not heard from her husband for a good number of months and called for Odhar. She asked him what her husband was doing and the seer's initial response was that he was in excellent health and very happy. Isabella was not satisfied with the response and pressed Odhar, demanding to know what he was up to as her husband did not write home and was also staying too long in Paris. Isabella got angry as time progressed and in the end, submitting to pressure, the seer declared that 'the Earl was in a handsome room and with him were two beautiful ladies, one sitting on his knee, the other playing with his curls.' Isabella did not like what she heard and flew into a rage. What upset her more was the fact that Odhar spoke in front of her friends and vassals. She accused him of making up defamatory lies about her husband. She ordered that the seer be taken away and executed.

Odhar was both surprised and taken aback by her reaction, but the die was cast. Isabella was very vindictive, and would not change her mind, or forgive him. Odhar was quickly taken away to the Ness of Chanonry. Realising that he was at the threshold of death and also that time was ticking away, he took out his stone and looked into it... and said:

> I see into the far future, and I read the doom of the race of my oppressor. The long-descended line of Seaforth will, ere many generations have passed, end in extinction and in sorrow. I see a chief, the last of his house, both deaf and dumb. He will be the father of four fair sons, all of whom he will follow to the tomb. He will live careworn and die mourning, knowing that the honours of his line are to be extinguished for ever, and that no future chief of the Mackenzies shall bear rule at Brahan or in Kintail. After lamenting over the last and most promising of his sons, he himself shall sink into the grave, and the remnant of his possessions shall be inherited by a white-coifed lassie from the East, and she is to kill her sister. And as a sign by which it may be known that these things are coming to pass, there shall be four great lairds in the days of the last deaf and dumb Seaforth — Gairloch, Chisholm, Grant, and Raasay — of whom one shall be buck-toothed, another hare-lipped, another half-witted, and the fourth a stammerer. Chiefs distinguished by these personal marks shall be the allies and neighbours of the last Seaforth; and when he looks around him and sees

316

them, he may know that his sons are doomed to death, that his broad lands shall pass away to the stranger, and that his race shall come to an end.

When the seer had ended this prediction, he threw his white stone into a small loch, and declared that whoever should find that stone would be similarly gifted. Then he was bound hand and foot and thrown, head foremost, into a barrel of burning tar which contained long sharp spikes driven in from the outside. This wild and fearful doom ended Odhar's life.

According to the register of Births and Christening of the Church of Saint Mary, Marylebone Road, London, Francis Humberston Mackenzie was born on 9 June 1755, the second son of Major William Mackenzie and Mary Humberston, daughter and heiress of Matthew Humberston of Humberston in Lincolnshire. William Mackenzie was the son of Alexander Mackenzie and the grandson of Kenneth Mackenzie, the 4th Earl of Seaforth. Francis was christened on 3 July 1755.

Very little is known of Mackenzie's early life except that according to Deaflore he attended a Royal Navy boarding school in England and took actual part in working on a warship. Francis was raised in England since birth and he had never been to Scotland until his early teens. In 1767, when a young midshipman, Mackenzie contracted scarlet fever and consequently became deaf. There is a legend referring to Mackenzie's dream on circumstances which led to his deafness. (See Appendix 6.) It is not disputed that Mackenzie was in fact a young midshipman when he went deaf, and this detail can also be found in pages 85-86 of *The History of Parliament: The House of Commons 1754-1790 — III: Members K-Y (Pub: 1964 by Secker and Warburg, London)*.

There is, however, another account of how Mackenzie became deaf. In John Knox's *A Tour through the Highlands of Scotland and the Hebridean Isles* (1787) a footnote on Mackenzie (Seaforth) states:

> This gentleman served when very young in the Royal Navy. While he was ill with fever, an engagement happened between the fleet on which he was on board and that of the French, when the noise of the cannon totally deprived him of his hearing, and under which calamity he still remains. The usual way of conversing

with him is by writing, or by the fingers, at which both his family and intimate acquaintance are very expert, and he is equally quick in anticipating the meaning.

Mackenzie's speech was initially intact, but as time went on, his speech deteriorated quite quickly. Mackenzie made his first visit to Scotland when his parents sent him to the Braidwood Academy in Edinburgh to cope with his new-found state of being deaf. Mackenzie learned to sign, fingerspell and lipread alongside3 normal educational studies. It is believed that he was enrolled in the Braidwood Academy around early to mid-1768, spending about two to three years at the academy. Mackenzie was never to master lipreading and he was to become very heavily reliant on fingerspelling and the written form of communication – that "pen and pad" method as present day deaf people call it. Mackenzie was to develop into a distinguished person with great intellectual ability and of extensive achievements.

Mackenzie's father William died on 12 March 1770 and his elder brother Thomas Frederick Mackenzie became the head of the family, but not the Mackenzie clan. It was not until Mackenzie's cousin Kenneth Mackenzie (b.15 January 1744) died on 27 August 1781 while sailing to the East Indies with the Seaforth (Highland) Regiment that Thomas Frederick Mackenzie became the clan leader and representative of the ancient house of Mackenzie of Kintail and the attained Earls of Seaforth, but not a member of the peerage. At the time of Kenneth Mackenzie's death at sea, Thomas Frederick Mackenzie was in the East Indies and he adopted the additional name of Humberston on succeeding to his mother's property and inherited considerable estates in Humberston, Lincolnshire from his uncle Thomas Humberston. Thomas Frederick then pledged his English property to purchase for £100,000 the remaining ancestral estates of the Earls of Seaforth from his cousin.

The Mackenzie family had a number of houses in fashionable parts of London and Mackenzie was in the main living in a house in Clarges Street, off Piccadilly, around the time he married Mary Proby (right, b.12 August 1754) on 22 April 1782. His wife was the daughter of the Very Rev. John Baptist Proby, the Dean of Lichfield, and his wife Mary, nee Russell.

Thomas Frederick Mackenzie Humberston held commissions in the 1st Dragoon Guards and the 100th Foot in India. Humberston with part of his troops joined the army under General Mathews in Malabar. He accompanied Colonel Macleod and Major Shaw to Bombay to make representations to the council relative to the conduct of General Mathews, which resulted in that officer's suspension.

After their mission was accomplished the delegates embarked at Bombay in the Ranger sloop, to rejoin the army on 5 April 1783. Three days later they were captured by the Mahratta fleet, when every officer on board was killed or wounded. Humberston, who received a four-pound ball through the body, died of his wound at the Mahratta port of Ghériah on 30 April 1783. Contemporary accounts described him as a young man of many accomplishments, and of brilliant promise in his profession. He was unmarried. He left a natural son, Thomas B. Mackenzie Humberston, who fell, a captain in the 78th Ross-shire Buffs, at Ahmednuggur, in 1803.

Upon the death of his elder brother, Mackenzie reluctantly succeeded to the Seaforth estates and became the chief of the Highland Clan Mackenzie. He was also known as MacCoinnich Bodhar (Deaf Mackenzie). Mackenzie also inherited vast debts that came with the estate: the extravagant lifestyle and poor financial housekeeping of the previous Seaforth chieftains contributed largely to the creation of the debts. Mackenzie initially put the financial worries aside and began his leadership deciding whether to campaign for a seat in the British Parliament. Mackenzie was keen on restoring the neglected Seaforth interest in Ross-shire and Lewis, but faced powerful opposition in Lord MacLeod, the powerful and highly respected chief of the junior branch of the Mackenzie clan. MacLeod had a lot of supporters and was all set to win the Ross-shire seat. In this election, Mackenzie would be the underdog should he decide to stand for the region's parliamentary seat and no one supposed, because of his deafness, that Mackenzie would take the plunge into politics — this was seen in the comments written by John Robinson in December 1783 (*The Parliamentary Papers of John Robinson 1774-1784*):

> As the chief of the Mackenzies, brother and heir of
> the late Colonel Humberston, is deaf and dumb, it is
> unlikely he will think of coming into Parliament and
> therefore it is most likely that Lord MacLeod will be
> elected again.

But Mackenzie did stand for election. He won against the odds and was returned, albeit in controversy. It was said that Mackenzie was assisted by a number of fictitious votes, but this was not proved and might be due to lies from the bitter supporters of the defeated MacLeod. Barely a year after taking up the clan chieftainship, Mackenzie was elected Member of Parliament for the County of Ross and took his seat in the House of Commons.

In 1771 the British Crown restored the Seaforth Estates as a favour and, in gratitude for restoring the family estates, Mackenzie, in 1787, offered to raise a regiment on his own estates for King George III's service in India, to be commanded by himself. In the same year the 74th, 75th, 76th and 77th Regiments were raised, but the Government declined his patriotic offer; the Seaforth recruits were taken only to complete the 74th and 75th Foot. In his last year as an MP in 1790, Mackenzie renewed his offer on 19 May but the Government declined his services again, saying that the strength of the army had been finally fixed at 77 Regiments.

As an MP for Ross-shire, Mackenzie made regular trips to London. There is a mention in *The Times* dated Friday 26 December 1788 of a deaf person sitting in the House of Commons debate:

> One of the Members who divided with Mr. Fox is perfectly deaf – and yet he had the patience to sit out the debates, - no doubt perfectly entertained, as well as convinced by the ARGUMENTS on both sides of the question.

This small item in *The Times* does not really make much sense and why the deaf MP was not named is typical of people's attitude towards the deaf in that era. Both Francis Humberston Mackenzie and Charles James Fox were able to hold lengthy conversations using fingerspelling; Fox had a deaf son at the Braidwood Academy, which moved from Edinburgh to Hackney in 1783 and Fox learned fingerspelling in order to communicate with his son Henry.

The Rev. Dr John Buchanan wrote around 1782 of Mackenzie, who was the President of the Society for Propagating Christian Knowledge, of which Buchanan was one of the officers:

> Mackenzie has a noble demeanour and a handsome open countenance that bespeaks the feudal baron

320

and the head of a great clan. He has excellent parts and almost universal knowledge, and is particularly distinguished by his enthusiasm and attainments in natural history. Though deaf from birth, he is very lively and pleasing in conversation. The company spell their words on their fingers and Mackenzie answers by speech.

Being extremely quick of apprehension, he will carry on a regular discourse on any subject with his guests. After seeing a few letters spelt on fingers, he immediately supplies the rest and saves them the trouble of going through the whole. Those who have the honour of visiting at his house are at pains to touch their fingers cleverly, and most of the gentlemen at Stornoway in the Isle of Lewis are adept at this kind of learning, in order to make themselves understood when in company with him.

(W. R. Roe — Peeps into the Deaf World, p356. 1917)

It appears that Mackenzie's residual natural speech was holding up well in 1782 at the time of Buchan's writing, but it was nevertheless on a gradual decline because, not long after, reports and writings appeared to say that he did not speak well and people used signs and writing as the main forms of communication with him.

He may be said quite to have recovered the use of speech, for he was able to converse; but he was totally deaf, and all communications were made to him by signs or in writing.

(Burke — *Vicissitudes of Families*, 3rd Series, 2nd ed. 1863)

Mackenzie decided not to seek re-election in the 1790 Parliamentary elections and offered the seat to William Adam, a fellow Whig and a businessman. Mackenzie was sure that Adam would be a success, but it was not a quiet election: several nobles staked claim for candidacy, and a number of them were scheming against Mackenzie and his choice. Despite being deaf, Mackenzie was aware of this scheming. Persistent 'surmises and whispers' of opposition prompted him and Adam to muster 'the most powerful and reputable attendance' possible, and the election went off quietly in the end. Mackenzie got his way, and his man.

There was a dark period in Scotland's history ongoing during Mackenzie's rule — the first phase of the Highland Clearances (1785-1820). This infamous chapter in Scottish history referred to the cruel events of how the Highland people were dispossessed of their homes and livelihood by their landlords who wanted land for sheep and cattle grazing because they gained more income from sheep and cattle farmers. Not all landlords, including Mackenzie, displayed little respect for their people: Mackenzie could not bear to evict any of his tenants. Despite being in heavy debt that came with his inheritance of clan chieftainship, Mackenzie chose to sell parts of his land to raise money to cover his debts. There were some accusations and suspicions that he sold some land knowing that the purchasers would evict the tenants.

Mackenzie was in the main quite comfortable with the state of affairs of Ross-shire and the Isle of Lewis: kelp and cattle were in demand and he treated his subjects well, unlike some landlords, especially the despicable Countess of Sutherland who, between 1811 and 1821, took to burning homes of many families to make them leave her land: it was written that in 1813 she had her agents burn 250 homes in one fell swoop and the fires raged for six days.

On 7 March 1793, a Letter of Service was granted to Mackenzie, empowering him, as Lieutenant-Colonel-Commandant, to raise a Highland battalion which, as the first to be embodied during the War of the First Coalition with Revolutionary France (1792-1797), was to be numbered the 78th.

On 13 October 1793, Mackenzie offered to raise a second battalion for the 78th, and on the 30th of the same month King George gave him permission to raise five hundred additional men on the original Letter of Service. This was not what Mackenzie wanted and on 28 December of the same year he submitted to the Government three alternative proposals for raising a second battalion.

On 7 February 1794, one of these proposals was agreed to: the battalion was to be formed of eight battalion and two flank companies, each to consist of 100 men, with the usual number of officers and non-commissioned officers. Mackenzie, however, was disappointed by the Government; Lord Amherst signed an order that it was considered to be a separate corps. This did not please Mackenzie and prompted him to write a letter of protest to the War Secretary, Henry Dundas (1742-1811):

St Alban Street
8th February 1794

Sir —I had sincerely hoped I should not be obliged to
trouble you again; but on my going to-day to the War
Office about my letter of service (having yesterday, as I
thought, finally agreed with Lord Amherst), I was, to
my amazement, told that Lord Amherst had ordered
that the 1000 men I am to raise were not to be a second
battalion of the 78th, but a separate corps. It will, I am
sure, occur to you that should I undertake such a thing,
it would destroy my influence among the people of my
country entirely and instead of appearing as a loyal
honest chieftain calling out his friends to support their
King and country, I should be gibbeted as a jobber of
the attachment my neighbours bear to me. Recollecting
what passed between you and me, I barely state the
circumstance; and I am, with great respect and
attachment, Sir, your most obliged and faithful servant,

F. H. Mackenzie.

The letter had the desired effect and the order for a separate corps was
rescinded. A Letter of Service was issued in Mackenzie's favour on 10
February 1794, authorising him, as Lieutenant-Colonel-Commandant,
to add the new battalion, the strength of which was to be one company
of grenadiers, one of light infantry, and eight battalion companies, to
his own regiment. The regiment was soon raised, inspected and passed
in June of the same year at Fort George, located on an isolated spit of
land jutting west into the Moray Firth at Ardersier, about 10 to 11
miles north east of Inverness. On the following month in July, King
George gave permission to have the battalion named "The Ross-shire
Buffs."

The formation of the battalion was not without controversy. Young
Scots were forced against their will into joining: a large number of
young men in their late teens and early twenties were snatched by
Mackenzie's Press gangs roaming the Highlands and the Isle of Lewis.
Mackenzie noted that these young men had nothing much to do and
they needed to contribute to the greater good of their country. Many of
the men never returned to their homes until they were away for at most
twenty years in the army.

Francis Humberston Mackenzie
by William Dyce after Sir Thomas Lawrence
According to the auctioneer Christies, the original by Lawrence
is in a private collection in France (2003).

(Reproduced with kind permission of The Highlanders' Museum
[Queen's Own Highlander Collection]}

Outside of politics, Mackenzie showed great interest in everything he was doing, in particular botany and natural history. He expressed a desire to become a Fellow of the Royal Society and on 20 March 1794 he was proposed for Fellowship. He was elected as a Fellow on 26 June 1794, becoming only the second Braidwoodian pupil to achieve the fellowship of the Royal Society since John Goodricke in 1786.

EC/1974/05 Letter of election for Mackenzie to become
a Fellow of the Royal Society

(Reproduced with kind permission of the Royal Society)

Mackenzie showed keen interest in the arts and he commissioned a few works by Thomas Lawrence, besides sponsoring other artists to execute paintings that Mackenzie wished to be undertaken. Lawrence was a famous portrait artist and he was celebrated by members of the Royal family, stars of the theatre and members of the ruling classes, including parliamentarians. There was a time when Lawrence, a former pupil of Sir Joshua Reynolds, hit hard times and got himself into debt.

Mackenzie lent Lawrence a sum of £1000 to get himself out of his dire financial situation and send him on his way. It was an expensive advance in those days: Lawrence was to repay Mackenzie partly with money and partly by commissioned paintings.

Thomas Lawrence

Mackenzie also commissioned Benjamin West in 1785 to paint Colin Fitzgerald saving the life of King Alexander III who was attacked by a stag. This fantastic painting, entitled *The Death of the Stag*, is 12 feet high by 17 feet across. The painting initially hung in Brahan Castle until it was demolished and it is now in the care of the National Gallery of Scotland. For this painting, Mackenzie paid West £800. Years later West bought back the painting from Mackenzie for the price he was paid for it - £800, as he needed it for his exhibition.

Mackenzie's interests were wide-ranging. Around 1782 he was the President of the Society for Propagating Christian Knowledge. He later added the role of Extraordinary Director of the Highland Society to his list of activities. In 1795, he was elected a Fellow of the Royal Society of Edinburgh. Botany and natural history remained Mackenzie's chief interests. On the list of Past Fellows of the Royal Academy of Edinburgh, Mackenzie's profession was listed as "Landowner, Soldier, Politician, Botanist."

Mackenzie usually spent two to three months annually on the Island of Lewis, living in a large white dwelling house named Seaforth Lodge on top of a hill overlooking the town of Stornoway. Lewis was a profitable island for Mackenzie due to its trade in kelp as well as fishing. Mackenzie took great interest in building and expanding the town of Stornoway as well as other villages scattered along the various bays which were plentiful in fish. In other times, he was usually found alternating between his main London home in Clarges Street and his Scottish home, Brahan Castle near Dingwall — his home was the traditional seat of the Mackenzie Clan and the Earls of Seaforth. He also had a number of houses in Edinburgh.

In 1794 William Adam surrendered his seat in the Commons and Mackenzie accepted the seat for Ross-shire, when Adam thought he was sure of an alternative berth in Banbury. Adam did not win the

Brahan Castle' near Dingwall
Seat of the Mackenzie Clan.
(Photograph - Doreen E. Woodford Collection)

Banbury seat, and Mackenzie, though uncomfortable 'at the idea of forcing' Adam 'out of Parliament', felt obliged to implement the change and come in himself. On 1 May 1794, Mackenzie became an MP for Ross-shire and he entered the House of Commons for the second time. Following his re-election as an MP, Mackenzie sought and employed one Peter Fairbairn from Kelso in the Scottish Borders as his secretary based at Brahan Castle. It was an important position because Mackenzie's speech deteriorated around that time and he relied heavily on both the manual alphabet and written communication. It was Fairbairn's task to ease the flow of communication between his employer and others. It can be safely said that Fairbairn was the first recorded employed sign language interpreter.

Some months before the dissolution of Parliament in 1796, Mackenzie, aware that he was to receive a peerage, had decided to retire from the Commons. One of his bitter political opponents, Mackenzie of Cromarty, reminded him of an earlier 'conversation' concerning his desire to enter Parliament. Mackenzie responded that he had no strong objection to Cromarty's coming in, provided he could win the seat on his own bottom, but rejected the implied assertion that he was obliged to give him a personal endorsement.

On 26 October 1797, Mackenzie was created Lord Seaforth and Baron Mackenzie of Kintail as a reward for his eminent services to the

Government. His new-found peerage titles were limited to the male heirs of his body. Mackenzie then became well known and formally addressed by the name Francis, Lord Seaforth. In 1798 he was appointed Colonel of the Ross-shire Regiment of Militia.

With his title of Lord Seaforth, more members of the upper classes had to learn to fingerspell in order to communicate with him. Seaforth commanded respect and his knowledge and views were readily welcomed. There is a little anecdote about a true event mentioned in *Recollections of the Table-Talk of Samuel Rogers* (1856):

> Lord Seaforth was invited one day to dine with Lord Melville. Just before the time of the company's arrival, Elizabeth, Lady Melville, sent into the drawing room a lady of her acquaintance who could talk with her fingers, that she might receive Lord Seaforth. Presently Lord Guildford entered the room and the lady, believing him to be Lord Seaforth, began to spell on her fingers quickly. Lord Guildford did the same, and they had been carrying a conversation in that manner for about ten minutes when Lady Melville joined them. Her female friend said, "Well, I have been talking away to this dumb man." "Dumb, bless me" Lord Guildford exclaimed, "I thought you were dumb!"

There were ventures by many enterprising Scots to the West Indies and the north coast of South America in search of quick fortunes. To many Scots, the prospects to make money in their homeland were limited and consequently they sought their luck overseas. Guiana was one of the countries the young Scottish entrepreneurs visited and they settled on the coastline of Berbice and Demerara, initially draining the land and building plantations. News of these adventurous Scots returning home "as rich as a Demerary man" came to Seaforth's attention and one James Fraser of Reelig had sons speculating in Demerara around 1795. Fraser of Reelig wrote to Seaforth in 1801 that:

> Fraser of Belladrum... was said to have made £40,000 by his last trip...

David Alston: Very Rapid and Splendid Fortunes?
Transactions of the Gaelic Society of Inverness, LXIII
(2002-04)

The Belladrum Frasers – Col. James Fraser and his sons, James, Simon and Evan – were also some of the first speculators in Berbice and Demerara, and their quick fortune tempted Seaforth to join in the Berbice and Demerara venture. Seaforth was not only struggling to balance the books on his vast Scottish estates, but trying to support their families.

In 1801, Seaforth became a part of a consortium which bought land in Berbice; Seaforth paid £8,000 and he brought his share on the West Sea Coast of Berbice into cultivation as Plantations Brahan and Kintail and on the East Sea Coast as Plantation Seawell. Seaforth made his secretary Peter Fairbairn manager of the plantations, providing him with £12,000 for the purchase of the land and stocking it with slaves. The following year his cotton plantation yielded a net profit of £3,000. Seaforth had in mind the expected rising value of land as a part of the attraction of investment in Guiana.

On 29 November 1800 Seaforth was appointed Governor of Barbados by Lord Portland. He did not set foot on this most easterly of the Caribbean islands until the following year and his position was taken up in a caretaker capacity by one William Bishop. To look after his Guiana investment and project, Seaforth sent his secretary Peter Fairbairn to Berbice and Demerara in the same year that he set off for Barbados.

Seaforth and his family boarded the ship *Topaze* under Captain Church on 12 February 1801. *Topaze* was a part of a convoy of 130 vessels setting out for Madeira on the day. The following day storms and gale force winds came, causing chaos to the convoy. Only 80 ships arrived in Madeira, including *Topaze*, which left Madeira for Barbados on 27 February.

Seaforth and his family arrived in Carlisle Bay on 26 March 1801 and he was soon sworn in as Governor. He was initially welcomed and popular but he was stepping into a different world – a world dominated by the brutal superiority of the white race over the black race, and the injustices and atrocities that flowed from the terrible prejudices of both the white plantation owners and the white authorities towards the blacks, both slaves and freedmen. Seaforth was aware of the situation, but he was plunged into it, with directions from the British Government to deal with, or sort out, certain legal irregularities; and he was to gain first-hand experience of what 'white superiority' meant. According to Jerome S. Handler in his 1974 work *Unappropriated People:*

Freedmen in the Slave Society of Barbados (John Hopkins University Press), Lord Seaforth arrived at Barbados with instructions from the British Government to:

1. Prevent corporal punishment for female slaves
2. Make the murder of slaves a capital offence
3. Modernise the 1688 slave code

The climate between the whites and the 'freed blacks' in Barbados at the time of Seaforth's arrival was very tense. Besides cruelty to slaves and related incidents, there were also freedwomen who made their way to a fortune and started to own property, or properties, mainly by "borrowing" sums of money from various white benefactors. The money lent by the whites represented a gift cloaked in legal disguise, and prostitution was rife within Bridgetown hotels and bars owned by the freedwomen who were mainly mulattoes. Local white Barbadians were expressing anger about the situation and they put pressure on the local colonial authority to curtail the property rights of the free coloureds. The whole situation was made clear to Seaforth by John Poyer, a native white creole, in his letter dated 22 June 1801, in which Poyer reminded Seaforth that...

> two grand distinctions characterised the Barbadian society. These distinctions existed, firstly between the white inhabitants and free people of colour, and secondly between masters and slaves. Moreover — nature had strongly defined the difference not only in complexion, but in the mental, intellectual, and corporeal facilities of the different species.
>
> John Poyer: *The History of Barbados, from the First Discovery of the Island, in the Year 1605, till the Accession of Lord Seaforth, 1801*

These distinctions, Poyer asserted, were recognised and adopted in the Barbadian legal and political system. Poyer's letter was written at the time of the growing debates on the abolition of slavery in Britain, and the white Barbadians felt that Seaforth's arrival was tied to this debate; there were suspicions that Seaforth's instructions from Britain required him to deal with such issues as the penalty to be imposed for the wilful murder of a slave. The white Barbadians, through Poyer's letter, were declaring their position on the social state of the island; they were resentful and also incensed at the possibility of the growth of a propertied free coloured class with the capacity to challenge the social and economic influence and authority of the whites. They wanted a law preventing property ownership by free negroes and mulattoes.

John Poyer was the author of *The History of Barbados, from the First Discovery of the Island, in the Year 1605, till the Accession of Lord Seaforth, 1801*. On page 132 of his book (Chapter IV, 1688) it was written:

> ...the legislature of Barbadoes enacted that famous statute, Number Eighty-two, for the government of negroes, which has of late years become a popular theme of declamation in England; and subjected the peaceable, unoffending West Indians, to the most illiberal invectives and the most virulent abuse. By this law, among many provisions made for the prevention of crimes and the punishment of offences; which, to the honour of the people, are executed with a spirit as mild and lenient as the object is just and laudable, it was ordained, "That if any slave, under punishment by his master, or his order, shall suffer in life or member, no one shall be liable to any fine for it. But if any person wantonly or cruelly kills his own slave, he shall pay into the public treasury fifteen pounds."

To the above was added a footnote:

> Though the punishment here prescribed may appear disproportioned to the enormity of the crime, it should be remembered that in a country where slaves compose the principal part of the property of the inhabitants and where their labour, or hire, is in many cases the only means of their owner's support, the loss of a slave is, of itself, a very heavy forfeiture, without an additional penalty.

It is of interest to mention here about the Barbados Slave Code of 1661, a law that was passed by the colonial legislature to provide a legal base for slavery in Barbados. The code's preamble, which stated that the law's purpose was to "prevent them (slaves) as we do other men's goods and chattels" established that black slaves would be treated as chattel property in the island's court. This slave code ostensibly sought to protect slaves from cruel masters and masters from unruly slaves; in practice it provided far more extensive protection for masters than slaves. The law required masters to provide each slave with one set of clothing per year, but it set no standards for slaves' diet, housing or working conditions. It also denied slaves even basic rights guaranteed under English common law, such as the right to life. It allowed the slaves' owners to do entirely as they wanted to their slaves, including killing, mutilating and burning them alive, without fear of reprisal. This 1661 law, which underwent minor modifications in 1676, 1682 and 1688, marked the beginning of the legal codification of slavery, and it was adopted by other British colonies such as Jamaica, South Carolina and Antigua.

Under the aforementioned circumstances and with his hands full in dealing with numerous issues on the island, Seaforth set about doing his task as Governor. He, however, took time in the early period of his arrival to familiarise himself with his new surroundings and, being a keen botanist, he was particularly interested in the diverse tropical plants, and began recording all he came across. He resided at Pilgrim, the residence of the Governor of Barbados (now Government House), and took on a number of slaves to work in his household. He employed one slave named Quaco as his cook. Unlike the plantation slave owners, Seaforth treated his own humanely and did not put them through strenuous and excessive tasks or hours. He often cared for the health of his domestic slaves and ensured that they all were not in want of decent attire and breaks.

Pilgrim (Governor's House)
The residence and office of Lord Seaforth

In 1802 Seaforth sent a message recommending to the island's His Majesty's Council and the House of Assembly, which consisted of twenty-two elected members, that they consider changing the law and making it a capital offence for anyone to wilfully murder a slave. This proposal caused uproar in the Assembly, and later the anger of the members of the House of Assembly was directed towards Seaforth, although the Council were more agreeable to his proposal. Some members of the Assembly labelled him "obnoxious." It must be mentioned here that the circumstances of the island of Barbados during that time was peculiar, containing a much larger number of white men of small property than in any other Caribbean islands; and in consequence there prevailed among the lower whites, the bulk of the white population, a most bigoted and vulgar prejudice against the African race. It was the influence of the low whites on the Assembly of Barbados that so long rendered the law of that island different from those of all the other British colonies, by punishing the wilful murder of a slave with a small maximum fine of £15 (which was later reduced to £11 4s) instead of making it a capital crime. The Assembly was under the powerful influence of the low whites and it remained so until 1818. The proposal from Seaforth that the wilful murder of a slave should be made capital stirred up the anti-African spirit in the Assembly, which responded by calling his proposal an insult and throwing it out. Seaforth expected such a reaction, but this was the beginning of his long battle with the Assembly. Seaforth even wrote home to Ministers in that year to say that he had offended the whole island of Barbados by endeavouring to persuade them that the wilful murder of a slave should be made felony, instead of being compounded for by a fine of £11 4s.

Again in the same year, taking advice from the Society for the Propagation of Gospel, which owned the Codrington Plantations, Seaforth put forward a proposal that slaves could and should be instructed in reading and writing, especially so that they could read the Bible. The planters and the House of Assembly immediately opposed the proposal and dismissed it outright. Seaforth again wrote in that year:

> The planters urge that such instruction could be of no avail to a race of men doomed to... slavery, that extending their means of information could only awaken them to a keener sense of their situation, which would... render them more unhappy in themselves and more dangerous to their masters.

Jerome S. Handler 1974: *Unappropriated People.* p183

Missioners and priests were in the main very unwelcome in Barbados. The Quakers were pushed out of the island when they tried to preach Christianity to the slaves; they were severely rebuked and immediately shunned for attempting to teach the slaves literacy. The Methodists faced the same situation. Seaforth brought with him a few men of the cloth attached to the Society for Propagating Christian Knowledge to Barbados, promising them his protection, and protect them he did for there were no reports of anything untoward happening to the priests, apart from being almost constantly cold-shouldered by the white Barbadians.

Seaforth quickly learned about Barbados, its people and its social system and he began to understand what was occurring. He understood the whites' labelling of Negroes; and he was concerned about the status of a certain section of free slaves, writing to Lord Hobart on 2 June 1802:

> There is, however, a third description of people from whom I am more suspicious of evil than from either the whites or the slaves: these are the Black and Coloured people who are not slaves, and yet whom I cannot bring myself to call free. I think unappropriated people would be a more proper denomination for them, for though not the property of other individuals they do not enjoy the shadow of any civil right.

Seaforth to Lord Hobart, letter 6 June 1802,
Seaforth Papers 46/7/7

Seaforth instigated a thorough and detailed investigation on the issue of cruelty and murder of slaves and this took a long time. The investigation eventually found only three instances of the wilful murder of slaves. The investigation was most probably hindered and stifled by the planters' deliberate withholding of the truth, imparting no accounts of incidents involving the murder or maiming of slaves.

Tensions and arguments between the House of Assembly and Seaforth intensified throughout the year and in the latter part of 1803, Seaforth suffered health problems and he was advised by his medical attendant to go to Tortola to recuperate. The advice was accepted and he left for Tortola, where he stayed for several weeks. His family remained in Barbados. On 3 December 1803, they were picked up by the ship Berwick and sailed for England, in part for him to seek further advice from the Colonial Office on the situation and also to take a short break from his labours in Barbados. In his absence, John Ince, the President of His Majesty's Council, became the acting Deputy Governor.

Seaforth had to return to Barbados in March 1804, having fully recovered and also taken instruction and advice from the British government. On Thursday 8 March, a party was held at the London Tavern by both the Colonial Office and a group of gentlemen from Barbados in honour of Seaforth. Those who attended included Lord Dartmouth, Lord Hobart, Lord Harewood, the secretary at War, several army colonels, Governor Beaujean and Van Battenberg, the Governor of Berbice. The event was a night of entertainment and full of good cheer. Midway through the party, which lasted into the small hours, a toast was proposed by one Mr Jordan, the agent for the colony of Barbados to Seaforth—

> ... I shall have the honour to name to you a Noble Lord, Chief of a colony, in the administration of the government of which he has displayed all of the talents that become so important and exalted a station. He has given energy to the legislature and the judicature, he has supported the dignity of his government on all occasions, he has concurred to establish and preserve those distinctions between the different classes of persons and inhabitants upon which the safety and happiness of the Colony depended; he has encouraged and improved the Militia, and he has secured the affections of the people of Barbadoes to his person and family. The organ of the Colony, I speak the language and sentiments of the Colony, and I propose His Excellency Lord SEAFORTH, his safe and speedy return in perfect health to the bosom of his family and the Colony.

> *Morning Post,* Monday 12 March 1803, p3.

Seaforth left England on 9 March and arrived in Barbados around the end of April 1804. Nothing had changed during his absence with regard to the whites/slave situation and Seaforth resumed his battle with the House of Assembly over the issue of slave killing.

In the meanwhile, his venture in Berbice and Demerara was not making as much profit as he hoped for. In order to increase his returns,

Seaforth purchased more land through his secretary Fairbairn. Despite this, Seaforth's business plan appeared to go wrong, and to overcome that Seaforth borrowed further and restructured his venture as "The United Ross-shire Company settled in and trading to Berbice" and he made Fairbairn his partner.

Seaforth invested an initial outlay of £12000 in establishing three plantations and in the first year, the venture made £3000, which was quite good since the enterprise was intended to be a mid-term project. After that, the weather in Berbice and Demerara was not good in subsequent years and barely enough money was generated to make the plantation business tick over, and break even. Seaforth relied on Fairbairn not only to purchase slaves to work on the plantations, but to ensure that the slaves were well treated, well fed, well clothed and received medical care.

Britain was at war with France and a large fleet of British warships led by Sir Samuel Hood and General Grinfield were sent to the West Indies in mid-1803. In the same year the fleet left Carlisle Bay on 19 June and the colonies of St. Lucia, Tobago, Demerara and Berbice fell into British hands. In the following year, Hood courted Seaforth's 21 year old daughter Mary Elizabeth Frederica Mackenzie, and they eventually married on 6 November 1804.

On the thorny issue of cruelty to slaves, Seaforth was persistent in his endeavours to change the Barbadian law to make the murder of a slave a felony punishable by death. On 13 November 1804, he wrote a letter addressed to Earl Camden and this letter became famous and it was also to play no small part in the anti-slavery movement. The letter contained a recital of cruelties said to have been committed upon slaves in Barbados. Three out of four papers are recorded here, taken from pages 359 – 366 in William Stevens' *The Slave in History: His Sorrows and His Emancipation* (Pub: The Religious Tract Society, London. 1904):

> The following, taken from *Substances of the Debates on a Resolution for Abolishing the Slave Trade* (London, 1806) furnishes an example of the evidence already at the disposal of the Parliament. We print it as it appears in the original:—
>
> In some papers presented to the House of Commons on the 25th February 1805, is contained a letter from Lord SEAFORTH, the Governor of Barbadoes, in which he thus writes to Earl CAMDEN:—

"I enclose four papers containing, from different quarters, reports on the horrid murders I mentioned in some former letters. *They are selected from a great number*, among which there is not one in contradiction of the horrible facts, though several of the letters are very concise and defective. The truth is, that nothing has given me more trouble than to get at the bottom of these businesses, *so horribly absurd are the prejudices of the people* (not of one or two, or of a few individuals, but of the PEOPLE).

"I enclose the Attorney General's letter to me on the subject of the negroes *so most wantonly murdered.* I am sorry to say SEVERAL OTHER INSTANCES OF THE SAME BARBARITY have occurred, with which I have not troubled your Lordship, as I *only wished to make you acquainted with the subject in general.*"

The letters to which Lord SEAFORTH refers, and which accompany the above extracts, are from four of the most respectable individuals in the island of Barbadoes, viz. Mr. INCE, *the President of the Council*; Mr. COULTHURST, *the Advocate General*; Mr. BECCLES, *the Attorney General*; and the Rev. Mr. PILGRIM. These gentlemen all agree in the material facts of the cases which they state. It would, therefore, be an unnecessary repetition to transcribe the whole of their letters: it will be sufficient to give the substance of the statements which they contain.

On the 10th of April, 1804, a militia-man of the name of Halls, of the St. Michael's regiment, returning from military duty, overtook on the road some Negroes who were going quietly home from their labour. When he came near, he called out that he would kill them, and immediately began to run after them. The Negroes, not supposing that he really intended to do them any injury, and imagining that he was in joke, did not endeavour to escape, but merely made way for him. The person nearest to him happened to be a woman, the property of a M. Clarke, the owner of Simmons's estate, who is stated to have been a valuable slave, the mother of five or six children, and far advanced in

337

pregnancy. Without the smallest provocation of any kind. Halls coolly and deliberately plunged his bayonet several times into her body, when the poor creature dropped, and expired without a groan. Two gentlemen were eye-witnesses of this horrid action. One of them, Mr. Harding, the manager of the Codrington College estate, went up to Halls and spoke harshly to him, and said he ought to be hanged, for he never saw a more unprovoked murder, and that he would certainly carry him before a magistrate. Halls' reply is very remarkable. "For what?" said he (with the utmost indifference as to the crime) — "For what? For killing a negro!"

This is a short but a significant sentence, strongly confirming an important truth, which has frequently been asserted, viz. that the Negroes are regarded by their white-skinned oppressors as an inferior order of beings, and, under the influence of this sentiment, are naturally enough denied the common rights of humanity, and excluded from the pale of that sympathy which a sense of a common nature and a common extraction is calculated to inspire. Mr. Harding, however, greatly to his credit, was proof against the force of Halls' compendious reasoning; and, having procured assistance, laid hold of him, and carried him before Mr. Justice Walton. Mr. Justice Walton, it would appear, was not indisposed to use the authority with which he was vested in bringing Halls to justice; but he found, that "in his situation as a magistrate, the law of the island gave him no jurisdiction or authority over him, and, in short, that he had no right to commit him. In this dilemma Mr. Walton applied to Mr. President Ince. "I told Mr. Walton," says the President, in his letter to Lord Seaforth, "that I regretted, with real concern, the deficiency in our law: but that there was a penalty due to the King in such cases," (viz. the eleven pounds four shillings); "and that, as Mr. Harding had sufficiently substantiated the fact, I would order him to be committed till he paid the forfeiture, or a suit should be commenced against him.' Accordingly he was sent to prison.

338

The second instance produced by Lord Seaforth is not inferior in atrocity to the first. A Mr. Colbeck, who lives overseer on Cabbage-tree plantation, in St. Lucy's parish, had bought a new Negro boy out of the yard (meaning the Slave yard, where Negroes are exposed to sale, in the same manner as the cattle and sheep in Smithfield market), and carried him home. Conceiving a liking to the boy, he took him into the house and made him wait at table. Mr. Crone, the overseer of Rowe's estate, which is near to Cabbage-tree plantation, was in the habit of visiting Mr. Colbeck, had noticed the boy, and knew him well. A fire happening one night in the neighbourhood, Colbeck went to give his assistance, and the boy followed him. Colbeck, on his return home, missed the boy, who had lost his way; and as he did not make his appearance the next day, he sent round to his neighbours, particularly to Crone, informing them that his African lad had strayed, he could not speak a word of English, and possibly he might be found breaking some sugar canes, or taking something else for his support: in which case he requested they would not injure him, but send him home, and he would pay any damage the boy might have committed. After a lapse of two or three days, the poor creature was discovered in a gulley (or deep water-course) near to Rowe's estate; and a number of Negroes were soon assembled about the place. The boy, naturally terrified with the threats, the noise, and the appearance of so many people, retreated into a hole in a rock, having a stone in his hand, for the purpose, probably, of defence. By this time. Crone, and some other White persons, had come up. By their orders a fire was put to the hole where the boy lay, who, when he began to be scorched, ran from his hiding-place into a pool of water which was near. Some of the Negroes pursued him into the pool; and the boy, it is said, threw the stone which he held in his hand at one of them. On this, two of the White men, Crone and Hollingsworth, fired at the boy several times with shot, and the Negroes pelted him with stones. He was at length dragged out of the pool in a dying condition; for he had not only received several bruises from the stones, but his breast was so pierced with the shot that it was like a cullender. The White savages (this is the language of Mr. Attorney

General Beccles) ordered the Negroes to dig a grave. Whilst they were digging it, the poor creature made signs of begging for water, which was not given to him: but as soon as the grave was dug, he was thrown into it and covered over, and, as is believed, while yet alive, Colbeck, the owner of the boy, hearing that a Negro had been killed, went to Crone to inquire into the truth of the report. Crone told him, that a Negro had been killed and buried, but assured him it was not his, for he knew him well, and he need not be at the trouble of opening the grave. On this, Colbeck went away satisfied! Receiving, however, further information, he returned, and had the grave opened, when he found the murdered Negro to be his own. Colbeck brought his action of damages in the courts of the island against Crone and Hollingsworth. The cause was ready to be tried, and the Court had met for the purpose, when they thought proper to pay double the value of the boy and 2$ for the use of the island, (being 5$ less than the penalty fixed by law, of 15$ currency each), rather than suffer the business to go to a hearing. "This, I am truly sorry to say," observes the Advocate-General, "was the only punishment which could be inflicted for so barbarous and atrocious a crime."

"This horrid recital (which is given almost in the words of the Report, merely avoiding repetition) seems to require little comment." One circumstance of it, however, may not strike the minds of some readers with its due force, although it appears to be the most affecting part of the whole case. Colbeck, it is said: on hearing that it was not his slave who had been murdered, went away satisfied! O most opprobrious satisfaction! The preceding part of the narrative had prepared us to expect in Colbeck some approximation to European feeling. But what is the fact? On being coolly told that a Negro had been killed and buried — told so by his neighbour, the murderer — is he shocked? Does he express any horror or indignation on the occasion? No! He goes away satisfied! Let the reader give its due weight to this one circumstance, and he must be convinced that a state of society must exist in the West Indies, of which, as an inhabitant of this happy island, he can scarcely form any adequate conception. Suppose, instead of a Negro Slave, that it had been a horse which had been thus killed: Colbeck, had his horse happened to be missing at the time, would have pursued exactly the same steps, and would have been affected in the same way as in the present instance. We may also learn, from this impressive circumstance, the value of West-Indian testimony when given in favour of West-Indian humanity. The moral perceptions and feelings which prevail in that quarter of the world, it will be perceived, are wholly different from those on this side of the Atlantic. It may be allowed that these men mean what they say, when they give each other the praise of humanity. But examine their standard. Who is this man of humanity? It is one, who, hearing that a fellow-creature has been cruelly and wantonly murdered, goes away satisfied because he himself has sustained no loss by the murder! An exception may be admitted in favour of a few men of enlightened minds; but the remark applies to the people — to the bulk of the community, whose prejudices are stated by Lord Seaforth to be so horribly absurd as to resist all measures for remedying this dreadful state of things. But, not to detain the reader any longer with reasonings on this subject, let us proceed to the third case communicated by Lord Seaforth, and which, if possible, is worse than either of the foregoing.

A man of the name of Nowell, who lives in St. Andrew's parish, had been in the habit of behaving brutally towards his wife, and one day went so far as to lock her up in a room, and confine her in chains. A Negro woman belonging to this man, touched with compassion for her unfortunate mistress, undertook privately to release her. Nowell found it out, and in order to punish her, obliged her to put her tongue through a hole in a board, to which he fastened it on the opposite side with a fork, and left her in that situation for some time. He afterwards cut out her tongue nearly by the root, in consequence of which she almost instantly died. No punishment followed this monstrous act of barbarity.

It will, doubtless, be argued, that individual instances of cruelty like those which have been cited, are no proofs of general inhumanity, any more than the annals of the Old Bailey can be considered as exhibiting a fair view of our national character. There is, however, this very remarkable difference in the two cases, a difference which is fatal to the argument. In this country, when we read of crimes, we read of their being followed by just retribution; by severe and exemplary punishment. In the West Indies, on the contrary, we not only hear of the greatest crimes escaping with impunity, but find the laws themselves conspiring to shelter criminals from justice: we find the most respectable and enlightened part of the community sanctioning the perpetration even of murder, by their refusal to recognize the commission of it as a felonious act.

Seaforth's determination to battle it out with the members of the House of Assembly and the planters finally paid off. As early as April 1805 the Council transmitted a bill to the House of Assembly, which had passed it unanimously, entitled an *"Act for the better protection of the Slaves of this island."* This Act repealed the disgraceful clause in one of the old statutes, punishing a slave owner or his agent merely with a fine of fifteen pounds currency for the murder of a slave. It was a small step but an extremely important achievement on a long road to secure the abolition of slavery.

On 17 February 1805 official information reached Barbados that England and Spain were now at war – and England ended up fighting both the French and the Spanish. Seaforth announced in a gazette extraordinary the declaration of war and his being authorised to grant letters of marque and general reprisals. On 20 February about twelve French ships with 4,000 troops arrived in Martinique. Information of the arrival of this formidable armament in the Caribbean Sea reached Barbados on 26 February, prompting Seaforth to deem it necessary to adopt the strongest measures to guard the island against surprise attack by the French. His call was quickly answered. On 6 March Seaforth called the Legislature together and recommended strenuously the furnishing of pecuniary means for putting the island in a state of defence. The House of Assembly quickly passed three bills; two of these bills for raising money to pay for the defence and the third bill to regulate the militia. To these bills, the Assembly added another bill giving the governor power, with the consent of the Council, to proclaim martial law upon receiving information that an enemy's fleet is at sea, but this law should not be longer than three days, unless the enemy should appear in sight.

Seaforth's daughter Mary and her husband Sir Samuel Hood left her family and Barbados for Europe on 18 April. However, Hood sailed first to Antigua to receive from Lord Lavington the investiture of the Order of the Bath.

On 16 May Seaforth issued a new proclamation informing the inhabitants of the island that a very large and formidable French force had arrived in the neighbouring islands, rendering it necessary to adopt every precaution; and as no house of Assembly was existing at that time due to elections, Seaforth, with the advice and consent of the Council, called on the inhabitants to assist in public service. The information received included a statement that the enemy fleet was in sight and as a consequence martial law was proclaimed to commence on 19 May until 21 May, and it was further prolonged until the evening of 25 May. It later transpired that this stringent measure was premature

The new Assembly was summoned to meet Seaforth on 29 May and Seaforth commended the spirit and patriotism of the militia during the recent alarms. He then drew the attention of the Assembly to the approaching expiration if the militia bill and the need to renew it. Seaforth did not mention at that meeting anything about the recent proclamation of martial law and the additional three-day extension, and this did not please the newly-elected members of the Assembly: they voted to resolve itself into a committee of the whole House, to take into consideration the legality of Seaforth's attempt to subject the island to martial law. The Assembly drew the attention of Seaforth to a clause in one of the colonial acts declaring that martial law should be put into force only when an enemy should be seen from the island and should cease in forty-eight hours after that enemy had disappeared: the assembly considered this act had been totally disregarded by Seaforth and elected to hold an inquiry.

Another battle between the Assembly and Seaforth reared its ugly head. The House of Assembly fired off by setting out five resolutions and requesting that

> ... a communication might be made to this House,
> stating the grounds of the late proclamation of martial
> law from the 19th to the 21st instant, and the

continuance thereof from the 21st to the 25th instant; and information given why the same proclamations were not prepared and made with the proper legal formalities.

Robert H. Schomburgk: *The History of Barbados* 1848.

As a consequence of the Assembly's proceedings, the Council adopted a resolution on 25 May exonerating Seaforth from any blame.

At a meeting of the Assembly on 18 June, they received a letter from Seaforth:

> Council Chamber, 18 June 1805.
>
> In answer to the address and resolutions of the Honourable House of Assembly of 29th May, the governor cannot but deeply regret that the Honourable House of Assembly should have thought fit, in the first instance, to vote him guilty of acting unconstitutionally, and then to call upon him for an explanation. Called upon for an explanation of his conduct in a proper manner, he should have been very happy to have given such an explanation, and is fully conscious he could give one satisfactory to every impartial mind; but situated as he is, he must refer the whole to the Sovereign, in whom alone he acknowledges any jurisdiction competent to find him guilty, and representing whom, he finds himself incapacitated from answering a charge of criminality before any other body.
>
> *Seaforth.*

Robert H. Schomburgk: *The History of Barbados* 1848.

Seaforth's letter was accompanied by a letter from the Council to the Speaker of the Assembly:

> The members of his Majesty's Council have herewith sent the Honourable House of Assembly a copy of their minutes from the 18th to the 22nd inclusive, and are sorry to find the House of Assembly should be so intemperate as to condemn by their Resolution the

measures of the Council, before an explanation has been laid before them.

Council Chamber, 18th June, 1805.

Robert H. Schomburgk: *The History of Barbados* 1848.

On 16 July, the Assembly met and noted the messages from Seaforth and the Council and took them into consideration. One member of the Assembly, a Mr Grasett made a long speech in condemnation of Seaforth's proceedings, and moved the two following resolutions:

> Resolved, 1st, That the answer of his Excellency the Governor to our resolutions and address of the 18th day of June is unsatisfactory, and highly disrespectful to this Honourable House.

> Resolved, 2ndly, That the grounds for continuing martial law from the 21st to the 25th of April, contained in the answer of the members of his Majesty's Council to the resolutions and address before-mentioned, were not sufficient to justify the same, no such circumstances existing at the time, by their own showing, as the law requires to sanction such a measure.

These resolutions were challenged by the Speaker of the House, John Beckles, who said he regretted the unhappy dissension that had arisen between the branches of the Legislature and urged the Assembly to seek reconciliation with Seaforth and the Council. The Assembly, however, voted through the resolutions by a majority of fourteen to four.

A message arrived from England declaring that Seaforth's proceedings in the proclamation of martial law were fully approved of by the Crown, and this put an end to the argument with the House of Assembly. The message instructed that his task was to preserve the prerogative of the Crown to declare martial law when he considered it necessary for the safety of the colony.

1806 turned out to be a memorable year for Seaforth. He received news that on the 10th of June a resolution was passed in the House of Commons by a majority of ninety-five to fifteen, declaring the slave trade to be founded on principles contrary to justice, humanity and sound policy, and engaging to institute measures for its total abolition. The House of Lords concurred in the vote by a majority of forty-one to twenty. This resolution was a huge step forward in the abolition of the transatlantic slave trade; and although its entire abolition had not yet been effected, those who assisted in the passing of this bill had the satisfaction of having largely contributed to saving thousands then unborn from the misery of slavery. (The statute 47 Geo. III., chap. 36, which was passed on 25 March 1807, utterly abolished the traffic and purchase of slaves from Africa after 1 May 1807).

Seaforth appeared to have completed what was required of him as Governor of Barbados and he made a decision early in 1806 to leave his post. His application to leave was accepted, and Seaforth informed the island of his impending retirement as Governor. On 22 July, the merchants and other principal inhabitants of Bridgetown gave a farewell public dinner in general estimation of the merits of his administration. Before leaving for England, Seaforth arranged for the slaves employed by him, including his cook Quaco, to be shipped to his Plantation Kintail in Berbice and Demerara. On 25 July, Seaforth boarded the ship Severn under Captain Watson, and accompanied by HMS Agamemnon, departed for England. The journey home took some time as according to the *Morning Post* dated Friday 24 October 1806 "*Seaforth arrived in Bristol a few days ago.*"

It appeared that despite Seaforth's achievement in turning the wilful murder of a slave into a capital crime punishable by death, both the planters and the low whites were able to find another way around this law. A hint was to be found in *Memoirs of an Old Army Officer: Richard A. Wyvill's Visits to Barbados in 1796 and 1806-7* (Edited by Jerome S. Handler, The Journal of the Barbados Museum and Historical Society, Vol. 35, no. 1, March 1975):

> Sept. 16th (1806). As I was riding up St Anne's barracks, I saw a poor Negro lying in the road in the agonies of death. A Barbadian gentleman, passing by, observing how anxious I was to get the poor fellow removed, exclaimed he was a runaway rascal that deserved no pity and rode on. I got some of the black soldiers to endeavour to take him to the barracks but he died on the way.

Seaforth's venture in Berbice and Demerara was not going well despite restructuring. There were more bad seasons, and by 1808 Seaforth, perhaps unfairly, lost confidence in his partner Peter Fairbairn, leading to a slow but steady deterioration in their relationship. Since 1805, Plantation Brahan, the first to be brought into cultivation, had fallen in value by 8% and was at best only covering its running costs from year to year.

The weather in the Berbice and Demerara region had not been kind and all speculators, including Seaforth, were struggling. Seaforth had to sell off some of his Scottish lands to cover expenses and the cost of running the plantations. At home, Seaforth was financed, for the time being, by the profits of kelp from his estate on the Isle of Lewis. As time went on, his reliance on kelp was not enough and Seaforth was in a desperate financial state, barely struggling along. Peter Fairbairn was also struggling in the management of the three plantations in Berbice and Demerara. He had planned to return home, but put it off many times. In 1810, Seaforth considered travelling to Guiana, but nothing materialised. Fairbairn was frantically buying, hiring and selling slaves as the weather and the workload demanded. Seaforth's relationship with Fairbairn deteriorated further and this led to a severe breakdown in his relationship with Fairbairn's family in Ross-shire. Fairbairn was never to return home to Scotland, and Seaforth was never to make a fortune from this venture. Fairbairn died at Plantation Kintail on 7 July 1822.

The whole idea of making a fortune in Guiana was a disaster from the beginning: in 1808 Fairbairn pointed out to Seaforth that his business plan had been based not on average crop over the years, but on a single season of 1799/1800, which produced almost double the crop. By 1814, Seaforth's affairs were desperate. He was advised to lose no time in selling his three plantations, being told that the slaves would fetch a good price, but the land and machinery would be worthless.

Come 1814, Seaforth was left with one son, his other son having died in 1813. His surviving son, the Hon. William Frederick Mackenzie was elected MP for Ross-shire in 1812 and had a promising future ahead of him. He was the most distinguished of Seaforth's sons, possessing intelligence and kindness of heart, which he used to the best advantages in his Parliamentary work. And let us take up an account from Sir Bernard Burke's *The Fate of Seaforth*, pages 277-8 from his *Vicissitudes of Families* (1845):

> One after the other his three promising sons were cut
> off by death. The last, who was the most distinguished

of them all for the finest qualities of both head and heart, was stricken by a sore and lingering disease, and had gone, with a part of the family to the south of England. Lord Seaforth remained in the north, at Brahan Castle.

A daily bulletin was sent to him from the sick chamber of his beloved son. One morning, the accounts being rather more favourable, the household began to rejoice; and a friend and neighbour, who was visiting the Chief, came down after breakfast full of the good news, and gladly imparted them to the old family piper, whom he met in front of the castle. The aged retainer shook his head and sighed: "Na, na," said he, "he'll never recover. It is decreed that Seaforth maun outlive all his three sons." This he said in allusion to the Warlock's prophecy: thus his words were understood by the family; and thus members of the family have again and again repeated the strange tale. The words of the old piper proved too true. A few more posts brought to Seaforth the tidings of the death of the last of his three sons.

William Frederick Mackenzie was only 29 years old when he died unmarried on 25 August 1814.

Seaforth was both heartbroken and inconsolable. It must have dawned on him that the prophecy of the Brahan Seer was about to be fulfilled with regard to his part. He received sympathy and commiserations from many people, among them the buck-toothed Sir Hector Mackenzie, Bart. of Gairloch; the hare-lipped Alexander Chisholm of Chisholm; the half-witted Lewis Alexander Grant of Grant; and the stammerer John Norman Macleod of Raasay. Every one of these named individuals were mentioned in the prophecy: it was foretold that when these individuals were around at the same time, the last of the line of the house of Mackenzie would meet his end.

Following the death of his last son, Seaforth locked himself away, becoming a recluse and communicated very little with the outside world.

News also reached Seaforth early in January 1815 of the death of his son-in law, Sir Samuel Hood, on 24 December 1814.

348

Francis, Lord Seaforth
By Henry Raeburn

(Reproduced with kind permission of The Highlanders' Museum
[Queen's Own Highlander Collection])

Next, an obituary appeared in *The Scotsman* and *The Inverness Journal* announcing the death of Lord Seaforth. *The Inverness Journal* reported:

> January 20 — Died, at his house in Charlotte Square, Edinburgh, on the 11th curt., the Right Hon. Francis, Lord Seaforth, his Majesty's Lieutenant for the County of Ross. "The death of this distinguished nobleman, in the 60th year of his age, although the rapid decline of his health during the last two years must have led to the expectation of that event, will give birth to very gentle feelings of sorrow and regret.
>
> The wonderful power of his mind, undiminished even by the privation of the sense of hearing, the stores of information which he had acquired in almost every branch of science, and his rare proficiency in several, his delightful talents for society, the nobleness of his person and elegance of his manners, the richness of his imagination, and his faculty of diffusing grace and lustre over every topic, whether of instruction or amusement, will be long remembered, but with peculiar fondness and deeper regret by those who had the happiness to enjoy his intimate friendship; and alas! By those related to him by still dearer ties, who had access to know the many virtues of his benevolent heart, of which his other qualities were but the decorations and embellishments."

On 9 February, Seaforth's remains were interred in the family vault at Fortrose.

There were numerous tributes paid to Seaforth from people of prominence and high repute and two are mentioned here.

The Honourable Henry "Harry" Erskine, a Scottish Whig politician and lawyer and the Dean of Faculty of Advocates mentioned that...

> Lord Seaforth's deafness was a merciful imposition to lower him to the ordinary rate of capacity in society.

The poet and author Sir Walter Scott added his tribute to Seaforth in his *Lament for the Last of the Seaforths* –

In vain the bright course of your talents goes wrong.
Fate deadened thine ear and imprisoned thy tongue,
For brighter o'er all her obstructions arose
The glow of thy genius they could not oppose;
And who in the land of the Saxon or Gael
Could match with Mackenzie, High Chief of Kintail?

Thy sons rose around thee like light and in love,
All a father could hope, all a friend cou'd approve;
What 'vails it the tale of thy sorrows to tell?
In the springtime of youth and promise they fell!
Of the line of Mackenneth remains not a male,
To bear the proud name of the Chief of Kintail.

The prophecy of the Brahan Seer did not end with Seaforth's death. Following the death of her husband Sir Samuel Hood, the widowed Mary, Lady Hood, returned to Scotland and entered into possession of the family estates, which had devolved upon her by the death of her father without male issue, when the titles became extinct. After two years of widowhood, Mary married for the second time on 21 May 1817 James Alexander Stewart of Glasserton, nephew of the seventh earl of Galloway. Following that marriage, Alexander Stewart inherited his wife's estates and added Mackenzie as his surname.

After years of happiness, Mary was one day driving her younger sister, Caroline, in a pony carriage among the woods in the vicinity of Brahan Castle. Suddenly the ponies took fright, and started off at a furious pace. Mary was quite unable to check them and both she and her sister were thrown out of the carriage much bruised and hurt. Mary soon recovered from the accident but the injury which her sister sustained proved fatal and after lingering for some time in a hopeless state, she died. As Mary was driving the carriage at the time of the accident, she may be said to have been the innocent cause of her sister's death, and thus to have fulfilled the last portion of Kenneth Mackenzie's prophecy...

> ... and the remnant of his possessions shall be inherited
> by a white-coifed lassie from the East, and she is to kill
> her sister.

The Appendices

Appendix 1. (page 46)

Of The Origin and Progress of Language - James Burnett, Lord Monboddo 1773, Vol. 1., Chapter 14, pages 177 - 186.

But what puts the matter out of all doubt in my apprehension, is the case of deaf persons among us. And their case deserves to be the more attentively considered, that they are precisely in the condition in which we suppose men to have been in the natural state. For, like them, they have the organs of pronunciation; and, like them too, they have inarticulate cries, by which they express their wants and desires. They have likewise, by constant intercourse with men who have the use of reason, and who converse with them in their way, acquired the habit of forming ideas; which we must also suppose the savage to have acquired, tho' with infinitely more labour, before he could have a language to express them. They want therefore nothing in order to speak, but instruction or example, which the savages who invented the first languages likewise wanted. In this situation, do they invent a language when they come to perfect age, as it is supposed we all should do if we had not learnt one in our infancy? or do they ever come to speak during their whole lives? The fact most certainly is, they never do; but continue to communicate their thoughts by looks and gestures, which we call *signs*, unless they be taught to articulate by an art lately invented.

The inventor of this wonderful art, which, I think, does honour to modern times, was John Wallis, one of the first members of the Royal Society, and a most ingenious, as well as learned man. He has written an excellent English grammar, which was reprinted in 1765, and subjoined to it is a letter of the author to one Beverly, wherein he gives an account of this art which he had invented, and mentions two persons upon whom he had practised it with success. I knew two professors of the art in Paris, one of them *Mons. l' Abbé de l'Epée*, with whom I was several times, and whose civility, and the trouble he took to shew me his method of teaching, I take this opportunity of acknowledging. He had brought some of his scholars a surprising length; and one of them I particularly remember, a girl, who spoke so pleasantly that I should not have known her to be deaf.—There is at present in Edinburgh a professor of the same art, Mr Braidwood, whom I know, and who has likewise been at the trouble of shewing me his method of teaching; of which I very much approve. He has taught many with great success; and there is one of his scholars particularly who is presently carrying out the business of a painter in London, and who both speaks and writes good English. But it is surprising what labour it costs him to teach, and his scholars to learn: which puts it out of all doubt, that articulation is not only an art, but an art of most difficult acquisition, otherwise by imitation, and constant practice, from our earliest years. For, in the first place, it is difficult to teach those scholars to make any sound at all. They at first only breathe strongly, till they are taught to make that concussion and tremulous motions of the windpipe which produced audible sounds. These are very harsh, low, and guttural, at first, and more like croaking than a clear vocal sound; which I think will account for what *Mons. la Condamine* tells us of the strange method of speaking of a people he found upon the banks of the river Amazons; for he sound of their language was so low, and so much inward, more resembling muttering than speaking, that he imagined they spoke by drawing in their breath: and a girl whom I myself saw in France, that had been catched wild in the woods of Champaigne*, when she shewed me how the language of her country was spoken, made a low muttering sound in her throat, in which I could hardly distinguish any articulation. After this difficulty, which is not small, is got over, then comes the chief labour, to teach them the pronunciation of several letters; in doing which, the teacher is obliged, not only himself to use many distortions and grimaces in order to shew his scholars the positions and actions of the several organs, but likewise to employ his hands to place and move their organs properly; while the scholars themselves labour so much, and bestow such pains and attention, that I am really surprised, that, with all the desire they have to learn, which is very great, they should be able to support the drudgery. And I am assured by Mr Braidwood, that if he did not take different methods with them, according to their different capacities, and the difference of their organs, it would be impossible to teach many of them. And this very well accounts for what seems so strange at first, that those Orang Outangs that have been brought from Africa or Asia, and many of those solitary savages that have been catched in Europe, never learned to

---

* There was an account of this strange phænomenon published in France by a lady, under the title, *Histoire d'une Fille Sauvage*, and revised by *Mons. la Condamine*. It was translated into English, and published in Edinburgh in 1767, with a preface, shewing it to be very probable, that she came from a country upon the coast of Hudson's bay, where she was taken, and carried to one of the French islands in the West Indies; from whence she was again imbarked, and the ship was wrecked somewhere on the coast of France or Flanders; and it appears, that only she and a negro girl escaped by swimming. At the time I saw her, she at been thirty years in France, but remembered many particulars concerning her own country.

speak, tho' they had the organs of pronunciation as perfect as we: for, as it is well known, savages are very indolent, at least with respect to any exercise of the mind, and are hardly excited to action by any curiosity, or desire of learning.

If, therefore, this art be so difficult to be learned without imitation, even by the assistance of the most diligent instruction, how much more difficult must the invention of it have been; that is, the acquiring of it without either instruction or example?

Having thus proved the fact, as I think, incontestably, it will not be difficult to assign the reasons, and explain the theory. For we need only consider with a little attention the mechanism of speech, and we shall soon find, that there is required for speaking certain positions and motions of the organs of the mouth, such as, the tongue, the teeth, lips, and palate, that cannot be from nature, but must be the effect of art: for their action, when they are employed in the enunciation of speech, is so different from their natural and quiescent situation, that nothing but long use and exercise could have taught us to employ them in that way. To explain this more particularly I think is not necessary for my present purpose. I shall have occasion to say more of it afterwards; but who would desire in the mean time to be better informed about it, may consult Dionysius the Halicarnassian, in his treatise of Composition, where he has most accurately explained the different operations of the organs in the pronunciation of different letters. And whoever would desire to be still better informed, let him attend Mr Braidwood when he teaches, who, from his practice in that way, has learned to know more of the mechanism of language than any grammarian or philosopher.

I shall only say further on this subject, that pronunciation is one of those arts of which the instruments are the members of the human body; like dancing, and another art more akin to this, I mean singing: and like those arts it is learned, either by mere imitation, man being, as Aristotle has told us, the most imitative of all animals; or by teaching, as in the case of deaf men; but joined with very constant and assiduous practice, that being absolutely necessary for the acquiring of any art, in whichever of the two ways it is learned.

And here we may observe, that it is a very false conclusion, to infer, from the facility of doing any thing, that it is a natural operation. For what is it that we do more easily and readily than speaking? and yet we see it is an art that is not to be taught without the greatest labour and difficulty, both on the part of the master and the scholar; nor to be learned by imitation, without continual practice, from our infancy upwards. For it is not to be learned, like other arts, such as dancing and singing, by practising an hour or two a-day, for a few years, or perhaps some months; but constant and uninterrupted practice is required for many years, and for every hour, I may say, every minute of the day. And even after it is learned with so much trouble and pains, it may, like other acquired habits, be lost by disuse: of which I mentioned a remarkable instance before, in a boy, who did not lose his hearing till he was after eight years old, and had learned, not only to speak perfectly, but to read; and yet, when he came to be taught by Mr Braidwood, which was at the age of five and twenty, he had absolutely lost the use of his speech, and had it to learn as much as any of his scholars. So that we need not doubt of what we are told of Alexander Selkirk, who was but three years in the desert island of Juan Fernandez; and yet during that short time he had lost the use of speech so much as to be hardly intelligible to those who found him there. They therefore who, from the facility of a performance, conclude, that it is not a work of art, but of nature, do not sufficiently consider how much of artificial habit there is in our natures, in the state we are in at present, and that is chiefly we differ from other animals; that most of them, I mean such as are wild, are altogether creatures of nature; and even such of them as we have tamed, and assimilated in some degree to ourselves, have still much more of nature in them than of art. Whereas a civilized man is so much more a creature of art than of nature, that his natural habits are almost lost in his artificial.

I will make another observation before I conclude this article. If it had not been for this new-invented art of teaching deaf persons to speak, hardly anybody would have believed that the material or mechanical part of language was earned with so much difficulty. But if we could get an Orang Outang, or a mute savage, such as he above mentioned, that was caught in the woods of Hanover, and would take the same pains to teach him to think that Mr Braidwood takes to teach his scholars to speak, we should soon be convinced, that the formal part of language was as difficult to be learned as the material. For my own part, I am fully persuaded that the minds of men laboured as much as first, when they formed abstract ideas, as their organs of pronunciation did when they formed articulate sounds; and till the mind is stored with ideas, it is a perfect void, and in a kind of lethargy, out of which it is roused, only by external objects of sense, or calls of appetite from within.

Appendix 2. (page 113)

Specimens of Writings and Letters of Pupils at the Edgbaston
Institution for the Instruction of the Deaf and Dumb 1821—1824

[Note: According to the 9th Annual Report (1821), all specimens of the
charity school pupils' writings published in the Report were written
unassisted and uncorrected.]

1.   Edgbaston, October 15, 1821.

My dear Mother,
      I am quite well and happy—I hope you are very well—I
love my brothers and sisters—Mr Braidwood tells me not to be idle—he
tells me to learn to read, and to understand my duty to God and man—
to understand accounts, to speak, to write, to draw very much—I do
love you very dearly—I suppose father is in London—I suppose he will
go home soon—I wish Mr Braidwood to teach me every day—I hope I
shall go home quite soon enough to learn to be a painter—I feel grateful
to Mr Braidwood, because he taught me every thing—I kneel down to
pray to God every night and every morning—we always go to the
church on Sunday—I like to draw—I love William Bayzand—I love
father and mother, and will be dutiful and obedient to them.

I remain, my dear Mother,
Your affectionate son,
JAMES WHITAKER.

2.   1821.

My dear Mr Braidwood,
      I am very well and happy—I think there was a thief here
last Thursday morning—Francis Hinckley, James Whitaker, John
Williams, and Jasper Gibson, and the dog, all ran very fast after a
man—the dog tried to catch the man—the man ran very fast, and the
boys ran after him—the man is gone to prison—I suppose the
Magistrate will say that he must be punished—I think the man is very
much afraid, and I hope he is sorrowful—I think he is silly.—The man
will give him some water and little bread in prison, and no meat—I
think he is to sleep on the straw—he will not go home very soon—I
think his mother, or his wife and his children, will be very sorrowful—I
think the man will tell the Magistrate when he comes next Thursday,
that he will never do so again—God can see a thief—He does not love

him to steal.—The wicked will be sent to hell at the last day.

I hope you are very well—I am grateful to you, and I love you—I hope your sister is very well.

I am your affectionate pupil,
THOMAS BOAZ.

3.   Edgbaston, October 25, 1822.

My dear Mr Braidwood,
I am an English boy, and I was born in Hexham. Hexham is in Northumberland. I think Hexham is about 200 miles from Birmingham. My parents lived at Hexham—they have left Hexham—they now live near Durham. My father is a farmer—he had many cows at Hexham—he had many horses in the stables, and many sheep and lambs in the fields, and many young pigs, and some sows and boars, and some calves; he had many hens, and two cocks, and two Guinea-fowls, and many ducks and geese, and many pigeons in the pigeon-house. I think he had perhaps no turkies, and he had no peacocks; he had many ploughs and harrows, and waggons and carts, and sickles and scythes, and rollers, and dung-forks and hay-forks, and a drill for sowing turnips, &c. and a winnowing machine to blow the chaff and dust from the corn, and a strike and bushel, a peck and half-peck, to measure corn, and a threshing machine, and many other things. He sent the wheat in sacks on a waggon to the mill, and when it was brought back it was flour. I remember that corn is ground in a mill, between two large stones, which are turned round very quickly;—they are made to turn round either by the force of the wind, as in a wind-mill, or by the current of water, as in a water-mill. Flour is made of wheat—wheat grows in the fields. My father and mother are alive. My name is Jasper Gibson, I am fourteen years old, and I was born in the year 1808.
I have four brothers and four sisters. My father's name is John Gibson; my mother's name is Margaret Gibson. My brothers and sisters are named William, John, Henry, Thomas, Jane, Isabella, Helen and Julia Gibson. My sister Margaret is dead; she was deaf; she was a very good girl;—I hope she will be happy forever in heaven. Your mother and you taught her at Hackney. Hackney is in Middlesex. I never was at Hackney.—My sister Isabella is deaf. Your mother and your sister taught her at the Mount. She is at home now. Your mother was a very good woman;—we all loved her. I hope she is gone to heaven.—I hope my brother Thomas will come here very soon—he is

deaf—I hope you will teach him at Edgbaston.—I hope you and your sister are very well and happy. You live at Highfields—your sister lives at the Mount.

I am, respectfully,

Your obedient, and humble, and

Affectionate pupil,

JASPER GIBSON.

4.   GENERAL INSTITUTION FOR THE DEAF AND DUMB,
Edgbaston, near Birmingham, Oct. 18, 1823.

MADAM,

We were all very happy to see you at the Royal Hotel last year. We are all thankful to you, you are so kind to us. We were all happy to see you at the Shakespeare last Saturday, the 11th of this month, and we hope you will come here to see us in the school soon. We will try earnestly to understand our lessons. Mr Braidwood teaches us to be generous and good-natured—we feel grateful to him. We all went to the Shakespeare last Saturday, the 11th of this month—there were Lords, Ladies and Gentlemen. They came to see that the Deaf and Dumb can be taught to know everything—they are our kind benefactors. Lords Newport and Calthorpe were speaking to the ladies and gentlemen.—Mr Braidwood told J. Haycock that he was to draw a house on the board, and a balloon, and lords, ladies and gentlemen looked at them. A girl made a sign of a house and balloon—W. Carter wrote the names on the board—G. W. Moore was spelling them on his fingers—a girl was speaking them—J. Haycock wrote on the board, 'a small house,' he read it aloud; I wrote over it the article, adjective and substantive, on the board. The company clapped their hands to see us. I think they were surprised. I wrote the pronouns on the board and signed them to Mr Braidwood, and then J. Haycock signed them; and I asked J. Haycock if he was quite glad to see our kind friends?—he wrote on the board and read it, he said 'yes, I am.'—I wrote on the board the Addition—W. Hockenall and S. Taylor wrote the sum of the addition very fast—S. Taylor was the first before W. Hockenall—I think they were happy to try the addition.

Mr Bingham wrote the names of the sum, and I wrote the Rule of Three in Fractions—J. Gibson wrote the Single Rule of Three— J. Haycock wrote the Rule of Three in Decimals.—Mr Braidwood was speaking to the lords, ladies and gentlemen.—Mr Braidwood wrote the substantives, verbs, and adjectives, and I spelled them;—the boys were classed to see me spell them—but they did not see the names on the board—I spelt on my fingers fast, and they were signing them. We are all very grateful for your kindness in asking Mr Braidwood to take us to see the balloon go up. The netting was made of string—the balloon was made of silk—it was not heavy—the balloon went up very fast—it was so light—the wind did not blow against it—I think the wind would make it fly fast.—Mr Busby and Mr Sadler sat down in the car, and I suppose they were not afraid to be killed. I remember we did not go to the Crescent on Saturday 11th of this month—because the wind was blowing too hard, and Mr Sadler did not like to go;—we saw the gentlemen go into the car—I should not like to go up with the balloon, I should be afraid to fall out of the car.

I am, dear Madam,
Respectfully,
Your affectionate and obedient servant,
WILLIAM FAIRHURST.

5.,   Edgbaston, March 27, 1824.

My dear Mr Braidwood,

I am very sorry to tell you that I have broken a pane of glass in the window—it was an accident—I did not wish to break the glass. I have been picking up the stone in our yard—and I have thrown it on the pane of glass—and it was broken. I will never break a pane of glass again—I must be careful of them—I did not deny it.

Mr Harrison brought a nest of young starlings with a large cage here from Hagley-row—they belong to Mr Bingham. I believe Mr Bingham paid some money for them. I think two of the starlings are very well—one starling is dead. The starlings can almost fly in the large cage. Mr Bingham gives them bread and worms—I think they like the bread and the worms. I never saw a starling before—I am surprised to see them—I never saw them hopping in the fields.

I am
Your affectionate pupil,
WILLIAM HOCKENALL

Appendix 3. (page 116)

The 1826 Edgbaston Rebellion
A Deliberately Erased Surdohistorical Event?

(This account by Raymond Lee was first published in the British Deaf History Society's official journal, *Deaf History Journal*, Vol. 10, Issue 1, 2006)

There was a time 180 years ago this year when deaf children stood up and fought for their rights to use their preferred method of communication only to be severely crushed to humiliating and painful defeat through the use of brute force by the hearing authorities. Such an event, unique in British Deaf history, was briefly reported in the two *Report of the Committee to the General Meeting* booklets in 1826 and 1827. The school concerned was the Edgbaston General Institution for the Deaf and Dumb, in Birmingham (below).

Details of the events are very sketchy and it is hoped that a deeper and probing research into the events will be carried out in the near future. It is imperative that a full and truthful account be recorded. For the present, one can only rely on the Reports and some newspaper cuttings.

The story began when the first head teacher of the Edgbaston General Institution, Thomas Braidwood (the grandson of Thomas Braidwood, 1715-1806) passed away unexpectedly in April 1825 after a short illness. His death left a situation which caused confusion among the members of the Committee, resulting in a split among its members. On one side were those who wanted the then assistant teacher, Henry Brothers Bingham, to take over as the head teacher. They saw in Bingham a natural successor after spending an initial training period of 4 years with private deaf pupils under Braidwood before he was promoted to Assistant Teacher in the charity school. On the other side were those who were swayed and influenced by the claims of an ailing and sickly American. This American, the Rev. William Woodbridge, was passing through England on his way to Switzerland to recuperate from his illness. He met some members of the Committee of the Edgbaston General Institution. Woodbridge was a former teacher at the Asylum for the Deaf and Dumb in Hartford, Connecticut and he used different means of signing and communication to that of the British. He was, however, invited to visit the Edgbaston School and observe the classroom. Woodbridge proceeded to give his opinion that the American and European systems (both using the one-handed method) be adopted as he considered them to be far superior to the British system. On the advice of that one man alone with his own bias towards the one handed sign method, and also with very little knowledge of what true deaf education involved, this small group of members of the Edgbaston Committee campaigned and pushed for the adoption of the allegedly "superior" sign system and a debate within the entire Committee ensued. At the end of the day, this small group won. Consequently the Committee had to find a teacher who would put into practice the so-called "superior" system and enforce the change.

In line with the Rev. Woodbridge's advice and recommendations, the current system used at the Edgbaston General Institution, which was the Braidwoodian system (also known as the combined system), was to be replaced by a system of signs only. The Committee initially approached Bingham and asked him to consider taking up and teaching under the new system of signs, abandoning the Braidwoodian method. Bingham declined and he further indicated that he was against the sign-only system, saying that it deprived the children of the variety offered by the Braidwoodian method.

Quite bizarrely, the Committee then took to seeking the advice of one Dr. Orpen at the Claremont Institution for the Deaf near Dublin, Ireland. There was a situation going on at Claremont at that time where its headmaster, Mr Humphreys, was to leave the school and the school had a teacher in mind to replace him. However, Dr Orpen managed to persuade Humphreys to stay on. Following that, Dr Orpen offered Humphrey's intended replacement to the Committee of the Edgbaston Institution. The intended replacement, Louis du Puget, had nil experience in the education of the Deaf prior to visiting the Claremont school, despite having been a pupil and assistant to the celebrated Pestalozzi in Switzerland. Puget had been a teacher for seven years in

Ireland but he had never been involved in teaching the Deaf. Dr Orpen, however, sang praises in favour of Puget and declared his confidence in Puget's ability to run the Edgbaston General Institution. Testimonials of Puget's ability and professionalism were produced from various sources, of which none were connected in any way whatsoever with the deaf, and the Edgbaston Committee decided to employ Puget. This decision having been made, Puget was put through a three month or so crash course on the instruction of the deaf at Claremont, and he was not taught signing...

When Puget commenced his work at the Edgbaston School, not one of the existing pupils could understand him. The pupils were taken aback when the method they used became forbidden. Puget was not using the American system, nor was he using any sign system at all. In short, he could not sign despite the fact that the Edgbaston Committee insisted on the change to sign only system! Henry Brothers Bingham protested to the Committee about the absurdity of the situation but he was told to toe the line. Rather than submitting to their instruction, he resigned. This upset the deaf children further, causing the situation to turn from bad to worse.

In protest, the deaf children took to a regime of disobedience, non-co-operation and wilful behaviour, and later persistent truancy. Puget was given a hard time and took to applying physical action against the children in his attempt to control them. Members of the Committee were shocked by the children's actions, and as a consequence several sturdy men were sent over to assist Puget in controlling the situation.

News of the rebellion spread to the surrounding neighbourhood and people were shocked to learn of what was happening. In a desperate attempt to subdue the rebellion and justify the appointment of Puget, the Edgbaston Committee issued a series of statements... an example was printed in the 14th Report of the Committee to the General Meeting:

> ... your committee, however, did not expect that a transition from the course of Instruction which had been for some time followed in your Institution, to one in several respects materially different, would be effected without some temporary difficulties...

> ... They were prepared also to accept some degree of unwillingness on their (the children's) part to transfer

their attention to an entire stranger from an Instructor to whom they had been so long and deservedly attached, as they were to Mr. Bingham...

... (the Committee) will not deny that their anticipations on this head (Puget) were painfully realized. The collision between different systems of instruction produced effects unfavourable to the docility and prompt obedience of the pupils; they became refractory, and even refuse to receive the instructions of their new Teacher, alleging (though as the event afterwards proved, not with perfect sincerity) that they could not understand them...

This report, based solely on the Committee's one-sided explanations, exploited the failure of the Committee members to observe that the British sign system could not be changed for a foreign system: after all other schools for the Deaf in Britain were using the British system. Deaf pupils had every right to feel aggrieved at the attempted change, but the hearing members of the Committee could not see it from the Deaf children's perspective and situation.

Despite the Committee's reassurances to the general public that the situation was under control, the rebellion continued. In fact, it lasted around three months until the Christmas period. In order to assist Puget, the Committee decided to employ a temporary assistant. This assistant was to be a young person who could liaise himself with the rebellious deaf children and win their confidence. This young man was Charles Baker, who was to go on and become the headmaster of the Yorkshire Institution for the Deaf and Dumb in Doncaster. Baker's involvement in the incident can be read through a brief account from an unpublished mss Memorials of Charles Baker by Thomas Baker. Written in 1874, the year of Charles Baker's death, page 10 stated:

... he (Puget) failed however in securing either the affections of his pupils or the respect of his Assistants and the result was a state of disorganisation which threatened the existence of the Institution.

... and the Committee was urgent that he (Baker) should go and assist its management... he was induced however to promise that he would next day visit the Institution. This he did and found the description of the state of things had not been overcharged. His (Baker's) reception was satisfactory. He saw that he should have the requisite influence to allay the storm. He thus describes what took place and the effect of his going there in his future life.

Page 11 (cont. of above) - in Charles Baker's own words:

In the course of the first day I was among them. The children all became calm; they had been literally prisoners for weeks. I obtained their confidence at once and without any imputation on the Master. They asked me to take them out. The Master and the Members of the Committee present said they would all run away if I did so. I told the children this and they scorned the idea, promising implicit obedience to me. Peace began to take the place of confusion at once.

After seeing them to bed and promising to go the next day, I went home. Gradually lessons commenced, my influence over them keeping all right except occasional ebullitions of temper.

The use of the phrase "except occasional ebullitions of temper" appears to indicate that Baker was economical with facts, for there were much worse and terrifying brutality on the part of Committee members towards deaf children to come later on.

During the Christmas period, there was an outrage when some of the pupils appeared before their families in what can only be described as "in battered physical condition". One pupil, 12 years old William Boote who was an orphan, appeared badly beaten. There were also printed circulars handed around among members of the public that deaf pupils were flogged and tortured. A complaint was raised against the school and the Committee found itself on the back foot, having to defend its position throughout the classroom rebellion. In issuing its defence, the Committee issued another report. In Supplement to the Report dated February 5 1827, the Committee wrote at the beginning...

The Committee of this Institution, having learnt with regret that rumours prejudicial to its character and interests have obtained extensive circulation, think it is their duty to lay before the Subscribers and the Public at large the following brief statement of facts.

... With regards to themselves - the Committee are fully persuaded that they exercised too much forbearance, not to say indulgence, in the first instance, towards the refractory pupils. Their extreme disinclination to the use of severe measures induced them to pass by, or slightly animadvert upon, several acts of insubordination which occurred in the earlier stage of the proceedings. The consequence was such as might perhaps have been expected. The children put a wrong construction upon the conduct of the Committee...

... the disaffection of the children towards Mr du Puget originated, it was unfortunately strengthened by manifest indications which they witnessed, from time to time, of a decided predilection, on the part of some members of the Institution, in favour of the late under master...

... several of the pupils continued to indulge a refractory and turbulent spirit for some weeks after the General Meeting (October 1826). They not only refused to attend to their lessons during school hours, but were very unruly and unmanageable at times. They went out of bounds... broke different parts of the furniture of the school-room... some of the older children proceeded so far as openly to incite others to rebellion... abuse his (the Master's) forbearance and that of his Assistant, as to strike them, and that repeatedly.

Various means were used to repress these evils: some of the offenders were confined for a short time to the sick room; one or two for still a shorter period were kept in a passage leading to the cellar; others were put on bread and water for two days at the utmost...

Whether the Committee was actually being truthful in its defence or not is easily perceived by its admission - the members of the Committee were lying about their methods and the severity of punishment meted out. The report continued:

... it was not till an ineffectual trial had been made out of these milder modes of punishment, that the

368

Committee had at length recourse to one more severe, which, if applied at the commencement of the disturbances to one or two of the most refractory, would, in all probability, have checked the evil on its first appearance.

The Committee's defence was quite poor. In the attempt to deny that William Boote was not flogged despite evidence that he was severely beaten as visible scars and marks on his person indicated, the Committee proceeded to shoot itself in the foot. In the same Supplement to the Report there was added a passage:

The names of the boys thus punished are Turner, Green, Cooper, Kirby, Thompson, Gibson, Wilkes and Swallow. This is mentioned because it has been stated that of a boy of the name of Boote was so severely flogged as to retain the marks of his punishment when he went home at the Christmas holidays. The fact is, that Boote was not flogged at all, nor any corporeal chastisement inflicted upon him.

In denying that they had one boy flogged, the Committee admitted they had eight boys punished! Boote most certainly suffered physical harm and the rest of the pupils also were harmed. Three boys and one girl were expelled from the school. The Committee was on a damage limitation exercise to hide its cruelty to the deaf children, and failed to cover it up.

Of great interest is the question - what was the root cause of the problem?

The problem was the Committee's attempt to copy and simulate the Hartford and Paris methods, using the one handed system. Why one thought such a system was superior to the British system is hard to understand, but it is most likely to be based on personal prejudices - it is natural that the Rev. William Woodbridge would choose the US method. The Edgbaston Committee learned a hard lesson when Woodbridge's choice was rejected by the deaf children themselves. If anything appeared to have triumphed out of that turmoil, British signs won and the foreign signs lost, but educationally, the Edgbaston General Institution lost. This was shown by the fact that Henry Brothers Bingham went on to become headmaster of both the Exeter and Manchester Schools for the Deaf as well as finally founding the

Rugby College for the Deaf which churned out a series of notable Deaf individuals.

As for Puget, Charles Baker had this to say in *Memorials of Charles Baker* (1874):

> Mr du Puget was an intelligent man and a good teacher. He thought himself specially qualified for the teaching of the Deaf and Dumb, which he was not.

And the deaf children knew it straightway. They were not stupid and yet they were made to suffer for their rightful protests through being flogged, brutalised and imprisoned. The severity of the beatings the children took so upset the Matron Mrs Vallant that she made a vehement protest about it to the Committee. She was quickly removed from her post.

It is hoped that a fuller and clearer picture of the event can be written in the near future once more facts and sources have been unearthed. Here is the list of the pupils who rebelled and fought for their rights and their names should not be forgotten. Ages shown are as at the time of the 1826 rebellion.

William Langley,	14.	Walsall, Staffordshire.
Reuben Turner,	14.	Eckington, Derbyshire.
Ann Dewhurst,	18.	Wigan, Lancaster.
William Cater,	14.	Wolverhampton, Staffordshire.
George Wright Moore,	13.	London.
Thomas Thompson,	13.	Newport, Salop.
Phoebe Turner,	15.	Tipton, Staffordshire.
Thomas Cooper,	14.	Stourbridge, Worcester.
Mary Swindal,	15.	Branstone, Burton-upon-Trent.
James Lockett,	18.	Tarvin, Cheshire.
Mary Stevenson,	12.	Tamworth.
Thomas Green,	13.	King's Norton.
Joseph Venables,	12.	Stourport, Worcestershire.
Martha Bagley,	14.	Tipton, Staffordshire.
Thomas Gibson,	12.	Heugh, Durham.
Margaret Thompson,	11.	Newport, Salop.
William Boote,	12.	
Lavinia Brookes,	15.	Birmingham.

Sarah Tomes,	14.	Coleshill, Warwickshire.
Ann Boden,	14.	Workhouse in Derby.
Mary Lea,	11.	Feckenham, Worcestershire.
John Kirby,	10.	Birmingham.
Charles Smith,	11.	Elmdon Heath, Birmingham.
Jonathan Wild,	10.	Winster, Derbyshire.
Richard Kear,	14.	Cheltenham.
Ann Houlgate,	12.	Alderwasley, Derbyshire.
Keziah Wilkes,	12.	Kingswinford, Staffordshire.
Samuel Wilkes,	10.	Brother of above.
Ann Shaw,	13.	Mear, Staffordshire.
John Swallow,	11.	Wath-upon-dearne, Yorkshire.
George Beetlestone,	10.	Faintree, near Bridgnorth,
Ann Bassett,	12.	Atherstone, Warwickshire.
Thomas Dunn,	8.	Kinver, Staffordshire.
Martha Turner,	9.	Sister to Reuben Turner.

Appendix 4. (page 262)

Pages 70-79 — An Essay on the Deaf and Dumb, 1829.

Mr Arrowsmith observes, that "Much has been written on the subject of educating the deaf and dumb, by gentlemen who have themselves taught and instructed them with great success, and who have been the means, through a bounteous public, of establishing asylums for the exclusive purpose of educating indigent persons of this description. It is feared, however, that those establishments have operated like scarecrows with the teachers in general, who have been induced, in consequence of the establishment of such asylums, to think there must be so much difficulty in educating these unfortunate mutes, that none are competent to undertake the charge but such as have attended an asylum for instructions, and have thereby acquired a thorough knowledge of all the mysteries of this seemingly occult science. These newly initiated artists, instead of taking off the mask which was worn by their predecessors, have put on another, still more hideous, and thereby dazzled the ignorant.

"The education of the deaf and dumb has for ages been conceived a matter of great difficulty, and even by some impossibility. Very few persons, consequently, have given themselves the trouble of investigating the subject; yet all who have attempted the education of them have succeeded beyond their own most sanguine expectations. Too much praise cannot be bestowed on the establishment of the benevolent institutions for educating the indigent deaf and dumb. These institutions were established when there was no apparent possibility of meliorating their condition by any other preceptors; consequently, every credit is due to a generous public for their philanthropy. I must beg leave to differ from the preceptors in one particular. Too much time and too much labour, as I conceive, have been bestowed upon teaching the deaf and dumb utterance, when the benefit of it to them is by no means adequate to the trouble of learning it, particularly in the manner in which they are now attempted to be taught. If it were of that utility which some have been pleased to ascribe to it, I would cordially subscribe to the propriety of every exertion being used to acquire speech; for, if man without utterance were void of reason, as some have pretended, speech would be indispensable. I will suppose, for a moment, that I was born deaf and dumb, had attended school, and learned every thing without utterance; and you, being alike situate, had learned every thing with utterance. I should be glad to know, under such circumstances, how it can be made to appear that I am less rational than you, and what can prevent me from exercising my reasoning faculties as well as any other person who can hear? The only difference, I conceive, is that I may be a little longer about it, but perhaps I may on that account be more correct; for it cannot be denied, that a written question or answer is more to be depended upon the verbal one. Does not reason tell us, there is no more connexion between ideas and sound, which affects our ears, than between those ideas and written characters, which affect our eyes? Speech is nothing more than a translation of writing. Those who can hear and speak make use of it as a more convenient mode of communication; while the deaf and dumb, for want of hearing and speaking, substitute the written language and signs.

"It has been observed, by an author who is a great encourager of utterance that this artificial speech is a medium which is found very useful for the indigent deaf and dumb; because children of this description are placed out in manufactories, and are thus enabled to communicate more easily with their masters. It is evident that the person who made this observation had never been a manufacturer; if he had, he would have given preference to servants who could not hear and speak. They make the best and most trusty servants, having nothing but their business to attend to; and they are not diverted from it by conversation, like the others, while they are no less useful and rational. I cannot help dwelling upon this subject, because I know the indigent deaf and dumb have lost much useful time in learning utterance, which, without being of absolute use to them, causes great pain and torture to themselves in learning, and makes them very disagreeable companions afterwards. If parents in affluent circumstances think proper to have their children taught utterance, in the name of fortune let them, as they can afford to pay for their education, and may be pleased to hear them speak; but do not let a public charity be occupied in any thing but what is useful and absolutely necessary.

"It is a great pleasure to see many gratuitous schools established for educating the poor, who can hear and speak; and I hope to see the indigent deaf and dumb admitted into those schools, confident as I am, that they can be taught, with great ease, to read, write, and understand so much as to render them useful, agreeable, and happy members of society. I have often thought, when I have met a man unable to read or write, but who could hear and speak that he was infinitely a more pitiable object than the instructed deaf and dumb. I know, if two men thus situated, of equal abilities, were to apply to me for employment in any trade, I should not hesitate a moment in fixing on the latter as a servant, in preference to the former.

"There are asylums established for the exclusive education of the indigent deaf and dumb, in most countries; and I shall be very happy to see the education of them introduced into all charity schools where children are educated who can hear and speak. The masters and mistresses would find little difficulty in beginning to teach them the letters and the meaning of words; but in case their pupils should not be quite equal to the children taught in the first asylums, it must be admitted, that a little education is better than none. But I am certain, from experience, that a child born deaf will have greater advantage from learning in a school where children are educated who can hear and speak, than at a school where none but deaf and dumb are taught; and the children who can hear and speak will be alike benefitted by being taught along with them. If the deaf and dumb were going to spend all their days in company with each other, then it would be as well for them to be brought up and educated together; but as they will have to depend chiefly upon people who can hear and speak, the sooner and oftener they join their society, the better it must be for them; and the children who can hear and speak will, from their infancy, become acquainted with the dumb language, and be able, when they grow up, to correspond with any person they may happen to meet with labouring under the like infirmity. If I had a child of my own born deaf and dumb, and could not afford to send him to any school, I would not let him go to an asylum, nor to a school where none but the deaf and dumb are taught, if he could be educated there for nothing.

"The asylums for the education of the deaf and dumb are so well filled, that thousands must remain without education, unless the parents or other teachers will undertake to instruct them.

"I have, for many years past, had it in contemplation to publish all I knew of the method of educating the deaf and dumb; but I could not make up my mind on the subject until lately, when Providence caused to be put into my hands a most valuable book, entitled 'The Method of Educating the Deaf and Dumb, confirmed by long experience; by the Abbé de l'Epée.' The moment I read this book, I was confirmed in the opinion which I had ever entertained, that there is no necessity for the education of the deaf and dumb to be confined to the teachers at the asylums; but that parents, or any schoolmaster or mistress in the world, might as usefully instruct them.

374

"It is somewhat extraordinary, that although there have been so many professors in the art of teaching the deaf and dumb, who have promised to publish to the world at large the knowledge of their advances and improvement in the art, no such publication has appeared; for what reason it may be difficult to conceive, unless they were afraid of exposing the simplicity and artlessness of their tuition, and thereby losing that popularity and general estimation which the public, for want of knowing better, has been pleased to bestow upon them. I will admit that it could not be expected, that gentlemen, whose labours had been crowned with such brilliant success, would have made known to the public the mysteries of their profession, by which they were making a fortune, without some handsome remuneration; nor can the public wonder that their mode of instruction has been kept so profound a secret. Indeed, this is the best reason I can assign, why children who can hear and speak are not allowed to be taught with the deaf and dumb. If they had, it is natural to suppose the magic secret would have long ago been known, because the method adopted at the asylums is perfectly explicable. There is no more useful knowledge to be obtained at a deaf and dumb asylum, that can be taught by any schoolmaster or mistress whatever.

"Nothing can possibly contribute so much to the information of the deaf and dumb as pictures; the vocabulary and plates published by Dr. Watson in 1809, would have been the most useful part of his publication, had the pictures been properly arranged and referred to; but they are jumbled together in such a manner as rather to confuse the ideas than edify the understanding.

"I have often asked those who have been taught utterance, whether they found it pleasant to speak, and whether it was not painful to them to learn? And I have always been answered, that they suffered so much in learning, and afterwards found it so unpleasant to speak, that they wished they had been made to depend entirely upon reading, writing, and the manual alphabet, as a medium of communication. It is painful to every body to hear them attempt utterance; and learning it spoils their features so much, that I have seen very handsome children so disfigured by it, that in a few years time I hardly knew them. I have before observed, that I lately met with a work published by the Abbé de l'Epée, on the subject of educating the deaf and dumb.

"For want of another and better system than that adopted at the asylums, thousands of our fellow creatures must continue little better than the brute creation. It is very extraordinary that this book of the

375

Abbé de l'Epée, which was published in 1801, should have entirely disappeared, and that there is not a single copy now to be met with. I am inclined to think that the work was suppressed; for, if publicity had been given to it, the deaf and dumb would have been educated in common with other children long before now. It is evident, from what appears in the Edinburgh Encyclopædia lately published, respecting the deaf and dumb and their education, that every pains have been taken to depreciate the method adopted The latter, I have no doubt, have been the principal cause of endeavouring to make the public believe that the system of education, in every respect, adopted and practised by the Abbé, was useless, and even an imposition upon the public. By these means they have endeavoured to establish their own magical and occult science, in teaching that which is of no use—utterance tending only to astonish the weak, and to acquire an unmerited applause. I will defy them, or any person, to instruct a deaf and dumb child without signs; and I challenge them to produce better signs than what the Abbé made use of. I do most positively deny that the Abbé ever taught his pupils words without explaining meaning of them; and every unbiased person, after perusing his method of educating the deaf and dumb, will be convinced of this fact. Could anything so chimerical have entered the mind of any one, as to attempt to teach a deaf and dumb child to write a word without explaining the meaning of it? No person, it may be presumed, would be so foolish as to do this, much less a man of such abilities as the good Abbé de l'Epée.

"The authors of the Edinburgh Encyclopædia, after having totally misrepresented the Abbé's method of education, say, 'we have done with the Abbé de l'Epée.' The teachers at the asylums may also say they have done with him; and they would, no doubt, be glad to find every body else of the same opinion. But I must beg leave to differ from these gentlemen, and wish I could find language sufficient to express the sense of gratitude I feel for so benevolent and good a man. The French nation has acknowledged to be the greatest character she ever produced by the following eulogy bestowed upon him, which diffused his fame to all nations: — 'Science would decide for D'Alembert, and nature says Buffon; wit and taste present Voltiare; and sentiment pleads for Rousseau; but genius and humanity cries out for De l'Epée, and him I call the best and greatest of all.'"*

*The Art of Instructing the Deaf and Dumb, by J. P. Arrowsmith.

Appendix 5. (page 291)

This is the Last Will and Testament of me Charles Shirreff now residing in Upper John Street Fitzroy Square in the County of Middlesex being in perfect health of body and mind, subject to the payment of all just debts and funeral expenses, I give and bequest all my Estate and Effects, Real and personal and all other my Estate and Effects in this Kingdom or otherwise unto my dear Wife Mary Ann Shirreff to and for her own absolute use and benefit and I nominate, constitute and appoint my said dear wife Mary Ann Shirreff Executrix to this my last will hereby revoking all former and other Will or Wills by me at any time heretofore made. In Witness whereof I have hereunto set my hand and seal this thirteenth day of December in the year of our Lord one thousand eight hundred and twenty four. Charles Shireff (signature) — Signed, sealed, published and declared by the said Testator as and for this last Will and Testament in the presence of – William Berry Brown, Artist, No. 15 Seymour Place, Bryanston Square, London — George Augustus Atkinson, Artist, 48 London Street, Fitzroy Square, London.

Codicil

Some years past I wished Louisa Honoria Brown to have £500 given to at my demise out of my property but my circumstances having become so much worse I wish the above to become null and void, but should my circumstances improve so to enable me to do it I will consider her and whatever property I have in Columbian bonds, my above and all Effects etc etc I bequeath to my beloved wife Mary Ann Shirreff — London, December 18th, 1826. I have wrote the above as I do not wish my wife to be injured.

Appeared Personally James Bakewell of Nr. 1 Lisson Street, New Bond in the parish of Paddington in the County of Middlesex, architect, and John Chippendale of Nr. 10 John Street, Adelphi, in the County of Middlesex, Navy Agent and being sworn on the Holy Evangelists made oath that they knew and were well acquainted with Charles Shirreff, late of Nr. 15 Upper Frederick Street Connaught Square in the parish of Paddington in the County of Middlesex, Gentleman for some time before and nearly to the time of death and also with his manner and character of handwriting and subscription having frequently seen him write and also write and subscribe his hand and having now with care and attention viewed and perused a paper writing hereunto annexed purporting to be and contain a codicil to the Last Will and Testament of the said deceased the said Codicil beginning thus "Some years past I wished" ending thus "I bequest to my beloved wife Mary Ann Shirreff" and thus subscribed and dated "Chas. Shirreff, London Decr 18, 1826" and an addition to the words following to wit "I have wrote the above as I do not wish my wife to be injured." They further made oath that they verify and in their consciences believe the whole body series and contents of the said Codicil beginning ending and subscribed as aforesaid together with the said addition and the aforesaid subscription thereto to be all of the proper handwriting and subscription of the said deceased — James Bakewell – Jno Chippendale — On the fifth day of Novr 1829 the said James Bakewell was duly sworn to the truth of this affidavit before Mr W. C. Curteis Surr. Pst. Fielder Not. Pub. — On the 10th day of Novr 1829 the said John Chippendale was duly sworn to the truth of this affidavit before Mr J. Phillimore Surr. Pst. Th. Ed. Fielder not. Pub.

Proved at London with a Codicil 11th Novr 1829 before the Worshipful William Calverley Curteis Doctor of Laws and Surrogate by the oath of Mary Ann Shirreff widow to the relict the sole Executrix to whom administration was granted having been first sworn duty to administer.

Appendix 6. (page 317)

Mackenzie had a dream, which was described by Alexander Mackenzie in *Prophecies of the Brahan Seer* (*Pub: 1899 by Eneas Mackay, Stirling*):

... we shall give the particulars of a curious dream by Lord Seaforth, which was a peculiar forecast of the loss of his faculties of speech and hearing during the latter part of his eventful life. It has been supplied by a member of the family, who shows an unmistakable interest in everything calculated to throw light on the "prophecies," and who evidently believes them not to be merely an old wife's tale. We give it *verbatim et literatim*:-

"The last Lord Seaforth was born in full possession of all his faculties. When about twelve years of age scarlet fever broke out in the school at which he was boarding. All the boys who were able to be sent away were returned to their homes at once, and some fifteen or twenty boys who had taken the infection were moved into a large room, and there treated. After a week had passed, some boys naturally became worse than others, and some of them were in great danger. One evening, before dark, the attendant nurse, having left the dormitory, for a few minutes, was alarmed by a cry.

She instantly returned, and found Lord Seaforth in a state of great excitement. After he became calmer, he told the nurse that he had seen, soon after she had left the room, the door opposite to his bed silently open, and a hideous old woman came in. She had a wallet full of something hanging from her neck in front of her. She paused on entering, then turned to the bed close to the door, and stared steadily at one of the boys lying in it. She then passed to the foot of the next boy's bed, and, after a moment, stealthily moved up to the head, and taking from her wallet a mallet and peg, drove the peg into his forehead. Young Seaforth said he heard the crash of the bones, though the boy never stirred. She then proceeded round the room, looking at some boys longer than at others. When she came to him, his suspense was awful. He felt he could not resist or even cry out, and he never could forget, in years after, that moment's agony, when he saw her hand reaching down for a nail, and feeling his ears. At last, after a look, she slunk off, and slowly completing the circuit of the room, disappeared noiselessly through the same door by which she had entered. Then he felt the spell seemed to be taken off, and uttered the cry which had alarmed the nurse. The latter laughed at the lad's story, and told him to go to sleep. When the doctor came, an hour later, to make his rounds,

379

he observed that the boy was feverish and excited, and asked the nurse afterwards if she knew the cause, whereupon she reported what had occurred. The doctor, struck with the story, returned to the boy's bedside and made him repeat his dream. He took it down in writing at the moment. The following day nothing eventful happened, but, in course of time, some got worse, a few indeed died, others suffered but slightly, while some, though they recovered, bore some evil trace and consequence of the fever for the rest of their lives. The doctor, to his horror, found that those whom Lord Seaforth had described as having a peg driven into their foreheads, were those who died from the fever; those whom the old hag passed by recovered, and were none the worse; whereas those she appeared to look at intently, or handled, all suffered afterwards. Lord Seaforth left his bed of sickness almost stone deaf..."

Appendix 7. (page 191)

Thomas Braidwood v. Thomas Bolling

Thomas Bolling's letter to Thomas Braidwood dated October 1783 mentioned from the second paragraph onwards:

> As to the balance due you, for the education of my Children, you may assume yourself it shall be paid, but [I] have been so much distressed by Lord Cornwallis's Army, when they were here, that [I] am much afraid, it will not be so soon as you expected, or as I should wish, they Burnt a very large Tobacco House for me, with all the Tob° I had made for two years, a good deal of Corn, and destroyed many other things too tedious to trouble you with., but Sir, you may depend upon being paid as soon as it is in my power to do it. I can not conclude , without returning you my most hearty and sincere thanks, for the great care & attention paid to my Dear Children in their Education & Morals, for they appear to be quite without any kind of Vice whatever, and as to their Improvement, it finally answers my most sangu^r expectations. Mrs Bolling joins me in kind Comp^{ts} & best wishes to your self, Mrs Braidwood and two Daughters to whom [I] may return our most Hearty & sincere thanks for the great care and kindness toward our Dear Children.
>
> I am Dear sir with great esteem
> Your most Obe^t Hble Servt
> Thos Bolling
>
> N.B.
> Your two Pupils wish you
> by this Opportunity.

As it turned out, Thomas Bolling did not make an effort to pay Thomas Braidwood for the education of his deaf children: it appears that Bolling was unwilling to pay and the situation dragged on for so long that in 1794 Braidwood had to hire an attorney to sue Bolling in the American courts for non-payment of monies due for the period between 12 May 1777 and 12 April 1783.

In May 1796, a writ was issued against Thomas Bolling for the non-payment of $6000 and Bolling had to attend before the judges of the Court of the United States, for the Middle Circuit, at Richmond, Virginia, on 23 May 1796. Bolling disputed the amount and was granted leave to come to a settlement on the agreed final account with Thomas Braidwood.

Braidwood's initial claim was for £601.1.0 for board, lodging, instruction, assistants and servants up to 9 April 1783 when all the Bolling children left the academy for America. On top of this claim, Braidwood added the sum of £493.7.4 for clothes and necessities for the use of the three children whilst they were under his tuition and care.

Braidwood mentioned that while the war was ongoing in America, he came to an arrangement with Bolling, via Bolling's representative in London, Mr John Hyndman, to reduce the annual tuition fees for his three children. Braidwood agreed to reduce John Bolling's fee from £100 per annum to £90 per annum and also the same for Thomas and Mary. However, despite the arrangement, Bolling could not find any money due to the ongoing war between America and Britain. Through his representative, Bolling asked for further reduction in payment and Braidwood agreed to reduce payment from £90 per annum for each of Bolling's three children to £40 per annum for John, and to £60 per annum each both Mary and Thomas, representing a saving of £140 per annum on the initial fee of £100 per annum per child to Colonel Bolling. This arrangement was sealed on 12 May 1777.

Despite reducing costs, Braidwood did not receive the agreed annual payment of £160 in full. This was shown in Braidwood's legal submission of accounts, a sample of which the year 1777-1778 read:

Balance owed as on 12 May 1777	66.13.2
Board, lodging & washing for Mr John	
6 June 1777 to 6 June 1778	40.0.0
Ditto to Mr Thomas and Miss Mary	
6 October 1777 to 6 October 1778	120.0.0
For shoes & soleing to Mr John from June 1777 to Dec	3.1.0
Ditto to Thomas & Miss Oct to Dec	4.9.0
For school necessaries 36/- Assist^s & serv^s for 1 year 46/6	4.2.6
Pocket money & material expenses for 1 year	3.6.6
	241.12.2

Note - the monetary system at that time was pounds - shillings - pence.

The accounts went on for the next year, and so on until 1783. In the six years between 1777 and 1783, Col. Thomas Bolling contributed a total payment of £500, that being £100 per annum between 1778 and 1783, but the outstanding costs of education and maintenance of the three children came to £601.1.0 after deduction of Bolling's payment of £500. Due to non-payment of full amount owed for every year, interest was added to the amount outstanding for each year and on April 12 1794, interest amounted to £433.7.4, making a grand total of £1034.7.4 owed by Bolling to Braidwood.

There was apparently a series of negotiations between Bolling and Braidwood's American legal representative, Phillip Richard Kendall, and the final claim was reduced and agreed by Braidwood for the sum of £999.7.4 plus legal costs/interest of £566 up to 12 April 1794.

The case of Braidwood v. Bolling dragged on: Bolling appeared to have formed a partnership with one William Murray in a business venture and as a consequence, Murray was drawn into the ongoing legal proceedings against Bolling. Some time before 1797, Bolling and Murray agreed to be bound under a bond to repay money due by a certain date. The amount bound for was $4964.06 each. However, in September 1797 both Bolling and Murray were summoned to court in Chesterfield County and they had to deliver a list of names of their 40 slaves to the court, and these slaves were put up for sale by the court to raise funds to pay off the debt to Braidwood.

The above represents in a nutshell all the information that is known of the case from the Bolling papers in the Library of Virginia. It is understood that the case dragged on well into the early part of the 19th century. There is a remote possibility that some of the land belonging either to Bolling or Murray, or their heirs, was seized to repay the debt in full. This is an area that needs to be thoroughly researched.

The 52nd Work of the
British Deaf History Society

© BRITISH DEAF HISTORY SOCIETY
WARRINGTON, CHESHIRE

ISBN 978-1-902427-42-3